P9-CQS-237

THE MANY LIVES OF

MARILYN MONROE

THE MANY LIVES OF
MARILYN

MONROE

Sarah Churchwell

METROPOLITAN BOOKS   HENRY HOLT AND COMPANY   NEW YORK

BOCA RATON PUBLIC LIBRARY
BOCA RATON, FLORIDA

Metropolitan Books
Henry Holt and Company, LLC
Publishers since 1866
115 West 18th Street
New York, New York 10011

Metropolitan Books™ is a registered
trademark of Henry Holt and Company, LLC.

Copyright © 2004 by Sarah Churchwell
All rights reserved.
First published in the United Kingdom in 2004 by Granta Books, London.

Lyrics from "Candle in the Wind" (John/Taupin) © 1974,
used by kind permission of Universal Music Publishing Limited.

Photographs reproduced with kind permission: Marilyn Monroe by Cecil Beaton, 1956 © Sotheby Picture Library; Marilyn Monroe, 1954 © Rex/Sam Shaw; Marilyn Monroe, 1955 © Rex/Sam Shaw; "Overexposure" © Bettmann/Corbis; Marilyn Monroe, 1954 © Christian Blau, 2003 (detail); Norma Jeane Dougherty, 1945 TM © Estate of André de Dienes © 2005 www.AndredeDienes.com Licensed by OneWest Publishing Inc. Worldwide, 9461 Charleville Blvd. #500, Beverly Hills CA 90121 USA www.OneWestPublishing.com; Marilyn Monroe, 1949 TM © Estate of André de Dienes © 2005 www.AndredeDienes.com Licensed by OneWest Publishing Inc. Worldwide, 9461 Charleville Blvd. #500, Beverly Hills CA 90121 USA www.OneWestPublishing.com; Marilyn Monroe and Joe DiMaggio, 1954 © popper foto.com; Marilyn Monroe and Arthur Miller, 1956 © Rex/Sam Shaw; Marilyn Monroe © 1962 Bert Stern; Marilyn Monroe, 1956 © Elliott Erwitt/Magnum Photos.

Library of Congress Cataloging-in-Publication Data
Churchwell, Sarah Bartlett, [date]
    The many lives of Marilyn Monroe / Sarah Churchwell—
    1st American ed.
        p.   cm.
    Includes bibliographical references and index.
    ISBN-10: 0-8050-7818-5
    ISBN-13: 978-0-8050-7818-3
    1. Monroe, Marilyn, 1926–1962.   2. Motion picture actors and actresses—
United States—Biography.   I. Title.
PN2287.M69C48   2005
791.43'028'092—dc22
[B]   2004053076
Henry Holt books are available for special promotions and
premiums. For details contact: Director, Special Markets.

First U.S. Edition 2005
Printed in the United States of America
10 9 8 7 6 5 4 3 2 1

CONTENTS

APR 2005

NOTE ON SOURCES

This book seeks to understand the myriad stories in circulation about Marilyn Monroe, to read the public myth. It does not promise (or indeed endeavor) to reveal the "private woman." I have in consequence restricted myself to publicly available stories, documents and images, in an effort to understand the story that is produced by, and for, our culture and that circulates within the public sphere.

In addition to the specific works cited in the text, the discussion that follows has been enlightened by the insights of many scholars and critics. Foremost among these are Susan Bordo, Judith Butler, Michel de Certeau, Michel Foucault, George Lakoff and Mark Johnson, Joan W. Scott and Eve Kosofsky Sedgwick. The discussion of "Snow White" at the end of chapter six is indebted to the reading offered by Sandra M. Gilbert and Susan Gubar in *The Madwoman in the Attic*. These thinkers have provided another key source for this book.

THE MANY LIVES OF

MARILYN MONROE

Marilyn Monroe, 1956. PHOTOGRAPH BY CECIL BEATON.

INTRODUCTION

You're always running into people's unconscious.

—MARILYN MONROE,
Life interview, August 3, 1962

Sometime during the night of August 4, 1962, Marilyn Monroe died of an overdose of barbiturates. She was alone in the bedroom of her new home at 12305 Fifth Helena Drive, an unpretentious Spanish bungalow in Brentwood, California, that she had only recently purchased. It was the first house she had owned by herself; in the summer of 1962, divorced three times, Marilyn Monroe lived alone. Her dead body was discovered in bed, naked. There was no note, but there were dozens of pill bottles on the bedside table, most of them empty. When the first policemen arrived they found Monroe's housekeeper doing the laundry. And they began to hear conflicting stories about the events that had taken place between 8 P.M. on August 4 and 4:25 A.M. on August 5, when they were notified.

These reports would only grow more confused and disordered as time passed and more voices added to an already convoluted tale. The disputes have never been resolved, and conflicting stories continue to spread, scrambling fact, speculation, belief and accusation. The coroner's official verdict was "probable suicide," but the myth is not satisfied with the probable. New stories appear regularly, each of which promises to deliver the truth—a different truth—at last. More often than not they only offer another tangled web of anecdote and conjecture, and these competing myths have become the only truth we have.

In some stories Marilyn kills herself, in despair over the end of her career, or a love affair, or both. In others, she was never happier: her career was flourishing, she was about to marry. Most of the tales, though, are murder mysteries, and the culprit varies from one account to the next. The Kennedy men (not just John and Robert, but in some variants their father, Joseph) are fingered most often, but she might have been murdered by the Mob—or Jimmy Hoffa, or the CIA, or J. Edgar Hoover and the FBI, or Communists (some prefer Khrushchev, others Castro). In some versions it was her psychiatrist whodunit, in others her housekeeper. It was assassination. It was accident. She was destroyed by the powerful men who manipulated her. She was her own worst enemy.

Each of these endings concludes its own plot, and each plot differs in key respects—yet they all insist that theirs is the true story of Marilyn Monroe's life.

The authors of these tales are not all paranoid cranks. Monroe's major biographers differ widely about her death, and many respected writers have accepted the possibility that Marilyn could have been murdered. After the Profumo scandal, Watergate, Vietnam, Iran-Contra and the Clinton-Lewinsky affair, the prospect of a cover-up at the highest levels of government is not only *not* paranoid, it is politics as usual. In his 1973 "novel biography" *Marilyn,* Norman Mailer lingered over the likelihood of Monroe's murder and on the "political stakes" riding on her death, before admitting that evidence of homicide was hard to find. Nearly thirty years later, in her biographical novel *Blonde,* Joyce Carol Oates attributed Monroe's death to a "Sharpshooter" working for "the Agency," who neither knows nor cares why he's killing her: the murder was either ordered by friends of "R.F." or else by his enemies. (And calling him a "Sharpshooter" can only invoke the death of J.F.K., for Oates's Sharpshooter never actually shoots anyone but rather kills Marilyn by lethal injection.) The stories that believe—or toy with—the possibility that Marilyn Monroe was murdered depend for their motive upon the assumption that she was having an affair with Robert Kennedy, but that theory itself is by no means proven; some of Monroe's biographers continue to dismiss it as unfounded.

What is the truth? And how can we possibly not know everything there is to know about one of the world's most oversold icons?

It is hardly news that Marilyn Monroe's death remains controversial. More surprisingly, the mysteries surrounding her death are not the only confusions in her story. Uncertainty *is* the story of Marilyn's biographical life: we don't know nearly as much about her as people may assume. Although Marilyn Monroe was one of the most famous, most photographed, most written-about people in the twentieth century, we know less about her for certain than about many far more distant historical figures.

It is not just the case that biographies of Marilyn Monroe disagree about the answers to charged questions about her life, her character and her experiences. They often do not acknowledge that other versions even exist. Each of Marilyn's many lives asserts as proven fact what another calls a total lie, and presents conjecture as if it were certain knowledge. Often only after several accounts have been compared does controversy emerge, and only by reading many do the stakes of the arguments begin to appear.

Whichever biography of Marilyn Monroe we read, however, we are instantly confronted with an identity that seems confused, secret, lost. Biographies then promise to clear up these confusions, reveal the secrets, reclaim the lost soul. But these many lives help to create the confusion in the first place.

"Why not assume that Marilyn Monroe opens the entire problem of biography?" asks Norman Mailer, with a characteristic mix of presumption and insight.[1] That problem, for Mailer, is "the question of whether a person can be comprehended by the facts of a life." But in Marilyn's case those facts cannot even be established with confidence in the first place. Much of what we think we know about Monroe the person is actually extrapolated from the persona of Marilyn.

The myth of Marilyn is not without correlatives: she can be (and has been) compared to other iconic figures who died young and have had their images endlessly reproduced and their stories forever recycled. She and Elvis often take a bow together; sometimes James Dean comes into the story. But Marilyn, that icon of über-femininity, is most often compared to other dead women. Or rather, other dead women are often compared to her. To take just one example, when Princess Diana died in September 1997 the *New Statesman* wrote: "By dying young, at the peak of her fame, she has taken her place in the holy trinity of immortal blondes. The more beautiful Marilyn Monroe overdosed wearing Chanel No. 5. The more intelligent Sylvia Plath died with her head in a gas oven like a Sunday roast."[2] Whenever a glamorous young woman dies, she is compared to Marilyn Monroe, whether she was a blonde—or dumb—or not. Plath, who was only blonde for one summer and died six months after Monroe, is regularly described as the "Marilyn Monroe of literature." Janis Joplin, far less blonde—and less likely to appreciate the comparison—is an even more incongruous member of the sorority, coupled to Marilyn in death with startling frequency. A study titled *Virginia Woolf: Icon,* by Brenda R. Silver, ends on a chapter called "The Monstrous Union of Virginia Woolf and Marilyn Monroe." She's been compared to Eva Perón and Marina Tsvetaeva. And of course, when Diana died, it wasn't just the comparison that was recycled—the myth's theme song, "Candle in the Wind," was, as well.

Marilyn has gone from sex symbol to a symbol of mourning, from a promise of the liberation of sex to a cautionary tale about the dangers of loneliness and spinsterhood. And chiefly it is the writing and rewriting of her life story that has achieved this transformation.

The many lives of Marilyn Monroe disagree about almost everything that might be held to characterize her, offering different versions of her name; the identity of her biological father; whether she was raped as a child; her mother's mental state—and her own; her sexuality, her beauty, her fame; the number of abortions she may have had, or whether she slept her way to the top; her relationships with powerful men—DiMaggio, Miller, the Kennedys; and of course, the cause of her death. Where there is consensus, this book will not linger: it is about the disputes, and tells the story of Marilyn's life through them; it looks at the pressure points where stories can't or won't agree. It is about the perilous and fascinating lines between fact and fiction, between desire and contempt, between knowledge and doubt. Most of all, it is about cliché.

Marilyn's lives promise the truth, but they more often recycle formula, telling us what we already think we know, satisfying our expectations. Images so fixed, so recognizable that they can tell an implicit story, icons are a kind of visual cliché, the stereotyping of an individual rather than of a group. Whereas icons are usually idealized, stereotypes can justify fears, anxieties and taboos: there is a strong association between stereotype and images of pathology, disease and filth (thus in anti-Semitic stereotypes Jews are not only greedy, they are "greasy"; in homophobic stereotypes homosexuals are not only promiscuous, they are dying of AIDS; in misogynistic stereotypes women who have sex too much are called "sluts," which also means dirty, etc.). The image of Marilyn Monroe is of an icon of desirability and a stereotype of pathological femininity, all rolled into one. She is desire, and she is death.

Stereotype, cliché and icons are all shorthands that do our thinking for us. Resisting stereotype is not simply a matter of overturning it, because every stereotype suggests its opposite already (as in virgin/whore), and is more than elastic enough to resist the assault of the counterexample: someone who says "For a blonde, you're surprisingly smart" won't necessarily be reconsidering his attitudes toward blondes in general.

Marilyn Monroe participated in creating her own image, worked industriously at playing into it, and then tried, and failed, to discard it. Stereotype proved, in the end, far stronger than she.

I never thought I was interested in Marilyn Monroe. Two obsessive love affairs (neither, I'm sorry to say, with a person) dominated my adolescence. The first was with novels, and the second with old black-and-white movies. When I was fourteen, Technicolor Marilyn appealed to me not at all: her films actually made me uncomfortable, though I never gave much thought as to why. I just knew I preferred the tough-talking, wisecracking, trousers-wearing comic heroines of the thirties and forties: Katharine Hepburn, Rosalind Russell, Carole Lombard, Irene Dunne. Marilyn Monroe was dumb, twittering, help-less. And somehow so *exposed.*

But when I began a study of Sylvia Plath, and realized that I was as interested in how she was written *about* as in what she herself wrote, I found that Marilyn Monroe kept popping up everywhere I looked. For someone so trivial, so hackneyed, she was remarkably tenacious. I read a biography, and was left with many questions; reading another, I found myself with different questions. It soon became clear that there was a story in the gaps and contradictions between them. The more I read, the bigger and more insistent this story became. Eventually it left even Plath behind.

When people hear that I am writing about Monroe, they usually assume that I want to defend her, to show that she was a misunder-stood genius, a great actress, a feminist, a victim. I'm not sure she was any of these things. I have come to admire her films, and much of her acting. (*Some Like It Hot* was already an exception to my long-standing indifference—but then it *was* black-and-white—and Marilyn had always made me laugh in *How to Marry a Millionaire.* Since then I have added her work in *The Prince and the Showgirl* and *Bus Stop* as two favorite performances, though they are problematic films. And she is very moving in *The Misfits,* a film I find unbearably cruel.) I hope that being a somewhat belated, even reluctant, fan helps me be fair-minded in my assessment of Monroe. But there is one charac-teristic of her story about which I am quite *parti pris:* I hate the con-tempt with which Marilyn is treated by the very people lining up to capitalize on her popularity. So I do hope to evoke an aspect of Marilyn Monroe that has been lost in the gaps between the many lives, one that surprised me, because it isn't in the films: it turns out Marilyn Monroe may have had a tough-talking, wisecracking and trousers-wearing side after all.

Or maybe it's just pretty to think so. Because I'm even more inter-ested in what *we* bring to the story of a woman we supposedly adore: usually it's shame, belittlement and anxiety. Marilyn Monroe pre-sents a series of problems, and this book is an attempt, if not to solve those problems, at least to explain them.

*   *   *

Repetition can itself be a pleasure: it creates and fulfills expectation at the same time, and provides an illusion of control. We get what we were expecting, and what we wanted. That is the satisfaction of formula fiction: we know the mystery will be solved, the girl will get the guy, the hero will kill the villain. And it happens every time, just the way we knew it would. The repetition, imitation and recollection of Marilyn is just such a pleasurable repetition, a looking forward to being satisfied. But it is also the painful repetition of being helplessly stuck in a pattern, in thrall to an obsession or grief, a destructive habit we can't break (thus, for Freud, repetition is a part of the process of mourning). The sheer enormity of the reproduction and repetition of the myth of Marilyn reflects both the pleasure and the fear that her story prompts.

The scale of the myth is impossible to measure. In addition to the dozens of biographies (purportedly nonfictional) of Marilyn Monroe in print, and scores more available through used-book sellers, there are biographical novels, "novel biographies," and fictionalized autobiographies about her historical life. There are countless memorabilia books, collections of photographs, anecdotes, trivia and quotations. There are books that say they are "in her own words" or that she "speaks for herself," and there are more conventional collections of interviews; there are books that mix text and photograph to provide "her life in pictures"; there is fiction that uses Marilyn Monroe as a character, and that invents sequels to her story; there are collections of poetry about her and by her; there are essays and elegies, scholarly articles, edited collections, and two academic monographs about her and her symbolic relationship to femininity, sexuality, Hollywood and celebrity. There is a flourishing subgenre of books dealing with her death alone. Documentary films—some "reenactments," some using only archival footage—appear with regularity, and there are more than twenty films that depict a fictional but recognizable version of Monroe's story. An Internet search of the name "Marilyn Monroe" reveals 1,720,000 entries. According to Adam Victor in *The Complete Marilyn Monroe:* "More books have been written about Marilyn

Monroe than any other entertainer. The most conservative estimates are in the low hundreds; more accurate guesses exceed the six-hundred mark, and at least half a dozen new Marilyn books are published every year in the English language alone."[3]

Put together, these texts create and circulate the myth of Marilyn Monroe. But that myth is more often referred to than it is explained, as if we all know what it is. The myth of Marilyn Monroe derives from the peculiarities of these accounts. Their dubious authenticity, their attempts to establish a truth about a mythical figure, their propensity for espousing cultural dogma (and for being sanctimonious while they're at it), their tendency toward the collective and the aggregate: all of these make the writings about Marilyn Monroe an apocrypha, which is how I will often refer to them. Which of the accounts are "canonical," as opposed to apocryphal, actually varies from interpretation to interpretation, as we shall see. Thus in one sense there is no such thing as a Marilyn canon; in another sense, the apocrypha *is* the canon.

A religious metaphor like apocrypha seems particularly apt in the case of Marilyn, our ultimate goddess, divinity, icon, idol. Her story is not just a myth because it is suspect, full of rumor and conjecture. It is a myth in the ancient sense of a tale invented to explain the inexplicable, of stories focusing on exemplary figures (gods or heroes) that reflect—and sanction—cultural values. No culture has ever failed to produce its own myths: Marilyn is one of our favorites. Myths always raise questions about their own veracity or meaningfulness; they offer belief in default of knowledge. Marilyn shows above all else what we believe, not what we know.

These religious metaphors provide at once figurative imagery and literal description: they are both trope and dead metaphor. A dead metaphor is not only a cliché, it is a metaphor that has lost its figurative power, and gets taken literally. Marilyn Monroe has become a dead metaphor.

The force of the dead metaphor affects the way her lives are narrated: they are told through cliché, presumption, loaded phrases and literal judgments. The story of Marilyn Monroe begins with the close unconscious association between dread and love, sex and death, that was so important to Freud; it ends having been translated into the conscious, resolved into the literal, turned into what we can see, what we can face, what we want to know. But as Monroe understood, "you're always running into people's unconscious." Underlying these "factual" stories is the unruly, symbolic, figurative world of the unconscious, of deep-seated anxieties and desires. By no coincidence, most biographers rely upon a reassuring, undemanding version of "psychoanalysis" to manage these fears, to translate our responses to Marilyn from the unconscious to the conscious, from figurative to literal. The many lives of Marilyn Monroe are a talking cure for our lingering, persistent fears about sex, knowledge, the female body and death.

Six weeks before she died, Marilyn agreed to do a photo shoot for *Vogue* magazine. She had been one of the biggest movie stars in the world for exactly a decade. Recently and publicly dismissed from her longtime studio, 20th Century-Fox, she had begun a publicity campaign to counteract the rumors that she was on the skids and was unemployable, even insane. She had just had a gall bladder operation; it had helped her lose the weight for which she had been attacked in the press over the last three years, and she was as slim as she had been in her starlet days (slimmer, actually). Photographer Bert Stern met with Monroe for several long days of shooting; the pictures they produced together became known as the Last Sitting, and would achieve their own mythical status as the legendary, elegiac final images.

Stern took nearly 2,600 pictures during the session. Some of them, in which Monroe has strings of beads in her mouth, or a glass of champagne tilted to her lips, have become nearly as familiar as the publicity glamour stills taken in the early 1950s, images of Monroe in plunging gold lamé with hands on hips, in strapless purple satin admiring her own reflection in a multiple mirror, or the head shots of Marilyn leering at the camera that Andy Warhol would reproduce on silkscreens after her death as the memento mori he called *Colored Marilyns*. The Last Sitting photographs, however, reveal a Monroe considerably more chameleon-like, less fixed and static, than the rigid stereotype represented by the iconic "Marilyn." Stern brought props to the shoot, which gave Monroe the opportunity to act: they used sheer colored scarves, black knotted veils, beaded necklaces, the champagne glass. Some of the pictures are in black and white of Monroe in an evening gown with her hair pulled back in a chignon and her back revealed; in some her hair is piled on her head and she hides behind a chinchilla coat; others show her almost unrecognizable in a black wig.

The jacket of this book presents one of the many Marilyns produced in the Last Sitting; it is not the Marilyn Monroe we usually see. Instead of studied, frozen glamour, we get tousled charm; instead of the overt come-on, a coquettish wide-eyed gaze. She stands with arms out, almost like a small child inviting an embrace; but the eyes and half smile are knowing. Marilyn is veiled not just by the scarf she holds in her teeth, but by the hair covering one eye from which she regards us so unwaveringly: each screen offers only a glimpse of what is behind it. Her direct gaze is challenging, mischievous, a little sly. Here I am, she seems to say. But are you sure you're ready for me?

Like her image, her story has been reproduced to the point of saturation. We may think there is nothing left to say, but there are still some surprises left. Most books telling the story of Marilyn Monroe offer to reveal the real woman behind the image, the truth behind the myth. But this assurance is a fundamental part of the myth itself: the story of Marilyn always includes the promise to unveil the true woman.

This book makes no such promise. This is the story of the stories of Marilyn Monroe. The photograph of Marilyn with a veil in her teeth is no truer than the picture of Marilyn in a white dress on a subway grating, or doing her makeup in a backstage mirror, or a candid shot of Marilyn laughing on her sofa. What truth we can find is in the composite, and the same can be said of Marilyn's many lives.

Since her death, Marilyn Monroe's story has been endlessly told and retold. Nearly every book begins with the same question: Who was the woman who became Marilyn Monroe? But this book asks a different question: Who was the woman Marilyn Monroe became?

PART ONE

PRODUCTION

Marilyn Monroe on Lexington Avenue, New York City, 1954.

PHOTOGRAPH BY SAM SHAW.

I

PRODUCING THE IMAGE, 1946–1962

People you run into feel that, well, who is she—
who does she think she is, Marilyn Monroe?

—MARILYN MONROE,
Life interview, August 3, 1962

BECOMING MARILYN

In the summer of 2002 a book of photographs was published called
Becoming Marilyn, featuring pictures taken in 1949 by photographer
André de Dienes of a young model who was preparing to make the
leap into Hollywood stardom. She had already changed her name to
Marilyn Monroe, but she had not yet developed the distinctive "look"
with which she would become so indelibly associated. These memorably beautiful images, many of which had never been published
before, are of a young woman (she was twenty-three) with shoulder-
length dark-blonde hair, lightened from its natural chestnut, but
many shades darker than the short white cotton-candy hair that
would be one of the movie star's trademarks. Happily smiling, rather
than seductively smoldering, she is poised on the brink of "becoming
Marilyn."* These pictures are recognizably Marilyn Monroe,

---

*See page 180.

and recognizably *not* Marilyn Monroe. The title of the book reinforces this idea: Marilyn is someone else, someone this young woman would become.

In reviewing *Becoming Marilyn, Newsweek* magazine commented that the book's "images [are] catching Norma Jeane as she mutates to 'Marilyn.' "[1] This statement reflects the basic premise of the myth of Marilyn Monroe: a real girl (often named Norma Jean or Norma Jeane) metamorphosed into something that was not a person, but a concept: "Marilyn."

As soon as one begins reading about Marilyn Monroe, one encounters immediately the idea that "Marilyn" was a persona so artificial, so manufactured and packaged, that it eradicated the person. In becoming "Marilyn," the image, this woman produced an ideal of female glamour that has endured for half a century. And it is an ideal seen as being distinct from the woman's reality. "Marilyn" was only a fantasy of femininity, an imaginary role the actress performed with immense success, but which eventually destroyed her. Thus the name Marilyn is relentlessly set off in distancing quotation marks by writer after writer as they attempt to distinguish the real woman from the artificial role:

By May 1953, Marilyn was nearing the end of her seventh full year as "Marilyn," a person with few determinable antecedents.[2]

The dumb if innocent blonde with the whispery voice that was "Marilyn Monroe" freed Norma Jean, but, paradoxically, became at the same time a means of enslaving others to an impoverished and demeaning conception of what it meant to be a woman. And Marilyn herself became the prime victim of this image.[3]

Who was the woman who turned herself into "Marilyn Monroe"?[4]

"Marilyn" is a man's "Marilyn," a manufactured dream of physical purity.[5]

She had finally resented and rejected the artifice of the manufactured Marilyn Monroe, realizing that was itself a role she could assume and put off.[6]

In the invented person of "Marilyn Monroe," Norma Jeane should have the opportunity to relive certain humiliations of her young life, not as tragedy, but as comedy.[7]

For thirty years, these very different writers have told precisely the same story: "Marilyn" was not a real person, but a product invented for the gratification of men in the 1950s.

Several things are worth noting about this interpretation. It is dominated by a suspicion of the manufactured and a preference for the natural: although she is supposed to be "our love goddess," many now regard Marilyn with misgiving, even hostility. It rapidly becomes incoherent, producing meaningless sentences like "Marilyn was nearing the end of her seventh full year as 'Marilyn.'" And it is a cliché, unvarying for more than thirty years, but one that is always presented as a unique insight. Joyce Carol Oates describes in an interview her motivation for writing *Blonde,* which was seeing a picture of the young "Norma Jeane Baker" and realizing, with "an almost rapturous sense of excitement, that I might give life to this lost, lone girl, whom the iconic consumer-product 'Marilyn Monroe' would soon overwhelm and obliterate."[8] In another interview she declares: "To me, she's always Norma Jeane." Oates seems to be unfamiliar with "Candle in the Wind," in which Bernie Taupin and Elton John realized exactly the same thing almost thirty years earlier:

> *Goodbye Norma Jean*
> *Though I never knew you at all [. . .]*
> *Goodbye Norma Jean*
> *From the young man in the 22nd row*
> *Who sees you as something more than sexual*
> *More than just our Marilyn Monroe*

What is remarkable about this chestnut is the way in which it creates in the beholder a sense of singularity, of novelty. Both Oates and Taupin/John seem to imply that they're the only one in on the secret, the only one who sees Marilyn as more than a sex symbol. "To me, she's always Norma Jeane." In fact, to most writers she's always

Norma Jeane, a real woman beyond (before, behind, above, below) the image. The refrain of "Candle in the Wind," "though I never knew you at all," is part and parcel of the myth of Marilyn Monroe. We see her, and we know that we don't really know her; we can enjoy the poignancy of what feels like a loss, when in fact not knowing her is the point. If Marilyn was invented, she was invented in order to be lost, in order to be lamented.

This story actually reinforces Marilyn's supposed artificiality while pretending to uncover the real woman. It allows for a literal, and easy, split between image and reality; it is founded on a simplistic notion of reality as a stable, prior truth entirely distinct from image, projection, reproduction. But of course, images have a reality, too, and reality can be made. This chapter is about the reality of the image: its interpretations, its history and its evolution. Or rather, its lack of evolution. The image of Marilyn Monroe has remained static for fifty years, which is surely one of the reasons for its durability. Marilyn is nothing if not a stereotype.

Andy Warhol's familiar *Colored Marilyns* silkscreens are a comment upon Marilyn as stereotype: his Marilyn is an image mechanically, invariably reproduced from a mold. The first *Marilyn* silkscreens were made in 1962 immediately after Monroe's death, as a memento mori. Although eventually Warhol would repeat the technique with other celebrities, including Elizabeth Taylor and Chairman Mao, Marilyn was the first to be figured in this way, and helped make the technique itself iconic. The same picture is repeated over and over: that is the portrait's most salient characteristic. But each image is also slightly different from the one that precedes it: Warhol's technique allowed for variations in the reproduction so that they are recognizably Marilyn, but a different Marilyn every time. The *Marilyn* screens reproduce a picture from 1952, a publicity still from Monroe's film *Niagara,* which was her first real starring role. Warhol took a Technicolor still, drained it of color and made a black-and-white image; he then painted bright colors over the face that suggested cosmetics, the garish fakery of Hollywood, and cartoons. As S. Paige Baty argued in her 1995 academic study *American Monroe,* in these pictures "Marilyn Monroe is a type, a reproduction; indeed her type stands in *as* reproduction. Here she is an icon *because* she is the subject of this repeated reproduction; Warhol shows us a Marilyn who radiates the power of reproduction."[9] His *Colored Marilyns* remark on her status as cliché, as someone made up. They suggest both her mutability and her immutability.

We remember Marilyn in kaleidoscopic pieces: she is written as a catalog of so many isolated, fragmented elements. If she were a sonnet, Marilyn would be a *blason,* that dissection of a beloved object into pieces that Shakespeare famously mocked in "My mistress' eyes are nothing like the sun." We all know the component parts of Marilyn's iconic look: her curly platinum-blonde hair; black arched brows; glistening, open red mouth; beauty mark; her white skin and white dresses ("I like to feel blonde all over," she is supposed to have said[10]); her prominent breasts; her equally conspicuous behind ("I've never seen a behind like hers, it was really remarkable, it was a very subtly composed ass," said one journalist[11]); her exposed legs elongated on stiletto heels. Just as symptomatic of her image are her whisper, her dumbness (or naïveté), her childishness, her vulnerability and her suffering. Thus a compendium of facts and trivia like *The Unabridged Marilyn* opens with a roll call of these stereotyped features:

> Her striking and unparalleled blonde luminosity; her hair thrown back in defiance and ecstasy; her lips suggestively parted; her breathy, baby-voiced whisper that seduced us with its innocence; her infectious mirth; and her transparent vulnerability that touched something deep in us all. We understood her pain, because we recognized it in ourselves.[12]

But the sum of these invariable parts adds up to many different Marilyns floating around our culture. She is figured by turns as heroine, martyr, bitch, victim, castrator; she is oppressed, vicious, promiscuous, frigid, dumb, sly, monstrous. As miscellaneous as this catalog might at first appear, however, it unwaveringly describes stereotypical Woman in all her extravagant contradictions.

As far as she represents a mythic version of Woman, Marilyn

tends to divide audience response across gender lines. No one has better rendered the stereotypical male response to Marilyn's image than Norman Mailer in his "novel biography" *Marilyn*. For those of us who are not titillated by Marilyn's figure, and who are too young to remember her career, Mailer's weird mix of sentimentality and satyriasis helps explain the sexual plenitude her image was held to offer the American male in the 1950s:

> Marilyn was deliverance, a very Stradivarius of sex, so gorgeous, forgiving, humorous, compliant and tender that even the most mediocre musician would relax his lack of art in the dissolving magic of her violin [. . .] "Marilyn Monroe's sex," said the smile of the young star, "will meet every human need."[13]

In other words, Marilyn's appearance of sexual availability protected the man watching from performance anxiety. The Marilyn image, in still photograph and in film, is of compliance, submission, of giving in and putting out. She was the world's sex object; her dream was to fulfill men's dreams. With her quivering mouth open, her hooded but direct gaze, her body yielding to the viewer, she was a woman always on the verge of an orgasm.

If she is the world's (or "our") sex object, then the world is not only male, it is straight: when Mailer declares that sex with her would fulfill "every human need," this cannot even begin to seem true unless every human is a heterosexual man (or a gay woman, but one imagines that's not what Mailer meant). Film critic Pauline Kael argued that Marilyn's appeal to gay men was, essentially, heterosexual: "her mixture of wide-eyed wonder and cuddly drugged sexiness seemed to get to just about every male; she turned on even homosexual men."[14] But insofar as Marilyn is a gay icon, it makes better sense to think of her as someone with whom gay men identify, rather than as someone they desire. The palpable artificiality of her persona lends itself to a camp sensibility, which, as Susan Sontag famously noted in 1964 (only two years after Monroe's death), is a "comic vision of the world," marked by "its love of the unnatural: of artifice and exaggeration." Because "Marilyn" is also seen as a production, an already self-parodic exhibition of female sexual allure, she suggests by extension

that any femininity can be a put-on: that it is not natural, but a performance. Marilyn is already a drag show; hers is a comic vision of
femininity.

If affirming a specific fantasy of female vacuity, naturalness and
readiness, Marilyn was also relentlessly portrayed as cheerful, light-
hearted, spontaneous, as a way of mitigating the implicit dangers of
female sexual availability. As Kate Millett described her image: "You
talked her into it—she was willing—she was even hot. She giggled.
You stuck it to her and she ate it up. When it's over, you remember
that. That she was willing."[15] The roles she played from *Monkey
Business* to *Some Like It Hot* were characterized by their happy
aplomb, impulsiveness and *esprit de jeu*. Writer after writer explains
that Marilyn's appeal in the 1950s was the way she made sex, hith-
erto seedy or menacing, seem innocent and sweet. In this sense, she
has often been hailed by her admirers as being in the vanguard of the
sexual revolution (while representing to her detractors precisely
the opposite, a woman who single-handedly pushed cultural images
of women back fifty years). Mailer said: "Marilyn suggested sex might
be difficult and dangerous with others, but ice cream with her."[16]
She did this, writers agree, by projecting a kind of childishness that
made the overt sexuality of her voluptuous body unthreatening
and safe: "The image of voluptuous womanhood and childish innocence which she embodied was unique."[17] The phrase "child-
woman" recurs throughout writing about Marilyn (though Mailer
doesn't even grant her that much adulthood, and calls her a "child-
girl"). Rollyson writes in his *Life of the Actress* (1986) that "she was
somehow able to exploit her sexuality in the most deliberate, self-
conscious way and yet appear to be an innocent, a naif, a child surprised at all of the commotion she has caused."[18] Richard Dyer, in an
academic consideration of Monroe as a star, agrees that innocence
was crucial to her appeal: "With Monroe sexuality *is* innocent [. . .]
Monroe knows about sexuality, but she doesn't know about guilt and
innocence—she welcomes sex as natural."[19] She was thus an appropriate symbol for that most childish of decades, the 1950s, when
America regressed, and developed a breast fixation. Marilyn's childishness becomes the obverse of a fantasy of maternity, a woman who
is as infantile as the men around her. "She would ask no price,"

Mailer rhapsodizes. No strings attached, no pressure—she would give, and men would take.

For some women, she came to symbolize the straitjacket of just such sexual fantasies, the high emotional cost of asking no price of men, and being left to pay it oneself. Both men and women emphasize how childlike she seemed: for Mailer, that is part of her appeal; for female observers like Gloria Steinem and Molly Haskell, that is part of her liability. Many feminists view Marilyn with weariness, contempt or overt hostility. In her review of Mailer's *Marilyn* in 1973, Pauline Kael wrote:

> She would bat her Bambi eyelashes, lick her messy suggestive open mouth, wiggle that pert and tempting bottom and use her hushed voice to caress us with dizzying innuendoes. Her extravagantly ripe body bulging and spilling out of her clothes, she threw herself at us with the off-color innocence of a baby whore.[20]

In *From Reverence to Rape,* her classic study of the representation of women in film, Molly Haskell responds with similar skepticism to the stereotype: "What was she, this breathless, blonde supplicating symbol of sexuality, the lips anxiously offering themselves as the surrogate orifice, the whisper unconsciously expressing trepidation? And who made her what she was?"[21]

Actually, Monroe's persona was always comprised of questions about its fabrication; the rhetorical question provides the writing about Marilyn with its grammar. And this question—"what was she?"—has been asked about Marilyn from the beginning. *Playboy* wanted to know exactly the same thing in 1953: "What Makes Marilyn?" was the headline of the article accompanying their first centerfold. The story doesn't change, as misogynists and feminists ask exactly the same thing of Marilyn twenty years apart and more— who, or what, made her? *Playboy's* answer, as we shall see, is that she was a "natural phenomenon," instinctive, artless. Haskell's answer is that Marilyn was anything but natural; she was a notional woman produced solely for the benefit of men, a celluloid blow-up doll: "She was partly a hypothesis. [. . .] She was the masturbatory fantasy that gave satisfaction and demanded nothing in return. [. . .] She was the fifties' fiction, the lie that a woman has no sexual needs, that she is there to cater to, or enhance, a man's needs."[22]

The idea that Marilyn was only a fantasy is by now a commonplace, extending to her many biographies, and (perhaps especially) her academic interpretations. In his 1988 scholarly monograph *Marilyn Monroe*, Graham McCann insists on the basic role of fiction in Monroe's identity: "The 'real Marilyn Monroe,' I want to suggest, is a proper appreciation of her fictions, even if they are facts; or her facts, as long as one is not certain that they cannot serve as fictions."[23] Now not only is the name "Marilyn Monroe" in scare quotes, but so is the idea of there being a real Marilyn Monroe at all. Her fictionality is her essential reality. Seven years later, Baty made virtually the same declaration in *American Monroe* when she argued that Monroe is only ever an imitation of herself: "The 'real Marilyn' is an oxymoron: she *mediates the real* by being a simulation of herself."[24] By 2002, this had become a truism, as the *Newsweek* review of *Becoming Marilyn* shows: "the real Marilyn Monroe (now there's an oxymoron for you)."[25] Eventually, the reality of Monroe comes to seem so remote that we believe she is nothing more than an image, which has the effect of flattening her back into the two-dimensional stereotype from which feminists like Haskell and Steinem were attempting to rescue her by recognizing her image as a fantasy produced for the benefit of men. She has mutated from totally natural to pure fiction, but either way, male desire is what makes Marilyn.

Although the idea of the "real Marilyn" is not at all an oxymoron (there was a real Marilyn), the image of Marilyn is very much an oxymoron, or rather a series of paradoxes. Which is to say, more accurately, that others see in Marilyn a series of paradoxes, contradictions that they find impossible to reconcile. The difficulty of reconciling these polarities would seem to owe more than a little to the infectious literalism of the split between image and reality. Once you believe in that split, everything about Marilyn starts to separate along fault lines; she begins to bifurcate. All of the oxymorons Marilyn is supposed to represent reflect the way stereotypical Woman has been viewed with fear and desire by the men who invented the idea and could not grant it reality. Again, Mailer shows this response par excellence in his notorious, ranting catalog of Marilyn's contradictions. She was, he writes:

> a queen of a castrator who was ready to weep for a dying minnow; a lover of books who did not read, and a proud, inviolate artist who could haunch over to publicity when the heat was upon her faster than a whore could lust over a hot buck; a female spurt of wit and sensitive energy who could hang like a sloth for days in a muddy-mooded coma; a child-girl, yet an actress to loose a riot by dropping her glove at a premiere; a fountain of charm and a dreary bore; an ambulating cyclone of beauty when dressed to show, a dank hunched-up drab at her worst—with a bad smell!—a giant and an emotional pygmy; lover of life and a cowardly hyena of death who drenched herself in chemical stupors; a sexual oven whose fire may have been rarely lit—she would go to bed with a brassiere on—she was certainly more and less than the silver witch of us all.[26]

Dyer has influentially argued that the concept of stardom always depends upon living contradictions: the star is at once ordinary and extraordinary, familiar and distant, ubiquitous and unattainable. Marilyn represents all of these contradictions and more.

The Marilyn apocrypha has produced a woman who is natural and artificial, innocent and sexual (madonna and whore), smart and stupid, safe and dangerous, victimized and powerful, beautiful and grotesque, sex and death, herself and someone else. Underlying the stereotype is a similar confusion of the literal and the figurative: Marilyn is a symbol, and she is the real thing. Her first biographer, Maurice Zolotow, declared in 1960 that she had the strange ability to be whatever a man wanted her to be:

> almost any man can find an element in Monroe to correspond to his interests. Lerner finds a woman with whom to discuss "ideas," Mailer a blonde hipster, Farrell a *femme du peuple*, Nabokov a comedienne of sex, Chayefsky a love-starved victim. And there is

something, either in Monroe's past history or in her complicated personality, in her eerie intellect, in her being rejected and seeking the love of older men, that lends a certain rationale to each of those responses to Monroe, just as there are two good reasons to justify those who see her as the ideal physical mate for bearing children.[27]

For men like Mailer and Zolotow, Monroe is a Rorschach inkblot, the screen for conflicting male desires, and she is the reality of that fantasy, someone who naturally embodies all of these contradictions. But her reality will always return to the sexual: if she can be anything, as Zolotow asserts, she can only be infinite variations on the theme of the desirable woman. Allied with nature and with body, idealized for her fertility and reviled for uncontrolled sexuality, Woman is conventionally figured as giver of life and as destroyer. Simone de Beauvoir wrote that Woman "is all that man desires and all that he does not attain."[28] Or, as director Jean Negulesco said of Marilyn, "she represents to man something we all want in our unfulfilled dreams."[29]

Thus Zolotow can declare in his next paragraph that Marilyn is authentically "all things to all men," which is why her imitators fail: "Because of the primal innocence within the Venus body, she was authentic. Her imitators were not authentic." For Zolotow, to be an authentic woman is to be both virgin and whore, Mary and Eve: suffering innocence and the origin of guilt. With somewhat more historical nuance, he also recognized that Monroe's popularity related to the fact that "the character she created coincided with a fundamental change in man's conception of woman's role in sexuality." This change was the evolution to the "mistress-wife," which Monroe epitomized:

she is voluptuous, but she admires Dostoyevski. She devotes endless hours to making herself look beautiful, but she reveres children and the home, and she cooks well and bakes her own bread. She, or the character she plays (which is partly she and partly a product of her imagination), experiences sex as a pleasurable act, and yet she is not wanton, for her libido arises out of love and pity and she is faithful to one man.[30]

She is body, but mind; desirable, but domestic; sensual, but chaste: Zolotow's paradoxes are defensive, demonstrating how uneasy Marilyn's projection of sexuality always made her audience. And this unstable movement between madonna and whore (as well as between authentic and fake, performance and reality) continues to define the myth.

For all the sentimentality of Zolotow's account, he is clearly correct that Monroe animated a set of questions about proper femininity in a time of changing sexual roles. Although Marilyn is often now invoked as the last gasp of conventional 1950s femininity, her image has also been seen by many as a harbinger of changes to come. In a feminist study of pornography in 1981, Susan Griffin argued that Monroe was "a rebel against society's double standard. She would not wear bras and girdles. She refused to be ashamed of having posed nude."[31] Most of Monroe's commentators credit her with having been instrumental in combating the sexual puritanism of the 1950s, as Adam Victor claims in *The Complete Marilyn Monroe*: "Although it is perhaps an exaggeration to say that Marilyn single-handedly pushed back the barriers of prudish fifties America, she certainly had a leading role in the process."[32]

Certainly many of the most frequently recycled Marilyn quotations (or "Monroeisms," as they were sometimes called) involved her "natural" attitude to sex: "sex is a part of nature," she said in 1956, "and I'll go along with nature."[33] But neither was Monroe's audience quick to abandon the fear and shame associated with such a natural attitude. The writing about Marilyn in the 1950s insists with such obsessive redundance upon her naturalness that it seems to be trying to persuade itself of something it is afraid isn't true at all. Thus the first issue of *Playboy* called her "natural sex personified" (as opposed to personifying unnatural sex, one gathers), and a natural phenomenon, and "the most natural choice in the world" for their first centerfold, while also declaring that "it seems perfectly natural to ask *why*" she was such a phenomenon (and it answered the question tautologically, by twice deeming her "the real article"). Her unrelenting naturalness rapidly became a term of contempt for some, like Nunnally Johnson, who called Marilyn a "phenomenon of nature, like Niagara Falls. You can't talk to it. It can't talk to you. All you can do is stand back and be awed by it."[34] For Johnson her naturalness is monstrous: she's a freak of nature. 1950s America wanted Marilyn's open sexuality to seem natural and innocent, but couldn't quite convince itself that it was.

Just as her "naturalness" was supposed to legitimate her open displays of sexuality, so was faith in her innocence used to mitigate the threat of sexual aggression and promiscuity. Words like "brazen and carnal" appear next to "cheerful and innocent" in many renditions, such as biographer Donald Spoto's: Marilyn was "the postwar ideal of the American girl, soft, transparently needy, worshipful of men, naïve, offering sex without demands. . . . But there was also something quietly aggressive in her self-presentation as a frankly carnal creature."[35] Or in Andrew O'Hagan's more pragmatic summary of her development of the persona: "After a spell modeling and flirting and screwing and practicing her walk, waiting in line with the other girls at Schwab's Drugstore on Sunset Boulevard, Marilyn emerged with a brazen sense of how to enliven the Fifties."[36]

If she was a force of sexual liberation, then, she was a compromised one. Marilyn is less feminist than postfeminist. She emerged on the cusp of feminism (she died the year before Betty Friedan published *The Feminine Mystique,* which identified the neo-Victorian attitudes to women that Marilyn would be held to exemplify), but her image paves the way for postfeminism in its suggestion that sexual display or conspicuous consumption can operate as a form of feminine power, or indeed that conspicuous consumption is distinct from a sexual ideology that sees women as ornamentation. Monroe spent her entire career on a tightrope between being popular and being cheap, between commercial power and commodification, between the power and the punishment of being a woman desired by men. She often equivocated about the links among commerce, power and sex, trying to have it both ways (that quintessentially postfeminist desire). She declared defiantly: "I don't want to be sold to the public as a celluloid aphrodisical [*sic*]," but then added: "It was all right for the first few years. But now it's different."[37] Another time she said, with equal contradiction: "If that part about my being a symbol of sex is true, it ought to help out at the box office, but I don't want to be commercial about it."[38] In her last interview Monroe similarly hedged when she discussed becoming "a thing": "I never quite understood it, this sex symbol. I always thought symbols were those things you clash together! That's the trouble, a sex symbol becomes a thing. I just hate to be a thing. But if I'm going to be a symbol of something I'd rather have it sex than some other things they've got symbols of."[39]

Marilyn did become a thing, a commodity, an image. She was at once complicit in and resistant to her own commodification. Since she died, that commodification has accelerated and multiplied. "Marilyn" is merchandise: photograph, poster, calendar, coffee mug, playing cards, handbag, T-shirt. Marilyn's material reality as a plastic icon—a dashboard Marilyn—appears in two critical contexts. She is either seen as irretrievably a commodity, one that can be analyzed in quasi-Marxist accounts of consumerism and cultural studies. This is the Marilyn-as-icon approach, exemplified in Baty's monograph. Or, in the other, much more common and popular strand, Marilyn is a real woman who has been obscured by this commodification, but who can be excavated and saved by telling her "true" story, finding the "real woman" behind the myth, offering Marilyn "in her own words," or in some other way rescuing Marilyn from pernicious consumer culture.

These two attitudes share the presumption that in becoming a sex symbol Marilyn became not only a thing, but a novelty, a knickknack. This sense of her triviality no doubt relates to her ubiquity: familiarity has only increased the contempt with which Marilyn was often treated during her life. The opening words of Gloria Steinem's feminist "defense" of Marilyn reinforces both her omnipresence and her insignificance:

It has been nearly a quarter of a century since the death of a minor American actress named Marilyn Monroe. There is no reason for her to be part of my consciousness as I walk down a midtown New York street filled with color and action and life.

In a shop window display of white summer dresses, I see several huge photographs—a life-size cutout of Marilyn standing in a white halter dress, some close-ups of her vulnerable, please-love-me smile.[40]

Steinem assumes that Marilyn doesn't matter—she was a "minor" actress, whose presence in Steinem's thoughts is arbitrary, even absurd—while at the same time noting Marilyn's durability as a cultural phenomenon, her intensity as an object of desire, her persistence as a symbol. The reason she is in Steinem's consciousness is, presumably, because she is in so many shop windows.

How can someone so recognizable, so sellable, so *valuable,* for so long, be so unimportant? There are many answers to that question, as we will see. One is that her "please-love-me" smile is also a "please-buy-me" smile: Marilyn was always recognized as a come-on, and many people reacted with suspicion to the hard sell.

The sense of Marilyn's calculatedness has a great deal to do with her derogation. We tell ourselves now that what people once were naïve enough to buy as an ideal of sexuality was only a fantasy anyway, and congratulate ourselves on our superior sophistication. Thus *Newsweek* on *Becoming Marilyn* again: "We still have versions of the Marilyn syndrome—women living up to, even parodying, men's bizarre and contradictory perceptions of them—but nowhere in a form so pure and naïve. The sweetly corrupt style of self-representation to which she aspired now seems both too coy and too raw."[41] In other words, not only was "Marilyn Monroe" a role played by Marilyn Monroe, but we no longer fall for the performance. We recognize that she's just a sex symbol—and in many ways, for all her continued popularity and recognizability, she seems an outdated one. She has kitsch or parodic appeal, but who would take her seriously anymore?

Viewing Marilyn through the lenses of postmodernism, feminism, or camp, she appears trite; as a standard of female beauty in an age of the disciplined hard body, she is obsolescent. Anecdotal accounts by straight men suggest that the kind of legendary desirability Mailer rhapsodizes about now seems something of a puzzle, or even a joke. Straight women today often see Marilyn as a joke too, but where once they saw her as a joke on them, now they may see her as a joke she played on herself, a woman destroyed by her own willingness to play up to (or down to) men's expectations.

In *American Beauty,* a history of changing perceptions about beauty,

Lois Banner argues that Marilyn represents the 1950s' two favorite modes of femininity, which were girlishness (Debbie Reynolds, Sandra Dee) and voluptuousness, the "mammary goddess" (Ava Gardner, Jane Russell). "Both ideals," writes Banner, "reached their apogee in Marilyn Monroe."[42] Although her supposed childishness is mocked, or pitied, now Marilyn's body is often invoked nostalgically as emblem of an age when women were "allowed" to be "womanly": voluptuous, curvy and fleshy. Marge Piercy maintains that "she was one of the last female stars who had a woman's natural body. She would be told now immediately to go on a strict diet and sent for liposuction, because we are no longer supposed to look womanly. Today's stars are carved and bony. She jiggled. She swayed. She was ripe and succulent. If she had bones, they were buried in flesh."[43] Or as model Elizabeth Hurley recently put it, in a rather less feminist register: "If I were as fat as Marilyn Monroe, I'd kill myself."

However, while it is certainly true that Monroe was rounder than the "carved and bony" stars of today, it is not true that she was allowed to be heavy, or that she lived in some prelapsarian moment when our culture adored women and permitted opulent displays of female sexuality. Nor is it the case—then or now—that only men attempt to regulate women's bodies (*vide* Elizabeth Hurley). In 1953, when Marilyn had her first starring role, in *Niagara,* a woman audience member wrote a letter to columnist Dorothy Kilgallen, in which she complained about Monroe's undisciplined body:

> I have a gripe. I am making my gripe to you because as a woman I feel that you will understand and maybe do something to help the movie-going women in America fight back. I refer to the phrase that is constantly being thrown to us: "Women who dislike Marilyn Monroe are just catty and jealous of her." [. . .]
>
> The other night I went to the Roxy to get a good glimpse of this bombshell. As I sat there in my seat in the balcony and watched Miss Monroe lying in bed with her legs flung about, I began to sink lower in my seat. When she tripped away into the distance with that ridiculously tight dress on and her derrière fanning in the breeze and that silly walk, I sank lower. [. . .]
>
> I said to myself, is this refreshing? Is this the most exciting

thing to come along in years? If so, then I suggest that every hard working student in dramatic school, every burlesque queen and pulp model just hire a press agent, pose in the nude, eat rich food and let their derrières get fat, and waddle. They can't lose.

No, Dorothy, I felt no jealousy, just shame and a little fear, too, that acting such as I saw portrayed by Miss Monroe should be the criterion by which so many foolish women will pattern themselves.[44]

"Ridiculous," "silly," "shameful," "foolish"—Marilyn Monroe was a joke to much of her audience, a joke that had more than a little to do with being "overripe," overavailable, overdone. She was an embarrassment.

As we shall see, Marilyn has always represented a lack of discipline, and has always been viewed with as much discomfiture as desire. Her undisciplined, embarrassing displays are both physical and psychological: she is unrestrained, uninhibited, disordered, hysterical. Outside, she is fat, and as we shall see, inside, she is mad: both figures represent feminine licentiousness, looseness, even rebellion. And her culture responded to such excess by shaming her as much as it celebrated her. In 1960, Marilyn was criticized for having gained weight in *Let's Make Love*. "Marilyn offers her famous curves, not a little on the fleshy side. Diet, anyone?" remarked one review.[45] Her former maid, Lena Pepitone, wrote a memoir that focused largely on Monroe's fat body, disordered closets, slovenly habits. Her biographer Barbara Leaming reports that Monroe was "in despair" after seeing a preview of *Some Like It Hot*, declaring: "Everybody's going to laugh at me. And not because of my acting. I looked like a fat pig. Those goddamn cocksuckers made me look like a funny fat pig."[46] Her "overripe" body and overt sexuality were just as likely to prompt derision as desire. In Arthur Miller's *After the Fall*, written after Monroe's death, a version of Marilyn called Maggie repeatedly worries that she is "a joke that brings in money"; her guilt-stricken ex-husband Quentin cries out at one point: "I should have agreed she *was* a joke, a beautiful piece trying to take herself seriously!"[47] She had lost weight the summer she died as part of an attempt at a comeback; the coroner weighed and measured her body and reported that she was 5' 5½" tall and weighed 117 pounds. In our cultural memory, she looms larger than life: she is the colossal *Seven Year Itch* cutout dominating Times Square, not the rather slight woman she actually was.

In fact, Marilyn has come to represent not just our notion (however nostalgic and inaccurate) of 1950s attitudes toward women's bodies, but of the 1950s itself, as critics like Richard Dyer and Paige Baty show. As Dyer argued in *Stars,* Monroe's image must be

> situated in the flux of ideas about morality and sexuality that characterized the 50s in America and can here be indicated by such instances as the spread of Freudian ideas in post-war America (registered particularly in the Hollywood melodrama), the Kinsey report, Betty Friedan's *The Feminine Mystique,* rebel stars such as Marlon Brando, James Dean, and Elvis Presley, the relaxation of cinema censorship in the face of competition from television, etc. [. . .] Monroe's combination of sexuality and innocence is part of that flux, but one can also see her "charisma" as being the apparent condensation of all that within her. Thus she seemed to "be" the very tensions that ran through the ideological life of 50s America. You could see this as heroically living out the tensions or painfully exposing them.[48]

For Baty, she also represents *our* attitudes toward the 1950s: "Marilyn is at once the seemingly innocent American 1950s—a decade that is already an iconic representation of itself, for its innocence repeatedly proves itself false—and the decadence that follows. [. . .] She is simultaneously the sunny, sexy, innocent cipher and the dark, dangerous and disillusioned marker of an American legacy."[49] Some versions, like Marge Piercy's, blame the messenger for the problems of the age she symbolizes:

> I approach her with boredom and disquiet, as if circling an exotic dump of fifties paraphernalia, Freudian texts, merry widows, brassieres built like rocket launchers, spike heels four inches high, canisters of hair spray the consistency of shellac, back-alley abortions you tell no one about, marriage as the Holy Grail, ruffled aprons, and plucked eyebrows. So much verbiage swirls around

her, so many egos have flirted with and co-opted her ghost, at first there seems little at the center but a vacuum.[50]

Piercy sees Marilyn as just one more discarded 1950s object, an exhausted commodity, a squeezed-out tube of toothpaste, an empty can of hairspray with "little at the center but a vacuum." In stories like these, Marilyn's is a discontinued model of femininity.

But to see Marilyn as simply a used-up commodity is to deny the desire her image still incites. That's why Piercy feels as much disquiet as boredom: Marilyn's not done yet. She is still out there, selling herself, and her culture is still consuming her image. In fact, it is consuming images of her producing the image: In our knowing, postmodern age, that's what we like to see, the "behind the scenes" footage, the outtakes, the effort.

Sam Shaw's brilliant *mise en abyme* of Marilyn watching herself in the mirror being photographed suggests some of the complexities of the way in which Marilyn's image evokes production and consumption at the same time. This is conspicuous consumption: perfume bottles (and we know the brand without seeing the label), jewelry boxes, cosmetics and compacts, all the paraphernalia of makeup is before her, making her up. But the camera makes her up too, and so does Marilyn herself. Marilyn is always being consumed by watching eyes: "the gaze that brought her into existence as 'Marilyn,'" writes Piercy "and kept her in existence just as long as she could keep that gaze on her, was also a judgmental and piercing gaze."[51] But the gaze that brought her into existence, as Shaw's image reveals, was not just the audience's, or the photographer's, but her own. She was self-fashioning. She sold herself to us, and we are determined to view that as a Faustian pact because we think that anything that can be sold is cheap. The disturbance is caused partly by how valuable Marilyn's self-advertising has become.

Monroe was associated with advertising from first to last. In 1945, she began a highly successful modeling career, and was soon named "The Most Advertised Girl in the World!" by the Advertising Association of the West.[52] As a model, she advertised a range of products,

Marilyn Monroe, 1955. PHOTOGRAPH BY SAM SHAW.

including American Airlines, Kyron Way Diet Pills, Pabst Beer and Tar-Tan Suntan Lotion. In 1950, as a starlet, Monroe appeared in her only television ad, for Royal Triton Oil; she stood next to a car, which she explained was the first car she had ever owned, and was called Cynthia: "She's going to have the best care a car ever had. Put Royal Triton in Cynthia's tummy."[53] As she became a rising star, Monroe began advertising herself as a product—and others advertised her, as well, in promoting her image, and her career. After she died, the Marilyn Monroe estate continued to license her name and image to sell, among other products, Chanel No. 5, "Marilyn Merlot" wine, Absolut Vodka, Mercedes-Benz and Gap khakis.

In 1999, the auction house Christie's sold off some of Monroe's effects for $13.5 million. They made an additional $2.38 million just

from selling the catalogs at $85 apiece; 75,000 visitors attended pre-
views of the auction in six cities across three continents. Marilyn's
driver's license sold for $145,500; a few snapshots of her dog Maf
(short for Mafia; she named him that because he was a gift from
Frank Sinatra) went for $222,500; her white baby grand piano,
which features in her autobiography, was eventually purchased by
pop star Mariah Carey for $632,500. The dress she wore to sing
"Happy Birthday" to John F. Kennedy at Madison Square Garden in
May 1962 was purchased for a whopping $1.26 million; the memo-
rabilia shop that bought it had valued the dress at $3 million and con-
sidered the purchase a "steal."

In 1997, Mercedes-Benz used a picture of Marilyn with only one
word—"glamour"—as an advertisement. Nowhere does the name
Mercedes-Benz appear on the ad; it is impossible at first glance to
discern what is being sold, except Marilyn herself. What are we supposed to want when looking at the picture? Glamour, to be sure.
Modern advertising associates an attribute with a product: buy the
product, and you will attain the attribute. But if you want glamour, as
the ad suggests you will, how do you know what to buy? The image
plays off the idea of the trademark by replacing Marilyn's iconic
beauty mark with a tiny Mercedes trademark; both Marilyn and Mercedes have what we could call trademark glamour. They are the
desired, the advertised, the symbolic. In addition, this advertisement
increases its sense of value by association in referring obliquely to
the immensely valuable Warhol silkscreens. Warhol used a slightly
different photograph from the same sitting (with Fox staff photographer Frank Powolny), a series of publicity photos to promote *Niagara*; while not identical, the pictures are similar enough that the
allusion still registers. This kind of allusiveness is not only pictorial;
all of the stories about Marilyn similarly cross-refer to one another,
and much of the meaning of Marilyn Monroe's image, and of her
many lives, resides in the relation of one image, or story, to another.
If this kind of interrelationship of image and story, person and persona, is a hallmark of the postmodern icon in general, Marilyn is
surely an exemplary, and ideal, instance. The icon is a trademark of
itself, a person turned into a brand. The trademark trades on stereotype, it makes stereotype valuable—or rather, it makes the value of

stereotype visible in economic terms. The trademarked image, or icon, is literally a brand, a claim of ownership over a stereotype. The image of Marilyn is branded twice over in the Mercedes ad, a trademarked trademark.

Marilyn has always been seen as a series of trademarks. In 1952 *Time* magazine wrote its first full-page profile of Monroe, describing the sudden success of

> an inexpert actress but a talented woman. She is a saucy, hip-swinging 5 ft. 5½-in. personality who has brought back to the movies the kind of unbridled sex appeal that has been missing since the days of Clara Bow and Jean Harlow. The trademarks of Marilyn's blonde allure (bust 37 in., hips 37 in., waist 24 in.) are her moist, half-closed eyes and moist, half-opened mouth. She is a movie pressagent's dream.[54]

Her "trademarks" are her sexual body, and particularly her "half-closed eyes" and "half-opened mouth." Why not eyes half-open, mouth half-closed? Because it is a cliché; the cliché is a kind of literary trademark, a reproducible phrase indelibly associated with a particular concept. Marilyn succeeded in part because she became a trademark. She not only had a trademark facial expression, and the trademark beauty mark, but trademark hair and makeup. She is so branded that we need only a glimpse to recognize her; the cover to a paperback edition of Joyce Carol Oates's novel *Blonde* showed only the edge of her hair and face, but it was obviously Marilyn. And when Monroe tried to escape the trademark, or even to vary the formula, she encountered audience resistance. She had so thoroughly identified herself with a brand, an idea, an image, that she could never entirely separate herself from the trademark again: the trademark had turned into typecasting. She had become a cliché, as Richard Woodward suggests: "Her synonymy with 'sex,' like the *Mona Lisa's* with 'art,' is so pervasive that the mention of her name often bores those who detest clichés of any kind." Although she was initially compared to other Hollywood sex symbols—especially Clara Bow and Jean Harlow, as in the *Time* article above, with whom she was supposed to share an approachable, girl-next-door appeal—she has far surpassed them in remaining *the* sex symbol, in representing sex itself.

MAGAZINES AND THE MODEL

Part of the reason Marilyn became so identified with a static concept of sexuality is that she began her career as a pinup, and the representation of the pinup stayed with her throughout her career. A pinup was not quite the same as a model, selling not fashion, but a coy, sanitized, image of the sexually available woman. The pinup was friendly; she was smiling and beckoning, as in the most famous pinup from World War Two, of Betty Grable looking over her shoulder—the story goes that Grable was shot from behind because she was pregnant; the picture was taken by Frank Powolny, the same Fox photographer who took the *Niagara* publicity stills just mentioned.

One effect of Marilyn's association with the pinup was that narcissism became central to her image. Many of Monroe's most famous images position her in front of a mirror, encouraging the viewer to perceive her as enjoying her own sexuality. The famous photograph of Monroe leaning over in front of a mirror to dab Chanel No. 5 between her breasts suggests the equivalence between Monroe as a sexual commodity and the perfume with which she is synecdochically associated. Narcissists treat themselves as an object of desire— and thus tacitly offer permission for the spectator's own voyeuristic gaze. By desiring herself, the narcissist (or exhibitionist, as Monroe's biographers would "diagnose" her) invites the viewer to desire her, as well. Both narcissism and exhibitionism make audience central to the image of Marilyn: she is on display, being watched, being desired—and she likes it that way. She wants you there, watching her. She is not performing sexiness to gratify an audience, but to gratify herself. Narcissism (and exhibitionism) make the performance of sexuality natural—to her.

Monroe was discovered in a factory during World War Two, and began posing for men's magazines with titles like *Peep, Laff* and *See*. She would never be separated from that image of still, cheerfully available sexuality, as Dyer has argued:

Monroe = sexuality is a message that ran all the way from what the media made of her in the pinups and movies to how her image became a reference point for sexuality in the coinage of everyday speech.

   She started her career as a pinup, and one can find no type of image more single-mindedly sexual than that. Pinups remained a constant and vital aspect of her image right up to her death, and the pinup style also indelibly marked other aspects, such as public appearances and promotion for films. The roles she was given, how she was filmed and the reviews she got do little to counteract this emphasis.[55]

Indeed, as I argue in the discussion of Monroe's films below, not only do the roles she was given do little to counteract this emphasis, they consciously play upon it, positioning Monroe as a spectacle whose narcissism and exhibitionism invite not only desire, but derision.

Monroe also posed for what were then euphemistically referred to as "art" photographs, which was a code for pictures of nudes (the pinup would tend to be in a bathing suit, or at most seminude). Art pictures were not pornographic; in fact, the difference between art photography and pornography at that point was whether pubic hair was visible; art pictures would reveal breasts, and perhaps nipples. (*Playboy* would make history when it first published a picture in which the model's pubic hair was barely visible, in January 1971.)

The best-known of Monroe's earliest photographers, André de Dienes, made his living primarily as an art photographer, although his pictures of Monroe are, for the most part, far less "artistic" (i.e., far more clothed) than were most art pictures. De Dienes took many of Monroe's most famous early photographs as "Norma Jeane," including those of her climbing a hillside in khakis and green sweater, and sitting on the highway, as well as the shots on Tobay Beach in August 1949 that were published as *Becoming Marilyn*. These pictures of Marilyn in a bathing suit recall the art picture, but they also subvert the pinup, in being far more active, playful, even romping, than the usually static pinup girl.[56] Monroe also posed several times for a painter and photographer called Earl Moran around the same time (c. 1946–49) in seminudes. Much of what scholarship there is about

Monroe—and there is surprisingly little—has focused upon the representation of her body in these images, and the effect of these
images on the way she was visually presented on-screen, in particular the emphasis upon tits and ass, and the tendency to shoot her figure in profile or focused on the rear.[57]

Monroe's most famous pinup came from a session she modeled
fully nude in 1949, as she was struggling to make ends meet as a starlet in Hollywood. The picture, which became known as "Golden
Dreams," earned Monroe a flat fee of $50, and was sold to a company
making calendars. Three years later, the nation was gratifyingly
shocked to learn that there were nude pictures of a rising movie star
in truck stops and gas stations around the country. Monroe admitted
that she was the model, declared she had nothing to be ashamed of,
and her fame was sealed.

A year later, a young entrepreneur named Hugh Hefner bought
the negatives from the calendar company for $500 and used "Golden
Dreams" to launch a new magazine, *Playboy,* which promised for the
first time to make the "famous Marilyn Monroe nude" available to a
mainstream audience, who could simply purchase it from a news-
stand. Hefner became a millionaire by selling the picture, which
never earned Monroe more than the $50 she received in 1949. That
picture, and the scandal accompanying it, would haunt Monroe's
public persona throughout her lifetime. The well-documented impression of friendly availability that so many viewers found in Monroe's
image no doubt owes much to the implicit promise of nudity. But it
also owes something to circulation: it was, and is, easy to get a picture of Marilyn Monroe.

Although Monroe's face is now the key to her image, during her
lifetime publicity remarked relentlessly upon her body. Fan magazines featured Monroe on their covers with headlines such as
"Marilyn Monroe: How the Body Built a Career," and "Marilyn
Monroe: The Body Is Paid For." In particular, the magazine writing
that launched Monroe's career (and kept her in the spotlight even
when her acting career slowed) asked questions about the reality of
Monroe's body, questions raised by the tensions inherent in the
pinup between availability and unavailability, friendliness and cheapness, the natural and the artificial. Monroe's star rose in the same

year that America embraced *Playboy,* and that the long-awaited Kinsey Report on female sexuality was published. Sex—and in particular, female sexuality—was on America's brain.

Playboy explicitly sold Monroe's body (without asking her permission, let alone offering payment) on its cover in order to sell itself. "First time in any magazine FULL COLOR the famous MARILYN MONROE NUDE." A brief two-column article appeared alongside the centerfold, and its wording makes it clear that the article is responding to a barrage of publicity about Monroe. The article serves as a barometer registering how Marilyn Monroe was received—and perceived—in 1953, as her career was taking off and her story was first beginning to be told. The article is titled "What Makes Marilyn?" and it opens:

> Some say her real name is Norma Jean Baker. Others claim it's Norma Jeane Mortenson. Her measurements have been reported as 35" 24" 37", 37½" 25" 37½", and 37½" 23" 37½". Sometimes, she's 5'4" tall and weighs 120 pounds, but she may shift unexpectedly to 5'5½" and weigh in at 118. Though the gentlemen who handle such matters for the magazines and newspapers of the nation seem to be working with a rich variety of statistics, their sum totals all come out the same.[58]

From the beginning of her career, as *Playboy* demonstrates, Marilyn was seen as equivocal, contradictory, shifty. The article outlines conflicting reports, and then tries to dismiss any uneasiness by declaring that despite the variation in the data, "their sum totals all come out the same." But facts are not supposed to vary; if they do, they look like fictions.

The *Playboy* article goes on to explain the reason for its interest, and its attempts to resolve these contradictory reports: because Monroe is "as famous as Dwight Eisenhower and Dick Tracy, and she and Dr. Kinsey have [. . .] monopolized sex this year," *Playboy* declares that "it seems perfectly natural to ask *why?*" The answer would seem to be suggested by the three other most famous figures of 1953 to whom *Playboy* compares Monroe: one is the president, one is the "sexologist" whose long-awaited *Sexual Behavior of the Human Female* had appeared that year, and one is a cartoon character.

These affinities with power, sex and fiction slide through the article's skeptical consideration of the role publicity might have played in creating Marilyn Monroe's popularity, to suggest that she is both made-up and "the real article":

> Publicity is the most obvious answer. Nobody climbs to stardom without a healthy boost from the rear by a Grade-A publicity man. In this case, there are two—Harry Brand and Roy Craft—both Grade-A. They do their boosting for 20th Century-Fox, and they outdid themselves on Marilyn. Yet some of the biggest publicity breaks were unplanned. Marilyn's romance with Joltin' Joe DiMaggio was on the up and up. [. . .]
>
> Yes, publicity is certainly part of Marilyn's popularity—but only a part. Promotion men grow gray trying to outpromote one another in the glamour girl field, for constant exposure to the cheesecake virus has left most citizens immune. Marilyn caught on in epidemic proportions because, as *Life* put it, she's "the real article."
>
> What makes Marilyn *the real article*?
>
> [. . .]
>
> More than either face or body it is what little Norma Jean has learned to do with both. [. . .]
>
> There is nothing else quite like Marilyn on this good earth—be it animal, vegetable or mineral. She is natural sex personified. It is there in every look and movement. That's what makes her the most natural choice in the world for our very first *Playboy Sweetheart*.[59]

Actually, *Life* called her the "genuine article." *Playboy* wants to know if she's the real thing, but starts out by strongly implying that she is indeed manufactured by the Hollywood studio system, and invented to be consumed: her stage name has been invented and her real name changes from one version to the next; her vital statistics also vary. But having acknowledged the possibility that Monroe was fabricated for its pleasure, *Playboy* insists that she was natural, "the real article." It finally concludes that she was made naturally, but the obsessive insistence upon her naturalness in an article so concerned with her dubiousness might suggest (to a suspicious reader) that *Playboy* is protesting too much.

One might be tempted to dismiss *Playboy* as unrepresentative of orthodox American attitudes to the female body in the 1950s. But this would be profoundly to misunderstand *Playboy*'s conventionality and popularity (by 1960, *Playboy* had a circulation of 1.2 million readers a month, and had built Hefner an empire worth $16 million).[60] Furthermore, inarguably mainstream magazines represented Monroe in exactly the same terms, as a naturally naked body. Monroe was a staple of national magazines for a decade, featured regularly in *Look, Collier's, Cosmopolitan, Esquire, Family Circle, Photoplay* and, of course, *Time* and *Life*. *Time* magazine referred repeatedly to the nude calendar scandal in its first full-page write-up of Monroe in August 1952:

> A loud, sustained wolf whistle has risen from the nation's barber-shops and garages because of Marilyn's now historic calendar pose, in which she lies nude on a strip of red velvet. Uneasy studio executives begged her last January to deny the story. But Marilyn believes in doing what comes naturally. [. . .]
>
> When she's alone, she often strikes art poses before a full-length mirror, admiring the beautifully distributed 118 lbs. that millions of moviegoers admire. [. . .]
>
> In one scene in *Monkey Business* [a Monroe film recently released], Charles Coburn tries, unsuccessfully, to explain the intricacies of typing to Marilyn, who plays his secretary. Coburn finally watches her make her hip-swinging exit, then shrugs and says to [Cary] Grant: "Anyone can type." Apparently Marilyn's avid, growing following feels strongly that anyone can act.[61]

This passage, written the year Monroe became a star, suggests many of the elements in the Marilyn image. It will always recall the photograph (and in particular the pinup). It will suggest that her open sexuality comes "naturally" to her, and that in fact, she poses when alone, and in the nude ("strikes art poses"), the implication being that these poses are not acting, but being herself. And finally, to reinforce this idea, it will position her as a natural model (she is there to be looked at) but as a nonperformer (what we are looking at is the real person).

Monroe was on the cover of *Life* eight times between 1952 and 1972, more than anyone else except Audrey Hepburn. Her first *Life* cover, on April 7, 1952, followed hard on the heels of the nude calendar scandal, which had broken in March. The magazine called her a "sturdy blonde" who was "the talk of Hollywood" because "somewhere between her ingenuous mind and voluptuous body came a spark of the kind that makes movie personalities."

> Because her movie role is always that of the dumb blonde, Hollywood generally supposes she is pretty dumb herself. This is a delusion. Marilyn is naïve and guileless. But she is smart enough to have known how to make a success in the cutthroat world of glamour, [. . .] being as wholly natural as the world will allow.[62]

Whether she was indeed naïve and guileless would preoccupy writers to come. But initially, she is innocent, glamorous and natural.

In 1956, Monroe had her only cover of *Time* magazine, which included a long feature-length profile. It declared that "Marilyn Monroe's hip-flipping, lip-twitching, frolicsomely sensual figure is the latest curve on the path of erotic progress that has led Hollywood from the slithering vamp to the good-natured tramp." It commented on her weight—"she is a little leaner (118 lbs.) than she looks on the screen"—and on her appearance. She

> looks a little too beautiful to be true [. . .] The eyes are large and gray, and lend the features a look of baby-doll innocence. The innocence is in the voice, too, which is high and excited, like a little girl's. [. . .] Monroe is for millions a figure of fantasy rather than of flesh. She offers the tease without the squeeze, attraction without satisfaction, frisk without risk.[63]

The original piece was researched and written by Ezra Goodman, but *Time*'s editors rewrote it. Goodman went on to publish a witty, intelligent history of the studio system, *The Fifty-Year Decline and Fall of Hollywood.* In it, he describes the way in which he carefully researched and substantiated a factual story about Monroe for *Time* that the editors promptly fictionalized:

> The editors commended "the absolutely first-rate" research, and then, as usual, proceeded to ignore it. What appeared in *Time* can be read in the May 14, 1956, issue of the magazine. It bears little or no relationship to the laboriously assembled and documented material that was sent to New York. Of course, some things could not be printed in *Time;* there are even, as you might imagine, some things that cannot be printed in a book. But the final result in the magazine was more fictional than factual. It blithely disregarded the reporter's report and was compounded mostly of hearsay, myth, old file clippings and just plain invention. [Columnist] Walter Winchell, no friend of *Time*'s, had taunted the magazine in his column with "What can the *Time* cover say that's new about Monroe?" The story that appeared in the magazine did nothing to offer a rebuttal to Winchell.
>
> If, as a Hollywood medical friend of mine maintains, "all actresses are made of steel," Monroe was cast in an even mightier mold than most of them. But what appeared in *Time* was a sort of high-toned, polysyllabic fan-magazine story about an innocent in the Hollywoods.[64]

The desire to view—or construct—Monroe as an innocent, a creature of natural, almost helpless sexuality is such a crucial part of the story that the magazine's editors were not interested in hearing anything else. This tendency to repeat what we already believe, to deny what we don't want to accept, will characterize the myth of Marilyn Monroe from beginning to end.

By 1958, the anxious insistence upon her naturalness, that she wasn't acting but just being herself, had become such a pervasive interpretation that when Monroe did a photo shoot for *Life* magazine in which she impersonated the earlier sex symbols with whom she was often compared, she was again declared to be not acting—and this time, by her husband at the time, Arthur Miller. In the December 22, 1958, issue of *Life*, Marilyn Monroe, working with photographer Richard Avedon, posed as famous screen "sirens" Lillian Russell, Theda Bara, Clara Bow, Jean Harlow, Marlene Dietrich—and herself. In fact, the imitations are uncannily accurate, and the startling resemblance Monroe created to these very different women might actually seem to prompt the article's dogged assertion that in these pictures Marilyn really is just being herself. Otherwise, lining up "Marilyn" alongside all the other iconic women she is performing might just suggest a bit too uncomfortably that Marilyn, too, was a performance. And in fact, the Marilyn shot by Avedon shows a rather different Marilyn from the studied, static glamour she had been projecting: her figure looks startlingly contemporary, displaying a much more relaxed and confident (rather than aggressive) Marilyn.

Arthur Miller extolled the layout as "a kind of history of our mass fantasy, so far as seductresses are concerned." Miller wrote a two-page introductory gloss for the layout, in which he explicitly, if a bit sententiously, historicizes Marilyn Monroe in the tradition of these other female movie stars: "In our time Marilyn is their heiress. The picture at the left is an attempt to portray her as 'herself' and it succeeds as much as any single picture can. For in anything she does she is 'herself.'" But why set off "herself" in scare quotes, if not to imply an ironic distance from the conception of her just being herself? Miller's uneasiness—is she herself, or isn't she?—is echoed by the magazine's editors, who caption a candid picture taken during the shoot: "Photographer Richard Avedon feels this is the real Marilyn, a loving wife playfully kissing her brilliant husband, playwright Arthur Miller." Marilyn Monroe may be a role, but Marilyn Monroe can't play it, she can only be herself. Everyone was always looking for the real Marilyn Monroe while insisting that she only did what came naturally.

Once Monroe became a movie star, she used the still photograph strategically to publicize her career. It is not the case that Monroe started out as a still model and became an actress; Monroe, perhaps more than any other movie star, not only used still photographs to further her career (a common practice) but *performed* in those stills.

Monroe was eventually photographed by some of the most important photographers of her day, including Henri Cartier-Bresson, Richard Avedon, Cecil Beaton, Milton Greene, Eve Arnold, Philippe Halsman, Elliott Erwitt and Bert Stern. Most wrote about her after her death, eulogizing her in glowing terms (although they tend to snipe at one another) as a "photographer's dream." As McCann notes, although Monroe's film directors comment repeatedly on her "insecurity, inconsistency, and panic," her still photographers "were aroused to passionate awe" by her mastery of the form, and what many of them consider her genius.[65] Richard Avedon said "she gave more to the still camera than any actress—any woman—I've ever photographed."[66] Eve Arnold declared:

> I never knew anyone who even came close to Marilyn in natural ability to use both photographer and still camera. She was special in this, and for me there has been no one like her before or after. She has remained the measuring rod by which I have—unconsciously—judged other subjects.[67]

Although Monroe reportedly started out early in her modeling career by asking constant questions of her photographers about posing, lighting, angles, and why certain pictures worked and others didn't, by the end of her career photographers were admitting to having learned from her. Douglas Kirkland, who was just starting out when he had the opportunity to work with Monroe in the last summer of her life, said that she taught him "the importance of movement in a shooting session. Things have to *jump*. . . . Everything must be bouncing and rolling."[68] Many photographers comment on the way she would transform or come to life for the camera, that she had a unique relationship with the camera eye:

> I worked with Marilyn Monroe. A rather dull person. But when I said "Now!" she lit up. Suddenly, something unbelievable came across. The minute she heard the click of the camera, she was down again. It was over. I said, "What is it between you and the camera that doesn't show at any other time?" She said, "It's like being screwed by a thousand guys and you can't get pregnant."[69]

Eve Arnold writes in perhaps the clearest terms about Monroe's technical skill with the still camera, and her insistence that she maintain control over the finished product:

> If an editor wanted her, he had to agree to her terms. She knew how she wanted to be seen, and if her cooperation was sought, she reserved the right of veto.
>
> She knew she was superlative at creating still pictures and she loved doing it. [. . .]
>
> She had learned the trick of moving infinitesimally to stay in range, so that the photographer need not refocus but could easily follow movements that were endlessly changing. [. . .]
>
> At first I thought it was surface technique, but it went beyond technique. [. . .] It didn't always work, and sometimes she would tire and it was as though her radar had failed; but when it did work, it was magic. With her it was never a formula; it was her will, her improvisation.[70]

Arnold quotes the photographer Burt Glinn saying: "She had no bone structure—the face was a Polish flat plate. Not photogenic in the accepted sense, the features were not memorable or special; what she had was the ability to project."[71] In other words, she was acting. According to one critic, Monroe was different from other pinups because "her pose, her expression, her costume, all encourage interaction rather anonymity [*sic*] on the part of the spectator," so that "the viewer is made to feel less a voyeur and more a participant"; "the quality that made her different from the hundreds of other sex-goddesses procured by Hollywood's system" is that she gradually came to appear ever more "natural and spontaneous" in her poses, which makes her seem even more attainable than the more static poses of the conventional pinup.[72]

Monroe often used props and costumes in her best photography sessions, which enabled her to perform different personas in the stills. This is perhaps clearest in two sittings: the beautiful costume pictures she made with Milton Greene in Hollywood in 1953 (instead of the usual "crappy pinuppy stuff," Greene "photographed her as if she were Garbo"),[73] and in the justifiably famous Last Sitting she produced with Bert Stern a few weeks before she died. In the Last Sitting, Monroe uses a variety of props: scarves, beads, necklaces, champagne glasses and different clothes to produce entirely different looks, moods and styles. Like Arnold, Stern writes about Monroe's active involvement in the shoot:

> She was much more of a partner than I'd expected. The first hour or two I had an idea of what I was after. I had all kinds of imagery floating around, and she was picking up on it, performing it all. I didn't have to tell her what to do. We hardly talked to each other at all. We just worked it out. I'd photographed a lot of women, and Marilyn was the best. She'd move into an idea, I'd see it, quick lock it in, click it.[74]

These are also the pictures that show most clearly Monroe's interest in—and control over—the finished image: she x'd out in orange marker, and with a pin, those images of which she disapproved. Stern complained about it:

> *she had crossed over half of them out.*
>   On the contact sheets she had made x's in magic marker. That was all right, although I didn't agree with her—I thought some of the ones she'd crossed out were beautiful. But she had x-ed out the color transparencies with a hairpin, right on the film. The ones she had x-ed out were mutilated. Destroyed.
>   I have to admit I felt some anger at her at that moment. Not that she didn't like all my pictures, but that she'd been so destructive about it! [. . .] I would have been kinder to her. She hadn't just scratched out my pictures, she'd scratched out herself.
>   When she made her mark on these pictures, she had less than two weeks to live.[75]

As we will see, this practice of interpreting Monroe retroactively through the hindsight of her eventual death is extremely common, and it is misleading. Perhaps she was scratching out "herself"; perhaps she was a professional scratching out an image to which she felt no attachment, because it was precisely not herself as she wished to see herself, or for others to see her. Perhaps she was controlling her performance.

Many of the most famous still photographs of Monroe were publicity shots for her films, in which she recognizably strikes poses associated with the characters. This is perhaps most obvious in her leering expression in the *Niagara* still that Warhol used; the character she played in the film is sexually aggressive and predatory. The most famous stills of all, of course, are the shots of Monroe in a white dress on a subway grating from *The Seven Year Itch* (1955), taken as a publicity stunt: none of the photographs taken on Lexington Avenue in New York in front of a crowd of thousands actually appeared in the film, which used a scene reshot in the studios. But the image of Marilyn in this picture is an image drawing on the character from the film. The famous gold lamé dress that features in many stills, and which caused an uproar at an awards ceremony in 1953, similarly came from a film: it was originally intended for *Gentlemen Prefer Blondes*, but never used in the film (but now features on the covers of many Marilyn books).

Another familiar pinup pose would appear to come from *How to Marry a Millionaire*, but never appears in the film. It does, however, *allude* to a scene in the film: Monroe wears a strapless purple evening gown and stands in front of a multiple mirror, which reflects her famous body from all angles. In the film, she is wearing glasses in order to inspect herself before meeting a man she hopes to marry: she briskly twitches the gown, checks herself over front and back, removes her glasses, and turns and walks into a wall. The film scene refers to her desirability but also mocks it, as critic Sabrina Barton has argued: "the glasses are a constant reminder that Monroe is indeed performing idealized femininity for a specific audience. Also, the fact that Pola cannot see well and is constantly embroiled in slapstick situations without her glasses, pokes fun at seamless images of (nonbespectacled) glamour such as the one frozen in the famous publicity still."[76] The still image entirely lacks such irony: Marilyn is without glasses, striking a pose, far more narcissistically positioned as someone implicitly enjoying her own sexuality (rather than anxiously checking it over for flaws) and inviting the viewer to share that narcissism. Moreover, she has her arm thrown up over her head at an angle, recalling the pose of the pinup, and specifically that of the nude calendar picture that had scandalized the nation the previous year.

The movement between pinup pose and film performance is not only in one direction, and this is the important point. Just as her photographic image drew on her film performances, so did her films position her as a model, striking static poses inviting the viewer to remember her as a pinup. In *The Seven Year Itch* she stands on the subway grating while her costar, and the plot, stop to admire her; in *How to Marry a Millionaire,* she is not only positioned in front of the multiple mirror, but there is a long set-piece in the film in which Monroe and her two costars, Lauren Bacall and Betty Grable, pose as models for the man—and the audience—watching them. In this scene, supposedly for a fashion house describing its autumn line, Monroe's character is introduced with the line "diamonds are a girl's best friend," the famous tag line from *Gentlemen Prefer Blondes,* which appeared only months before *Millionaire.*

This self-referentiality would increase as the Marilyn persona became more stereotyped, and more familiar. This was part of a general (and generally postmodern) trend in Hollywood films toward the kind of intertextual references that undermine a film's realism and self-consciously joke about its own status as a Hollywood film. (To take another example from a Monroe film: when Tony Curtis's character does a Cary Grant imitation in *Some Like It Hot,* his friend Jack Lemmon responds exasperatedly in the same accent: "Nobody talks like that!" The joke of course is that only Cary Grant talks like that.) The two film roles that most pointedly recalled her persona as "Marilyn" were in *The Seven Year Itch* and *The Misfits.* Although, particularly in terms of *The Misfits,* these roles are frequently described as alluding to Monroe's *life* offscreen, this is only partly the case. They refer more obviously to her *persona* offscreen, and that persona developed through the evolution of her visual image and her film roles.

THE FILMS

Whether Monroe was a good actress continues to be a matter of debate; if anything, most people simply assume—usually without having seen her films—that she wasn't. Although she was never nominated for an Oscar or received any real public accolades as an actress, she did win awards in Europe, and a Golden Globe in the United States. More important, many of her coworkers on film, including directors and some legendary stage actors, consider her to have been a "genius" at film acting. A fair amount of commentary on Monroe's acting is available in scholarship and in the biographies; Carl Rollyson's "critical biography," which anchors Monroe's life in her work, offers the most sustained, insightful account of her performances and the evolution of her technique (although his account of her offscreen life is far more problematic, as we shall see). Director Billy Wilder, who worked with Monroe on two films, declared that she was the "meanest woman in Hollywood," and that working with her required "nerves of iron and total dedication, like climbing the Himalayas." He said she was plastic, "a DuPont product," with "breasts like granite and a brain like Swiss cheese, full of holes."[77] But he also said: "She was an absolute genius as a comic actress, with an extraordinary sense of comic dialogue. . . . Nobody else is in that orbit; everyone else is earthbound by comparison."[78]

But the clichés about the Marilyn persona have overtaken the reality of her performances. The presumption that she was not an actress (but a model) is just the most obvious instance of an interpretive practice that colors all aspects of what we think we know about Marilyn Monroe. To take a smaller example, the whisper. When commentators refer now to Monroe's persona, they will inevitably mention the iconic, supposedly childish "whisper" with which she is associated. In point of fact, Monroe only whispers like that in a few comic roles, and really only in the two films she made in 1953, *Gentlemen Prefer Blondes* and *How to Marry a Millionaire.* Even in *The Seven Year Itch,* which represents the Marilyn persona par excellence, her voice is high-pitched and chirpy, in keeping with the comic insouciance of the role (whereas she plays the femme fatale in *Niagara* in a much deeper vocal register), but it is by no means always breathy. In many scenes in the film (for example, when playing "Chopsticks") her voice is merrily robust. Monroe used breathiness when playing a certain kind of role, when creating a seductive moment.

Similarly, if her persona is that of a "dumb blonde," the dumbness is not general, but specific: her comedy was based on wide-eyed literalism, on non sequiturs and misinterpretation. Literalism suggests innocence, naïveté, even naturalness: it is unconscious, unknowing, unsophisticated. For example, two famous quips with which Monroe was associated were both dependent for their comedy upon the suggestion of literal-mindedness. The first is the famous reply to being asked what she wore to bed: "Chanel No. 5." Similarly, one of the jokes she delivered to the servicemen in Korea expressed bewilderment over all the fuss about so-called sweater girls (pinups): she artlessly asks, "Take away their sweaters and what have you got?" The most famous of all may be her response, quoted in *Time* in 1952, when asked if she had anything on during the nude photo shoot: "I had the radio on." This literalness became part of her comic persona, on-screen and off, helping to blur the boundaries between the two. One of the few lines in which Lorelei Lee, in *Blondes*, explains that she is smarter than she seems was, reportedly, suggested by Monroe: when a man exclaims that he thought she was dumb, she replies, "I can be smart when it's important, but most men don't like it." Later in her career, as with so many aspects of her persona, it became so familiar that it was joked about in the scripts of her films: in *The Prince and the Showgirl,* Elsie listens to the Regent deliver a long, trite, seduction speech and then translates it as, "You mean you want me to kiss you," to which he responds, complainingly: "You're so literal." As we shall see, such literalism becomes so strongly associated with Monroe that it defines her biographical interpretation, as well; literalism seems contagious in the Marilyn myth, as if her biographers catch it from her persona (or from one another).

In her earliest films, however, before she became a star, Monroe was typecast less comically: initially she was a troublesome sexual schemer. Of the seventeen films in which Monroe appeared through 1954, she played some version of a sexually opportunistic woman—gold digger, prostitute, or woman "on the make"—in nine. In three more, she was an ambitious showgirl or a model: less predatory, but no less professionally sexual. The roles that got Monroe noticed by the critics and by the public were without exception playing sexual opportunists: gold diggers in *The Asphalt Jungle, All About Eve, Gentlemen Prefer Blondes* and *How to Marry a Millionaire,* and a sexual predator (femme fatale) in *Niagara.* Lorelei Lee, from *Gentlemen Prefer Blondes,* is only the most famous role of a series that helped define Monroe's public persona. In the roles she played in these early films, Monroe played a woman literally selling sex, and thus she was also figuratively "selling sex" (i.e., emphasizing her desirability) as an actress. As such, she became identified with the type of the gold digger, and the notion of a woman on the make has never been far from the story of her life. As Rollyson persuasively argues: Monroe was only "given credit for skillfully playing parts according to her type, and not for imaginatively exploring a type according to her talent."[79]

The type of the gold digger was itself a source of enormous cultural anxiety in the American 1950s, an unsurprising if unfair reaction to the sexual economics of marriage. In an era of unprecedented prosperity and of sexual conservatism, sex and commerce were strongly associated culturally with Monroe's persona. For example, the first issue of *Playboy* featured not only Marilyn Monroe on the cover and the nude photograph of her inside as its first playmate (or "Sweetheart," as Hefner then called her); its very first article is called "Miss Gold Digger of 1953," and is a harangue against alimony that complains that "it doesn't matter who's to blame. It's always the guy who pays and pays, and pays, and pays." The article ends with a caveat to the reader: "it's important to remember that the modern gold digger comes in a variety of shapes and sizes. She's after the wealthy playboys, but she may also be after you." Innocence, cheerfulness and comedy became a crucial way of managing not just the aggression, but the cupidity implicit in Monroe's sexual come-ons.

From 1946 to 1950, while she was making a living as a model, Monroe had bit parts in a series of films that are now only remembered as the

films that launched her, including *Scudda Hoo! Scudda Hay!*, *Dangerous Years*, *A Ticket to Tomahawk*, *The Fireball* and *Right Cross*.*
Monroe had signed a standard studio contract with 20th Century-Fox in 1946; they dropped her a year later, and in 1948 she had a brief stint as a contract player at Columbia Pictures. It was at Columbia, in 1949, that she had her first substantial role in a B-grade support musical, *Ladies of the Chorus*, in which she sang and danced for the first time on-screen, and for which she received her first press reviews. (It was in this film that she sang "Every Baby Needs a Da-Da-Daddy," a song that would be echoed at the end of her career when she sang "My Heart Belongs to Daddy" in *Let's Make Love*.)

In 1950 Monroe appeared in three films that garnered her the attention of audiences, press and film distributors. The first was *Love Happy*, a Marx Brothers film in which Marilyn had a brief but conspicuous "walk-on" part that featured her walking away from Groucho, hips swinging. It was the first of many early emphases upon Monroe's walk, which would culminate in her long walk in *Niagara*, which received an amazing amount of attention ("like Chaplin," photographer Eve Arnold opined, Marilyn "built her film character around her walk").[80] The next two films, and roles, were considerably more memorable: she played the gangster's moll Angela in *The Asphalt Jungle*, directed by John Huston, and the aspiring starlet Miss Caswell in Joseph Mankiewicz's *All About Eve*. These were Monroe's first bona fide "A-grade" ventures, when she was in the company of Hollywood's biggest name directors and stars. Her performances were favorably reviewed and duly noted; her career had acquired the momentum it needed to take off.

Although she continued to be cast in a series of unmemorable films over the next two years (*Hometown Story*, *As Young as You Feel*, *Love Nest*, *Let's Make It Legal* and *We're Not Married*), Monroe began

---

*There are also rumored early appearances in several other films. Richard Buskin, in *Blonde Heat: The Sizzling Screen Career of Marilyn Monroe*, "carefully reviewed" each of the following films, and found "no evidence" of Monroe's presence: *The Shocking Miss Pilgrim*, *Mother Wore Tights*, *The Challenge*, *You Were Meant for Me*, *Deep Waters*, *Green Grass of Wyoming* and *Meet Me After the Show*. He also refutes the persistent rumor that Monroe appeared in a stag film called *Apples, Knockers and Coke*. Rumor has tenaciously associated Monroe with pornographic films early in her career, but all of her principal biographers agree that these rumors are false.

to be given larger parts. These films tended to be lightweight romantic comedies, but Monroe's role as the sex object meant that she was in a sense the straight man; certainly her talent as a comedienne had not yet revealed itself. In these films, for the most part Monroe's acting is definitely strained, and often awkward: in particular, she speaks in a noticeably mannered way, with exaggerated lip movements and diction. These exaggerations make them easy to parody, and they became remembered as part of the Marilyn persona; for those dismissing Monroe, these mannered speech patterns became part of the ammunition used against her. (However, Monroe was at this time being coached on every film by Natasha Lytess, a failed actress on Columbia Studio's payroll who signed on as Monroe's full-time acting coach. Monroe checked every take for Lytess's reaction, so presumably Lytess approved Monroe's pronunciation. Certainly when Monroe fired Lytess, at the time of *The Seven Year Itch,* she stopped talking like that.)

In 1952 Monroe had her biggest year yet, with substantial parts in several more memorable films. *Clash by Night* was a political drama based on a Clifford Odets play; Monroe was the second female lead in a film starring Barbara Stanwyck. Generally acknowledged as one of her best early performances, it is also one of the few in which she plays someone down-to-earth; neither a sexpot nor a schemer, her character is natural and feisty. The film is also remembered as the first to follow the nude calendar scandal, which occurred in March of that year; the film was released in June, and did consequently healthy business at the box office. Monroe's name was above the titles for only the second time in her career, and would stay there. That year she also made *Monkey Business,* with Cary Grant and Ginger Rogers; directed by Howard Hawks, this film was the first to cast Monroe in what would become her fixed type: the dumb, childish blonde innocently unaware of the havoc her sexiness causes around her. By no coincidence, the same director would cast Monroe in the part that defined her persona forever after.

The most important film for Monroe of 1952, however, was *Don't Bother to Knock,* her first lead role in a major film. She played the extremely implausible part of a psychotic babysitter, deranged by the death of her fiancé in World War Two. "A so-so psychological thriller hampered by an improbable plot and sometimes laughable dialogue," as Richard Buskin notes, in his history of Monroe's films, *Blonde Heat: The Sizzling Screen Career of Marilyn Monroe,* most agree that the film was not the right vehicle for Monroe. Although she had been studying hard with acting teacher Michael Chekhov since the autumn of 1951, as well as with Lytess, she had nothing like sufficient technique to make such a silly role seem persuasive. Rollyson is more generous, considering her acting in the film good, and the flaws to be all in the way the part was written: "Monroe declared that *Don't Bother to Knock* was one of her favorite films. She believed that in it she had given one of her strongest performances."[81] Although the film received mixed reviews at best, having been released only six weeks after *Clash by Night* and one week after *We're Not Married,* it benefited from the continued publicity from the nude calendar scandal, tripling Fox's investment.[82] She next appeared in *O'Henry's Full House,* a star-studded "anthology" of five short vignettes, in which she featured opposite Charles Laughton as a nineteenth-century streetwalker.

These four movies were rapidly followed by Monroe's first real star vehicle, *Niagara,* which began filming on May 26, 1952. *Niagara* consolidated not Monroe's persona, but her look (the whole Marilyn persona would take another year to emerge clearly). Both the look and the image were being carefully produced: Buskin reports that her longtime makeup artist and close friend Allan "Whitey" Snyder believed that, after several years of work, they had achieved her "look" by the time of *Niagara*: "By that time we both knew exactly how she wanted to look, and we used that look for several pictures in a row. [. . .] Slowly but surely we changed the eyebrows and the eye shadow and things like that, and the look was established."[83] Once it was established, it was modified, but did not vary again in any substantial way.

Rose Loomis is the most consciously sexual of all of Monroe's characters, and the only true femme fatale she would play, an amoral, adulterous and homicidal wife in classic noir style. For all the distinctness of this character, Rollyson argues that "*Niagara* initiates the many 'Marilyns' to come, a point Andy Warhol has grasped brilliantly in his many portraits of 'Marilyns.' "[84] This is true up to a point, but unconscious, rather than conscious, sexuality would become the Marilyn hallmark after 1953.

An extraordinary amount of *Niagara's* publicity concentrated on the 116-foot walk that Monroe's character takes toward Niagara Falls, in which the camera focuses upon her swinging hips; it was dubbed "the longest walk in movie history." Reviewers and movie columnists asked one another how this supposedly remarkable walk was "achieved"; Monroe was quoted as commenting: "I learned to walk as a baby and I haven't had a lesson since." Arthur Miller said in his autobiography, *Timebends,* that "it was, in fact, her natural walk: her footprints on a beach would be in a straight line, the heel descending exactly before the last toeprint, throwing her pelvis into motion," although this does not of course mean that she could not have learned to walk that way.[85] But other people proffered the following explanations for what was seen as so remarkable a method that it required explanation: Emmeline Snively, the head of Monroe's former modeling agency, said her walk was due to weak ankles; Monroe's acting coach, Lytess, claimed to have invented it; and gossip columnist Jimmy Starr said that Monroe shaved off part of one high heel so that her walk would become uneven. The dispute, if it can be called that, over how "the walk" was developed is entirely typical of the controversies about Marilyn Monroe. It focuses on her body, and in particular on its sexuality (in this case, hips, buttocks and legs), and argues over whether it was produced naturally or artificially.

In *Gentlemen Prefer Blondes* Monroe played Lorelei Lee, now one of her most iconic roles; it was Monroe's largest-grossing film to date, making more than twice its cost at the box office; it was the third-most commercially successful film of her career.[86] With *Some Like It Hot* and arguably *The Misfits,* it is the film that has received the most scholarly attention, primarily for its visual presentation of Monroe. Monroe's biographer Barbara Leaming argues convincingly that *Gentlemen Prefer Blondes* is the first performance of "The Girl," or the Marilyn persona, who would come to dominate the majority of

Monroe's roles after 1953, and that it was in this film that she "transformed herself into a star of the first magnitude":

> Bits and pieces of "the girl" may have emerged in previous films,
> but this was the first time Marilyn had put them all together. Thanks
> to [director Howard] Hawks, her look in the film was blonder,
> sleeker, cleaner-lined than in the past. Thanks to Hawks, her per-
> formance was supported by a beautifully made film. But the
> essence of Marilyn's own creation was a perfect balance of sex and
> humor. [. . .] In an important twist, "the girl" has wit but—unlike
> the tougher, more knowing character Mae West once created—she
> doesn't use her wit as a weapon. The character Marilyn created is
> totally unthreatening to men. Also, unlike West, "the girl" seems
> completely unaware that she is being funny. That made the char-
> acter difficult to play, but Marilyn brought it off to perfection.[87]

Leaming appears not to have read McCann's study of Monroe, in
which he quotes her as saying about Mae West: "I learned a few
tricks from her—that impression of laughing at, or mocking, her own
sexuality."[88] As noted above, this character had really only been
hinted at in one other Monroe film, also directed by Howard Hawks.
Although Leaming surely gives Hawks far too much credit (and others might want to give him blame), it does seem clear that he helped
Monroe develop the Marilyn persona. She would never fully abandon it again.

Blondes is a bold, over-the-top Technicolor musical about performance: Lorelei is an actress on and off the stage, whose depths
the film never establishes. She knows more than she lets on, but is
never "off." The idea that this character is "totally unthreatening to
men," as Leaming would have it, makes no sense; the plot revolves
around the anxiety she causes all four male principals. That she is a
performance is highlighted by the fact that Jane Russell does a burlesque imitation of Marilyn-playing-Lorelei at the end of the film.
"What is thrown into relief" by these constant performances, as Barton
argues, is "how the Monroean character thereby thwarts efforts (on
the part of the other characters or on the part of viewers) to discover,
diagnose, and define a real woman behind the bombshell persona."[89]

In this sense, Lorelei would seem an iconic role because she so closely approximates the cultural fictions about Marilyn herself, which are so entangled with the facts.

Up until Lorelei Lee, Monroe was not cast in especially comic roles, nor was she particularly associated with "dumb" characters. If anything, the schemer is reasonably smart, or at least shrewd in her manipulativeness. Lorelei Lee was a turning point, the hinge from sexual schemer into innocent dumb blonde. Lorelei is both, and neither: the film refuses to fix how much she knows, exactly. *Blondes* features the show-stopping "Diamonds Are a Girl's Best Friend" number, in which sex and money are conflated with Marilyn's body, but she is also performing this song onstage. Lorelei, like Marilyn, begs the question of how much is a performance, how much is natural. What is she *really* like? Lorelei cemented not only Monroe's fame, but also her wide-eyed, artfully delivered unwittingness. Although it is true that Monroe played some version of a showgirl for nearly all of her career—a role predicated on the professional exploitation of sexuality, which created excuses to put her on display—it is also true that the girl she played became ever more recognizable as a variation on the theme of "Marilyn" after *Gentlemen Prefer Blondes*.

Capitalizing on the success of *Blondes,* Fox cast Monroe in another role as a gold digger in *How to Marry a Millionaire,* the first film shot in CinemaScope (although released after *The Robe*), in which her costars were Lauren Bacall and Betty Grable. Screenwriter Nunnally Johnson adapted the three characters to the actresses; the script also has an in-joke reference to each of them: Lauren Bacall's and Betty Grable's characters both refer to their real-life famous husbands (actor Humphrey Bogart and bandleader Harry James), while Monroe is introduced, as I noted above, with the phrase "diamonds are a girl's best friend," and she later reads a book called *Murder by Strangulation,* which was her character's fate at the end of *Niagara*. Johnson later claimed that he made Monroe's character nearsighted in order to reflect "what he saw as her insensitivity—her way of cutting off the world—and her self-absorption."[90] Such cinematic references to Monroe's ostensible offscreen reality do not simply blur boundaries between performance and self, as it is important to bear in mind that Johnson was already interpreting Monroe. Pola Debevoise is his comic reinterpretation of his opinions about Monroe, and as such the role helps to suggest that the fictions about the persona are natural, for her.

By the end of 1953, Monroe was an undisputed international superstar, bringing enormous revenue to Fox. "In 1953, Fox's two greatest assets were CinemaScope and Marilyn Monroe, in that order."[91] Her popularity was such that, with the new widescreen process, she was heralded as Hollywood's defense against the incursions of television.[92] According to *Time* magazine in 1956, at the end of 1953 she had made more money for her studio than any other actress in Hollywood.[93] After *How to Marry a Millionaire,* Monroe's career would begin to take a sharp turn, as she fought to be given a chance to play a part other than a sexy showgirl on the make.

Fox next cast her in *The River of No Return,* in which she plays a nineteenth-century sexy showgirl on the make, although she did at least get to wear Levi's as she stood on a raft floating down the river. Monroe angrily later denounced the film as "a grade-Z cowboy movie in which the acting finished second to the scenery and the Cinema-Scope process." This isn't entirely fair: although it suffered from an inane script, the film had reasonably high production values and big names in director Otto Preminger and costar Robert Mitchum. More important, Monroe's character does evolve: although the part is trite (the woman with a past and a heart of gold), she is not a flat one-dimensional joke. The film certainly didn't make the most of Monroe's increasingly specific talent for comedy, however, and she gave her most mannered performance for some time, overenunciating and overacting. Nonetheless, the combined popularity of Monroe and Mitchum, along with the new CinemaScope process, were enough to make the film profitable, although not nearly as successful as her two previous films. Fox followed this by casting Monroe in the musical "extravaganza" *There's No Business Like Show Business,* in which she plays a sexy showgirl on the make who is only revealed at the end to have a heart of gold. Unlike *River, Show Business* didn't turn a profit; it didn't break even at the box office. Both of these films are notable for the weakness of their scripts and the thinness of Monroe's characters; Monroe only accepted the part in *Show Busi-*

ness as a compromise for turning down an even weaker part in *The Girl in Pink Tights,* and in exchange for the lead role in the film version of the stage hit *The Seven Year Itch.* In fact, Marilyn would be dogged by weak scripts for her entire career; only *Some Like It Hot* would give her anything like scope for her talent.

The Seven Year Itch contains what may be the single most recognizable scene from any movie ever made: Marilyn Monroe in a white dress on a subway grating, enjoying the breeze that fans the skirt up around her waist. Ironically enough, the familiarity of the image comes not from the film itself, but from the photographs publicizing the film. Monroe's character is called only "The Girl": her type is so familiar that she needs no more back story than that. In fact, her type is that of a girl without back story: The Girl never mentions friends or family, only the men who try to seduce her. She exists only in relation to men's fantasies: her character provides the film simply with an occasion for a series of jokes about male desire. The film, based on a hit stage play, concerns a married man's adulterous fantasies about the girl upstairs. On Broadway the affair was consummated, and his guilt-stricken fantasies and projections fueled the play's comedy. However, the Hays Office, Hollywood's censorship board, had banned any scripts that associated adultery with comedy. In the film Tom Ewell's character must therefore have guilt-stricken fantasies based solely on his desire for her, which has the effect of making both characters even more childish. Rollyson provides a nice summary of The Girl's characteristics and appeal:

> Sherman, like the moviegoer, only has to dream about her in order for her to appear. She remains accessible even after Sherman blunders badly in his seduction of her; she is, in short, the perfect plaything, a *living* doll, as one of the characters in the film keeps insisting. [. . .] She constantly strokes [Sherman's] middle-aged ego.[94]

However, although The Girl's innocent sexuality is certainly crucial to her character, she is not as dumb as some writers make out, as

Rollyson also observes: "there is a matter-of-factness about her, a down-to-earth directness reminiscent of Clara Bow that is disconcerting for Sherman."[95] The Girl is artless and unsophisticated, but she is not stupid.

Sherman's fantasies are partly lifted from Hollywood clichés, in which he imagines The Girl as vamp and as gangster's moll (in a scene cut from the final version): finally, when questioned as to the identity of the girl upstairs, he declares sarcastically: "Maybe it's Marilyn Monroe!" In a clear sense it *is* Marilyn Monroe: by this time, Monroe herself was so famous, such a stereotype, that her screen roles were playing on the type: innocently desirable, cheerfully dim but occasionally shrewd, the constant "butt" of puerile jokes about her body (carrying an electric fan, she is positioned so that the camera is pointed at her backside when she requests help, because her fan is stuck in the door). In an even clearer allusion to Marilyn's off-screen image and history, Sherman discovers that The Girl has posed nude in an "art" book that he has on his shelf. Later The Girl proudly shows the picture to him: "Look! That's me, right there on the beach. My hair was a little longer then, did you notice?" To which Sherman, looking at the picture, responds (predictably): "No, actually I didn't." She offers to autograph it for him, artlessly commenting: "People keep asking me to." Writers often complain that the anonymity of Monroe's character in this film reflects only the misogynistic self-absorption of the fantasy she was portraying. This is inarguable, but it is also true that the character didn't need a name because everyone in the audience already knew her name: Marilyn Monroe.

After *The Seven Year Itch*, Monroe left Hollywood for New York, mostly in rebellion against Fox's insistence that she continue to play the formula that was bringing them so much money, and her so little. Her motives were both personal and professional: her contract hadn't changed although her career had skyrocketed, so she was being paid a fraction of her market value, and less than most of her costars (Jane Russell was paid approximately ten times more than Monroe for *Gentlemen Prefer Blondes*, for example, while Monroe reported later that she had to fight even to be given a dressing room by a studio that kept informing her she wasn't a star). She was also in rebellion against being typecast. Monroe formed her own production company and announced her intention of improving her acting and having greater control over her roles and films. She was promptly accused of pretension, and the papers were filled with outright derision.

The next film she made, after winning her yearlong battle with Fox, was *Bus Stop,* with director Joshua Logan. There is no doubt that the part of Cherie is considerably more nuanced and subtly written than Monroe's previous cartoon roles; Cherie has a past, dreams and desire; an "abused, tired-looking nightclub singer with a checkered past and uncertain future," she is more knowing and mature than the naïve cowboy who falls in love with her. Far and away Monroe's best performance to date, and arguably her best performance ever, Cherie is by turns wistful, bemused, sad, hopeful and angry. "Cherie is not just another one of Monroe's dumb blondes; there is a difference in the writing and the performing of this character and her successors."[96] Like Elsie Marina, Sugar Kane, Amanda Dell and Roslyn Taber, the characters Monroe played in her next, and final, four films, Cherie is worldly-wise, more mature than the men around her, "more of a whole person, less of an unblemished character, not so unreal as The Girl or Pola or Lorelei Lee."[97] Although Monroe's reputation for behavioral problems on set (lateness, not knowing her lines, demanding scores of takes and retakes) was by now preceding her, her director and her costar, Don Murray, both finished the film convinced of her genius. Logan said: "I finally realized that I had a chance of working with the greatest artist I'd ever worked with in my life, and it was Marilyn Monroe. I couldn't believe it."[98] Don Murray, a successful stage actor making his film debut, who clashed with Monroe several times during filming, nonetheless concluded that she was a far better screen actor than he: "When the first preview took place, we were all stunned. We couldn't believe how good Marilyn was. That's when all of us stage people came to realize that the screen medium is a totally different animal."[99] The critics agreed, *The New York Times* declaring: "Hold onto your chairs, everybody, and get set for a rattling surprise. Marilyn

Monroe has finally proved herself an actress in *Bus Stop*. She and the picture are swell."[100] The film doubled its cost, earning $4.25 million in its first run.

The only film that Monroe's production company independently made was *The Prince and the Showgirl,* with Laurence Olivier costarring and directing. Shot on location in London, the film was an extremely difficult experience for all concerned. Monroe's personal problems were escalating, and in Olivier she encountered a director with no intention of indulging her anxieties. Although a showgirl, Elsie Marina was something of a departure from The Girl because she is perfectly intelligent, even wise; not only the catalyst, she is in control of much the film's action, outmaneuvering the grand duke and his son, the prince. Monroe turned in another nuanced performance in a film that wasn't up to her standard, and that astonished the coworkers who suffered through the difficulties she caused during production. Oscar-winning cinematographer Jack Cardiff described the frustration of take after take during which Monroe forgot or blew her lines, and their subsequent amazement when viewing the rushes. He concluded with a backhanded compliment: "She wasn't an actress, she was a genius."[101] Dame Sybil Thorndike was more generous: "She's the only one of us who really knows how to act in front of a camera."[102] Dame Edith Evans visited the set, and told Monroe afterward: "When I saw you on the set, I thought you weren't even working. Then I saw the rushes in the projection room, and the scenes are all yours."[103] The film itself was not successful in America, receiving mixed to bad reviews. But Monroe won the DiDonatello award for her performance, the Italian equivalent of Hollywood's Academy Award.

Some Like It Hot is undoubtedly the best film, as a whole, in which Marilyn Monroe participated: performances, writing and direction were all at their peak. It was also one of the most successful films of the decade, grossing more than three times what it cost to make. Monroe gives one of her best performances, but so do her costars, Tony Curtis and Jack Lemmon. Sugar Kane is a singer with a small band, a girl with a past who says she's "not very bright"; but unlike previous Monroe characters, she's smart enough to consider herself "not very bright" for always falling for the wrong men and "ending up with the fuzzy end of the lollipop":

> I'm not very bright, I guess . . . just dumb. If I had any brains, I wouldn't be on this crummy train with this crummy girls' band . . . I used to sing with male bands but I can't afford it anymore . . . That's what I'm running away from. I worked with six different ones in the last two years. Oh, brother! . . . I can't trust myself. I have this thing about saxophone players, especially tenor sax . . . I don't know what it is, they just curdle me. All they have to do is play eight bars of "Come to Me, My Melancholy Baby" and my spine turns to custard, I get goose pimply all over and I come to 'em . . . every time . . . That's why I joined this band. Safety first. Anything to get away from those bums . . . You don't know what they're like. You fall for 'em and you really love 'em—you think this is gonna be the biggest thing since the Graf Zeppelin—and the next thing you know, they're borrowing money from you and spending it on other dames and betting on horses . . . Then one morning you wake up, the guy is gone, the saxophone's gone, all that's left behind is a pair of old socks and a tube of toothpaste, all squeezed out. So you pull yourself together. You go on to the next job, the next saxophone player. It's the same thing all over again. You see what I mean? Not very bright . . . I can tell you one thing—it's not gonna happen to me again—ever. I'm tired of getting the fuzzy end of the lollipop.[104]

Rollyson argues that *Bus Stop* and *Some Like It Hot* together are "the two films that most fully bring out the comic myth of Monroe's persona"; McCann says that *Some Like It Hot* "is the quintessential fiction *on* Monroe."[105] If so, once again, as in *The Seven Year Itch,* the stupidity of the character has been exaggerated, even misrepresented. Monroe reportedly objected to being forced back into playing a showgirl so dumb that she can't tell that the women she is becoming friends with are men in drag. She also insisted that Wilder and Diamond write a better opening for her: "I'm not going back into that fucking film until Wilder reshoots my opening," she is supposed to have declared.

"When Marilyn Monroe comes into a room nobody's going to be looking at Tony Curtis playing Joan Crawford. They're going to be looking at Marilyn Monroe."[106] But Monroe's character is not the only one in the film who falls for the comically bad disguise; in the convention of farce, all the characters are fooled by it. Other than that, Sugar Kane is not particularly dumb. The speech above reflects experience, self-knowledge, bitterness. The "dumbness" of Monroe's persona had become so axiomatic that it overpowered all else.

Let's Make Love was a film Monroe was forced into by her revised contract with Fox; it was a script she disliked, and which was turned down by no fewer than seven leading men, who are said to have either shared Monroe's distaste for the film, or to have declined to work with someone with her growing reputation for behavioral problems. Fox eventually hired Yves Montand, who barely spoke English, to make his first film. Monroe was even more difficult than usual, refusing to show up for work for days at a time, leaving her costars cooling their heels while she, depending on whom you read, fought stage fright, chemical dependency, her husband or her studio. By this point her reputation had become part of her press. *Life* ran a profile promoting *Let's Make Love* headlined "A Legend Is Costly but It's Worth It." The article opens:

> Even Hollywood, which has long held the copyright on psychological whim and fancy, has never found a way to handle the drives and compulsions of Marilyn Monroe. In the filming of *Let's Make Love* her little ways cost 20th Century-Fox 28 days' extra shooting time, nearly $1 million in added costs.
>
> The movie executives were glad enough to put up the money— a Monroe picture can hugely fill up the till—and her colleagues were glad enough to put up with Marilyn. They know her as a perfectionist who never gives up trying, even if she is chronically unable to get to work on time.[107]

Faced with an inert, inane film, the studio supposedly resorted deliberately to publicizing Monroe's on-set affair with Montand in order to inject the frisson of scandal into the project. The tactic failed, however, and the film flopped, earning only a third of what it cost to make.[108]

Monroe's character, Amanda Dell, has only a little of what had by this point become her persona's trademark self-referentiality: she takes night classes, hopes to improve herself, and is worldly-wise, even a little weary, all of which were features associated with Marilyn Monroe offscreen. She is another showgirl, but Monroe was essentially cast as straight man, against Montand (who also played a straight man; they forgot to write a comic role, which is one of the reasons why the film is so dire). Still, Amanda Dell is rather more competent and human than some of the earlier cartoons Monroe played, if underdeveloped and profoundly uninteresting. The film was noteworthy primarily for a few musical sequences, in particular an opening rendition of "My Heart Belongs to Daddy" (a song reminiscent of Monroe's first song on-screen some eleven years previously, "Every Girl Needs a Da-Da-Daddy"), prompting Steinem's acerbic observation that it is impossible to imagine a leading man of comparable stature to Monroe sucking his thumb and singing "My Heart Belongs to Mommy."

The Misfits would be Monroe's final completed performance, and the problems filming it were legendary, even for a Monroe picture. Monroe reportedly collapsed during filming. Although one of her biographers, Donald Spoto, insists that she was fine and taking the public fall for financing problems caused by director John Huston's gambling, photographs of Monroe returning to work show a physically ravaged face that belies such a sunny claim. The part of Roslyn Taber was written for Monroe by Arthur Miller, and would be the culmination of the self-referential roles Monroe had been playing since 1953. Roslyn is a version of the Marilyn persona, half-fact, half-fiction, leaving Monroe playing "a misconstrued concept of herself."[109] "The line between art and life was perilously thin" for all involved, writes Rollyson:

> Montgomery Clift, in particular, felt the self-reflexive quality that informed his as well as Monroe's role. In a naked admission of the

lifelike nature of film [. . .] Clift commented: "Someone said, 'My God, it's exactly like you.' Now it's just a question of can I do it? It's a wonderful part, and if I don't do it justice I'll shoot myself." Miller denied having written the character specifically for Clift, but like Gable and Monroe, Clift would inhabit his role, making it look like a fusion of art and life.[110]

The Misfits is a deeply sad movie, but critics are divided on its worth. Most seem to agree that although the performances delivered by leads Monroe, Gable (also in his final film) and Clift are among their best work, the script suffers from leaden pretension, and nothing much happens. The characters are flat, one-dimensional allegories of loneliness. In particular, Roslyn, who was conceived as a "valentine" to Marilyn's humanity, remains a symbol of nature and of generously available sexuality: she even hugs trees to show how natural, earthy and artless she is. In the film's most self-referential—and arguably cruelest—moment, Marilyn's character enters a room in which the inside of a closet door has six taped-up pictures that are clearly of Marilyn Monroe. One is a large, instantly recognizable glamorous head shot; one is a *Seven Year Itch* still of the white dress blowing up around her legs; two are pinups in bathing suits; and one shows her with bent arms thrown up over her head in a pose reminiscent of the "Golden Dreams" nude. The camera lingers on the pictures while Roslyn (Monroe) and Guido (Eli Wallach) enter the frame, and Roslyn shuts the door to the closet. When Guido opens it again, looking the pictures up and down, Roslyn shuts the door once more, saying, "Oh don't look at those, they're nothing. Gay just had them up for a joke." Guido opens the door again, and Roslyn looks briefly annoyed before firmly fixing her smile back on her face as she shuts the door for a third and final time.

"He could have written me anything, and he comes up with this," Monroe would later say. Roslyn is just an older, sadder and wiser version of The Girl: a showgirl who is remarkable only for the desire she inspires in the men around her. Most important, she has none of the power or professional success that marked Marilyn Monroe—Roslyn is a failed dancer, rather than the biggest movie star in the world; her only talent is her natural, artless, outpouring of love. Roslyn is the

Marilyn stereotype, made natural. Everyone knew that Miller was writing *The Misfits* to celebrate his wife's humanity; he ended up just affirming the truth of the cliché.

In 1962, Monroe began work on *Something's Got to Give,* a remake of a twenty-year-old Cary Grant comedy. Since *The Misfits* ended, she had lost between fifteen and twenty-five pounds (depending on whom you read); some critics say she looked radiant, others that she looked haggard. Certainly she began displaying her body again, and stripped off the flesh-colored bikini she was wearing for a "skinny-dipping" scene in the film and posed nude for the first time since the beginning of her career: she was the first major movie star to pose for nude pictures on set, while a star.

At this time, television was seriously challenging the cultural, and fiscal, supremacy of Hollywood film in the world of American entertainment. Fox was filming *Cleopatra,* starring Elizabeth Taylor, who was being paid a $1,000,000 salary and allegedly received $50,000 a week overtime; she was therefore being made rich from the delays she caused to an already exorbitantly priced project. Taylor's affair with costar Richard Burton was dominating the world's headlines, but Monroe's nudes knocked Taylor off the front pages (Monroe was reportedly exultant at triumphing over her longtime rival). But the problems with *Cleopatra* continued; Fox shut down most other productions except for *Something's Got to Give* and gambled everything on their two divas. Monroe was only being paid her contractual salary of $100,000, for which she had fought so hard in 1955; her costar Dean Martin, who had nothing like Monroe's box office power, was being paid $500,000 and Cyd Charisse, in a supporting role, was getting $50,000. Monroe caused some delays to the production, attending the Madison Square Garden benefit for John F. Kennedy's birthday despite studio orders that she stay and work on the film; she then called in sick for several days afterward (though whether she was struggling with sinusitis or with her drug addiction remains a question, as we shall see).

On June 7, Fox fired Monroe from the film, issued a barrage of negative publicity about her, including accusations of insanity, and sued her for $750,000 for breach of contract. In retaliation, Monroe went to work on her publicity, and began granting interviews and holding photo shoots (it was at this time that she held the two taped interviews with Richard Meryman and Georges Belmont that are the basis for the documentary film *Marilyn on Marilyn*), offering her side of the story and showing her fitness for work, including the photo sessions with George Barris on Malibu beach in a handmade Mexican cardigan (which Christie's sold for $167,500), and the Last Sitting for *Vogue* with Bert Stern. She died on the night of August 4, 1962.

Fact and fiction, performance and the real, are always part of the Monroe story. Most writers have contented themselves with discussing one or the other: either promising to reveal the "real" Marilyn, or analyzing the effects of her many representations. Although it is common practice for academic or analytical discussions to assume that Monroe's reality cannot be recovered, and that therefore the image is all we have, this is not the whole story. In fact, it is far too easy to treat Marilyn Monroe, as for example Baty does, as merely a cultural phenomenon, a series of iconic representations that have no particular relationship to the facts of her life. Barton even goes so far as to argue that such a reading, taking Marilyn at "face value," is politically resistant: "the absence of an inner depth or truth of self, as performed by Monroe through displays of stunning unwittingness, functions very usefully to produce impenetrability. If no one really knows what is going on inside her, that is because her identity can only be accessed at face value."[111] But this simply evades the ethical question about representation. Marilyn was not only a fiction; she was not simply an icon. And it is wishful thinking to believe that focusing exclusively on the surface does anything other than make her seem superficial.

Where academia has focused on the play of surface and façade, biography has promised depth and truth. But it must do so by reproducing the fictions. As we shall see, biographies about Marilyn Monroe have a very problematic relationship to fiction. Although biography depends upon an implicit contract with the reader that documented fact is being accurately represented, in Monroe's case this obligation is rarely, if ever, met. Although the promise of fact in Monroe's case is a deeply *problematic* one, as I shall show in the rest of this book, it is not nonsensical or trivial. Unless we are to embrace psychosis, we must agree that there *is* a difference between fact and fiction, between historical reality and individual imagination: biographies about Marilyn Monroe are interesting precisely because they reveal, and inhabit, a very murky space between the two.

The truth about Marilyn Monroe's life and self exceeds the commodification of her image and the literary representations of her self: as Lee Siegel memorably put it in an incisive review of Oates's *Blonde,* if Marilyn Monroe is an icon, then it follows that "to be an iconoclast today would be to assert the worth of human beings beyond the marketplace, to become a fine Kantian pain in the ass." We should remember to be Kantian pains in the ass: representations of Marilyn Monroe are indubitably commodities; she clearly felt treated like a commodity while she lived (and resisted that feeling); but this does not mean that she is *only* a commodity, even once she is dead. The person does not collapse into representations of her: she had and has a reality that escapes our efforts to represent, to understand, and to sell it.

Marilyn Monroe is not best understood as only an image, or as an "artificial creation of a woman," and the "real Marilyn Monroe" is not at all an oxymoron. For all our fascination with the artifice of the media with which we surround ourselves, we remain naïvely, nostalgically suspicious of the manufactured, and pious about the natural. Marilyn Monroe was not completely natural. She seems indeed to have developed out of a performance that was deliberately played; the person she grew into may well have been fabricated out of a blend of real materials. None of these renders her false, imaginary or unreal. Something that is not natural can still be real: it has been made. One of the questions the stories about Marilyn's life beg, therefore, is how much any of us is natural, whether any identity is not-made. Monroe's quest for self-improvement meant that she evolved, her image resisted that evolution, and the tension between the two produces the many lives of Marilyn Monroe.

Marilyn Monroe, leaving the press conference at which she announced she would be divorcing Joe DiMaggio, 1954.

2

PRODUCING THE LIFE, 1946–2003

Please don't make me a joke. End the interview
with what I believe. I don't mind making jokes,
but I don't want to look like one.

—MARILYN MONROE,
Life interview, August 3, 1962

The image that opens this chapter was used by Maurice Zolotow for
the cover of his revised 1990 edition of *Marilyn Monroe,* usually considered the first major life of Marilyn. The photograph was taken in
1954, when Monroe drove away from the press conference at which
she announced her intention to separate from Joe DiMaggio; she
clutches a handkerchief, and is weeping. With all the benefit of hindsight, twenty-eight years after she died, Zolotow and his publishers
choose an image of a "tragic" Monroe: this is the emblematic
Marilyn, beautiful but sad. We have made Marilyn into our secular
lady of sorrows.

But in her 1998 biography, Barbara Leaming claims that the
entire press conference was one of Monroe's better performances, in
which she was weeping crocodile tears to gain public support for
what would be an unpopular divorce from a national hero, baseball
star Joe DiMaggio: "there must be no trace," Leaming writes, "of her
steely determination to be rid of him." Which is the real Marilyn,
tragic victim, or devious manipulator? The biographical battles to
produce, and reproduce, the *real* Marilyn Monroe, to tease her out
from the image of natural, cheerful sexuality on permanent offer, are

the subject of the rest of this book. In revision, the myth of Marilyn moves from joy to sorrow, from innocence to cynicism, from comedy to tragedy.

The story goes like this: trapped behind the innocent, happy fiction of "Marilyn Monroe" there was a suffering real woman, whom we hardly know. She became a cautionary tale in death, a casualty of her attempts to live a lie. "Marilyn Monroe was nothing if not a sacrifice to her own mythology," Andrew O'Hagan recently observed in *The London Review of Books,* even as O'Hagan's summary of Marilyn's fate itself exemplifies that mythology:

> Marilyn invented a persona—The Girl—that would at first seem to release her from the bad things of her childhood, but which later became like one of her childhood ghouls, leaning over her, making her all sex, suffocating her. The Girl was a fiction and a mask—"Mae West, Theda Bara, and Bo Peep all rolled into one," said Groucho Marx—which served to turn a case of ordinary, everyday wishing into a triumph of calculated stardom. [. . .] The Girl, the resulting character, would seem to carry vulnerability and sexual freedom to a new place in the movies, but in real life, in the decompression chamber of overblown ambition, the person who called herself Marilyn Monroe could only unravel in a miasma of loneliness and uncertainty and pain. And worst of all, even this, her bad times, her suffering, came in the end to add to the myth of her specialness. In her own lifetime she became the patron saint of sex; and afterwards, in her very modern martyrdom, she made us feel that an engulfing sadness does not in any way preclude a giant success. Marilyn's fans find the combination fatal. And so unfortunately did she.[1]

That's the myth in a nutshell. Or, as Monroe herself is supposed to have dejectedly said when her marriage to Arthur Miller unraveled, "I guess I *am* a fantasy."[2] Biographies have promised since the beginning of Marilyn's life in print to unveil the real woman behind the fantasy, but the "truths" that they reveal are a fable we already knew. The moral of the story of Marilyn Monroe is that trying to be someone other than your real self will destroy you: counterfeit kills, to thine own self be true. At least, such is the distilled wisdom of thousands of magazine and newspaper stories, sixty full-length biographies, forty-odd bio-pic and documentary films, twenty or so plays, a dozen scholarly articles, at least ten novels, two academic monographs, two musicals, a ballet, an opera, and an Elton John song. (And that's just in English.) As news goes, it is a somewhat belated revelation.

The fictions running so rampant in the Marilyn image become an essential aspect of the supposedly nonfictional story of her life. The "fiction and [the] mask" that O'Hagan believes "suffocated" the woman smother the story as well. Journalism, novels, films, biographies—they all dutifully recite the same tale, trot out the same bromides right on cue, and it rapidly becomes difficult to distinguish truth from truism.

Its blending of fact and fiction makes the "Marilyn" persona seem especially suited to hybrid works that cross conventional boundaries of genre, compounds of fact, fiction and fantasy. There are "novel biographies," biographical novels, and fictionalized autobiographies about her life. Books that claim to be told "in her own words" and those in which she "speaks for herself" were not written by her. There are novels and short stories that use her as a fictional character, and that invent "sequels" to her life (such as *Marilyn's Daughter*, which features a daughter with the improbable name "Normalyn"). There were several stage dramatizations of Marilyn, all of which, with the exception of Miller's *After the Fall*, were notable commercial failures: musicals, opera and Norman Mailer's play *Strawhead* all disappeared; *After the Fall*, a cause célèbre, was commercially successful but initially a critical failure, although its reputation has improved over time. As I write, Miller has just produced a new play entitled *Finishing the Picture*, which is about working with Monroe on the set of *The Misfits*. Marilyn remains a highly desirable—and profitable—piece of merchandise; it is hardly surprising that new objects from the same mold keep being produced.

Unlike other pop-cultural icons, however, such as Elvis Presley or James Dean, Marilyn has been written about by some of our culture's more respected authors, including not only Miller (four times and counting), but also Norman Mailer (three times), Joyce Carol Oates (twice), Truman Capote, Thomas Pynchon, Ayn Rand and Diana Trilling. Jean-Paul Sartre said Monroe was the finest actress alive; Saul Bellow discussed her when he was interviewed by *Playboy*; Vladimir Nabokov said she was superb. While Marilyn is like other pop icons in prompting adoration from fans and facile comments from pundits, she is unique in being someone sufficiently interesting for highbrow writers to devote entire works to her. If anything, her viability among the literati has increased with time, despite her persistent cultural belittlement. The reasons for this are diverse (to take just two examples, Mailer wrote for money, Miller for absolution), but one more covert explanation for Marilyn's popularity with "serious" authors may be that she offers a writer instant fiction, ready-to-hand. She herself is seen as someone made-up, and her story is tragic fairy tale: small wonder so many writers have succumbed to temptation and reproduced her myth. But because the shape of the story is prefabricated and predetermined, writers find what they sought, and Marilyn stays a cliché, a dead metaphor.

The first half of this chapter provides an overview of the development of Marilyn Monroe's many lives. The second half offers some thoughts on the problematic role of fiction in a few of the principal texts in genres other than putative biography (which will be the subject of the rest of the book). The first is Marilyn's so-called autobiography; it is followed by a look at the ways she has been authored in different modes by three influential writers: Arthur Miller's memoirs of Marilyn in his play *After the Fall* (1964) and his autobiography, *Timebends* (1987); Norman Mailer's idiosyncratic blends of fantasy and fact in *Marilyn* (1973); and Joyce Carol Oates's roman à clef, *Blonde* (2000).

1946–1953

The story of Marilyn Monroe's biographical life opens with the first studio biographies, written to promote a new contract player; they helped establish the legendary aspects of Marilyn's life. These aspects read like fiction because they are: from the outset, her life story was always partly made up. Initially, the fictions in her studio biographies were no different from those of many other Hollywood stars in the heyday of the studio system, which sanitized and manipulated the images it was selling. Attempting to make Monroe's potentially controversial early life respectable, these mini-lives cheerfully blend error, euphemism and outright fabrication. What is particularly interesting, in hindsight, is their equivocation over Marilyn Monroe's real name.

The first Marilyn biography was a brief description of "Marilyn Monroe, 20th Century-Fox discovery." Issued in 1946, by the head of 20th Century-Fox's publicity department, Harry Brand, it claimed her real name was "Norma Jean Daugherty," which it was not, and that her age was eighteen, when in fact she was twenty. Five years later, Brand issued another biography to follow up on Monroe's growing fame after her small but conspicuous roles in *The Asphalt Jungle* and *All About Eve*. This time her real name was "Norma Jean Baker," another inaccurate—if more tenacious—name, and she was twenty-two, instead of twenty-five. This second account was both more detailed and more fictional than the first. It explained that her mother was "a helpless invalid" and that her father had died in a motorcycle accident, neither of which is quite true. The story made much of Monroe's childhood in and out of foster homes and orphanages, ending with a paean to Hollywood, which, although "often the scene of heartbreak, has been the scene of her success." The same year, 1951, Monroe was loaned out to RKO, which wrote its own biography. The first sentence announced: "From lonely orphan to sought-after motion picture star is the true life Cinderella story of Marilyn Monroe." This brief chronicle, too, made much of her childhood in foster homes and an orphanage, and her new success, "in which the heartaches of the past will be remembered only as inspiration for the future."

Although popular myth holds that Marilyn Monroe was forced to change her name by her pernicious studio, these earliest publicity accounts, from several studios, promptly admit that Marilyn Monroe was not her real name. They even offer that real name to the reader. More ironically still, the supposedly real name changes from account to account, while the "artificial" name Marilyn Monroe remains consistent. From the beginning, that is, she was presented as "someone artificially called Marilyn Monroe who is really called Norma Jean."

The name change was always part of the story: this is a tale of trans-formation, and has been from the start. Her real name has thus con-sistently been part of writing about her, as has her troubled childhood, the Cinderella story of leaving the past behind for new success and glamour.

By the end of 1953, Marilyn was an international celebrity; that year saw the first of three full-length biographical profiles that would appear during the next few years. None of them were fully researched, independent biographies; rather they were recapitula-tions of the fan-magazine profiles that had been appearing for several years. The first two were Joe Franklin and Laurie Palmer's *The Marilyn Monroe Story* (1953) and Sidney Skolsky's full-magazine issue *Marilyn* (1954). Both versions are now extremely difficult to find; the Franklin and Palmer is the highest-priced Marilyn life today, worth between $800 and $1,500. In 1956, after Marilyn abandoned Hollywood, proclaiming her desire to improve herself as an actress, journalist Pete Martin published *Will Acting Spoil Marilyn Monroe?*, which began as a series of articles for the *Saturday Evening Post*. Martin, too, relied upon circulating fan-magazine fare about Monroe's deprived childhood, and stories about her lateness, her marriage to DiMaggio, and her desire to improve herself, but he interviewed Monroe as well.

All of these versions portrayed Marilyn Monroe as a poor orphan girl, raised in a series of foster homes and orphanages, who had refused to allow her (sexual) standards to be compromised on the mean streets of Hollywood, and who had become a star thanks to the public's spontaneous (natural) liking. Although the facts were never reliable in these accounts, some of the themes that would persist were already stressed, particularly the hardship of her early years, art-lessness, and innocence.[3]

MY STORY: 1954

By March 1954, twenty-seven-year-old Marilyn Monroe had become one of the biggest movie stars in the world. She had married baseball legend Joe DiMaggio a month earlier, and had just come back from a triumphant honeymoon tour of Korea, in which she had entertained thousands of American GIs to thunderous acclaim. Upon returning to Hollywood, where her hand- and footprints had already been preserved in front of Grauman's Chinese Theater, she was persuaded to capitalize on her newfound celebrity by beginning an autobiography. It was born out of a collaboration with journalist and screenwriter Ben Hecht, hired as ghostwriter, and with movie columnist Sidney Skolsky, who was a friend of Monroe's and sat in on the writing sessions. Throughout the spring, she and Skolsky met with Hecht. While Hecht wrote, Marilyn Monroe talked, often, according to Monroe's biographer Donald Spoto, with "Skolsky ready to chime in."[4] The story they produced was almost certainly sanitized for a mainstream 1950s audience, but to what degree one can only speculate.

Unfinished, the manuscript was pirated by Hecht's agent and sold to the London *Empire News,* where parts of it were serialized. Monroe threatened to sue, but eventually the book was simply abandoned.

LA MONROE DESNUDA, THE FIRST LIFE: 1960

The first substantive Marilyn biography, Maurice Zolotow's *Marilyn Monroe* (1960), actually commenced, like the first three lives, as a series of magazine articles. It was based on several interviews Zolotow held with Monroe for *The American Weekly* in 1955, and also relied heavily upon recycling previous magazine stories, including the pirated portions of *My Story.* It received some good reviews when it first appeared, including one in the *Times Literary Supplement,* which declared that Zolotow's "persuasive case" for Marilyn's "historical significance as a symbol of certain important American desires and aspirations is both interesting and important. There is no denying that the hefty volume which has resulted from his labours is not only highly literate and documented to the hilt but also compulsively readable."[5] Both the review and Zolotow himself (in his preface) note that it was unusual to bestow upon a movie star such "serious" attention, but none of the editions of Zolotow I have seen could be said to document "to the hilt" by today's biographical standards. None of his quotations or facts are attributed directly to named sources, and many of his stories are a mélange of anecdote and conjecture.

Monroe is said to have expressed "reservations" about the finished product, and it is not hard to see why. Zolotow's book is an eccentric mixture of the censorious and the celebratory, the liberal and the chauvinist, offering "La Monroe Desnuda" (in his phrase) to the reader. Many of the aspects that would characterize future accounts of Monroe's life are already present: in particular, his account stresses her troubled childhood as a cause of later psychological insecurity, finding her to be a personality ultimately "split" between "dark" impulses and the moral codes she had been taught in religious foster homes. Zolotow will be the first in a long line of biographers who projects a justification for his own voyeurism into Monroe's head: "his eyes, consuming her, expressed great admiration. She felt good about this. Beautiful women, more than any other kind, need to be constantly assured that they are beautiful."[6] Most important, his narrative stresses her fundamental innocence and naïveté, locating in the real woman the essential quality of the "Marilyn" stereotype. In the U.K. edition of Zolotow's book, which came out in 1961, after Monroe and Miller divorced, Zolotow makes a prediction that says little for his powers as an oracle: whatever her suffering, he explained, Marilyn Monroe was ultimately a survivor. Although it turned out to be inaccurate, his assessment does seem, however, to reflect the "steely determination" that many who knew her say characterized Monroe.

Between 1961 and 1964, Marilyn would be the subject of much magazine writing, but no serious full-length consideration. In 1961, another expanded magazine interview appeared as a biography, George Carpozi, Jr.'s *Marilyn Monroe: "Her Own Story."* Like Zolotow, Carpozi relied upon a series of interviews from 1955 with Monroe; he produced a largely recycled biography, which reprints some of the earlier material virtually word for word. Over the course of the next year, Marilyn would be more newsworthy than ever, as her career was perceived to be in a tailspin. After she was fired in June 1962,

Marilyn held a series of interviews calculated to prove she was ready and able to go back to work. The most famous of these was one she gave to Richard Meryman for *Life* magazine, which appeared on August 3, 1962, the day before she died.

After her death, there were hundreds of magazine tributes all over the world. An anonymous book of dubious origin surfaced soon after she died, in 1962, called *Violations of the Child Marilyn Monroe,* by "Her Psychiatrist Friend," but not until 1964 would the sudden death of a screen goddess start to accrue the trappings of a legend. *Life* magazine published a cover story on August 7, 1964, offering thoughts by Clare Boothe Luce on "What Really Killed Marilyn" (the answer: spinsterhood). But 1964 was a watershed year in the Marilyn myth primarily because it saw two very different, though equally controversial, renditions of Marilyn: Arthur Miller's play *After the Fall,* and Frank A. Capell's pamphlet *The Strange Death of Marilyn Monroe.*

SUICIDE AND MURDER: 1964

In 1964, Arthur Miller produced his first play since 1956, the year of his marriage to Monroe. *After the Fall* concerns the memories of a man named Quentin, whose life and experiences clearly reflect Miller's own. The play is about betrayal: guilt ripples out in concentric circles with one man at the center, from his intimate relationships with the women in his life, to professional friendships with men in the context of a national witch hunt (the House Un-American Activities Committee, HUAC), to the global scale of the Holocaust. Like Miller, Quentin has left his first wife of many years because she insists upon her own innocence while accusing him of failing her and their marriage; he has since fallen in love with Maggie, an internationally famous pop singer bewildered by her own success, and torn between terror and resentment that no one takes her seriously ("I'm a joke that brings in money!").

After the Fall reunited Miller with Elia Kazan, the acclaimed director who had been Miller's close friend (he directed *Death of a Salesman*) and who had first introduced Miller and Monroe in Hollywood in 1951, while the married Kazan was evidently having an affair with Monroe. Miller and Kazan had parted company over Kazan's decision in 1952 to collaborate with the HUAC and name names; Miller had publicly snubbed Kazan after his capitulation. That their reconciliation took place over Marilyn's dead body is more than a little ironic, an irony that did not escape the notice of critics, who were fairly unanimous in their recoil from what they saw as Miller's exercise in self-justification. *The New Republic* called *After the Fall* a "shameless piece of tabloid gossip," and declared it "astonishing that a playwright, whose major business is perception, could live with this unfortunate woman for over four years, and yet be capable of no greater insight than those of [. . .] a professional theater columnist."[7]

The same year that brought *After the Fall*'s portrait of a Marilyn at once suicidal and psychotic also saw the publication of a seventy-page pamphlet called *The Strange Death of Marilyn Monroe,* by Frank A. Capell, which is widely acknowledged as the first published text to imply that Marilyn Monroe had been sexually involved with Robert F. Kennedy during the last summer of her life, and to suggest that the Kennedy brothers might have been implicated in Marilyn's death. The pamphlet was published by Capell's own imprint, called "Herald of Freedom," which describes itself as "a national anti-Communist educational bi-weekly." The title page explains that its author and publisher, who "maintains files on two million people who have aided the International Communist Conspiracy," "has been fighting the enemies of our country for twenty-six years in official and unofficial capacities." Capell is also the author of "Freedom Is Up to You," "The Threat from Within," "857 Reasons for Investigating the State Department," and *Henry Kissinger, Soviet Agent.* He apparently was one of the first writers to link Lee Harvey Oswald with the Soviets, as well. Although the newsletter circulated widely in intelligence and other "patriotic" circles (supposedly J. Edgar Hoover gave a copy of it to Robert Kennedy, with reported "glee"), it was by no means a mainstream text. It would only come into the orthodox story of Marilyn's life with the onslaught of conspiracy texts citing it as a key source, beginning in 1973 with Mailer's *Marilyn.*

*   *   *

Over the next few years, several other minor accounts of Monroe's life appeared. When Edwin P. Hoyt's *Marilyn: The Tragic Venus* was published in 1965, *Time* magazine tempted fate by exclaiming: "Not another biography!" Little did they know. Hoyt based his book primarily on interviews with screenwriter Nunnally Johnson, who had worked with Monroe on *How to Marry a Millionaire* and on *Something's Got to Give*; he detested her while she lived, but seems to have done an abrupt about-face in the last weeks of her life, at which point he began offering sentimental bromides. Hoyt relied primarily upon Johnson's loathing, and produced the first Marilyn life that was more or less openly contemptuous of its subject. Nineteen-sixty-six brought *Who Killed Marilyn Monroe?*, by Charles Hamblett, although Marilyn was the subject of only one chapter. In 1968, James A. Hudson's *The Mysterious Death of Marilyn Monroe* again mentioned the Kennedys, but did not explicitly associate them with her death.

GUILES: 1969

Fred Lawrence Guiles began what would become the first significant biography of Marilyn Monroe as a screenplay, in 1963; called *Goodbye, Norma Jean*, it was to be "a motion picture biography." This screenplay was shown to Marilyn's press assistant, Pat Newcomb, who assisted Guiles in expanding it into a series for the magazine *Ladies' Home Journal*, published in 1967 as "The Final Summer of Marilyn Monroe." Guiles interviewed dozens of people who knew Monroe well, including her first husband, James Dougherty; her third husband, Arthur Miller; her teacher and mentor, Lee Strasberg; and many of her friends and associates, including directors, costars and coaches.

The Marilyn that Guiles produced, he said later, is "an amalgam of innocence and power," of "naïveté and muscle," who died of "terminal frustration." She was a woman in thrall to her own "powerful sexual drives," who engaged in a "lifelong quest for affection and love" to overcome her family's history of insanity. But she was also obsessed with success, which she hoped would obliterate memories of her deprived childhood. Guiles, like Zolotow, produces a Marilyn consistent with the persona. Thus he captions a famous romantic Cecil Beaton photograph of a reclining Marilyn clutching a rose, with a note that the image was her favorite (this claim is made about several pictures), and that only the rose suggests it was posed, rather than "an intimate glimpse of the vulnerable innocent who inhabited Marilyn/Norma Jean."

Guiles would popularize this use of a double moniker, and the influential notion that she was split between her past and present selves. Although he distinguishes between the "two" personalities, however, Guiles treats the supposed split between Norma Jean and Marilyn with rather more nuance than would subsequent accounts (including his own revision fifteen years later):

> Only rarely does a stage or film name give its owner an entirely new identity. For Marilyn Monroe, it meant the abandonment of a hand-me-down kind of existence.
>
> [. . .] Marilyn quickly turned her back on Norma Jean and Norma Jean's associates and began to identify totally with her new self, her role as a film actress. It has been an enduring myth that Marilyn suffered from loss of identity. The truth was that she soon felt completely at home with *Marilyn*. The only uncomfortable element in her life was the intrusive past, the ghost of Norma Jean. At times Marilyn would regress to a giggling young woman and Norma Jean seemed about to reappear, but the point had to be conceded eventually—it was *Marilyn* giggling. The new person of Marilyn was to be accepted finally as half-child, half-woman.[8]

This comes in a chapter entitled simply "Marilyn." By 1984 it would be "Marilyn: Her Life Begins," as the cliché becomes literalized and exaggerated. The final sentence of this first fully researched life expresses a wish that the symbolic personas might not overtake Marilyn's interpretation: "Perhaps in the future people will come to see her not as a symbol, not as Maggie, not as Roslyn, not as Norma Jean, but will remember her as a unique human being and as the person she wished to be: Marilyn."[9] Not only would Guiles's wish not come true, he himself would lose sight of it. The plot, too, would become cruder as it evolved: in this version, Guiles claims that Monroe died of an accidental overdose, but by 1984 he would be writing of her "determination" to take her own life. Over time the story calcifies, and conjecture becomes conviction.

In 1969, the magazine serial was published as a book under the title *Norma Jean: The Life of Marilyn Monroe,* and became a best seller. *The Times* declared it "well researched and badly written."[10] *Norma Jean* was for many years the undisputed "definitive" biography of Marilyn and is still highly regarded; as late as 1998, Cunningham declares in his compendium *The Ultimate Marilyn* that it remains the "best" of Marilyn's many lives. Mailer would base his *Marilyn* in 1973 on Guiles and on Zolotow; Joyce Carol Oates would also rely heavily upon Guiles in her novel *Blonde* (2000).

MAILER: 1973

Four years later, in 1973, Norman Mailer received an enormous amount of publicity, much of it negative, for his admitted readiness to fictionalize and fantasize about Marilyn while purporting to tell the story of her life. Unwilling to devote the time and effort required to produce a biography—this is "a work done in greater haste" rather than a "formal biography," which "can probably not be written in less than two years since it can take that long to collect the facts"— Mailer decided instead to write "a species of novel," what he called a "novel biography."[11] Mailer based *Marilyn: A Biography* largely on Guiles's book, wrote it in the omniscient third person, and granted himself as a (quondam) novelist the "sanction" to fantasize at will:

> he [Mailer] would never delude himself that he might be telling a story which could possibly be more accurate than a fiction since he would often be quick to imagine the interior of many a closed and silent life, and with the sanction of a novelist was going to look into the unspoken impulses of some of his real characters. At the end, if successful, he would have offered a literary hypothesis of a *possible* Marilyn Monroe who might actually have lived and fit most of the facts available.[12]

When his Marilyn doesn't fit all of the facts available, Mailer makes her up, speculating, assuming and imagining. *The Times* acidly observed of this "extraordinarily batty" enterprise that "the word 'if' is the conceptual lynch-pin of the whole book; add 'not' at any point and it shivers to the ground."[13]

Mailer's fantasies both describe and invent the mythical Marilyn. In particular, Mailer's Marilyn is a screen for a series of nostalgic projections about the "cornucopia" of sex she promised.[14] Mailer was the first mainstream author to name Robert Kennedy as a possible lover of Marilyn's (Guiles had only alluded to an anonymous "Easterner"); his speculations about conspiracy and cover-up helped transform the legend of Marilyn's death into a myth.

"Stealing Marilyn" is Mailer's secret ambition, as he himself admits early on. When he couldn't steal the real Marilyn from his neighbor and rival Arthur Miller, Mailer not only invented his own, he appropriated other biographers' Marilyns in the process. A young Clive James declared that "Mailer's fantasizing goes beyond expediency: Maurice Zolotow, poor pained scrivener, can sue Mailer all he likes; neither he nor the quiescent Fred Lawrence Guiles will ever get his Marilyn back."[15] Critics have since called the book "a postmortem proposal" and, less politely but more accurately, "a sustained masturbatory reverie."[16] Ten years after her death, there were already competing versions of Marilyn that belong to a series of male writers who vie for control over her story. Her life had become just as much a commodity as her image, the ground for a contest of male authority over the right to (his) own Marilyn.

The early years of the 1970s yielded a bumper crop of Marilyn biographies: in addition to Mailer's conspicuous entry into the lists, Norman Rosten, a friend of Arthur Miller's and then of Marilyn's, who is a much-quoted source in the later biographies, wrote a memoir called *Marilyn: An Untold Story,* and Joan Mellen produced the first avowedly feminist life, *Marilyn Monroe.* Monroe's "autobiography," *My Story,* was published in book form in 1974.

In 1975 a man named Robert Slatzer brought forth *The Life and Curious Death of Marilyn Monroe.* Slatzer has been a subject of immense controversy in the Marilyn apocrypha for two reasons. First, in this book he claimed to have been married to Marilyn for three days during 1952. Second, he claimed to have remained a close friend right up to her death, and offered "testimony" of the truth of the Kennedy rumors. Slatzer insisted that Monroe was assassinated and called for a review of the circumstances of her death. For some years, although a series of conspiracy narratives were produced on the coattails of Slatzer's claim, he was not included in any main-stream accounts of Monroe's life story. Ten years later, however, one principal biographer (Summers) would endorse Slatzer's claims; several years after that, another one (Spoto) would insist that no one had ever heard of Slatzer before he published his book in 1975 (although, as we shall see in chapter five, George Carpozi's 1961 account, which is based on interviews he held with Monroe during her life, claims that Carpozi met her longtime friend and "noted literary critic" Robert Slatzer on the set of *Niagara* with her in 1952).

In 1975 Marilyn's housekeeper, Eunice Murray, who was in the house the night Monroe died, published *Marilyn: The Last Months.* The following year Monroe's first husband, James E. Dougherty, produced *The Secret Happiness of Marilyn Monroe,* which attempted to "set the record straight" by combating stories of her neuroses, psychoses and despair. At the same time, another conspiracy book appeared, by Anthony Sciacca, who apparently also publishes as Anthony Scaduto.[17] Scaduto wrote an article for the soft-core pornographic magazine *Oui* in 1975, an expanded version of which was published as *Who Killed Marilyn?* in 1976. Sciacca/Scaduto relied upon Slatzer as a source, and told a story of a "red diary" kept by Marilyn that recorded all of the political secrets told to her while she was having her (alleged) affairs with the Kennedy brothers. He also claimed that her house had been bugged and that tapes existed of her in conversation with the Kennedys. In 1979 Monroe's New York maid, Lena Pepitone, published a clean-and-tell revelation entitled *Marilyn Monroe Confidential.* Many of Pepitone's stories would be repeated by subsequent biographers. With Rosten, the controversial Slatzer, and Monroe's last psychiatrist, Dr. Ralph Greenson, she is one of the Monroe biographers' key sources.

MAILER AGAIN

In 1980, Mailer produced another book about Marilyn Monroe; in this case it was not a "novel biography" but rather a fictional memoir (he called it "an imaginary diary") entitled *Of Women and Their Elegance*. Like *Marilyn*, *Of Women and Their Elegance* is partly an excuse to reprint many photographs, in this case pictures taken by Milton Greene not only of Marilyn but of other actresses, including Marlene Dietrich, Joan Crawford and Elizabeth Taylor. It is also like *Marilyn* in being a recycled version of someone else's redaction of Marilyn: this time Mailer relies upon anecdotes and interviews with Milton Greene and his wife, Amy, with whom Monroe lived in 1955, to project himself into Marilyn's head and offer up what he imagines are her words and thoughts.

Mailer disclaimed the voice in this book, declaring in an author's note that he "in no way wishes to suggest that these are the actual thoughts of Marilyn Monroe." This claim is hard to reconcile with the book he wrote, given that it is an imaginary diary in the first-person voice of Marilyn Monroe. At the end of *Of Women,* Mailer runs through a taxonomy of genres in an attempt to categorize what he has produced by means of his admittedly "dubious method": "It arises from certain facts, and there are several sections within it that are all made up, and it cannot be said that the fact is wholly factual in other places [. . .] perhaps we may call this an imaginary memoir, an as-told-to-book, a set of interviews that never took place between Marilyn Monroe and Norman Mailer." Or we might call it fiction.

A private detective named Milo Speriglio who had been hired by Robert Slatzer published *Marilyn Monroe: Murder Cover-Up* in 1982, which alleged that Robert Kennedy was responsible for Monroe's death, and made a series of related claims about wiretaps, taped conversations, secret diaries, and the destruction of evidence including phone records. Speriglio offers his own useful summary of his story's outline: explaining that Monroe died because of the secrets in her "little red diary," he then elaborates: "Naïvely, she stumbled into secret domains. She knew too much. A man had scorned her. She was about to tell all. Then she died."[18] Beginning with her naïveté and ending with her death, this pretty much sums up the legend of Marilyn Monroe.

In 1983, a musical written by Norman Thalheimer was produced on Broadway called *Marilyn: An American Fable,* which closed after just sixteen performances, acquiring the distinction of being one of Broadway's biggest failures. *Time* magazine wrote that it was "perhaps the most bizarrely acute rendering of the Monroe parable":

> A flop with endearing qualities—mostly in its determination to print the legend, not the facts, about a shooting star—the show rendered her life in the form of an old-fashioned backstage musical, complete with an improbable, inevitable happy ending. Marilyn doesn't die; she is reunited with her second husband, Joe DiMaggio, and walks into the sunset hand-in-hand with her childhood self, Norma Jean. More pulp than poetry, the show gave audiences the wish-fulfillment climax to a real-life tragedy whose ending they wished they could rewrite.[19]

The *New York Post* was less forgiving: "There was once a controversy as to whether Marilyn Monroe was, in fact, murdered. Well, she certainly was at the Minskoff Theater last night."[20]

MARILYN REDUX: 1984–1988

Between 1984 and 1988, in addition to the steady stream of rehashed photobiographies, tributes and tell-all memoirs that appear annually, no fewer than five major contributions to Marilyn's life and myth emerged. In 1984, Guiles reissued *Norma Jean* as *Legend* in the United States and as *Norma Jeane* in the United Kingdom, in which he revised certain details (including the spelling of her first name) and changed the anonymous "Easterner," the "lawyer and public servant" with whom he claimed Marilyn Monroe was having an affair before she died, into Robert Kennedy. In the wake of fifteen years of speculation about murder and conspiracy, Guiles changed his verdict on the death, and argued that Monroe set out deliberately to kill herself that night, because Robert Kennedy had left her. Guiles also added more elaborate detail about Monroe's sexual life that had developed in the intervening years, including more about her earlier sexual relationships in Hollywood and some of the rumors about her supposed bisexuality.

It is around this time that the story of Marilyn Monroe's life begins to become circular, as biographers start quoting one another quoting the same earlier sources. For example, in the revised *Norma Jeane* Guiles describes an affair that most of her biographers agree Monroe had near the end of her first marriage, with the photographer André de Dienes; Guiles's primary source in the passage is Norman Mailer's "thorough account" in 1973 of that affair.[21] What Guiles doesn't mention for the unversed reader is that Mailer was using Guiles for the outline of his own narrative, and that he admitted in his acknowledgments that he didn't take the time to do much additional research. Thus Guiles offers Mailer as providing the best version of the story Guiles is revising, but Mailer relied upon Guiles to research and write it for him first: Guiles ends up simply affirming his own story.

Anthony Summers's 1985 *Goddess: The Secret Lives of Marilyn Monroe* began, like so many Monroe lives, as a commissioned article for a magazine, the *Sunday Express*, in the wake of the Los Angeles district attorney's decision in 1982 to reopen the investigation into the circumstances of Monroe's death. Summers interviewed 650 people (although neither DiMaggio nor Miller consented to participate) for *Goddess*; the sheer wealth of anecdotal material might seem to overwhelm doubt, but these sources for the most part relate what they believe, not what they demonstrably know. The interviews often repeat second- or thirdhand accounts of what someone else said, and neither Summers nor his sources is particularly dispassionate (Summers calls Monroe psychotic, for example; he quotes Milton Greene, her ex-partner, calling her "schizo," and Billy Travilla, a dress designer who considered her a "prick-teaser"). A "trained investigative journalist," Summers has also written *The Kennedy Conspiracy*, which offers "evidence" that Lee Harvey Oswald did not act alone in killing John F. Kennedy. Similarly emphasizing the conspiracy theories surrounding Marilyn's death, Summers proffers—but does not prove—a series of sensational claims, including the secret marriage with Robert Slatzer (Summers is the first major biographer to endorse Slatzer's story), an aborted Kennedy child, illegal wiretapping, and the seizure of Monroe's phone records by the FBI. *Goddess* was immensely successful, and remains one of the most popular and influential of the Marilyn lives. It scores highly on Amazon.com's Web site with customers, many of whom consider it the "indispensable" Marilyn biography. (Summers also features frequently in academic consider-ations of Marilyn Monroe, perhaps because the extremity of his views—and his language—lend themselves to skeptical debunking.)

Three Marilyn lives appeared in 1986 alone. Gloria Steinem pub-lished *Marilyn: Norma Jeane,* a self-styled feminist history of Marilyn Monroe's victimization by a culture that preferred her dependent and childish. Seeking the "real" Marilyn in the shape of lost and aban-doned Norma Jeane, Steinem's account began as an article for *Ms.* magazine, "The Woman Who Died Too Soon," in 1972. Although relying on the research of Guiles and Summers, Steinem is critical of earlier male writers, like Mailer, whose misogynistic assumptions color their interpretations of Marilyn's story. Ironically, however, her life shares some striking characteristics with Mailer's. Like Mailer, Steinem began in collaboration with a photographer, in this case George Barris, whose photographs of Marilyn in the summer of 1962 are one of two legendary sessions Monroe held weeks before she died. Barris had conducted some interviews with Monroe, intending a collaboration with her on a biography and photographs that would, Steinem says, "set the record straight." They completed one inter-view, of which Barris took notes; it was not recorded. From these evidently twenty-five-year-old notes, Steinem produces a chapter narrated in the first person, as if dictated by Monroe herself. Like Mailer, Steinem relies upon Guiles for her facts; unlike Mailer, she also treats Monroe's autobiography as a source of Marilyn's authentic voice.

That same year Carl E. Rollyson, Jr.'s *Marilyn Monroe: A Life of the Actress* came out, which interpreted Marilyn Monroe's biography through the framework of her screen career, and Milo Speriglio published another tale of assassination, *The Marilyn Conspiracy*. Rollyson's book is halfway between a biography and a more academically inclined consideration of her film work; his work on her films is sensitive and persuasive, but the biography is largely rehashed, tending to transform earlier conjecture and interpretation into hard fact. (Thus, for example, Rollyson omits years of controversy over whether Monroe was raped as a child, and settles for the flat—and rapid—assertion that she had fabricated the story.) But Rollyson provides the most detailed look at the work Monroe put into preparing for her roles, and into analyzing the resultant performances. As such, it is probably the only biography that Monroe—who said after her marriage to Miller ended that she would never like a writer as her judge—could have borne to have read (although she would no doubt prefer to be spared its psychosexual condescensions).

The year 1986 also saw the production of Norman Mailer's play *Strawhead*, which starred his daughter Kate as Marilyn. The play ran for two weeks at the Actors Studio in New York, and replayed, once again, Mailer's obsessive fantasies about Monroe. The play was apparently never published in its entirety, but *Vanity Fair* printed an extract from act one, with photographs by Bert Stern of Kate Mailer as Marilyn. The following exchange is supposed to take place between Marilyn and her friend Amy Greene, circa 1955, and demonstrates Mailer's continued fascination with Monroe's alleged gynecological problems (if not his talent for realistic dialogue):

Amy: My God, what's the matter?
Marilyn: I'm sorry. It's my period. I have periods that are like catastrophes.
Amy: We're going to the hospital right now!
Marilyn: No, it's all right. I have some pills. I'll be O.K.
Amy: Are you sure?
Marilyn: Oh, yes. Don't you ever get cramps like this?
Amy: It may get better after you have a baby.
Marilyn: Amy, the last doctor said he found a lot of scar tissue in there. He wanted to hear how many abortions I had. I told him I didn't know.

Amy: You don't know?

Marilyn: Twelve.

Amy: You must be shreds inside.

Marilyn: *(Pause)* Tatters.

Amy: What did you do, get pregnant every month?[22]

Subsequent plans to produce the play off-Broadway were announced, but were "postponed for undisclosed reasons."[23]

In 1988, the first full-length academic consideration of Marilyn was published by Cambridge University sociologist Graham McCann. *Marilyn Monroe* is sometimes referred to as a biographical study, but it only has one chapter of biography, which recycles some of the half-truths and errors circulating in the Marilyn story. Undeniably sentimental in places, McCann has nonetheless produced what is arguably the smartest reading of the implications of the Marilyn myth to date, offering some pungent commentary on Mailer, Steinem and Summers along the way.

But the influence of previous renditions, the aftermath of constant recycling, is powerful enough by this point that the subtle (and not so subtle) effects of earlier attitudes can linger in even avowedly revisionist accounts. McCann explicitly deplores what he considers the misogyny of men like Mailer, Zolotow and Summers, but virtually quotes Summers without attribution in his "own" characterization of Marilyn's contradictions. McCann writes, in 1988:

[Marilyn Monroe] was labeled with love whilst forced into loneliness, [she] died publicly but in pain at the age of thirty-six. She was marketed as the modern mistress, yet she yearned for monogamy and motherhood. The profile was cast as crude whilst the passion was for culture. The genius of the performer masked emotions marked with pain and insecurity.[24]

Compare McCann's words with Summers's passage, published three years earlier:

[Marilyn Monroe was] a woman [. . .] who was a symbol of love yet essentially lonely, who died famously but in folly at the age of thirty-six. She postured as the world's mistress, yet yearned for monogamy and motherhood. The profile was crude while the pursuit was for culture. The brilliance of the actress masked a seriously disturbed psyche.[25]

McCann neutralizes Summers's tone somewhat, tempering his judgmental assertions of Marilyn Monroe's "folly" and "seriously disturbed psyche," but the interpretive presumptions informing Marilyn Monroe's story are so pervasive that even a writer who, like McCann, is consciously protesting against misogyny, still finds Summers's contemptuous characterization apt enough to be worth lifting (without acknowledgment). In both renditions Monroe is in tension between two poles of (equally stereotypical) femininity, mistress and mother, while her career as an actress is associated with her "emotional problems." There is Marilyn, in a nutshell: revision and reinterpretation become not only unnecessary, but impossible.

1990-2003

In 1990 Maurice Zolotow reissued his 1960 *Marilyn Monroe,* unrevised but with a new, remarkably self-satisfied prologue, concerned primarily with Zolotow's great insight into Monroe and his greater access to exclusive Hollywood circles back in the day: "I was one of those who was admitted to the Stork Club," he announces, before adding:

> There was a time when only a few of the cognoscenti could gain admittance. And to be allowed to go into the hallowed Cub Room of the Stork—and to sit at Table 50, Winchell's favorite table—ah, that was indeed an accolade.
> I have sat at Table 50.
> How many of you reading this remember the name of Walter Winchell?[26]

Zolotow reiterates his own prescience (no less than one would expect from a cognoscento) in knowing that Monroe was going to be a big star in 1952—although she was already well on her way by then—

and the struggles he had to get anyone to take seriously his proposal of a biography (this despite the fact that "at the time, I was one of the highest-paid magazine writers"). But he persevered, interviewing along the way a great many people who worked with Monroe (Jane Russell, Betty Grable, Lauren Bacall, Clark Gable, Billy Wilder, Henry Hathaway), some who knew her intimately (Lee Strasberg, Milton Greene, Arthur Miller), and some who never met her but would hitch their wagons to her star (Hefner, Mailer). What Zolotow doesn't add to his prologue is anything new about Marilyn Monroe.

Marilyn: The Last Take, by Peter Brown and Patte Barham, appeared in 1992, detailing the last fourteen weeks of Marilyn Monroe's life, and arguing that she must have been assassinated. The following year brought Donald Spoto's *Marilyn Monroe: The Biography,* which became the new "definitive" biography. The author of biographies of Laurence Olivier, Alfred Hitchcock, Jacqueline Kennedy Onassis and Saint Francis of Assisi, Spoto also argued against suicide, partially in light of new evidence (also published by Brown and Barham) that Monroe had been quietly rehired by 20th Century-Fox in the weeks before she died, thus eliminating the primary motive for deliberate suicide. But Spoto does not believe that Monroe was deliberately murdered either, and entirely exonerates the Kennedys.

Where Summers touted his 650 interviews, Spoto emphasizes documentary research—35,000 pages of new documents, in fact. Spoto also conducted interviews, but often with different people from Summers. Spoto is the debunker: he repudiates many of the Marilyn myths, including those about her traumatic childhood, and especially her sexual relationships with Hollywood studio executives and the Kennedys. He does not consider her mad, but rather the victim of a 1950s fad for pop-Freudian psychoanalysis, which was the last thing her "intuitive genius" required. Spoto is recuperating the glamour; occasionally sentimental and sometimes pious, he writes for the most part in a more balanced manner than many of Monroe's earlier biographers, whose own biases about femininity (whether for or against) seem to have predetermined their judgments. But Spoto, too, has an idée fixe or two about Marilyn's death that can lead him astray into the ranting denunciations that are the hallmarks of the conspiracy theorists. Spoto was the first writer in thirty years to offer a new version of Marilyn's death: Spoto's "truth behind her death" is that her psychiatrist killed her by injecting a lethal enema.

The early 1990s saw two new renditions by those who knew Marilyn. On October 6, 1993, the New York City Opera premiered an opera called *Marilyn,* with libretto by poet, Monroe friend and biography stalwart Norman Rosten and music by Ezra Laderman. It was commissioned as part of the City Opera's fiftieth-anniversary celebration, and advance interest was sufficiently high to prompt them to offer an extra third performance. But it was not well received: "Laderman's score," wrote one review,

> was a well-constructed, expertly orchestrated and thoroughly conceived triumph of soporific note-spinning. Everything was there except musical content. [. . .] Some music is bad, some is fraudulent. Laderman's was neither, but it was extraordinarily boring. [. . .] In spite of its contemporary American subject matter, *Marilyn* seemed more of an exercise in an essentially nineteenth-century, European art form—complete with drinking song and mad scene.[27]

A year later, Monroe's half sister, Berniece Baker Miracle, published a memoir, *My Sister Marilyn,* including some new letters and photos. Over the next few years, the usual books of memorabilia, compendia of quotations and photograph collections continued to appear. *Marilyn: Shades of Blonde* (1997) collected twenty-one short stories, all fictional, based on Marilyn.

In 1995 political scientist S. Paige Baty published an academic monograph called *American Monroe: The Making of a Body Politic,* which analyzed the posthumous circulating Marilyn images and paraphernalia, including billboards, mugs, playing cards, fan clubs and female impersonators, as well as looking at delimited, political aspects of some of the major biographical representations (including Mailer's misogyny, Steinem's feminism and Summers's writing about Monroe's postautopsy corpse). Baty reads Marilyn the icon as a kind of imprint of the postmodern condition (what she calls a "post-mortem condition"). Fragmented, hypermediated, a simulation of the real, Baty's Marilyn-as-icon is an emblem of postmodern academic arguments about America as a land of simulacra and a society of the spectacle. In her *New York Times* review of *American Monroe,* Michiko Kakutani angrily denounced Baty for ignoring Monroe's reality in favor of analyzing her iconic representations. In her review, called "The Commodified Blonde, or, Marilyn as Text," Kakutani scathingly condemns *American Monroe* as "pretentious, solipsistic and utterly devoid of humor and common sense," declaring:

> By dwelling on Monroe's death and on her corpse, Ms. Baty argues, these works effectively turn a mythic superstar into dead meat that is "both more real and democratically accessible." . . . Such "readings" of Monroe completely ignore the reality of her life and art, never mind such unfashionable, humanistic concepts as emotions. Indeed, Ms. Baty has succeeded through this book in furthering the "commodification" of Marilyn Monroe.[28]

Kakutani's resistance to Baty's "commodification" of Marilyn Monroe, as if she were ever not commodified, seems like blaming the messenger, but Kakutani is right that Baty's argument is too easy (and that its impenetrable style "embodies much of what is wrong with academic writing today"). Marilyn Monroe is not merely a series of iconic representations that bear no particular responsibility to the facts of her life. The theoretical contention that Marilyn is *only* a simulacrum may at one point have been fashionable in certain academic circles, but it has the disadvantage of being untrue.

Two new biographies appeared together in 1998, Barbara Leaming's *Marilyn Monroe,* which insisted that Monroe deliberately committed suicide, and Donald H. Wolfe's *The Last Days of Marilyn Monroe,* which argued that she was assassinated. Like Spoto, Leaming had written conventional biographies of performers (Orson Welles and Katharine Hepburn) before, and she is even less of a believer in conspiracy than he. Not just agnostic toward the stories of cover-up,

Leaming omits them, eschewing any mention of some of the most controversial of the stories. Slatzer does not appear in her biography at all, even to be derided; she makes no mention of the alleged affair with Robert F. Kennedy; and entirely ignores the fact that the accounts of Monroe's last hours from those involved were, indeed, contradictory in many key respects.

Leaming fixes Marilyn's story around two central spectacular dramas: her relationship with her mother, and with her third husband, Arthur Miller. Leaming is particularly interested in (and persuasive about) Monroe's professional negotiations with her agents, lawyers, and with 20th Century-Fox; she consulted newly available archives of studio documents, as well as the papers of Monroe's quondam agent and lawyer, Charles K. Feldman, and the papers of Joseph Rauh, who was instrumental in Miller's defense against the HUAC. Such research, while valuable, can also mislead in suggesting a centrality to each of these persons that they may not actually have had in Monroe's life. Although Leaming's notes name her sources, they are not precise about attribution. Instead she chooses to catalog for each chapter a list of the sources upon which she "drew" for what becomes a novelistic story with Leaming as omniscient narrator. In particular, Leaming shares Zolotow's penchant for unsubstantiated generalizations, and Mailer's for mind-reading. For Leaming, almost all of Monroe's adult behavior can be traced to one of two sources: her need to disprove her mother's supposed assessment of her as disposable, and her need for Miller to accept her disreputable past.

Donald H. Wolfe's biography was called *The Last Days of Marilyn Monroe* in the United States; in Britain it was given the rather more candid title, *The Assassination of Marilyn Monroe*. Wolfe relies heavily upon Summers, but trumps him: bringing in the evidence brought to light in Brown and Barham's and Spoto's research of Monroe's rehiring by Fox Studios in the weeks before she died, Wolfe argues that this shows even more clearly than before that Marilyn had no motive to kill herself. Since she couldn't have wanted to die deliberately, apparently there is only one other possible cause of death: Robert Kennedy had her injected with enough pentobarbital to kill a horse. There isn't a conspiracy theory that Wolfe doesn't endorse; if someone said it, that seems to be proof enough. Although Wolfe's credulity about Monroe's death is immense (in one sense, although it defies Occam's razor), he does, however, bring a persuasive rational skepticism to bear on Monroe's notorious problems on film sets. Like Spoto (whom he reviles), Wolfe maintains common sense about one aspect of Monroe's life, and labors under obsessive fixations in regard to others. In his review in the *London Review of Books,* O'Hagan suggested that Wolfe's "hysterical" narrative might prove "the conspiracy sub-genre's reductio ad absurdum: Bobby Kennedy and Sam Giancana and Marilyn's psychotherapist tripping over each other in an effort to commit the great pointless homicide."[29] But little did O'Hagan know: there was worse to come.

In 2000, Joyce Carol Oates produced her roman à clef *Blonde,* a book that, like Mailer's and Steinem's, acknowledges a reliance upon Guiles for the "factual" outline of the narrative—but radically departs from Guiles in its account of Monroe's death. Also like Mailer, Oates chooses to fictionalize at will; one could argue over whether her claim to have written "a novel" is more or less candid than Mailer's to have written a "novel biography," given that Oates's "imaginary" Marilyn Monroe bears a striking resemblance to the historical Marilyn Monroe. *Blonde* was a notably successful book in America, both commercially and critically (it was short-listed for both the National Book Award and for the Pulitzer Prize). Many considered it a tour de force; like Mailer's *Of Women and Their Elegance,* *Blonde* purports to go inside the head of Monroe and to show us what it was like to be Marilyn. At 738 pages in hardback (939 in paperback), *Blonde* clocks in as the longest narrative devoted to Marilyn (and as Oates's longest book to date). Oates said that her story was a mixture of psychological realism and fairy tale:

> I saw her story as mythical, archetypal. [. . .] It was my intention to create a female portrait as emblematic of her time and place as Emma Bovary was of hers. (Of course, Norma Jeane is actually more complex, and certainly more admirable, than Emma Bovary.) Norma Jeane dies, and "Marilyn Monroe," the role, the concoction, the artifice, would seem to endure.[30]

Like Mailer, Oates repudiates any claim to historical veracity:

> So much of "Blonde" is obviously fiction, to call it "nonfiction"
> would be misleading. (I explain in my preface: if you want histor-
> ical veracity, you must go to the biographies. Even while perhaps
> not 100% accurate, they are at least predicated upon literal truth,
> while the novel aspires to a spiritual/poetic truth.)[31]

The problem is, which parts are obviously fiction, and how does the
reader tell? And on what basis does Oates confirm that the biographies do provide historical veracity? Although Oates was criticized by
some reviewers for her technique, she explained (again in an interview) that this was because America was unready for such an "experimental" book by a woman writer. Be that as it may, the singularity of
the book she produced is arguable. Certainly in terms of the Marilyn
apocrypha what Oates has produced is far from experimental: it is
typical. She is quite right, though, that literalism will always be what
is at issue: where do we draw the line between the literal and the figurative in the story of Marilyn Monroe?

In 2001 the BBC produced a documentary film entitled *Marilyn on
Marilyn*. It begins silently, with a printed title that explains: "In the
many documentaries about Marilyn Monroe, her own voice is
absent. Despite her fame, she gave few broadcasts or filmed interviews. But towards the end of her life, two magazine journalists,
Georges Belmont and Richard Meryman, tape recorded their interviews with her." The film does not distinguish between the two interviews, but cuts out the voices of the journalists: the entire film,
composed of still photographs and footage of Monroe and the Los
Angeles in which she was raised and worked, is narrated by Monroe's
speaking voice. The film opens, cannily, with a preamble that raises
the question of her relationship to her own words and to the truth.
The first sound of the film is her voice saying: "They ask you questions like 'What do you wear to bed? Do you wear pajama tops, the
bottom of pajamas, or a nightgown?' So I said, 'Chanel No. 5,' 'cause
it's the truth. And yet, I don't want to say, 'Nude,' you know? But it's

the truth." Then another printed title is shown: "On these recordings she talks frankly about her childhood in Los Angeles, her desire to act, her attitude to her own celebrity and sexuality, and her state of mind." The next words are Monroe's, and spoken: "No, I don't think I lie. I leave things out. You know, and I'll elaborate sometimes. But it'll be from the truth. Cause otherwise it's hard to know where to start. If you don't start with the truth." The film then "officially" begins, presenting its title: "Marilyn on Marilyn."

In other words, even Monroe's speech is (rightly) problematized by the film from the beginning, in raising the questions of how deliberately she presented her "self" to her audience; of the way in which answers were elicited by the simple fact of being interviewed, by a self-conscious presentation of her identity as a performance; and of whether she might be lying. There is another question raised by these tapes, which the film doesn't acknowledge: Monroe's speech (to my ear, at any rate) sounds decidedly slurred in these interviews; they were given in the last months of her life, when her addiction to barbiturates and alcohol is beyond serious question. Certainly Meryman later reported that they drank champagne through much of the second day of interviewing, and that she was a little "high" by the end. Her words then, by implication, might be strategically produced for the benefit of the audience; they might be self-censored; they might "elaborate" upon the truth; they might lie; and they might be rendered dubious by chemicals. Thus even speech (as opposed to writing) does not simply equal truth: but these tapes do present a unique opportunity to establish that at least these words were spoken *by* Monroe, and I will on occasion use them as such.

Finally, in 2003 Matthew Smith published *Victim: The Secret Tapes of Marilyn Monroe*. It is a memorable book in the Marilyn apocrypha because this latest "biography" has gone the furthest toward presenting a tissue of conjecture and unsubstantiated claims as documentary fact; even Mailer admitted to the vagaries of his methodology. Smith, by contrast, blithely offers what is arguably the least factual of all of the Marilyn lives. This latest reproduction of a series of Marilyn reproductions is like an eighth-generation photocopy, an indistinct, grainy blur of a portrait. With the exception of less than twenty pages of newly revealed "transcripts" of Marilyn Monroe allegedly speaking into a tape recorder just before she died, Smith's book recycles not only twenty years of conspiracy theories, but also his own 1996 *The Men Who Murdered Marilyn*. Smith tells essentially the same story, using many of the same photographs, even some of the same paragraphs, only slightly revised. For example, in 1996 Smith addressed the claims made by James Hall, who told Anthony Summers he was the ambulance driver called to remove Monroe's body, and that he witnessed a doctor administering a shot to her heart:

> The statement regarding the production of a syringe complete with large needle from a doctor's bag merits challenge of itself. It would have been highly unlikely. Doctors do not carry syringes around in their bags already fitted with needles of any kind: to do so would be dangerous, unhygienic and risking breakage.[32]

In 2003 Smith goes over the same "evidence" in essentially the same language:

> Hall must also have known that doctors do not normally walk around with hypodermics fitted with needles in their bags. Quite apart from it being quite dangerous and unhygienic, the needle was also subject to damage in that state. Such a suggestion was somewhat ludicrous.[33]

Although Smith has added a grand total of eight footnotes to his 311-page biography (whereas his 1996 narrative was unmarred by a single note or citation), *Victim* similarly relies upon claims that for the most part soar above petty concerns like attribution: none of the eight footnotes bothers with page numbers. Nor do any of the passages above identify the source of any of these tales: they are seamlessly incorporated into Smith's narrative.

This strategy demonstrates the way in which writing itself is part of the problem of the many lives of Marilyn Monroe. Assertion is not the same as fact, and the apocrypha's reliance upon soi-disant "proof" that has been assimilated right into the text actually makes its claims that much harder to credit. There is no reason for a skeptical reader to accept that the "transcripts" which Smith "summarizes" in *Victim* are anything other than sheer invention. And there are several reasons to believe that invention is precisely what they are, as we shall see. Detail and nuance are lost through repetition; like the children's telephone game, the recycling of the story of Marilyn grows increasingly garbled, and unintelligible. Finally we can only guess what we think we heard.

For the purposes of the four chapters to follow, the principal Monroe biographies—which is to say, professedly nonfiction accounts that undertook primary research in the form of both personal interviews and archival work, that were carefully documented, and that developed a strong interpretive line—are those by Guiles, Summers and Spoto. All three writers disagree, often strenuously, with one another about a great many of the basic facts concerning Marilyn Monroe's life and death (let alone about the correct interpretations of those facts). Indeed, Summers sued Spoto over the latter's allegations that Summers manipulated and misquoted statements by those he interviewed. In an out-of-court settlement, Summers received a "sizeable" sum of money and a "print retraction" of Spoto's accusations in the paperback and any other future editions of the book.[34] When these three principal biographers achieve consensus about a given fact (if not interpretation), I will usually accept their collective version, not because their agreement makes anything ipso facto true, but because it seems paranoid to dismiss it out of hand, and because radical disbelief is surely as foolish as absolute credulity. Skepticism is an attitude, not a dogma: it allows for persuasion.

Although Guiles, Summers and Spoto are, in my opinion, the predominant archivists of the Monroe apocrypha, many other texts contribute to this collective enterprise and will appear in the pages to follow. Although both Leaming and Wolfe also brought new research to bear on their accounts, each also follows an interpretive plot already established by an earlier biographer: Leaming concurs with Guiles, while Wolfe is quite heavily indebted to Summers. Both writers will appear frequently here, if only because of their currency.

However, Marilyn's many lives would not be complete without consideration of the influential accounts by Arthur Miller, Norman Mailer, Gloria Steinem and Joyce Carol Oates; the sheer prominence of these authors means that their versions have figured centrally in the Marilyn apocrypha. Finally, when it comes to Monroe's death, the books that focus particularly on her "last days" will become more conspicuous.

If nothing else, the many lives of Marilyn Monroe show that belief precedes the "facts." Like Othello turning a handkerchief into what he will call proof of an adultery in which he already believes, so too can biography build a framework upon evidence whose very flimsiness demonstrates the firmness of the opinions it already holds. Its strategies for dealing with evidence become circular, as we will see. For now, one example will suffice: in response to Leaming's 1998 life, which seeks to establish (by asserting) that Monroe committed suicide, an irate "reader from mass" [*sic*] wrote in to Amazon.com's website to offer potential readers the following advice: "don't bother" to read Leaming's book if you "already believe and have instilled in your mind" that Monroe was assassinated. The reviewer calls into question the source of Leaming's facts because Leaming "makes MM out to be a suicidal freak" whereas the reviewer doesn't "see her that way at all."* This reader already knows how she or he "sees" Monroe, and wants only to have those preconceptions reconfirmed; not knowing where Leaming got her facts implies sarcastically that these are not facts if the reader doesn't believe them. Facts must be false if they challenge the conviction of a mind already made up.

AUTOBIOGRAPHY: MARILYN MONROE, INC.

Where is the more accurate likeness of a person to be found—in self-portrait, or in a sitting for someone else? If biography is a conversa-

---

*The review (December 14, 1998) granted Leaming one star out of five, calling the book "depressing" for arguing that Monroe committed suicide. (Would her assassination represent a rosier outlook?) A more recent review (March 5, 2004) offers strikingly similar advice: "If you believe Marilyn was a smart, witty, loveable, strong role model type of woman," don't read Leaming. This reader concedes Leaming four stars *despite* her book's persuasiveness: "As much as I have to say that I hate the way this biography changed my view of Marilyn, I have to give it a good rating."

tion among the writer and many other people about the subject, autobiography is often assumed to be more truthful or accurate, a firsthand account of experience, memory and consciousness—a more or less immediate presentation of individual reality. That this is a rather hopeful view is apparent upon reflection: few of us are without confused or lost memories, or moments of self-delusion or self-justification; none of us is without bias. By definition an autobiographical account is subjective; in the case of Marilyn Monroe, it is also fictional.

In 1974, after Monroe and her two collaborators, Ben Hecht and Sidney Skolsky, were all dead, the autobiographical fragment "My Story" that Monroe had begun and abandoned in 1954 was published in book form by New York publishers Stein and Day as "*My Story,* by Marilyn Monroe," with no mention of Hecht or Skolsky anywhere in its pages. One paperback edition reprints a review quotation on the front cover, which reads: "Obviously authentic. Reveals Marilyn's most private thoughts and feelings." But its authenticity is highly questionable. Guiles declares that at least half the book was "pure invention by Marilyn."[35] In his autobiography, *Timebends,* Arthur Miller quotes Monroe as saying: "I never intended to make all that much about being an orphan. It's just that Ben Hecht was hired to write this story about me, and he said, 'Okay, sit down and try to think up something interesting about yourself.' Well, I was boring, and I thought maybe I'd tell him about them putting me in the orphanage, and he said that was great and wrote it, and that became the main thing suddenly."[36]

My Story is not copyrighted in Monroe's name, or in the name of her heirs, but in the name of Milton Greene, though nowhere does the book clarify who Milton Greene is, or what his connection to Marilyn Monroe's autobiography might be. In fact, Greene was a photographer and the cofounder of Monroe's film company, Marilyn Monroe Productions; their partnership lasted from 1955, after *My Story* had been abandoned, until 1957, when Monroe bought him out (some say forced him out) after the difficult production of *The Prince and the Showgirl,* the only movie that Marilyn Monroe Productions made. Save for the copyright claim, Greene gives only one other indication of his presence at all, which appears abruptly, without explanation, as the last words of the book: "This is where Marilyn's manuscript ended when she gave it to me. MILTON H. GREEN. [*sic*]" Given that *My Story* ends before Monroe's partnership with Greene began, he is never mentioned in the text; any reader unfamiliar with the specifics of Monroe's life could be forgiven for finding Greene's relationship to Monroe—and thus to her autobiography—obscure.

Although Greene implies that the book simply reproduces "Marilyn's manuscript," which she gave to him, he probably revised the manuscript, perhaps with the help of other writers. One Monroe annotator claims that Greene "threatened legal action against anyone who questioned the book's authenticity. Additions had been made to the 1954 version, to make it sound tragically prophetic."[37] At the end of chapter thirteen, for instance, "Marilyn Monroe" announces without any mention of suicide before: "I was the kind of girl they found dead in a hall bedroom with an empty bottle of sleeping pills in her hand."[38]

Monroe biographer Spoto, who had access to Greene's papers and who also interviewed Hecht's widow and saw Hecht's drafts, offers further reason to believe that Greene altered the manuscript:

> By careful comparison of the published version with the unpublished Hecht draft, it is clear that none of the first sixty-six pages of *My Story* was composed by Hecht at all [. . .] the vocabulary and diction of *My Story* in these sections bear scant resemblance to anything ever written by Ben Hecht. [. . .] "Sit down and try to think up something interesting about yourself," Hecht said to Marilyn when they began their task. She did, he did, Sidney did (and later Milton Greene did).[39]

According to at least two writers, that is, not only was Marilyn Monroe's "autobiography" *not* produced by Marilyn, much of it isn't even written by the acknowledged ghostwriter, and was most likely produced some time after Monroe was dead.

But anyone who did not happen to pick up—and believe—Spoto's account would have no particular reason to doubt that Marilyn Monroe wrote Marilyn Monroe's autobiography. Someone who happened instead to read and believe Steinem's *Marilyn: Norma Jeane* would never encounter the possibility at all. Indeed, Steinem opens her biography with her intention to use as many of Monroe's "own words in this book" as possible, quoting Monroe "from many sources, including her own unfinished autobiography, *My Story*."[40] Steinem treats *My Story* as a record of Marilyn Monroe's authentic voice, an attitude consonant with the strand of feminism that finds truth in personal testimony—a common-sense, but deeply problematic, assumption. Certainly such uncorrupted truth would be valuable if it could be located, but it tends to be a chimera, as *My Story* demonstrates. Using *My Story* to find an authoritative Marilyn is wishful thinking at best. Given Steinem's efforts to reclaim Monroe's voice from a feminist standpoint, it is certainly ironic that she overlooks the degree to which that voice was filtered through an all-male coterie of writers, editors and defensively litigious ex-business partners.

The role of fiction and other voices in *My Story* becomes part of the story of Marilyn Monroe's life: whose line is it, anyway? Some of Monroe's most famous quips have been consistently attributed to scriptwriters and publicity men: did she really say that she wore only Chanel No. 5 when she went to bed, or was that a line written for her? In discussing the implications of the conflicting stories about whether Marilyn traded sex for money in her days as a struggling starlet, Steinem quotes from *My Story* again, taking the line at face value without comment: "'Hollywood's a place where they'll pay you a thousand dollars for a kiss, and fifty cents for your soul. I know, because I turned down the first offer often enough and held out for the fifty cents.'"[41] In Steinem's sentimental rendering, it is not just that *My Story* tells the truth: truth will prove Monroe's moral worth, showing that she resisted the contemptible efforts of the Hollywood studio system to exploit her. Steinem does not admit even the outside chance that, *had* Monroe prostituted herself, she might possibly have been unwilling to admit it in 1954 (or ever), nor does she acknowledge the vested interests of all the other writers involved in producing the text and in safeguarding Monroe's reputation.

But precisely the same quotation that for Steinem proves Monroe was genuine, for other Monroe commentators reveals that the autobiography is corrupted. Cunningham finds Hecht's "fingerprints [. . .] all over that quote," comparing it to a line from a 1946 Hecht screenplay: a character is asked what is in his briefcase and responds: "Very little—my soul. And an extra can of tobacco."[42] The similarity of the two lines seems hard to ignore: it's a very hard-boiled and writerly quip. But that doesn't mean Monroe *couldn't* have said it; if she had, it might be because she too had learned the effective language of the hard-boiled—or, for that matter, had been watching Hecht's films.

Anthony Summers is at the other end of the spectrum from Steinem, both in terms of sexual politics (he tends to leer at Monroe, whereas Steinem tries to rescue her) and in terms of the credibility of *My Story*. Actually both writers treat the manuscript as a patent indication of Monroe's own worth, but for Steinem it is the truth incarnate, while for Summers it is a pack of self-serving lies. Summers treats Monroe as a pathological liar and "fantasist," while granting Hecht authority over the truth about her story. Summers explains that he will rely on *My Story*, even though it is unreliable:

> the truths in her story were highly selective. Hecht reported to his editor during the interviews that he was sometimes sure Marilyn was fabricating. He explained, "When I say lying, I mean she isn't telling the truth. I don't think so much that she is trying to deceive me as that she is a fantasizer." Hecht found himself struggling to interpret Marilyn's "odd little physical body language, to read when she was going into something fictional or when she was leveling."[43]

Despite Summers's agreement with Hecht that Monroe's story is questionable, nonetheless he depends upon the manuscript as a source for information about her childhood, relying upon Hecht and "other witnesses" to sift through the fictions for him and leave the facts. If enough people believe a story, does that make it true?

It is Norman Mailer who is most skeptical of *My Story*; he considers *both* Monroe and Hecht completely dubious sources, who together produced "a prodigiously factoidal enterprise printed as

Sunday supplement pieces in 1954. Hecht was never a writer to tell the truth when a concoction could put life in his prose, and Marilyn had been polishing her fables for years. No team of authors contributes more to the literary smog that hangs over legend than Marilyn ben Hecht."[44] Unless it is Norman Mailer, that is.

There does seem to be a sexual dimension to the question of Monroe's veracity: the more misogynist the writer, the more focused on Monroe's body, the more he dismisses *My Story*, whereas those writers who want to believe in Marilyn seem to need also to recuperate this highly problematic text as an outpouring of her "voice." What would happen if we considered the text to be entirely distinct from the question of Marilyn Monroe's moral worth or sexual character?

In point of fact, Marilyn Monroe's "autobiography" is an unfinished fragment, likely composed of omissions and half-truths, created through dictation, collaboration, ghostwriting, ventriloquizing and invisible editing, a narrative in which fact and fiction are often indistinguishable; and it is interpreted very differently through the lenses of varying sexual and textual attitudes. It is undoubtedly a fictionalized account. But neither is *My Story* entirely spurious: presumably *some* of it does accurately reflect Marilyn Monroe's true experiences and feelings—at least, in 1954. But we don't know which parts, and moreover the fact that she experienced or felt something in 1954 does not make it a consistent, stable "truth" of her "experience." Maybe she changed her mind later.

But in the end its very doubtfulness, its collaborative authorship, its alternate disparagement and aggrandizement, and its endless recycling in further accounts, does make *My Story* look, colloquially speaking, like the story of Marilyn Monroe's life.

MEMOIR: ARTHUR MILLER

Traditionally, the distinction between memoir and autobiography is that in autobiography one writes about oneself, while in a memoir one writes about another. Although this boundary has blurred in recent years, it provides a useful way of thinking about Arthur Miller's various depictions of Marilyn Monroe, given the ways in which they bridge not only memories of self and memories of another, but also fact and fiction. Miller has produced four clear versions of Marilyn to date (as well as several others arguably modeled upon aspects of her character): his film *The Misfits* (1961); his play *After the Fall* (1964); his autobiography *Timebends* (1987); and his recent *Finishing the Picture* (2004), a play about the making of *The Misfits,* in which Marilyn does not appear onstage, but is a central character and concern, the subject of much of the play's drama and dialogue. The title would certainly seem double-edged, suggesting not only the legendary difficulties in completing the film, caused in large part by Monroe's own problems, but also, presumably, that Miller is trying to finish his own picture of Marilyn and, at the end of his long career, achieve a literary closure adequate to a playwright of his standing. The implication seems to be that not only is this Miller's latest in a long line of dramatic attempts to come to terms with Marilyn, but his last.

In *After the Fall,* Miller's subject is not Marilyn alone, but rather a broader exploration of one of the abstractions she represents: innocence. Miller's Marilyn is neither sexually nor morally innocent. The play insists that ultimately no one is guiltless, and that the greatest guilt is trying to maintain one's own innocence. Miller's alter ego, Quentin, is not a writer, but a lawyer, whose career is threatened by accusations of Communism. For all his self-questioning, however, Quentin does lay down the law throughout the play; he is confused, but his motives are pure. Quentin has two wives, first Louise and then Maggie (clearly a Marilyn figure), both of whom accuse Quentin of treating them like they don't exist, which makes him cry out against bringing "two such very different women to the same accusation." He countercharges both women with parallel crimes, insisting that neither will admit to her own share of culpability in their relationships' failures. Ironically, for all that Miller sees the dangers of maintaining one's own innocence, he seems to indict all his characters but Quentin for that crime ("These goddamned women have injured me; have I learned nothing?")[45] To reinforce these themes, Miller's directions call for the stage to be dominated by a concentration camp tower, while Quentin has an irresistible urge throughout the play to spread his arms as though he were being crucified.

The similarities between Maggie and Marilyn are unmistakable:

the play begins fourteen months after Maggie has died by her own hand—which is how much time would have elapsed since Marilyn's death when rehearsals of *After the Fall* commenced. Maggie is child-ish, vivacious and spontaneous. She is uneducated, and touchy about it (Quentin responds by being unfailingly patronizing: when she wishes she were better educated, he says: "Honey, you know how to see it all with your own eyes; that's more important than all the books").[46] Maggie has been both sexually indiscriminate and exploited; she tries intensely to be "all love" and fears that anger is "forbidden"; she is a perfectionist; she is given to adorable literalism and non sequiturs. When Quentin first meets her, he describes her as

> Quite stupid, silly kid. Sleeps in the park, her dress is ripped; she said some ridiculous things, but one thing struck me, she wasn't defending anything, upholding anything, or accusing—she was just *there,* like a tree or a cat. And I felt strangely abstract beside her.[47]

After she becomes a star and they reunite (in another piece of verisimilitude), Quentin must cope with his "own contempt" for Maggie, even as Miller suggests how sensitive Marilyn was to ridicule:

> Quentin: In the office, I'd hear people laughing that Maggie had the world at her feet . . .
>
> Maggie, *hurt, mystified*: They laughed!
>
> Quentin: In a way.
>
> Maggie, *in pain*: That's what I mean; I'm a joke to most people.
>
> Quentin: No, it's that you say what you mean, Maggie. You don't seem to be upholding anything, or . . . You're not ashamed of what you are.
>
> Maggie: W—what do you mean of what I am?
>
> > *Louise appears; she is playing solitaire.*
>
> Quentin, *suddenly aware he has touched a nerve*: Well . . . that you love life, and . . . It's hard to define, I—
>
> Louise: The word is tart. But what did it matter so long as she praised you?

Quentin, *to [Audience], standing, and moving within Maggie's area*:
　　But there's truth in it—I hadn't had a woman's praise, even a girl
　　I'd laughed at with the others . . .
Maggie: But you didn't, did you?
　　　　He turns to her in agony; Louise vanishes.
　　Laugh at me?
Quentin: No.
　　　　He suddenly stands and cries out to [Audience]:
　　Fraud—from the first five minutes! . . . Because—I should have
　　agreed she *was* a joke, a beautiful piece trying to take herself seri-
　　ously! Why did I lie to her, play this cheap benefactor, this . . .
　　What? *Listens, and now, unwillingly*: Yes, that's true too: she had;
　　[*sic*] a strange, surprising honor.[48]

Miller memorably renders the sense of resentful insecurity that many who knew her say characterized Marilyn, but he also shows that she had reason to be anxious, since even he apparently concurs that her attempts to take herself seriously were a joke, and finds it strange and surprising that such "a tart" should have any sense of honor.

　　Like Marilyn, Maggie has had a difficult early life; her struggles have made her both more shrewd, and more vicious, than Quentin. She tells him: "you're like a little boy, you don't see the knives people hide," and "I've seen such terrible things, Quentin. [. . .] Ask my doctor—I see more than most people, 'cause I had to protect myself."[49] As a consequence, Maggie cannot distinguish mastery from cruelty: she is spiteful in her own exercise of power, while para-noid in her acuteness to it in others. She is, in fact, a one-woman embodiment of the fine line between sadism and masochism.

　　Maggie is described as a "nut" more than once; given Monroe's sensitivity to her mother's institutionalization for mental problems, and what most say was her own terror of going insane, this seems the unkindest cut of all. Maggie is unremittingly suicidal; although Quentin does everything he can to save her, finally he admits that she was "doomed"; she "needed more love than [he] thought" and in the end, despite his promises, he must leave her, not only to save him-self, but to save *her*:

I'm not your analyst, but if this is how you create a happy reunion, forget it [. . .] I'm just trying to remove one of the motives, if a happy reunion is one of them—because I'm not going to be the rescuer any more. It's only fair to tell you, I just haven't got it any more. They're your pills and your life; you keep the count [. . .] The question is no longer whether you'll survive, but also whether I will.[50]

She says: "you wanted a happy whore. Right?" and he responds: "Not a whore, but happy, yes. I didn't want too much trouble."[51] Searching for a "clue" to the "truth" about their impasse, he seems to locate responsibility for it in her:

You eat those pills like power, but only what you've done will save you. If you could only say, I have been cruel, this frightening room would open! If you could say, I have been kicked around, but I have been just as inexcusably vicious to others; I have called my husband idiot in public, I have been utterly selfish despite my generosity, I have been hurt by a long line of men but I have coop-erated with my persecutors.[52]

This particular speech makes Maggie, who is, according to Miller's directions, *"writhing, furious at this exorcism,"* shout: "Son of a bitch!"[53] As well she might; it must be uncomfortable to be exorcised. Quentin has become not lawyer, but priest. "There is a shocking absence of love in this play," observed Graham McCann, and it is hard not to concur; if it is there, it is certainly obscured by sanctimony.[54]

Maggie is a fiction; she neither *is* Marilyn, nor purports to be. But given that she recognizably reflects Marilyn, it is also fair to point out that Miller's portrait is certainly one-sided. Including only her unde-niable need for power, he omits Monroe's intelligence and curiosity; he forgets her struggles for self-improvement, in taking classes on lit-erature, modeling and acting; most unfairly, he neglects the strong political convictions that led her to throw the weight of her popular-ity behind him during the HUAC hearings. The play uses the HUAC and "Maggie" as separate crises that explore the issue of Quentin's guilt (or lack thereof), but it leaves a void where in reality the two precisely coincided: when Monroe risked her career to defend Miller's politics. He only allows Maggie to represent personal, domestic, sexual, emotional guilt. The "larger" political and ethical questions of the play are addressed by other characters, but in life Marilyn Monroe played an active role in resolving just those problems for Miller.

Miller's Maggie reproduces the Marilyn stereotype. He omits generally how aspirational she was, how idealistic. Maggie says "s'uze me" (in a particularly snide bit of spelling); Monroe read Dostoyevsky, Joyce, Freud; she liked Sean O'Casey's autobiography, and admired Colette. Marilyn was by most nonfictional accounts very witty, and verbally adept; Maggie is dim-witted (Miller retains all the verbal agility for Quentin). Two themes that characterize Marilyn's lives emerge strongly in Miller's depiction: shame and guilt. Miller ascribes both crimes to Maggie; shame is the projection of guilt, it keeps the viewer innocent.

The character of Maggie may also have given rise indirectly to some of the myths of Marilyn. In particular, there is a frequently cited biographical story about a journal Miller kept, which supposedly Marilyn read a few weeks into their honeymoon in England in 1956. The account, in which she was distraught to find Miller criticizing her in his notebooks, figures almost universally in the lives as the moment when she lost faith in him and in their marriage. Marilyn supposedly reported to friends that Miller had written that he had thought she was an angel, and now could not defend her from charges that she was a bitch; in another version, Marilyn said he called her a whore.

In the play, what Quentin has written is significantly more reasonable.

> Maggie: You know when I wanted to die. When I read what you
> wrote, judgey. Two months after we were married, judgey.
> Quentin, *stricken, afraid, but remorseless*: Let's keep it true. It's not
> some words on a piece of paper destroyed us. You told me you
> tried to die long before you met me. [. . .][55]

Looking for a pen to sign autographs, Maggie had found a piece of paper upon which was written: "The only one I will ever love is my daughter. If I could only find an honorable way to die"; she shouts at Quentin that up until that point "I was married to a king, you son of a bitch!"[56] In fact, Quentin explains, she has misunderstood. Faced with his own sexual jealousy and her reaction to it ("betrayed, screaming that I'd made you feel you didn't exist"), he had simply written down his worst fear: "I wanted to face the worst thing I could imagine—that I could not love. And I wrote it down, like a letter . . . from myself."[57]

If one comes to *After the Fall* knowing the Marilyn biographies, it might look as if Miller were sterilizing the incident. But, of course, *After the Fall* pre-dates all of the principal Monroe lives, and according to biographer Guiles, Miller said that the incident he recorded more or less accurately in the play was later adapted and twisted into a new biographical myth, a distorted and exaggerated version of the "facts" that is recycled from one biography to the next.

On the other hand, one of the sources of that "myth" is Miller's own university friend Norman Rosten, who met Marilyn when she married Miller and became a good friend of hers; he reports hearing the story from Marilyn herself. Whom does one believe? That may depend as much upon whom one likes as upon what one knows.

In his 1987 autobiography *Timebends*, Miller maintains that *After the Fall* was written before Marilyn died, and that Maggie's death followed the pressures of fiction, not fact: "I had not begun with the idea that Maggie would die but that she and Quentin would part. [. . .] But as the character formed, she seemed more inescapably fated, and I could feel the bending of that arc toward death."[58] He says that at this point, while Monroe was still alive, such a death seemed actually to distinguish the fictional character from Marilyn, who as far as he knew was alive and well in Hollywood. After Monroe died, when the play was produced, he says, it was the lead actress who chose a platinum blonde wig; he later had much cause to regret allowing her to do so. "Coming so soon after Marilyn's death, *After the Fall* had to fail," Miller observes.[59] But he seems to see this as a coincidence, presenting himself as the blameless messenger killed:

"in time, and with much difficulty, I saw the justification for the [crit-ical] hostility toward me, for I had indeed brought very bad news."[60]

Miller's Marilyn in *Timebends* is also almost purely suicidal. The first time he ever hears her seriously agitated, on the set of *Bus Stop* in 1956, when she was under enormous pressure to succeed, he reports that, in listening to her pleas over the phone that she couldn't make it alone, "her suicide leaped up before me, an act I had never connected with her before."[61] His Marilyn is also childish, innocent, generous, irrational and intuitive. One of the key ways in which he defines his own authority, even superiority, over Marilyn is in relation to their different approaches to books: given that he was an eminent author when they met, and she was sensitive about her lack of formal education, this again seems like a cheap shot. He considers her a curiously "literal" reader; when he says that he can't imagine how she would survive without him, his example is that she couldn't spell. Thus Miller takes two aspects of the stereotype—her literalness, her childish helplessness—and reaffirms their natural or true place in Monroe's character. The aura of truthfulness surrounding a distin-guished author's autobiography may overwhelm the question of sub-jective viewpoints: suddenly these aspects of Marilyn become fact, rather than interpretation.

In his first extended description, Miller describes Marilyn as a "self-destroying babe in the woods absentmindedly combing back [her] hair with a loaded pistol"; later he calls her the saddest girl he ever met, which she learns to take as a compliment, a welcome relief from the burden of always performing rapture for the gratifica-tion of men.[62] (This line had also appeared in *The Misfits*, spoken by Gable to Monroe.) Miller reports that when he first met her he sus-pected "how tough she must be to have survived" Hollywood, but he also comes to see that she idealizes those she admires, including himself, "beyond all human weakness."[63] One could say the same thing about his depiction of Marilyn, which overall gives short shrift to toughness:

To be with her was to be accepted, like moving out into a kind of sanctifying light from a life where suspicion was common sense. She had no common sense, but what she did have was something holier, a long-reaching vision of herself of which she was only fitfully aware [. . .] she was part queen, part waif, sometimes on her knees before her own body and sometimes despairing because of it—"Oh, there's lots of beautiful girls," she would say to some expression of awed amazement, as though her beauty betrayed her quest for a more enduring acceptance. [. . .] She was finally all that was true.[64]

He is convinced that "the simple fact, terrible and lethal, was that no space whatever existed between herself and this star. *She was 'Marilyn Monroe,' and that was what was killing her.*"[65] In other words, she was an artifice, and a lethal one. But maybe being Marilyn Monroe wasn't killing her. Maybe it kept her alive; if Marilyn was a role, she was also the victory of ambition and hard work over deprivation and neglect. Miller does do Monroe the justice of understanding that her stardom was her life's triumph: it was her art and her self and she could no more give it up than he could give up writing. Leaming makes the strongest case in her biography that Monroe terribly needed Miller to accept her distressing past; the best Miller can do is acknowledge his inability to do so:

> The terrible irony was that I had reinforced the idea of her innocent victimization because I could not bear to accept her life as it was, because I had wanted to heal her of it rather than acknowledge it as hers. I had rejected the horrors she had lived, denied their power over her, but she felt herself rejected. [. . .] All that was left was for her to go on defending her innocence, in which, at the bottom of her heart, she did not believe. Innocence kills.[66]

Despite this realization, Miller's Marilyn is ultimately a muse: first of creation, then of destruction. His desire for her is important only because it gives him "the certainty that I could, after all, lose myself in sensuality. This novel secret entered me like a radiating force, and I welcomed it as a sort of proof that I would write again [. . .] I sensed a new play in me, and a play was my very self alive."[67] For Miller, then, no less than for the rest of her audience, Marilyn was a symbol of creativity, a symbol who inevitably reflected the solipsistic desires of those watching her, rather than a differentiated human being. He told a reporter in 1955:

> She is the most womanly woman I can imagine. Being with her, people want not to die. This girl sets up a challenge in every man. Most men become more of what they are natively when they are around her: a phoney becomes more phoney, a confused man becomes more confused, a retiring man more retiring. She's kind of a lodestone that draws out of the male animal his essential qualities.[68]

Although this passage is clearly imagined as a "tribute," not only does it locate her meaning in the reactions of men to her: those reactions are all negative. If she is a lodestone, she brings out the worst in men, amplifying their anxieties. When a force to be reckoned with, Marilyn becomes not creator but destroyer. For Miller she was "condemned from birth—*cursed* might be a better word—despite all she knew and all she hoped [. . .] she would turn cruelly against herself, so worthless, the scum of the earth, and her vileness would not let her sleep, and then the pills began and the little suicides each night."[69] To say that she was cursed is to return this "factual" picture of Marilyn to fairy tale; like Maggie, Marilyn was doomed by narrative, not life.

Monroe was asked by a reporter after her divorce from Miller whether she believed that Miller had "sought her out" in the first place as some sort of a real-life muse, because he had "come to an end in his writing" (having not published anything successfully for several years). Monroe told the reporter that if she answered, he would need to print her answer in its entirety. He agreed, and after a pause, she said: "No comment."[70]

FICTION: NORMAN MAILER AND JOYCE CAROL OATES

If Marilyn Monroe has always been seen as a made-up identity, it is not surprising that she has been of particular interest to fiction writers, even two writers as superficially different as Norman Mailer and Joyce Carol Oates. Despite Mailer's renowned misogyny and Oates's

avowed feminism, the Marilyns both novelists produced are not, ultimately, very different from each other, or from the many Marilyns
already circulating throughout our cultural myths. Both Mailer and
Oates explicitly argue that fiction is the best way to understand
Marilyn, to "inhabit" her completely. For Mailer, fiction is warranted
by Marilyn's own deceptions ("a life like hers," he declares, "is antipa-
thetic to biographical tools");[71] for Oates, only fiction can achieve her
project of liberating the real Norma Jeane from the carapace of the
artificial Marilyn (Oates felt that a novel might let her "give life to
this lost, lone girl, whom the iconic consumer-product 'Marilyn
Monroe' would soon overwhelm and obliterate").[72] Both of these
claims presume that Marilyn Monroe is already a fantasy, and thus
not only particularly suited to fictional exposition, but dependent
upon it. Rather than offering what novelist Don DeLillo calls a fictional "disinvention" of a familiar historical character, neither Mailer
nor Oates estranges Marilyn or offers an alternative to the myth.
Instead, each of them reincarnates the stereotype.

Although Mailer only promises to offer a *"possible* Marilyn
Monroe," the woman he concocted has become notorious, a blend of
Mailer's own fantasies of Marilyn and his resentment at her refusal
to fulfill them. Mailer's overt competition with Arthur Miller
throughout *Marilyn* for literary supremacy is inextricable from his
desire to "steal Marilyn" from him. Mailer writes that when he and
the Millers were neighbors in Connecticut, he "waited for the call to
visit, which of course never came."[73] In fact, Monroe had several
opportunities to meet Mailer, and declined, according to Miller, who
reports that she only agreed to invite Mailer to a party she knew he
would be unable to attend. She told journalist W. J. Weatherby, who
gave her Mailer's *The Deer Park* to read, that she didn't care for it
because Mailer was "too impressed with power, in my opinion," and
that he obviously knew nothing about how it really works.

Mailer's misogyny has been well scrutinized by academic writers
like S. Paige Baty, Graham McCann and William H. Epstein:
McCann is particularly good on Mailer's identification and rivalry
with Miller; Baty explains the ways in which Mailer's sexualized portrait of Marilyn Monroe is an attempt at masculine knowledge as
"mastery" (because, as she says, "he who truly knows her is who

'fucked her' ");[74] and Epstein uses *Marilyn* to construct a psychoana-
lytic postmodern reading of biography as a form riven with symbolic
struggles for phallic power over its subject.

Not only is Mailer's account troubling for all of these reasons (and
they are good ones), however, but also because Mailer frequently
claims the "rights" of the novelist in order to save himself from the
effort and responsibility of the biographer. Mailer's bad-faith strategy
throughout *Marilyn* is to offer a baseless speculation, dwell on it, and
then withdraw it, because actually it is baseless. The rhetorical term
for this tactic is *paralipsis*: emphasis is created through denial ("to say
nothing of . . ." is a standard example). For instance, in discussing
why Monroe consented to marry her first husband, James Dougherty,
when she was only three weeks past her sixteenth birthday, Mailer
comments:

> why not assume she is playing her role with such invention she is
> ready to enter an actor's arena where reality can be measured only
> by the intensity of emotion. That is all that is real. So she adven-
> tures out for the first time into that psychic territory where fantasy
> can reach into terrors never confessed before to anyone alive, and
> she confesses to him, her first actor, that she lives in terror of
> doing away with herself, yes, she knows she will kill herself one
> day.
>
> There is no record of such a conversation, no particle of evi-
> dence to underwrite it, except that she is forever ready to tell him
> in their marriage that if he were to die or go away she would jump
> off the Santa Monica pier.[75]

Mailer uses a series of strategic words relating to the imaginary—
role-playing, invention, emotion, nonreality, fantasy—in order to
cloak a crucial psychological interpretation (that Monroe planned to
die a suicide from the age of sixteen), which is, as Mailer admits in
the next sentence, utterly unsubstantiated. Why not interpret her
threats as ordinary, sentimental adolescent histrionics, instead?

A novelist can assume anything he likes about his characters,
because they don't exist except in his head, and on his page, but even
if we accept that biography exists at the intersection of history and

fiction (rather than being undeniable fact), a biographer still has less license to presuppose than a novelist. What is the point of biography if it only tells us what we already believe? *Marilyn* is littered with locutions like the "why not assume" that opens the previous passage: "we can easily assume," "let us assume," "let us dare the argument," "let us assume it even happened," all of which grant Mailer the *permission* to assume.[76] Mailer's assumptions then become part of the true story of Marilyn Monroe. Because Mailer has literary authority, his account becomes, tautologically, authoritative. Mailer appropriated the cultural clout of biography, which derives from its claims to truth, without accepting its obligations, its scruples—or, quite simply, its labor. The plain fact is that in some cases fiction is *easier* than meticulous research, especially for a fluent, gifted writer like Mailer—although of course such research alone will not produce truth either.

Joyce Carol Oates went rather further than Mailer, in one sense, repeatedly denying any particular obligation in *Blonde* to biographical fact. Oates explains:

> *Blonde* is a work of fiction. While many of the characters portrayed here have some counterparts in the life and times of Marilyn Monroe, the characterizations and incidents presented are totally the products of the author's imagination. Accordingly, *Blonde* should be read solely as a work of fiction, not as a biography of Marilyn Monroe.[77]

This familiar legal disclaimer does not offer a particularly helpful account of the complex relationship among biography, fiction and history, however. Oates repeatedly protests in interviews against the "literalism" of critics who disliked her extravagant fabrications, but it is not crudely literal to acknowledge that Marilyn Monroe is not totally a product of Joyce Carol Oates's imagination, and that the story Oates tells is also not entirely a product of her imagination. Although Oates can (and does) hide behind the intellectual justification that the novel is postmodern in its "experimentations" with blending fact and fiction, it is hard not to conclude that the experimentation is expedient, and arbitrary. For example, although some characters in *Blonde* retain their historical names (Norma Jeane; John Huston), and others are abbreviated (Mr. Z for Darryl F. Zanuck), some are renamed outright (first husband James Dougherty turns into Bucky Glazer), while others become, according to Oates, "archetypes" (Norma Jeane marries first "the Ex-Athlete" and then "the Playwright"). At the same time, Oates doesn't, to my knowledge, introduce any entirely fictional major characters, so her project is not really akin to generally innovative works like E. L. Doctorow's *Ragtime* or John Dos Passos's *U.S.A.* trilogy (both of which Oates cited as *Blonde*'s progenitors), because those works follow fictional protagonists' encounters with real history. Oates explained at least her reason for the sobriquets given DiMaggio and Miller: "It was not 'Marilyn Monroe' about whom I wrote. Norma Jeane marries mythic individuals, not 'historic' figures. Her husbands include the Ex-Athlete and the Playwright. (If I wanted to write about Joe DiMaggio and Arthur Miller, I would need to write about these complex men in a different mode.)"[78]

None of this really makes any sense, however. If Oates is not writing about "Marilyn Monroe" (a name Oates relentlessly sets off in scare quotes), why does ordinary Norma Jeane require a mythic mode? And why is this a mode that would not accommodate such "complex" men as DiMaggio and Miller? So much for needing an epic novel to explore the intricacy of being Marilyn Monroe. In fact, as Oates acknowledges in this interview, when Miller enters the scene she abruptly abandons "Norma Jeane's" point of view and suddenly lets Miller—the Writer—provide the book with its perspective and conscience. Presumably because his point of view is more complex than Marilyn's. Oates's postmodern "experimentation" reconfirms the Marilyn Monroe we've known since 1946: artificial, one-dimensional and dim. Oates's technique is not archetype but stereotype, not only of "the Ex-Athlete" and "the Playwright," but particularly of breathless, confused, stammering, disintegrating "Marilyn."

The dead metaphor actually resists the inventiveness of fiction. In her author's note, Oates claims a novelist's right to abridge, explaining that "synecdoche is the principle of appropriation," in which she chooses one emblematic figure or episode to represent many in

Marilyn Monroe's life: "in place of numerous lovers, medical crises, abortions and suicide attempts and screen performances, *Blonde* explores only a selected, symbolic few." As we shall see, there are already presumptions embedded in this decision (in particular the question of whether Monroe even *had* "numerous" abortions and suicide attempts is a subject of much biographical contention). But in Oates's approach, Marilyn's life is such an open secret that we need not bother with its details: we can simply stand back and take in the whole as a panorama adequately represented by selected symbolic "truths." The logic is circular: it means assuming first that a fixed pattern existed, and then presenting one example that represents that pattern (so that, for example, even assuming that Marilyn had "numerous" love affairs, they were all so equivalent that only one need be represented). Offering only one example has the effect of effacing difference, it negates the possibility of *discovering* change, and confirms the truth of the "type," an endlessly repeated symbol that bears out our sense of immutable patterns. If "synecdoche is the principle of appropriation," it is also the instrument of stereotype. Someone who skims across the surface of a life should not be surprised to find superficiality.

"Poor Marilyn," observed Michiko Kakutani in her *New York Times* review of *Blonde*.

> She has been commodified by sleaze merchants and deconstructed by academics. Her life has been pawed over by conspiracy theorists and sifted by scandal mongers; her image, appropriated by Madonna and dissected by everyone from Norman Mailer to Gloria Steinem. Now comes along Joyce Carol Oates to turn Marilyn's life into the book equivalent of a tacky television miniseries. In "Blonde," she does to Monroe what she did to Edward M. Kennedy in "Black Water," her embarrassing 1992 fictionalization of Chappaquiddick, playing to readers' voyeuristic interest in a real-life story while using the liberties of a novel to tart up the facts.[79]

Kakutani seems to be the *New York Times*'s resident Marilyn critic: she has reviewed not only Oates, but also Baty and Leaming. She is not without her own axes to grind (her review of Baty was particularly ungenerous), but in pointing a finger toward Oates's propensity to "tart up the facts" she is not being unfair. Lee Siegel puts it more bluntly in his astute review of *Blonde*: "It is something of an accomplishment, to make a novel so riddled with facts and yet so unwarranted in its imaginings."[80]

Both Mailer and Oates cultivate certain mythic fantasies about Marilyn, particularly sexual fantasies, but also the persistent idea that Marilyn was assassinated by a political directive from the Kennedys. While it might be convenient to protest that in writing fiction they are permitted poetic license, in the case of Marilyn this is disingenuous, because the central question about the myth of Marilyn Monroe is precisely the question of where fiction stops and fact begins (or vice versa). The clearest example of the pitfalls of such fantasies is in the fictional writing about Monroe and sex. The moments when writers like Oates and Mailer *choose* to claim the "right of a novelist" to invent are those moments that relate to sex and shame. This lets them treat Monroe as a fantasy in the Freudian sense, as a way to articulate unacceptable, even terrifying desires.

IS YOUR ASSHOLE SHOWING?

The biggest fictional license Oates takes in *Blonde* is what she portrays as an ongoing ménage à trois of Monroe, Charles Chaplin, Jr., and Edward G. Robinson, Jr., an evidently imaginary threesome that Oates presents as the primary sexual and emotional relationship of Monroe's adult life. The so-called affair endures for some 250 pages, between 1949 and 1956, through Marilyn's marriage with DiMaggio and ending only with the arrival of the authoritative "Playwright" onto the scene, at which point he takes over the story in more ways than one.

However, neither Chaplin nor Robinson even appears in most Monroe biographies. Summers alone gives a brief affair with Chaplin, Jr., in 1947 three paragraphs; fifty pages later he reports that one lover of Monroe's in 1953, "for a month or so," was Edward G. Robinson, Jr. Summers's source, a friend of both Chaplin's and Robinson's, calls the three men a "trio" and explains that "Marilyn saw us all occasionally, together or separately, for the rest of her life. They were all depressives, Marilyn, Charlie, and Eddie, and they would hunt each other down when things were bad."[81] Summers is telling the story in terms of the beginning of Monroe's drug use, explaining that both men were "pill freaks" and that in his opinion they were probably the ones who introduced Marilyn to barbiturates and amphetamines.

Oates repeatedly insists in interviews that hers is a corrective view of the real Norma Jeane, who was destroyed by her sexual commodification by sleazy men. One wonders what resistance to such sexual exploitation is achieved in scenes like this one, in which Oates's "Norma Jeane" participates in her first sexual threesome on a beach:

> Eddy quick and deft as if he'd practiced such a maneuver many times shifted his position to crouch over her, as Cass was now crouching over her head, and both men penetrated her, Cass's slender penis in her mouth, Eddy's thicker penis in her vagina, pumping into her swiftly and unerringly until Norma Jeane began to scream as she'd never screamed in her life, screaming for her life, clutching her lovers in such a paroxysm of emotion they would laugh ruefully over it later.
>
> Cass would display three-inch scratches on his buttocks, mild bruises, welts. In a parody of a Muscle Beach bodybuilder, strutting naked for them to admire, Eddy would display plum-colored bruises on his buttocks and thighs.
>
> "It must've been, Norma, you were waiting for us?"
> "It must've been, Norma, you were starved for us?"
> Yes.[82]

Oates ends the chapter there, on the affirmation that Norma Jeane needed and was starved for sex. So much for experimental fiction.

Sex remains definitive in these portraits: it is who Marilyn Monroe is, even when she's Norma Jeane. And she will continue to be marked, even by those writers intent upon rescuing her from the misogyny of previous accounts, by what is imagined as pathological excess: excess partners, excess pleasure, excess need. Pornography marks the point at which fiction and fact collide: such scenes of graphic sex are presumably meant to represent the *real* (this is what she "really" did) but require fiction to write them.

Similarly, Mailer argues in *Marilyn* that the moment at which Monroe acknowledged she had posed in the nude was the moment at which a novelist becomes *justified* in putting words in her mouth:

> Now when Twentieth learns from her lips that she has, yes, posed in the nude, a novelist has a right to invent the following dialogue. "Did you spread your legs?" asks a studio executive.
>
> "No."
>
> "Is your asshole showing?"
>
> "Certainly not."
>
> "Any animals in it with you?"
>
> "I'm alone. It's just a *nude*."[83]

Only when she has admitted to posing nude does Mailer invoke the right of a novelist to invent. Mailer grants himself a droit du seigneur to invent scenes of sex with impunity because he is "a novelist" (having written novels in the past?) and calls this a "novel biography"— but he doesn't imagine scenes of Monroe reading Dostoyevsky, meeting Carl Sandburg, or attending literature classes at UCLA, all of which she actually did. Mailer's logic seems to be twofold: first, that in posing nude Monroe had already exploited the image of her body, and thus he is permitted to exploit it as well. Analogous is the implication that Monroe has already exposed herself in such a way historically that any fictional exposure is now sanctioned: in this (Victorian) view of female sexuality, having posed nude, Marilyn was asking for it, and any amount of fantasy is now Mailer's right. But this fantasy is Victorian indeed, for Mailer also constructs Monroe as an outraged Puritan shocked at his salacious suggestions: this is sexual role-playing with a vengeance, which lets him indulge his fantasies about her while keeping her pure.

The novelist's "right to invent" is not characterized as a right to imagine *incident,* but rather explicitly as a right to invent *dialogue,* which is to say, Mailer claims the right to replace her voice with his at the point when she admits to having been photographed nude. This is one of Mailer's few ventures into dialogue in *Marilyn,* and it is the only time in the book when Mailer puts words in Monroe's mouth that he admits to having made up himself. Despite all Mailer's protestations that the rights are the novelist's, the very language of rights and justification needs to be invoked because it is *not* fiction, but biography. Novels rarely invoke their right to invent; they don't have to.

Rights, justice, ethics are much less at issue in fiction, because power is much less at issue. Mailer asserts his authorial power at the point when he narrates one of the watershed moments in Monroe's career, a pivotal struggle over the right to determine her public identity. In most biographical accounts, the nude calendar scandal is treated as a David and Goliath story, in which Monroe was pitted against the powerful studio executives who wanted to shut her up, who enjoined her silence or repudiation of her own self-exposure. Monroe refused, and her voice thus becomes an image of personal power and populist resistance against the all-male commercial power of the studio. For most biographers this incident reveals Monroe's ability to finesse and beguile her public. Mailer inserts his authorial voice at just this point, demeaning her at the very moment when she refused shame, by associating the incident with bestiality and with her asshole.

As singular as this chain of associations might seem, Mailer's is not the only account to fictionalize the same conjunction of Marilyn's voice, her asshole, and the studio system: indeed this triangle of symbolic power becomes a recurrent motif in the fictional writing about Marilyn. In 1996, Kathryn Hyatt reproduced this triangle in a graphic novel (i.e., comic book) called *Marilyn: The Story of a Woman* (U.K. title: *Marilyn for Beginners*), which Hyatt describes in an afterword as "a fictionalized biography." Hyatt mixes direct quotations from *My Story*, biographies and magazine interviews, with imagined dialogue: "As for Marilyn's 'voice,' I built my dialogue from existing interviews and my own sense of how Marilyn would speak."[84] The back cover claims that in this book "Monroe speaks for herself—to her psychoanalyst, to a reporter—and ultimately to the reader of this book." Hyatt stages a series of interviews that are meant to stand in for naturalness: for example, a quotation that first appeared in a newspaper travels from Marilyn Monroe to a journalist to an editor to

Hyatt to her fictional Marilyn Monroe to a fictional psychiatrist to the reader. This is Marilyn Monroe speaking for herself?

Like Mailer before her and Oates after her, Hyatt creates representative encounters that are meant to suggest a lifelong pattern of abuse and then associates them with Monroe's anus. Unlike the mouth, which is associated with voice (as identity), control and agency, the anus is associated with waste, shame and vulnerability. Thus in Hyatt's vision of shameful, filthy studio exploitation, Marilyn, speaking for herself, says: "Wait a minute, I don't do this . . . You want to BUTT FUCK me. You want to hurt me."[85] Like Mailer, Hyatt simultaneously associates Marilyn Monroe with a "filthy" sexual act and sanitizes her, as one who categorically doesn't "do" anal sex.

Oates creates exactly the same motif of a fictionalized voice, anal sex and studio moguls. Oates lingers for an entire chapter over an imagined scene in which the young aspiring starlet is sodomized by the head of her studio, Mr. Z. Although much of *Blonde* is narrated in the third person, this particular chapter is written entirely in Monroe's voice. The punctuating breath-spaces are Oates's, presumably intended to suggest Marilyn's famous breathiness:

> Mr. Z was impatient   he was not a cruel man I believe but one accustomed to getting his way of course & surrounded by "little people"   there must be the temptation to be cruel when you are surrounded by such & they cringe & fawn before you in terror of your whim   I'd been stammering & now could not speak at all I was on my hands & knees on the soft fur rug (Russian fox, Mr. Z wld boast later) & my sharkskin skirt shoved up to my waist & panties removed [. . .]   I would not remember Mr. Z afterward except the small glassy eyes & dentures smelling of garlic & the sweat-film on his scalp visible through the wiry hairs   & the hurt of the Thing   of hard rubber, I think greased & knobby at the end shoved first between the crack of my buttocks & then up inside me   like a beak plunging in   *In, in* as far *in* as it will go   I wouldnt remember how long was required for Mr. Z to collapse like a swimmer upon the beach panting & moaning   I was in terror the old man wld have a heart attack or a stroke & I wld be blamed   you hear of that all the time, cruel crude funny

stories   you laugh to hear yet wld not laugh if you were the victim. My contract was a $100 a week.[86]

In Oates's version all-powerful Mr. Z exploits his victim, little Norma Jeane, in the most sadistic possible way. Oates writes Norma Jeane as coy, childish (even inside her own head, Marilyn can't spell, for some inexplicable reason thinking in shorthand),* and terrified, understanding her violation in terms of the "Thing" hurting her. Oates's "Norma Jeane" always stammers, throughout the novel; Monroe did have a stammer as a child, which would occasionally resurface under stress (Guiles tells a story in which Monroe once began stuttering during the filming of a scene, and was shouted at by the director: "But you don't stutter." Monroe responded: "Th-th-that's what you th-think!").[87] But it was by no means constant or debilitating—as her performances show. In Oates's rendition, however, the woman can't get a sentence out without stammering: thus in 1961, she asks: "Am I d-divorced now? Is it over?" Like the cliché of the whisper, the stammer represents her fear, paralysis, childishness, all of which are italicized, as it were, by fantasies of anal violation.

In fact, Monroe survived for years on the fringe of the Hollywood party circuit, and was known for some fairly tough talk. Several of the widely circulating statements ascribed to her involve obscenities; one of the most famous is a declaration of independence, attributed sometimes to her first big studio contract, and by Summers to her marriage to DiMaggio: asked how she felt about getting married, Monroe is said to have announced: "I have sucked my last cock."[88] Whether she really said it—as Mailer notes, "one can better ask about which Hollywood star it has not been told"[89]—interests me less than the selectivity Oates displays here. Not only will the possibility of Monroe's voice being cynically, knowingly obscene be effaced and rewritten as innocent shock and outrage; when the fiction does imagine Marilyn engaged in fellatio, it is not as a more active form of capitulation, but still as "helpless" subjugation. When

---

*In fact, typographical shorthand is a favorite strategem of Oates's for representing her characters' interior thoughts, but as an introspective reliance on ampersands and abbreviations is something she particularly associates with serial killers in books like *Zombie* and *The Barrens*, it is not clear that this technique does Monroe any favors.

Oates's Marilyn goes down, she is forced down on President Kennedy in a haze of drugs and self-loathing; regressing to "Norma Jeane, confused and frightened," she is in "terror that she might vomit, gagging, no sensation worse than helpless gagging."[90] None of these three writers will use the far more familiar story of a starlet using her mouth to get what she wants, in however compromised a manner: she can only be exposed, penetrated, and shamed.

Anal sex clearly signifies, for all three writers, a metaphor for exploitation, and provides shock value—but it also symbolizes a strange mode of confession and self-invention. Oates's Norma Jeane ends the story of her violation by brandishing her new contract and referring to "that day the start of my NEW LIFE": she will be cast in her first role (stammering at the news, of course) and renamed Marilyn Monroe—against her will—in the next two pages.[91] The back cover to Hyatt's *Marilyn* promises that its story is "seen through the prism of Marilyn's own inner world." But this is of course *not* "Marilyn's own inner world": it is in fact an outer portrait of her inner world, it is public. Our stories about Marilyn Monroe, from Mailer to Oates, imagine her interiority only in order to publish it. The violation of the anus seems to symbolize this necessary movement between inner and outer: Marilyn Monroe must always be exposed to our gaze, and that gaze will only see her as sexual. These three fictional lives imagine scenes of anal sex as the most private scenes they can think of only in order to "strip away the veil" and reveal them. An even more figurative reading might suggest that the tension is ultimately between Monroe's mouth, as a sign of her power, and her asshole, as a sign of her shame. The two remain opposed—Marilyn vocally repudiates anal sex in all three accounts—because Marilyn represents both power and shame.

This motif of voice, power and anal sex can *only* be read figuratively and not literally, because anal sex, with or without studio executives, is not mentioned in any of the principal biographies of Marilyn Monroe. This is a cultural fiction, and it is produced over, and through, Marilyn Monroe's dead body. Its consistency and repetition mean that this fantasy must articulate what seems to these writers a truth about Marilyn and her story. When Mailer's studio executive asks, "Is your asshole showing?" he is seeking the limits of exposure, testing the extent of her degradation. The image of Marilyn may symbolize innocence, childishness, deliverance, but her story represents the perversion of these qualities: mortification, victimization, penetration. If the image of Marilyn is plenitude, her story is about surfeit: almost anything can be shoved into her, and she will take it. But eventually she will spill over, as well—into madness, emptiness, and death. She will be ritually evacuated—if not cleansed—by story's end.

PART TWO

REPRODUCTION

Norma Jeane Mortenson, c. 1942. This photograph has been reworked and juxtaposed with a photograph of Marilyn Monroe's postautopsy corpse as a work of art entitled "Overexposure" BY CHRISTIAN BLAU.

3

"GOODBYE NORMA JEANE," 1926–1946

Reporter: "Is this the new Marilyn?"
Marilyn Monroe: "No, I'm the same person—
but it's a different suit."

—ERNEST W. CUNNINGHAM,
The Ultimate Marilyn

In a *New York Times* interview promoting *Blonde*, Joyce Carol Oates explains that, despite the erroneous impression one might receive from reading its more than nine hundred pages, it is not actually a novel about Marilyn Monroe:

> I never had any interest in Marilyn Monroe and I have to tell you immediately that I never would have written any book about Marilyn Monroe [. . .] I got very interested in writing about an American girl who is Norma Jeane Baker who becomes a celebrity later in life. I was focusing on her when she was about 17 years old. I have a beautiful photograph of her and she doesn't look anything like Marilyn Monroe [. . .] Her hair is dark brown and curly, her face does not look like Marilyn Monroe. She's smiling in a very girlish and yearning and hopeful way. She's not glamorous. She's not even especially beautiful, but she's very pretty. And I thought, I would love to explore the possibility of what it would be to be that girl and then a few years later to have become Marilyn Monroe. [. . .] Actually I never wanted to write about Marilyn Monroe. It was something that happened to me, the way her life happened to Norma Jeane. To me, she's always Norma Jeane.[1]

Although *Blonde* is supposed to be about Norma Jeane, in Oates's account Norma Jeane is defined as much by *not* being Marilyn Monroe (or glamorous or beautiful) as by what she is (brunette, girlish, yearning, hopeful, pretty). Oates presents her decision to write about Monroe in similarly negative terms: it "happened" to her, against her will. Joyce Carol Oates never would have written a book about Marilyn Monroe—and yet that would appear to be what she's done.

Like Elton John in "Candle in the Wind," Oates presents herself as remarkable for recognizing the real Norma Jeane obscured behind artificial Marilyn Monroe. She has to repudiate ("immediately") the impression that she would ever have written a book about Marilyn Monroe, because Oates is too clever and too feminist to be interested in an invented persona, a dumb blonde manufactured for the fantasies of men. The appeal of what I am going to call the "Norma Jeane story" is evidently not least the way that it enables writers to present themselves as more discerning than everyone else: "To me, she's always Norma Jeane." Oates's misrepresentation of her motive is extremely representative of the writing about Marilyn; most of us consider ourselves too knowing to be fascinated by false, glamorous movie stars, or so we profess: we want to know what happened to an ordinary, pretty "real girl" who coincidentally just happened to *become* a movie star (as if other movie stars did not start out as and remain real people, too).

Although we accept that Marilyn's image of natural sexuality was artificially produced, the natural has not left the story. Instead, we've split her in two. Marilyn represents the artificial, glamorous, made-up image, and Norma Jeane symbolizes the private, natural, real woman. Norma Jeane is nothing if not natural; this is clear from one of the Gap store's khaki ads from 1993, in which a series of celebrities were shown wearing khakis in natural-looking photographs; the campaign emphasized the candid aspects of these pictures to suggest stars caught offstage, in "real-life" clothing. The photograph shows the Norma Jeane described by Oates, with the caption "Norma Jeane wore khakis."

In this picture, taken in 1945 by André de Dienes, Norma Jeane is in the country, on a rugged mountainside, wearing a wool sweater, with her dark hair blowing in the wind—all symbols of the natural

Norma Jeane Dougherty, 1945. PHOTOGRAPH BY ANDRÉ DE DIENES.

Norma Jeane™ wore khakis.

and ordinary. This image is thus not Marilyn Monroe, it is Norma Jeane: can one imagine Marilyn Monroe wearing khakis? Marilyn Monroe wears glittering evening gowns that were, according to her publicists, sewn onto her. Marilyn was all about unreality.

But of course, Marilyn Monroe did wear khakis, at least once in her life, because there she is. Although Marilyn is supposed to be the icon, and Norma Jeane the real woman, Norma Jeane has become just as iconic as Marilyn Monroe: the name "Norma Jeane" is even trademarked, as can be seen in the ad. Norma Jeane just symbolizes the other half of the story: the natural world of girlish, light innocence that Marilyn Monroe the movie star abandoned on her dark journey into the artificiality that would, the story goes, kill her.

The story of Marilyn Monroe is a story of metamorphosis, a Cinderella tale in which poor Norma Jeane goes to the ball as Marilyn Monroe—but, in a compelling tragic twist, instead of living happily ever after, dies alone. As we saw in chapter two, the magical transformation from neglected Norma Jeane into desirable Marilyn Monroe was always part of the image. In its traditional European variants "Cinderella" is a story in which undeserved persecution and suffering (usually prompted by sexual jealousy) is followed by a supposed "transformation" that actually reveals the true self. This revelation in turn is followed by further jealous punishment, before recognition of the newly unveiled true self (if the shoe fits) leads to a "happily ever after" as atonement and compensation. "Cinderella" is a satisfying story not simply because it shows life as a beauty contest, as some have complained; such an interpretation only reads the tale literally. The tale certainly exalts physical beauty, but "Cinderella" is primarily a story about identity, about being recognized by one's culture (represented by the Prince) for one's true worth. The fairy tale itself dwells upon the process of transformation, not the marriage; similarly it is the metamorphosis from Norma Jeane *into* Marilyn Monroe that interests us. And if the comparison to Cinderella is apt, it ought to mean that Marilyn Monroe is the real identity, and Norma Jeane the role (of drudge) that a natural heroine was unfairly forced to play.

Although likening Marilyn to Cinderella is central to the apocrypha, it gets the fairy tale backward and makes the drudge the reality. Certainly her story can be made to conform to some of the fairy tale's archetypal structures: an absent father; a violent, dangerous mother figure; travail and neglect; the fairy-tale alteration and the recognition by "everyone" (whether the tale's courtiers, or real-life Hollywood and then the world) that this mythical creature was a golden girl. In particular, the fairy-tale logic that exterior appearance must reflect interior character (which is why in fairy tales good people are beautiful and bad people are ugly) recurs, as we are about to see, as do two other potent symbols of the fairy-tale heroine: blondeness as desirability, and the capacity of names to reflect one's true self. Part of the reason that Marilyn is such a powerful myth is that her life seems to correspond to some of our most symbolic tales. But as this chapter will show, those symbolic parallels are as much made as they are natural.

NAMING NAMES

The belated and oxymoronic revelation that the real Marilyn is really Norma Jeane is constantly rediscovered in the pages of the Monroe biographies, as if it had not been stated in the first studio biography in 1946 and a basic part of the tale ever since. In fact, the Monroe apocrypha presents a vast array of "real" names for the most famous woman in the world.

> Norma Jeane Baker, the real Marilyn Monroe, was born on June 1, 1926.[2]

> She was born on June 1, 1926 in the Los Angeles General Hospital and registered as Norma Jeane Mortensen. (The surname was evidently speculative: the "e" on Jeane was never used again.)[3]

> No one could have foreseen the impact that a newborn named Norma Jeane Mortenson ultimately would have on a generation of people. No one then would have believed that she would transform herself into the ultraglamorous enigma Marilyn Monroe.[4]

She was born Norma Jeane Baker (although her birth certificate reads Norma Jeane Mortenson) in Los Angeles on 1 June 1926. [. . .] She died Marilyn Monroe on 4 August 1962.[5]

These claims rapidly become nonsensical: how could she have been "born" anything other than the name on her birth certificate? They are also all founded on the idea that she became, in Rooks-Denes's phrase, an "ultraglamorous enigma." If Marilyn is a mystery, Norma Jeane is the solution. From the beginning of her biographical life, Marilyn is written about as someone other than herself, and, as Steinem's representative assertion shows, as someone unreal, so that "the real Marilyn Monroe" is actually Norma Jeane. Biographies will pretend to discover the "real" Marilyn by renaming her: Norma Jean or Norma Jeane, Baker, Mortensen, Mortenson, Dougherty, Daugherty—the proliferation of possibilities betrays that it isn't the name itself that matters, it is what the idea of the real name symbolizes: the lost reality that Marilyn shed when she became a movie star and embraced a poisonous artificiality.

"Norma Jean" was the consistent spelling of Marilyn Monroe's given first name in public accounts in her lifetime and in the first biographies, including Fred Lawrence Guiles's *Norma Jean* in 1969. It was in Guiles's 1984 revision that "Norma Jeane" was first offered as Monroe's preferred spelling:

> "Norma Jeane" has been used throughout this present volume rather than the more common rendering of her given name, "Norma Jean," principally because that was the way Marilyn herself consistently wrote it. The simpler spelling did not just happen; it was the way many of her close friends and at least two of her husbands thought it was spelled. [. . .] But I must assume some of the guilt for popularizing the simpler spelling through its use as a title, and it is my hope that this present work will give currency to Marilyn's preference, since it is my intention to correct here all previous errors of mine and others.[6]

Guiles's intention to correct all previous errors is either endearing or egotistical, depending on your point of view. Either way, it is unrealistic: the spelling "Norma Jean" persists in any number of accounts published after 1984. The link between names and identity is clear: How can anyone know this woman if we don't even know her name? How can she know herself? The proliferation of names alone creates the impression, from the beginning of her life story, of a precarious identity, an unstable self. This figurative implication will rapidly be offered as the literal truth of Marilyn Monroe's (always lost) identity.

Although uncertain of the name she was born with, we have no doubts as to the name she died with. By the end of all of the versions quoted above, Norma Jeane has become Marilyn Monroe and in many of them she will have died Marilyn Monroe. The specter of a dead Marilyn haunts many accounts of Norma Jean's birth:

> The baby was born on 1 June 1926 at 9:30 am in the Los Angeles General Hospital, and the birth certificate identifies her as the daughter of Gladys Monroe of 5454 Wilshire Boulevard. [. . .] The child's birth registration in the California Board of Health's Vital Statistics stated her name as Norma Jeane Mortenson. In her youth, she was sometimes known as Norma Jeane Baker. From the age of twenty, she was Marilyn Monroe, but she declined to make that her legal name until seven years before her death.[7]

Spoto's retrospective turn of phrase, constructed in the knowledge of her early death, implies not only that she rejected the name Marilyn (and thus rejected the identity) much longer than she did, but also that she changed her name knowing that she had only seven more years to live. But she was twenty-nine, and presumably believed that the name would be hers for decades to come: in fact, she legally changed her name in March 1956, the same year that she wed Arthur Miller and won her major battle with 20th Century-Fox for more control over her films. The name change might rather be inter-preted as a triumphant *assertion* of her identity, at the point at which she assumed command of her career and image. Seeing "Marilyn Monroe" as a fatality is not only a foregone conclusion, it determines the plot of her life story, her psyche, and identity itself.

FATHERLESS CHILD

If Marilyn Monroe's "true" identity has been *mis*named, it is *un*named as well. The confusing array of possible last names for Norma Jeane arises from several sources: Monroe's illegitimacy, her mother's several marriages, Norma Jeane's status as a foster child, and her own early marriage.

In a culture in which last names are conferred by the father and secure one's social identity, Monroe is a problematic case, because not only is her given last name a misspelled fiction, used by her mother to disguise Monroe's illegitimacy, but there is also no consensus about the name of Monroe's biological father. Actually the famously "artificial" name Monroe has considerably more claim to be her real name, given that it was her mother's maiden name, than all of the supposedly real names offered by various biographers; those names are the fictions.

Zolotow's 1960 biography offers a characteristic blend of inaccuracy and misunderstanding when he writes that her real name was "Norma Jean Baker," and that her biological father was a man called "Edward Mortenson," to whom her mother was not married. In 1969 Guiles explained, apparently correctly, that Zolotow's version was exactly backward. "Norma Jean" (as it was still being spelled) was indeed illegitimate; her father was *not* Mortenson, but her mother *was* married to him, although not when the baby was born.

Gladys Monroe's first husband was a man named Baker (whose own first name has many biographical variants, including John, Jack and Jasper), with whom she had two children. They divorced, and Baker took their children with him to Tennessee (as a teenager, Marilyn would be reunited with her half sister Berniece; her half brother died as a child). According to both Summers and Spoto, Gladys then married a "Martin Edward Mortensen," from whom she separated after several months; he was, apparently, not even in California when Gladys became pregnant in 1925. "It appears he was a Norwegian immigrant, a baker who died in a motorcycle accident in 1929, but even that," writes Summers, "is disputed."[8] She gave birth to a girl on June 1, 1926, ascribing paternity to "Edward Mortenson," whose whereabouts she declared "unknown." The birth certificate confirms this version of the tangle.

Spoto is the only major biographer to explain that she was enrolled in school as Norma Jeane Baker, and frequently called Baker during her youth, because her mother often went by the name of her first husband; according to one ancillary account, Monroe herself did not know that Baker wasn't the name on her birth certificate until her first marriage, at sixteen; the information is said to have come as a shock to her.

The birth certificate that should certify the existence of Marilyn Monroe confuses more than it clarifies: indeed, as Spoto explains, it is partly fictionalized, "so easy was it, then as now, to omit, invent, and alter one's record."[9] But most biographers will nonetheless treat "the record" as a source of proof, rather than as a written (and thus modifiable) text. "The record" is an imaginary ideal of documentary truth, but it is invoked by some writers as if the word "record" itself counts as evidence, as the irrefutable clincher to any argument. Thus Summers at one point pronounces that despite Monroe's claim that she was always faithful to her first husband, "the record, though, says Norma Jeane was unfaithful." Since we do not, in fact, have documents that certify sexual encounters, there is no record that says this—except Summers's, and the other accounts he is quoting.

If Mortensen wasn't Marilyn Monroe's father, who was? Guiles asserted flatly in 1969 that the biological father of Norma Jeane was a traveling salesman called C. Stanley Gifford; Gifford's paternity was accepted by writers including Mailer, Steinem and Rollyson for the next ten years. But subsequent accounts have contradicted this, too. Summers, characteristically, pronounces that Monroe believed Gifford was her father, and then blames her for being wrong: he asserts that Gifford's paternity is only "possible" but that Monroe's mind "became scrambled on the subject of paternity," when it is of course the paternity that is scrambled.[10] Spoto declares that

the simple truth is that the father could have been any of her boyfriends in 1925—Harold Rooney, a co-worker who was besotted

The birth certificate of Norma Jeane Mortenson, 1926.

with her; or the adoring Clayton MacNamara; or, perhaps most likely of all, Raymond Guthrie, a film developer who ardently courted her for months that year.[11]

An encyclopedia of Marilyn facts and fables called *The Complete Marilyn Monroe* repeats this list of possible fathers more skeptically, as evidence of historical mystifications rather than of Gladys's implicit promiscuity, and adds that the confusion was compounded by "another man called Martin Edward Mortensen" who died in 1981 and "long claimed he was Marilyn's father."[12] Sandra Shevey's *The Marilyn Scandal* is even more confusing: when describing Monroe's conception and birth in the text, she writes that Gladys "had recently been deserted by her second husband, Edward Mortensen. [. . .] It was generally believed that Norma Jeane was the result of Gladys Baker's relationship with a co-worker at the Consolidated Film Industries lab where she was employed, though Stanley Gifford did not accept parental responsibility."[13] Her discussion of paternity ends there. But the photographic insert includes a picture with the following caption: "Reputed to be Marilyn Monroe's father, Edward Mortensen, shortly before he died aged 85. He never acknowledged paternity." Spoto declares that Gifford's paternity cannot be proven:

> As for the child [Norma Jeane], she never met Gifford and was never certain he was her father. To be sure, she tried to contact one or two men she said *might have been* her father (and Gifford *may* have been among them), but the accounts of her attempts at a meeting are notoriously contradictory. Evidence that Charles Stanley Gifford was the father of Gladys's child is, in fact, utterly lacking.[14]

Summers says the same thing, even more bluntly: "We do not know who Marilyn's father was."[15] Although Wolfe relies heavily upon Summers for his 1998 life, and has clearly read Spoto, he opts simply for announcing that Gifford was Monroe's father, expunging from the story fourteen years of expressed doubt. In the same year, Leaming said that Gifford was "possibly" Monroe's father, but offered no other possibilities.

Not knowing the name of Monroe's father—moreover, the multiplication of possible candidates—makes her identity seem all the more unsettled. The name on her birth certificate is Norma Jeane Mortenson; the name on her baptismal certificate is Norma Jeane Baker; the name on her first marriage license is Norma Jeane Mortensen. The name by which her "original" identity is popularly known is Norma Jean Baker. She could be almost *anyone*; these incarnations function like aliases, suggesting a fluid, even volatile, character. The fact that there is no consensus about the name of Marilyn Monroe's father is rarely interpreted as indicating only that sexual and social mores in 1926 meant that Gladys Monroe Baker Mortensen had to falsify the paternity of her illegitimate daughter; nor is it considered to suggest how little we in fact know about Marilyn Monroe in particular and about other people in general.

The search for a "Daddy" is something that all of the biographies emphasize. Oates goes furthest, making the lost father (transposed into lost daughter) *the* childhood trauma, the essence of Marilyn Monroe's identity, source and explanation for most of her problems. The woman without a father is doomed by the force of fiction: thus Mailer will end *Marilyn* by comparing her to Little Nell: "Goodbye Norma Jean. Au revoir Marilyn. When you happen on Bobby and Jack, give the wink. And if there's a wish, pay your visit to Mr. Dickens. For he, like many another literary man, is bound to adore you, fatherless child."[16] Even more strongly, Oates suggests that "Norma Jeane" dies to join her father: the last words of *Blonde* are: "Norma Jeane—see? That man is your father."[17] But do we really believe that not knowing one's father is fatal? The same story is told about Sylvia Plath and Eva Perón, aligning these quondam peroxide blondes along the axis of abandonment, promiscuity, seduction and self-destruction. All of these themes not only locate sexuality firmly in the woman (who is seductress, a danger to herself and others) but emphasize the need for a woman to be legitimated by her relationship to men. The witch, the siren, the vampire and the suicidal daughter are cut from the same cloth: female power (as sexuality) will be aligned with illegitimacy and violation; it will be punishable, in fiction, by death.

None of this is to dispute whether Monroe in fact felt that she had been traumatized by the absence of her father: apparently she did, and certainly she called all three of her husbands "Daddy." But it is to point out how arbitrary, and how excessive, is the prominence fathers are given in the story of Marilyn Monroe's life. In the *Marilyn on Marilyn* interview tapes, Monroe describes a fantasy she had when she was a child: "Clark Gable—I'm sure he won't mind if I say it—I used to always think of him as my father, I'd pretend that he was my father. I never pretended anyone was my mother! I don't know why—but I always pretended he was my father." If Monroe herself believed that the loss of her father was more important than the loss of her mother, this may not indicate anything other than that she had been taught that fathers were more important than mothers and interpreted her experience accordingly.

Although Marilyn Monroe's mother was also absent and "lost," the stories told about Gladys are quite different in emphasis. Only the female biographers, Steinem and especially Leaming, think about Monroe in terms of needing to be mothered, rather than fathered. Maternity in Monroe's story must come back to her sexuality, so that it is her own status as mother that is in question; all the biographers, including Steinem and Leaming, link Monroe's need *for* a mother with her need to *be* a mother. But when Monroe is discussed in terms of abandonment, she is a "fatherless child." Stories about maternity are more censorious, and lead most of the biographers into diagnosis, judgmentalism, and accusations of failure. The story of Marilyn Monroe's mother is not a story symbolizing abandonment (though it might have been), but about insanity and murder.

BORDERLINE PERSONALITY

When Marilyn Monroe was not yet eight, her mother was hospitalized for mental illness; she would be in and out of institutions for the rest of her long life, dying in an old age home in Florida in March 1984. Monroe's own adult battles with what we classify as emotional problems—addictions, depression, attempted suicide—would always be biographically linked to her mother's institutionalization, and it seems clear that Monroe herself was (understandably) terrified of going mad. That Monroe was clinically disturbed, even "psychotic," is accepted by many of her biographers. The most extreme are Summers and Leaming, who believe that by the end of her life Monroe was insane. Summers opens his book by warning the reader never to believe Marilyn's own words: "We must treat what she tells us with informed skepticism. [. . .] Marilyn, an international fantasy figure, constructed her image, both public and private, from a blend of fact and self-serving fantasy. She exercised to excess a common human license. Fantasy was part of this creature and part of the challenge is to discover the woman who sheltered behind it."[18] Excess is the appropriate crime of the most womanly of all women, as these stories will reveal. By the end of the book, Summers is paraphrasing Monroe's psychiatrist asserting that she was psychotic, "a candidate for an institution."[19]

The question of hereditary insanity is nearly as fraught as that of Monroe's paternity. Not coincidentally, it is also like illegitimacy in being a question laden with cultural value: mental illness continues to bear a stigma, and implies for some people a lack of discipline, an excessiveness with which Marilyn will always be associated. More obviously, madness has been linked with female sexuality since at least the Middle Ages. Marilyn's reputed insanity adds the finishing touches to the melodrama of her life, making it read more like a Victorian novel than ever.

Gladys Monroe was diagnosed as paranoid schizophrenic by her doctors, but biographers nonetheless continue to argue about what precisely her illness was. There are two main reasons for the dispute. The first is a common confusion about what "schizophrenia" actually means as a clinical psychiatric disorder: psychiatry does not use schizophrenia to denote split or multiple personality (which psychiatry today terms dissociative identity disorder, or DID).* This frequent mistake leads to arguments like the one Baty advances, in *American Monroe,* that the proliferation of images of Marilyn Monroe is a sign

---

*According to the fourth edition of the *Diagnostic and Statistical Manual* of the American Psychiatric Association (APA) (*DSM-IV*), which is the official diagnostic handbook for psychiatry, schizophrenia is "*neither* split personality" nor "multiple personality" (original emphasis). It is, rather, characterized by an "array of symptoms" that demonstrate "profound disruption in cognition and emotion." The criteria for schizophrenia include psychotic manifestations such as hallucinations, delusions, hearing internal voices, disorganized speech, and disorganized or catatonic behavior.

of postmodern "cultural schizophrenia," in which "hosts of 'real, final, and true' Marilyns are reproduced in various media, each version claiming to most realistically re(as)semble the star."[20] Baty's confusion of schizophrenia with multiple or dissociated personalities lets her read Monroe's own life as an example of this "cultural schizophrenia," a reading dependent upon (Baty's mistakenly literal interpretation of) her mother's diagnosis. Baty declares that Monroe herself "suffered from mental illness all her life," but although she was clearly unhappy, even desperate, it is by no means unanimously agreed that Monroe suffered from clinical "mental illness" as distinct from the damage caused by her undisputed addiction to drugs.[21] The confusion with "split personality" derives from the etymology of the term *schizophrenia,* which translates as "split mind": psychiatry uses it figuratively, whereas in common practice it is understood literally.

In her study of femininity and insanity *The Female Malady,* Elaine Showalter suggests the way in which "schizophrenia" came to dominate discussions of female madness in the mid-twentieth century:

> Schizophrenia offers a remarkable example of the cultural conflation of femininity and insanity. First of all, unlike hysteria, anorexia nervosa, or depression, schizophrenia is *not* a predominantly female disorder. Most studies seem to show that the incidence is about equal in women and men. Nevertheless [. . .] the schizophrenic woman has become as central a cultural figure for the twentieth century as the hysteric was for the nineteenth. Modernist literary movements have appropriated the schizophrenic woman as the symbol of linguistic, religious, and sexual breakdown and rebellion.[22]

It is by no means clear that Marilyn Monroe was clinically schizophrenic; my own armchair diagnosis, for what it's worth, is that she certainly wasn't. She didn't have delusions, or hallucinations, or any of the dissociative linguistic hallmarks of schizophrenia; she wasn't catatonic; she didn't hear voices. She even more clearly had none of the symptoms of DID, which is marked by amnesia and fugue states (i.e., extended blackout periods, often lasting days, and in some extreme cases reportedly as long as months or years). She was

depressed, although whether her depression was caused and/or exacerbated by her circumstances is impossible to tell; her general practitioner, Hyman Engelberg, is interviewed in one film documentary
(*The Final Days*) saying: "We knew that she was a manic-depressive,
which is now called bipolar personality," a diagnosis not reported in
any principal biography. Monroe may have become paranoid before
she died, as some writers (notably Leaming) claim, but this is also a
symptom of drug addiction. The cultural association of Monroe with
schizophrenia shows yet again how Marilyn is representative of so
many postwar versions of femininity.* It also shows the pathology of
the literal: when she looks like two different people she will be diagnosed as "schizophrenic," in common parlance.

Presumptions of Gladys's "insanity"—variously characterized
not only as schizophrenia but as depression, "congenital manic-
depression," violent outbursts and lack of affect—structure three of
the principal biographies: both Guiles and Summers interweave their
accounts of Monroe's birth with their insistence that Monroe's
maternal family provided her with an inescapable legacy of hereditary insanity, and Leaming accepts the diagnosis (also offered by
Summers) that Monroe had what psychiatry unhelpfully terms "borderline" disorder. For a biographer like Summers, the presumption of
Monroe's hereditary predisposition toward mental illness determines
his entire story—its origin, its shape and its conclusion. He opens by
quoting a psychiatrist—who never knew Monroe—who labels her as
a "borderline personality."[23] Summers offers a narrative of the borderline personality, and then assures the reader that the story that
follows will fulfill the expectations he is creating:

---

*Anecdotal evidence for my claim that there is a persistent "cultural association" between Marilyn and
schizophrenia *as* multiple personality can be found on the Internet, which shows the following associations on the first page of a Google search conducted on June 23, 2003: in 2001 a German playwright
named Gerlind Reinshagen mounted a play in which he hired six actresses to play Marilyn Monroe's
"schizophrenic tendencies"; a review of *Blonde* notes "the fact that Gladys is committed as a schizophrenic is not unrelated to her daughter Norma Jeane's double life as 'Marilyn'" (www.etext.org/Zines/
Critique/article/blonde.html); "Marilyn was a suicidal depressive and quite probably schizophrenic"
(www.pharo.com/intelligence/marilyn_monroe/articles/ifmm_03_eunice_murray.asp); "Marilyn's psychiatrist at the end of her life, Dr. Ralph Greenson, is said to have suggested to colleagues that he believed
Marilyn was schizophrenic. It has been said that Marilyn appeared to have 'two people inside her'"
(www.pennylaing.freeserve.co.uk/what_really_killed_marilyn.htm).

"Borderlines" tend to have had a mother who could not cope, or who suffered from overt psychosis. [. . .] The "borderline" person is likely to be emotionally unstable, excessively impulsive, and to show the world a mood that seems expansive and active. He or she is likely to be histrionic or seductive or overly concerned with good looks. A "borderline" depends on constant external approval, loves applause, cannot bear to be alone, and suffers "depressive, crashlike reactions" to rejection by others. A "borderline" tends to abuse alcohol and drugs, and to make suicide threats as gestures to obtain help.

This personality profile . . . is chillingly recognizable in Marilyn Monroe. Marilyn's life was to be remorselessly faithful to the blueprint of her background, a scenario for brilliance and tragedy.[24]

Apparently, "borderlines" do not tend to have had absent fathers: perhaps this is so ordinary a phenomenon in our society that it cannot be considered a cause of "abnormal" psychology? Judgmentalism is implicit in all of these criteria; later Summers will declare that Marilyn Monroe was an "emotional mess" when judged "by any normal standards."[25] But what are those normal standards? Summers thinks she suffers from excess. Everything he describes would be normal in moderation, but Marilyn Monroe is too much, she is excessively impulsive, overly concerned with good looks. What is the *right* amount of impulse, of concern with good looks? Leaming offers the same diagnosis, in more neutral, but no less absolute, terms:

Borderline personalities dread abandonment. They fear that being left means they are evil or bad. Faced with even a routine separation, they react with anger, cruel sarcasm, and despair. [. . .] Borderline personalities, perceiving themselves to have been abandoned by those whom they have idealized, are apt to threaten or attempt suicide. The diagnosis fit Marilyn to a tee.[26]

Maybe so, but it hardly accounts for her entire personality: Where does Monroe's own ability to abandon her lovers and husbands—she left all three of her husbands—fit in? Other personality traits are erased altogether by such a reductive diagnosis. And it does not allow for the possibility of overcoming emotional problems, of growing, or learning, or saving oneself. The childhood trauma story forecloses maturity itself, keeping Marilyn an eternal child waiting to become her mad mother.

Guiles's opening pages juxtapose a brief foreboding account of Monroe's "chaotic" and "desperate" "final summer" with a claim that *both* Monroe's maternal grandmother, Della Monroe, and her maternal grandfather, Otis Monroe, were mentally "unstable" and that her mother, Gladys, had "inherited her parents' mental illness."[27] Only once her death and putative insanity have been darkly hinted at will Guiles turn to Marilyn Monroe's birth. Summers also opens his book with a quick summary of (in his order) Monroe's death, birth, and the fact that her mother and maternal grandmother were both institutionalized.

Many stories involve Gladys Baker attacking someone violently before she was institutionalized: in some she tries to suffocate her daughter, in others to stab a neighbor, a friend, or herself. Leaming writes that Monroe's "earliest, inexplicable memory" was of "Gladys's attempt to smother her in her crib," a memory that will resurface (in Leaming's narration, if not in Monroe's mind) whenever suicide is mentioned.[28] In other versions, it is not her mother, Gladys, but her grandmother Della Monroe who attacks the child. Wolfe's chronicle of Monroe's early years begins sensationally with this story, offering it as a fact: "Marilyn Monroe's first childhood memory was of being suffocated by her mad grandmother, Della."[29] Although Summers, with equal drama, begins his book by pointing out (accurately) that Della Monroe died in an asylum, he nonetheless dismisses Monroe's account of her grandmother's attack as a "little" story picked from her endless "ragbag of fantasies":

> The adult Marilyn would claim that she remembered her grandmother trying to smother her shortly before she was sent to the mental hospital. Since Marilyn was only thirteen months old at the time, it is highly unlikely she really remembered any such thing. Her little horror story almost certainly belongs to the ragbag of fantasies from which Marilyn embroidered her youth.[30]

This double bind is typical of Summers's account, blaming Monroe for dramatizing an aspect of the story upon which Summers himself will capitalize. Guiles believes the story of Della's madness, asserting that she was schizophrenic, and he observes in a footnote that Arthur Miller believed the story of her attack on the child, too.[31]

Spoto, however, insists that Della Monroe simply suffered at the end of her life from hallucinations caused by the untreated physical infection that killed her. Debunking the myth, as usual, he also claims that Gladys didn't even have the paranoid schizophrenia with which the hospital diagnosed her, and that the Monroe family's entire supposed history of mental illness was itself a series of confused fictions:

> Her father, she [Gladys] had been incorrectly told, had died of lunacy; her mother's death had been erroneously reported as caused by manic-depressive psychosis; now, her grandfather's death by his own hand convinced her that there was virtually a blight of mental illness on the family tree. [. . .] After several weeks of Gladys's depression, [her friend] Grace took matters into her own hands and called in a neurologist [who prescribed drugs to which she had "a violent reaction"]. [. . .] By February 1934, Gladys was still withdrawn and depressed—although once again there were no sure signs of outright psychosis: her inability to cope seems to have derived more from her own background (and perhaps, too, from guilt and remorse over neglect of her children) than from real psychiatric illness.[32]

In Spoto's diagnosis, Gladys Monroe breaks down over guilt and remorse for neglecting her children, and a reversed causal link between insanity and bad mothers is suggested, in which a woman does not become a bad mother because she is schizophrenic, but has a breakdown because she is a bad mother.

Madness and motherhood will remain linked in Marilyn's story, and will always suggest sexuality and the divided self. The madwoman is associated, traditionally, with sexual licentiousness, rage and rebellion. The mother is, in some sense, the madwoman's opposite, her sexuality channeled and legitimated as nurturing. Marilyn is not just split against herself, but against her mother: these women double and redouble, as her mother implicitly mirrors Marilyn. Finally Marilyn's associations with madness and maternity will bring death into the story. In *Blonde,* Marilyn goes crazy when she fails to become a mother; in many of the lives, Monroe's alleged abortions will be interpreted as self-hatred: a woman killing her child is represented as a woman killing herself.

INNER CHILD OF THE PAST

All of these stories locate the roots of insanity in childhood and heredity, but the etiology of mental disorder remains confused and disputed. Even those who don't see Marilyn as insane per se believe in a garbled popular version of the case stories of DID, in which a "childhood trauma" is responsible for the dissociation of personality. Gloria Steinem, who will argue for Monroe as a victim of her culture, does not liberate Monroe from being the source of her own problems, but rather, ironically enough, uses Norma Jeane, the child, as a symbol for Marilyn's losing her mind. Like Summers, Steinem partly relies upon medical "testimony" from a doctor who never met Monroe: her 1986 biography devotes pages to a 1963 popular self-help book by Dr. Hugh Missildine called *Your Inner Child of the Past.* Missildine is a popularizer of childhood trauma as a narrative; he argued that "seeking" the "inner child" and "integrating" it into one's adult personality will constitute an "empowerment system." The need for integration suggests the presence of disintegration, or indeed, dissociation (which takes us back to split personality, or DID). The inner child is written as a different person. For Steinem, Monroe is a "classic" example of precisely this (metaphorical) "disorder." The "inner child of the past" is an extremely literal version of the idea that identity lodges discretely inside us, the Cartesian pilot inhabiting the ship of the body, although the lost inner child is a stowaway, less pilot than hijacker—and suicide bomber. The past is encrypted inside Marilyn Monroe, killing her. And in Steinem's extremely representative narrative the past has a name: Norma Jeane. When the figurative becomes literal, it becomes fatal, too.

The lost inner child is a symbol of innocence, and of victimhood. It is no accident that Missildine calls his an "empowerment" system.

Steinem consistently writes Monroe as the childlike, innocent victim of men's pernicious power plays. Symbolically, this story inhabits the same space as the anal rape stories in the biographical fiction discussed in chapter two: it is a story about abusive men victimizing female innocents. It is also a story that locates the essence of Marilyn as a child: she is a vulnerable child who "inhabits" the voluptuous body of a woman. This feminist "revision" recycles the same sentimental myth of Marilyn's fundamental, eternal innocence; Steinem just renames innocence Norma Jeane.

The wholeness Steinem imagines for Marilyn Monroe is only ever a regressive return to the un-integrated "lost child" Norma Jeane, instead of as the phenomenally successful professional adult Marilyn Monroe. Steinem believes that Norma Jeane should have "realized" herself as a "whole self" by becoming: "a student, lawyer, teacher, artist, mother, grandmother, defender of animals, rancher, homemaker, sportswoman, rescuer of children—all these futures we can imagine for Norma Jeane. [. . .] But Norma Jeane remained a frightened child of the past. And Marilyn remained the unthreatening half-person that sex goddesses are supposed to be."[33] Actress is not an option for a whole self?

The possibility that Norma Jeane did in fact realize herself in Marilyn Monroe—that a self-destructive actress might be the "whole self"—is one that Steinem doesn't admit, because she sees realization as itself triumphant. Thus if Monroe didn't survive, she could not have been realized, QED. That a realized self could encompass not only contradictions, but manipulativeness, chicanery, self-destruction, is something that Steinem's blithe psychology doesn't acknowledge. Steinem insists upon the childishness of "both" Norma Jeane and Marilyn ("because she was a woman Marilyn was encouraged to remain a child"),[34] which has the effect of doubly effacing the possibility that one might take Marilyn Monroe seriously as an adult woman: if Norma Jeane is a child, Steinem doesn't let Marilyn grow up either.

This may sound like blaming the messenger; certainly Steinem is quite right that Monroe was encouraged by a patriarchal culture to behave in childlike ways. But while artificially separating Norma Jeane from Marilyn, Steinem doesn't grant normality or adulthood or indeed competence to either half, and does this in the name of feminism. Finally Steinem, like Mailer, locates Monroe's personal appeal in her childishness, but feels not sexually drawn toward that "fatherless child" but rather maternally "protective" toward "the endlessly vulnerable child who looked out of Marilyn's eyes."[35] Steinem's account is as dependent upon gender stereotype as Mailer's; each first insists upon the childishness of Norma Jeane *and* Marilyn Monroe, and then responds in ways conventionally appropriate to their respective sexes to such a "girl-child." Like the male biographers, Steinem emphasizes Monroe's vulnerability—she doesn't eroticize it, but she does patronize it.

HOMELESS WAIF

Marilyn Monroe was given to a foster family, the Bolenders, in the first weeks after she was born. Her earliest years were spent with them, with her mother, with other foster families, and in an orphanage, until she was sixteen. This erratic upbringing became another symbol of the way in which she was "lost": she didn't know where she belonged. Home symbolizes family, history, safety; Marilyn Monroe is perceived to have been dangerously dislocated, traumatically rootless, a child-woman always in search of a home and a father (or sometimes a mother).

My Story opens with an account of the narrator remembering her mother going mad, and being taken to an orphan asylum as a small child. Before her mother's breakdown, she had tried to keep a small white house for herself and her daughter, bringing in an "English couple" as boarders; their prize possession was a white grand piano once owned by the movie star Fredric March. The narrator explains that she had found the piano again when she became a movie star, and that it was in her apartment as *My Story* was composed. She goes on to explain that she "lived in the orphanage only off and on [. . .] I was placed with nine different families before I was able to quit being a legal orphan."[36] Her dreams as a child, the narrator says, were not of love but of being admired, and being able to wear something other than the drab orphanage uniform.

The importance of home and its loss to the Cinderella story is why Guiles opens *Norma Jeane* not with her birth but with the purchase of Monroe's first home, which is also the house in which she died. He thus incorporates loneliness, childhood and death into the symbol of the home in his first sentence: "In February 1962, when Marilyn Monroe was thirty-five, she moved into the first house she ever owned completely on her own."[37] Steinem similarly uses the home as the mark of authentic selfhood ("That she often ignored her own security was more than just the neglected Norma Jeane recreating a feeling of 'home' by treating herself as she had been treated").[38] Marilyn Monroe represents in part the dislocation of modern identity. She confirms our belief that "broken homes" lead to broken people.

When her mother was hospitalized, *My Story* says that her best friend, Grace McKee, had herself made the child's legal guardian; most biographers say that Monroe was made a ward of Los Angeles. She was certainly placed in more than one foster home, the number of which varies from biography to biography: Zolotow's version implies at least six, although he never offers a number; Guiles says "she was in exactly three homes as a foster child prior to moving in with the Goddards"; Summers counts twelve; Spoto argues that these numbers are inflated and reduces the claim to "two or three"; Leaming doesn't bother with numbers at all and merely says that the child was "passed from one grim foster home to another."[39] Spoto quotes Monroe's close friend Sidney Skolsky, who knew Monroe for years, saying that in his experience she herself altered the story:

> "How much of the story about her bleak childhood is actually true, I really can't say," Sidney said years later in a rare moment of understatement. "But she was not quite the poor waif she claimed to have been. When I first met her, she was supposed to have lived in three foster homes. As time went on it became five, eight, ten, because she knew it was a good selling point."[40]

Everyone agrees that the child was placed in an orphanage on September 13, 1935, at the age of nine: some accounts have her staying there for nine months, others for two years. The quantitative analyses are less significant than the qualitative interpretations. What interests chroniclers much more than the question "How many were there?" is the question "How bad was it?" The lower the start, the more impressive the rise—and the sharper the subsequent fall, the more poignant the loss she represents.

Most of the biographies tell a story in which she was dragged through the orphanage doors, kicking and screaming, "I'm not an orphan." They add that while there she washed dishes and stared out the window at the RKO backlot, dreaming of becoming a movie star. She refers to this briefly in her last interview, with *Life* in August 1962, explaining that she told her stepchildren about working in the orphanage: "I used to tell them, for instance, that I worked for 5¢ a month and I washed one hundred dishes, and my stepkids would say, 'One hundred dishes!'" The fairy-tale inflection is clear: a hundred dishes, always replenishing themselves, in an endless magical task.

The clichés create unvarying interpretive patterns and a sense of inevitability. "Both her desire for love and fear of it," writes Guiles,

> had their origins in the twenty-one months Norma Jeane spent within the walls of the Los Angeles Orphans' Home Society. When she was finally liberated from there, a few weeks after her eleventh birthday, the pattern she had begun earlier—a continuing quest for affection broken by occasional recoils from it—was set for life.[41]

This emphasis upon homelessness functions like madness, as an early foreshadowing of the inevitable plot. Monroe's homelessness is not just her beginning, it is her ending: when she fails at domesticity, when her marriages are over and she is not a mother, but a spinster, she will die in an empty home that is compared to her empty womb. The story will come full circle.

CHILDHOOD MOLESTATION

As an adult, Marilyn Monroe told many people that she had been sexually molested or raped as a child: biographers name innumerable witnesses who claim to have been told such stories. These stories are treated with a remarkable degree of skepticism, even sarcasm, by biographers who in other places rhapsodize about Monroe's sexual allure.

From the first, as Summers rather unwittingly reveals, Monroe's claim that she was molested as a child was treated with derision by the powerful men around her:

> the first firmly recorded reference to the violation of Norma Jeane seems to have been in 1947, when she offered it to Lloyd Shearer, a journalist who interviewed her at the request of the Twentieth Century-Fox publicity office. He listened to a horrific package story, and his reaction was this: "She confided to us over lunch that she had been assaulted by one of her guardians, raped by a policeman, and attacked by a sailor. She seemed to me then to live in a fantasy world, to be entangled in the process of invention, and to be completely absorbed in her own sexuality." Shearer was so skeptical that he decided to write nothing about Marilyn.[42]

Summers shares this skepticism; every time a story is raised in which Monroe was abused or exploited, he accuses her of living in a "fantasy world." But most of the stories that involve her own sexual insatiability he treats not as fantasy, but as truth. The lines between fantasy and fact blur in stories about Monroe and sex; they are particularly loaded in the stories told about Monroe and childhood sex. Anglo-American culture is today in the grip of an obsession about sex with children that, for all its self-righteousness, is not without its prurient side. Part of its appeal as a story, surely, is the way in which it so clearly locates blame and innocence. The prevalence of guilt— symbolized as sexual guilt, but in fact encompassing ethical, moral, legal and political guilt—in the Monroe apocrypha is nowhere clearer than in these writers' attitudes toward the question of Monroe as a childhood rape victim.

The story of the childhood rape determines Monroe's identity— and character. Is she a liar, or a victim?

In truth childhood trauma works in these narratives as evidence of a character that has already been interpreted. It is sadly not at all remarkable how few men were or are prepared to believe that even a woman they consider a "goddess" might have been sexually attacked, whether as a child or as an adult. Even Spoto, one of her most sympathetic biographers, tells of two friends reporting that she told them of a thirteen-year-old male cousin who "sexually assaulted" Norma Jeane when she was nearly twelve; Spoto accepts the story, but nonetheless finds it droll enough that he describes the cousin only as "importunate."[43] The fact that these writers are sarcastic does not mean that they must be wrong, but the selectivity of the story is significant. Biographers project cultural sexual attitudes onto Monroe, so that she is a siren who must herself be fantasizing (about herself, just as they do). These stories keep Monroe's sexuality safely in the realm of fantasy, preserving "her," and us, from the reality that sexuality is often violent, that desire is not always distinct from fear. These stories keep Monroe's sexuality "innocent" of such things by blaming her for being too desirable and for being a liar, a double bind if there ever was one. They also thus maintain the truth of the persona: sex with Marilyn will always be innocent for men, and pathological for her.*

The specific story that is most often repeated is that she was raped by an adult male in a foster house as a child. This allegation first appeared in *My Story,* which said only that at the age of eight, Monroe "learned about sex" from a boarder, "Mr. Kimmel," who locked the door, put his arms around her, and kept "whispering to [her] to be a good girl." The child, says the narrator, then ran to her foster mother to report "what Mr. Kimmel had done," although what exactly that was remains unclear. The foster mother slaps her face for telling lies, and Mr. Kimmel, adding insult to injury, attempts to purchase her silence with a nickel, which she throws in his face.

This story has become extremely charged in the Monroe apocrypha. In 1960, Zolotow offers the tale of molestation by a man in one of the foster homes as fact, repeating the *My Story* version without significant alteration. But in both his original (1969) and revised

---

*Thus Summers, introducing Robert Slatzer to the reader, writes: "'I think we had an instant affection towards each other,' says Slatzer, as though a man need apologize for having slept with Marilyn Monroe."[44] It's Marilyn who has to do the apologizing.

(1984) lives, Guiles asserted that the story of molestation (in which "an old man attempted something akin to rape") was a complete fabrication: "This invention was accepted as truth by several of her future biographers, but there are a number of reasons why it simply will not wash. Most important," Guiles concludes triumphantly, "Norma Jeane never lived in a boardinghouse."[45]

But then he offers another story that he feels "may very well have triggered the rape story": when her foster father "Doc" Goddard got drunk, "staggered" into her bedroom when she was fourteen, and "gave her what is commonly known as a French kiss." Goddard charitably felt bad afterward (he was "abashed and contrite for days"), but for Guiles, Monroe's tight sweaters, lipstick and "flirtatious manner" meant that she had "been courting just such a response," she just didn't expect to get it from her foster father. He deems it "not at all surprising that, when she told the story to Hecht, she changed her beloved Doc into an anonymous dirty old man who gave her a nickel to keep silent about what he had done to her."[46] Whether one finds that surprising depends upon one's point of view.

Guiles does not document specific sources for the quotations in his book; however, in his acknowledgments he lists interviews with Erwin Goddard, who is thus presumably a source for this story, and hardly a disinterested witness. The belief that a girl who is sexually accosted, in whatever manner, was "courting" such a reaction is too perfidious to require much comment beyond noting both its ubiquity and its iniquity. But not only does Guiles presume the adult male is reliable (although surely the older man who lived in loco parentis had sufficient reason to whitewash his tale), he considers both the child "Norma Jeane" and the adult "Marilyn" untrustworthy and confused.

In the mid-1980s, two biographies appeared that are even more suspicious toward the story of childhood rape, and consider Monroe not confused, but mendacious: Summers and Rollyson both dismiss it prima facie. Summers's tone in 1985 is derisive:

[In 1962] she was still rambling on interminably about the assault. Was the story true, or was it a perennial, self-serving fantasy designed to get sympathy? [. . .] Dr. Ralph Greenson, the

Hollywood psychiatrist who treated and befriended Marilyn in her last years, accepted the fact that she had a "terrible, terrible background." However, he also referred to her "mistreatment fantasy."[47]

Summers's rhetorical questions exclude the possibility that the story was accurate, without categorically denying it. That would be left to Rollyson, who flatly characterizes the story as a "fabrication."[48]

Steinem's account appeared in the same year as Rollyson's, and was the first to take the crucial step of setting Monroe's story of rape within the larger context of the way in which women's stories of abuse have historically been ignored, contradicted or ridiculed by patriarchal society. However, in Steinem's interpretation, feminism and skepticism seem mutually exclusive, so that to recuperate Monroe negates the possibility that the story might be untrue.

> But of all Marilyn's stories of her early years, the account of rape by an elderly boarder when she was eight was the most disbelieved. Guiles, the careful researcher, discounted the story because he could not find one of Norma Jeane's foster families who also ran a boardinghouse. On the other hand, he did support through interviews the fact that Aunt Grace's husband, Doc Goddard, once stumbled into the teenage Norma Jeane's bedroom, and terrified her by sitting on the bed and giving her what Guiles described as a "French kiss." [. . .] Neither he nor other biographers pursued the possibility of the Englishman, though he and his wife could have been considered boarders in the white bungalow, and Norma Jeane was then an eight-year-old. In many cases, the tendency to disbelieve Marilyn's story is reinforced by Jim Dougherty's remembrance of his sixteen-year-old bride as a technical virgin, and thus someone who could not have been raped. Norman Mailer flatly asserts that her virginity as a bride makes the story of her childhood rape impossible. He seems unaware of the statistics that show many rapes, especially those of very young children, consist of oral and other sexual humiliations, not intercourse. Dougherty and Mailer especially seem to depend only on their own imaginations of what a rape should be.[49]

Steinem is right, of course, in her insistence that Mailer's interpretation is colored by his prejudices (he euphemizes Guiles's already
understated "French kiss" as an "embrace"),[50] but what she doesn't
acknowledge is how much her interpretation, too, is affected by her
own assumptions—in this case, that because our culture has tended
to disbelieve women who claim to have been sexually assaulted, we
should counteract this by taking them at their word. She may be
right, ethically speaking, but she is not right logically: the fact that
these commentators were prejudiced does not prove that they were
wrong; the fact that Monroe is disbelieved for specious reasons does
not prove that she told the truth.

According to Spoto, however, the tale of Mr. Kimmel does not
appear in Hecht's handwritten draft of *My Story,* which suggests it is
a belated fiction, produced by someone other than Monroe. Spoto
tells two stories of molestation in the course of narrating Monroe's
childhood: the Doc Goddard story, and the incident, already mentioned, of the "importunate" thirteen-year-old cousin.[51] Confusingly,
he never addresses the question of rape by a boarder at all in the
course of describing Monroe's childhood; but later, when he comes
to 1954 and the composition of *My Story,* Spoto refers to the "actual
childhood rape" discussed in it, without ever acknowledging the fact
that this "actual" rape does not appear in his own account of her
childhood. He does repeat the story about Goddard, but unlike
Guiles refuses to justify Goddard's action, calling it "singularly
unpleasant and even traumatic." His source is first husband Jim
Dougherty, who said that it wasn't just a kiss, but that Goddard "tried
to force himself on her": this incident, Spoto adds, would have been
"especially" troubling for "so vulnerable and fatherless a girl."[52]
Although Spoto does not justify these violations in the patriarchal
terms of previous biographers, he still somehow sees Norma Jeane's
"special" distress as related to her being fatherless—as if having a
father would have made the incident less alarming and repellent.

Despite Guiles's declaration that the rape story had to be invented
because Monroe never lived in a boardinghouse, it is a fact that
Gladys bought a little house for herself and her daughter shortly
before her breakdown, and in order to help pay its expenses rented
out most of it to an English couple who worked in the movies: this is

the "possibility of the Englishman" that Steinem notes in 1986 had not yet been pursued by biographers. Wolfe pursued it in 1998, and pretty much accuses the Englishman in question of raping eight-year-old Marilyn Monroe. He gives Monroe the benefit of the doubt (as "the only reliable source regarding the incident") but then reveals that his source for Monroe's "reliable" testimony is *My Story*, which he describes quite misleadingly as "an interview with Ben Hecht in 1953." Wolfe thus turns the story full circle back to Zolotow's 1960 account and the problem of the credulous reader who simply buys into *My Story*, erasing Spoto's research showing that the rape story did not appear in Hecht's draft.[53]

Wolfe explains that the Englishman who boarded with Gladys and her daughter was named Murray Kinnell, a character actor whose photograph Wolfe reproduces with the ominous caption "Actor Murray Kinnell. He was the boarder at Gladys's home when Norma Jeane was molested." In my edition of *My Story*, the boarder's name is "Kimmel"; Wolfe argues in his discussion of the rape story that *My Story*'s name for the boarder, "*Kimmell* [*sic*], is scarcely a disguise for *Kinnell*, but in referring to her mother as her 'aunt' or 'foster mother' Marilyn was protecting Gladys."[54] The mystery would appear to be solved—were it not for the rather significant fact that, according to Spoto, the name of the Englishman who boarded with Gladys and her daughter was George Atkinson, an actor who occasionally appeared in George Arliss films (Guiles never names the Englishman, but does say that he worked with Arliss).[55]

By 1998 the story of childhood rape had become accepted, doubtless due in no small part to our culture's gradual reluctant acceptance of how common such stories have proven to be, and to Steinem's important positioning of this story within that context. But perhaps the story was accepted for a less gratifying reason, as well: it may have been treated as "fact" simply because of its repetition. Our familiarity with this story, and with other such stories, had made it part of "the record." In Leaming's 1998 account the rape has become plural instances: "By the time Norma Jeane was twelve, she had been assaulted in at least two of these [foster] homes, and possibly others."[56] The "truth" finally will be determined entirely by bias: one either believes Monroe—and/or the victim—or one doesn't. Again we see the movement between the figurative and the literal: Where do we locate guilt and innocence? The Monroe apocrypha will always move between the two, keeping both in the story—and in a sexual register.

Neither Mailer, Steinem nor Wolfe mentions in this context the 1979 account of Lena Pepitone, who worked for Monroe for several years as a maid and seamstress, and who reports that Monroe said that her "foster father" raped her while she lived with the Goddards, and that she became pregnant and had the baby and that he was taken from her by Grace McKee Goddard.[57] Summers, who protests against Monroe's tendency to exaggeration and fantasy, and who treats the molestation/rape story with sarcasm, also spends a page elaborating the stories of those, like Pepitone, who claim Monroe told them that as an adolescent she had a baby that was given up for adoption. After a page of elaboration, and quotes from three "witnesses," Summers dismisses the claim: "this may have been the fantasy of a woman who, by the time she was telling the story, feared she would never bear children."[58] Summers claims not to believe these stories, but he doesn't admit it until after he has spent pages on their sensationalist details, much as Mailer will spend pages elaborating a sexual fantasy and then admit that there is not a "particle of evidence" to support the story he has just told. Paralipsis can occur on a narrative scale: one indulges in a story that one then dismisses. (This will also be Summers's strategy for dealing with the question of whether Monroe was murdered, as we shall see.)

Not one of these accounts, in citing other contradictory accounts and complaining about their inaccuracies or presumptions, acknowledges clearly and plainly that we simply don't know what happened, and that part of the reason for the doubt is the proliferation of these competing versions themselves, which have been predetermined by what they already believe—whether about Marilyn Monroe, about sex, or about the authority of the male record.

CHILD-BRIDE

On June 19, 1942, less than three weeks past her sixteenth birthday, Monroe married James Dougherty, a twenty-one-year-old neighbor in Van Nuys, California. Whether Monroe was pressured into marrying Dougherty is a subject of some debate, and most of the stories about the first marriage circle around blame and guilt: who was to blame for this "abnormally" young marriage? Was it a calculating, domineering older woman, Grace McKee Goddard? Or was it a manipulative, opportunistic younger woman called Norma Jeane? Furthermore, what was to blame for the failure of the marriage? Some will blame youth and inexperience; some will blame Monroe's latent professional ambitions; few will blame Dougherty's expectations of his wife (which, naturally, did not include a career), which they will excuse as understandable for an average guy in 1942. Monroe's professional ambitions are evidently much less understandable.

Most of the stories about Monroe's first marriage attempt to establish, almost diagnostically, an invariable *attitude* to sex, as if that would explain all her subsequent sexual moods and sentiments. According to Guiles, Norma Jeane married to please her guardian and because she had "a crush" on Dougherty; although she was a virgin when she married, she was fortunate in the "substantial legacy" she received from Dougherty (whom Guiles interviewed, and is presumably the source for the claim): Dougherty "had an innate wisdom about sex. He knew all the turns in the road, and the way back. He taught her that sex is a gift, and the treasure each piled up at the feet of the other during their time together was staggering."[59] For Marilyn, Guiles says, sex came "as naturally as peeling a banana."[60]

Mailer offers what may be the silliest explanation for Monroe's marriage, but it is still sexualized: the agonizing menstrual periods that everyone acknowledges that Monroe suffered from her entire postmenarchal life. Mailer admits that they were "unendurable" and "excruciating," but then (erroneously) implies that menstrual cramps are a sign of lust.[61] As for Jim Dougherty's motivation in agreeing to marry a fifteen-year-old girl, Mailer finds this not at all difficult to understand: "We need only remember it is *Marilyn* we are talking about." According to Mailer, Dougherty was "unwitting," just "hopelessly entangled" by Monroe's "insane sexual musk."[62] But Mailer differs from Guiles on how much the young Norma Jeane enjoyed sex, declaring authoritatively that "the word from Hollywood over the years" was that she was "frigid."[63]

Summers offers a he-said, she-said tale in which Monroe claimed that she didn't enjoy sex with Dougherty, and that he wanted her to have a baby, a thought that, she said, "stood my hair on end. I could see it only as myself, another Norma Jeane in an orphanage." Dougherty contradicted her on both counts, claiming that she "loved sex. It was as natural to her as breakfast in the morning" and that she wanted to have a baby while he persuaded her it would be a mistake. Most principal biographers accept that Monroe terribly wanted to be a mother, at least in her marriage to Miller; but some ancillary accounts insist that she ruthlessly had many abortions to safeguard her career. Only Summers, in having-it-both-ways mode, has Marilyn both desperate for mother-hood *and* having fourteen or more abortions. All of which shows, Summers says, that "even this side of Marilyn was a sad confusion."[64]

Spoto gives rather fairer play to Monroe's account of her first marriage, quoting not *My Story* (which Mailer uses to discuss the marriage although he has disparaged its reliability) but an interview that Monroe gave to a journalist much later: "Grace McKee arranged a marriage for me [. . .] I never had a choice. There's not much to say about it. They couldn't support me, and they had to work out something. And so I got married. [. . .] It didn't work out—just like Jean Harlow's didn't work out. I guess we were too young."[65] Spoto notes that Dougherty was "publicly rhapsodic" about their "intimate life," but that Monroe's later accounts were rather different, emphasizing her confusion and discontentment: "the marriage itself left me cold."[66]

Spoto understands all of Monroe's marriages as a failed search for a surrogate father, claiming that "far from finding security with a 'daddy' during the first year of her marriage," she felt "nonessential."[67] That is not the case in Oates's account, written five years later: fictionalizing Dougherty's name into Bucky Glazer, Oates suggests that Monroe simultaneously discovered a surrogate father and her own carnality: "she called him Daddy. Sometimes he was Big Daddy, proud possessor of Big Thing. She was Baby, sometimes Baby-Doll, proud possessor of Little Thing. She'd been a virgin, sure enough. Buck was proud of that too. How well they fitted together! 'It's like we invented it, Baby' [. . .] loving it when Bucky made lusty vigorous love to her."[68] Here are the two (antithetical) versions of Monroe's sexuality, in which she is either virgin or whore.

She is not only seen as contradictory in these lives, but as a pendulum swinging between extremes. Monroe's own account, which Spoto quotes, was that "there's not much to say about it." But this doesn't stop writers from diving into their first fantasies about Monroe actually having sex. The content of these dissenting interpretations (whether she was indeed "frigid" or "loving it") is not as different as it might seem: they are united by their faith in her excess, her extremity. The one possibility that is not admitted is that Marilyn Monroe might have liked sex about the same amount as everybody else, enjoying it when it was pleasurable, uninterested when it wasn't: she must be exaggerated, abnormal, pathological, and defined by her relationship to sex.

In 1944, after two years of marriage, Jim Dougherty, who had joined the Merchant Marine, shipped out to war in the Pacific. Monroe moved in with his family and took a job working in an aircraft plant. Later that year the U.S. Army's First Motion Picture Unit sent a crew of photographers to the plant to photograph women contributing on the "home front" to the war effort. One photographer, David Conover, quickly singled out Monroe and asked her to pose several times over the next few weeks, and then returned through the summer of 1945 to continue photographing her. On August 2, 1945, she applied to and was accepted by the Blue Book modeling agency, run by Emmeline Snively, who gave her lessons in walking, dressing, makeup and grooming, and who recommended that she lighten her hair, because "a blonde could be photographed in any wardrobe and in any light."[69] By the spring of 1946, Spoto reports, "Norma Jeane Dougherty" (sometimes billed as "Jean Norman") had appeared on thirty-three men's magazine covers.

In late 1945, before Dougherty had returned from the Pacific, Monroe met a photographer named André de Dienes, who took some of the most famous "Norma Jeane" photographs (including the one *Life* magazine would use as a memorial when Monroe died, and the picture of Norma Jeane in khakis discussed above). All three principal biographies agree that the two had an affair. (Other claims about Monroe's alleged sexual promiscuity in these early years of her modeling and while she was trying to become an actress are much more widely disputed, as we shall see.) At the same time, her mother, Gladys, was released from the hospital and into her daughter's care, where she remained for a few months. In July 1946, Monroe had a screen test at 20th Century-Fox studios, and was signed to a standard contract. The head of casting, Ben Lyon, told her that she should change her name, and she signed the contract as Marilyn Monroe on August 24, 1946. On September 13, 1946, at the age of twenty, she divorced Jim Dougherty, and, with her mother also returned to the state asylum, she was free, the story goes, to begin her "new life" as Marilyn Monroe.

THE END OF NORMA JEAN

In *My Story* the divorce from Jim Dougherty signals "the end" of Norma Jean: "This is the end of my story of Norma Jean. Jim and I were divorced. And I moved into a room in Hollywood to live by myself. I was nineteen, and I wanted to find out who I was."[70] But Norma Jean lingers on even in this early incarnation of the myth: "this sad, bitter child who grew up too fast is hardly ever out of my heart. With success all around me, I can still feel her frightened eyes looking out of mine. She keeps saying, 'I never lived, I never loved,' and often I get confused and think it's I who am saying it."[71]

In the Norma Jeane story, the past does not merely affect identity, it defines it: she has no identity other than the lost and all-but-dead ("I never lived") Norma Jean. Thus at the end of the passage, the split between the "two women" becomes literal: "I get confused and think it's I who am saying it." But this is only confusing if one treats as literal the metaphor of becoming a different person when one grows or evolves. In fact, she *was* the same person; she had just changed. It is only the language that is confusing, not the concept. But from the outside, the change in her appearance is so dramatic that it seems to require a comparable inner shift. As the biographical narrative develops, this literalism hardens into a story of confused, lost and even split identity.

"Marilyn Monroe" is, by definition, not the self, and not a whole person, in part because she is endlessly represented as having been created by external pressures, rather than being a more "natural" expression of some internal, invariable self. But again, most people develop in response to external forces as well as to internal desires: the interplay between the two makes us who we are. What in any other story might be evolution is mistrusted in Marilyn Monroe's case a posteriori because we are suspicious of the woman she "became." Thus Summers declares flatly of this particular claim from *My Story* ("I get confused and think it's I who am saying it") that it was *not* figurative but the literal truth: "the confusion was real. As her actual psychiatrists would discover, and as armchair ones have insisted ever since, Norma Jeane did not cease to exist when Mrs. Dougherty became an actress."[72] But does one need a psychiatrist, whether qualified or amateur, to discover that Norma Jeane didn't *really* die when Marilyn Monroe was invented?

Although biographers insist that the "other person," Marilyn Monroe, is artificial, they will also define that person as natural—for her. Like Holly Golightly in *Breakfast at Tiffany's,* she's a "real phony" because "she honestly believes all this phony junk she believes" (the similarity is no coincidence: Truman Capote, who knew Monroe well in New York, drew on her for the character of Holly in the novella, and George Axelrod, who wrote the script for the film version, also wrote both *The Seven Year Itch* and *Will Success Spoil Rock Hunter?,* a satirical play about Monroe). The idea that this "new identity" called Marilyn Monroe is artificial and yet natural to her is the central, paradoxical motif in the stories about the invention of that persona.

Over and over again biographers will comment upon how "artificial" this new incarnation was—but at the same time they will insist that it is real and natural. Several of the stories rely upon the metaphor of rebirth: Wolfe transforms her not from Norma Jeane but from an anonymous orphan number to emphasize the idea of renaissance in which "orphan number 3,463 became Marilyn Monroe, reborn on August 24th, 1946."[73] Guiles says goodbye to Norma Jeane just before a section entitled "Marilyn: Her Life Begins": "Now all of the baggage she had carried as Norma Jeane was gone. She was completely free to be this new creature with the golden hair: Marilyn."[74] But on the next page, having declared that Marilyn's life hasn't begun until twenty years of it have elapsed, Guiles will insist that this "new creature" was not just a role: "It has been an enduring fiction that Marilyn suffered from confusion over her identity. The truth was that she felt completely at home with this new creature, Marilyn."[75] For Guiles, Marilyn is a completely new identity with whom she nonetheless feels at home, and yet not a role ("she was a real person quite distinct from Norma Jeane").[76] But Norma Jeane is still there, too, not quite disappearing: "She was half child, half woman, but all Marilyn. Even so, Norma Jeane was not entirely dead, as we shall see."[77] But only someone who thinks they are two separate people would find it noteworthy that Norma Jeane wasn't dead: as Marilyn enters the narrative, so does the rhetoric of death. The transformation comes to seem monstrous because Marilyn Monroe is being depicted as a chimera, half one beast, half another: half Norma Jeane, half Marilyn; half child, half woman; half dead, half alive: and then this monstrous "fusion" together will be pronounced to be "all Marilyn."

"YOU ARE TO ME A MARILYN"

If Marilyn Monroe's given name is charged with questions about her identity, her manufactured name is no less so. Guiles tells the story of the invention of her name in the words of Ben Lyon, the talent agent at 20th Century-Fox credited (or blamed) in most stories with suggesting she change her name, who reported that he said to her: "You are to me a Marilyn" and that she responded by asking if she could use her mother's maiden name of Monroe.[78] In this version, Marilyn is already there, waiting to be recognized. Spoto also credits her with the suggestion of Monroe, and reports a spontaneous cry of recognition from Lyon ("I know who you are, you're Marilyn!"), but unlike Guiles he claims that Marilyn resisted her new name because, like the identity it would denote, it "sounded strange, artificial." But before long Monroe acquiesces to this new, and yet obviously comfortable, persona: "She smiled. 'Well, I guess I'm Marilyn Monroe.' "[79]

In all of these accounts, Marilyn is recognizably Marilyn, despite being an artificial creation; soon she will accept this manufactured identity as her own. But it is an artificial person that her audience feels is so natural to her that they know she is Marilyn before she does: "I know who you are, you're Marilyn!" She is recognized even as she is invented, a fiction who knows she's really a fiction—which makes it an authentic identity, after all.

The more mythical version, recounted by Steinem and Oates, is the victim story encapsulated in the line "they made you change your name" from "Candle in the Wind." In fact most of the biographies represent her as either willing enough to assume the new name, or even jubilant, as do Summers and Wolfe ("'That's a wonderful name!' Norma Jeane exclaimed").[80] Steinem reports a popular anecdote in which Monroe says that "after the studio gave me the name Marilyn Monroe" she had to ask an autograph seeker how to spell her new name. "Perhaps the spelling incident expressed her feeling of distance from that artificial creation called Marilyn Monroe," Steinem opines.[81] In this story, Marilyn is not a Cinderella hiding inside drab Norma Jeane waiting for release, but rather a mask inflicted upon her, so that the persona of "Marilyn Monroe" is a male fantasy foisted onto the real Norma Jeane. The story of renaming thus becomes a parable for women's lack of power and self-determination, in which the studio executives refuse Norma Jeane any participation in deciding on the name. In Oates's account she strenuously resists this imposition, but only in interior monologue (never spoken: Norma Jeane is always interior) for nearly a page. For Oates, the name change symbolizes Norma Jeane's manipulation and victimization at the hands of the studio executives; Oates even invents an orphanage matron named Marilyn to provide Norma Jeane with a childhood (i.e., real) reason for finding the name Marilyn "hateful." This renaming immediately follows the scene of anal rape with Mr. Z: in Oates's version, "Marilyn Monroe" is always associated with an imposition of men's desires, and bears no responsibility at all for the creation of Marilyn Monroe.

According to André de Dienes, who was a friend during the summer she changed her name, he watched her try writing out her new name with "two large, curly, romantic Ms on a notepad. She was getting acquainted with her new identity, saying 'Marilyn Monroe' as if tasting a piece of candy." From that point on, he said, "no one was allowed to call her by any other name."[82] Monroe does comment on the name change in the taped interviews in the documentary *Marilyn on Marilyn;* her description is notably matter-of-fact: "I wanted the name Monroe, which was my mother's maiden name. He always said, you know, I reminded him of Jean Harlow and Marilyn Miller. He said, well Marilyn goes better with Monroe." Far from being a portentous, symbolically charged moment of manipulation and resistance, in Monroe's account the change of name is a simple, pragmatic decision, and beautifully anticlimactic.

BLONDES ARE DIFFERENT

As her name changed, so did her appearance. In particular the new look is defined by Monroe's hair: the manufactured and yet natural identity of Marilyn is associated with Monroe's artificial blondeness, a change in appearance that is consistently rendered as an essential alteration of the self. Rollyson's account is typical of the way in which her altered appearance is construed as a new identity: her new hair color "imposed a welcome redefinition of her person; now she had a specific role to play. Yet she had not chosen this identity and she resisted. [. . .] Thus a role was grafted onto her, and she had to fuse herself to it."[83] When her appearance changes, her essence changes, and a disastrous pretense comes rushing into the story.

The idea that bleaching her hair would be as momentous, and eventually as deadly, a transformation as changing her name is a theme that goes all the way back to Zolotow. Like everyone before and after him, Zolotow sees "Marilyn Monroe" as a fabrication, and his is one of the first accounts to suggest that such fabrication could be perilous:

> She was uneasy when she first saw herself in the mirror. "It wasn't the 'real me.'" Then she saw that it worked. Being a pragmatist, she remained blonde. [. . .]
>
> A bleached blonde is not natural; therefore she cannot wear ordinary clothes or make-up, or *be* ordinary. She becomes, in a sense, an assembled product. To be artificially put together

by modistes, couturiers, cosmeticians and coiffeurs, leads to a profound loss of one's identity. Motion-picture actresses often lose all sense of who and what they really are. They are wraiths, reflections in a mirror, existing only in an audience's reaction to them. They hardly exist apart from an audience. If they lose the appeal, because of a change in type or because they have become middle-aged, they, as it were, die.

Whether she knew it or not, the moment Marilyn bleached her hair, she made a serious commitment. One is never the same afterward.[84]

Marilyn loses her identity when she becomes blonde because blondeness is not natural (to her). The portentousness with which Zolotow pronounces that bleaching one's hair was a "serious commitment" and so transfiguring that "one is never the same afterward" might be funny were it taken less literally. The logic is simple, if illogical, and it is fairy-tale logic, magical thinking: she must be what she looks like. "A bleached blonde is not natural; therefore she cannot wear ordinary clothes or make-up, or *be* ordinary": the emphasis is Zolotow's. Looking fake means that you become fake; looking extraordinary means that you must become extraordinary (and ordinariness will kill you). Being "a bleached blonde" means becoming "an assembled product," in Zolotow's pejorative phrase. She becomes this, we are told, on the inside, but only because she looks like it on the outside.

Zolotow's construction was either influential, or he was on to something: future accounts of the change in hair color are certainly "colored" by this interpretation. In 1973, Mailer, too, read "becoming a blonde" as identity-forming. Mailer claims that her resistance to bleaching her hair was "intense" because she "has so little identity to give away" that she needed to hang on to her hair color to know who she was.[85] Wolfe shows the limits of the reinterpretation of Marilyn when in 1998 he restates (without acknowledgment) Zolotow's thirty-eight-year-old reading:

But to be a blonde demanded a certain commitment. Blondes are different. Shapely blondes fall into a mythological morphology.

They dress differently, think differently, act differently. Studying the reflection of the blonde in the mirror, she must have recognized something that was true to herself—something that was blonde inside. And as she stared at the image of the other woman, Norma Jeane stepped through the looking glass and became a blonde forever.[86]

Wolfe returns us to the same corkscrew logic that characterizes the name change: the new Marilyn is different, but the same; artificial, but natural. She was "blonde inside." Because it is being reconstituted as part of her natural identity, blondeness must ipso facto be "inside" her, despite the manifest idiocy of saying that someone is blonde inside. Becoming a blonde apparently means becoming an altogether different kind of person, but just what is "a blonde" anyway?

First of all, blondes are dumb. Blondeness as a marker of stupidity is such a truism in our culture that Oates offered it as a definition for how Monroe "turned out." In the *New York Times* interview promoting *Blonde,* Oates says of her: "she just is lost in this 'blondeness'— the whole idea of blonde. How do you sell yourself? She wasn't blonde, yet that was how she turned out." But what exactly is "the whole idea of blonde"? Is the whole idea of blonde that she sold herself? That she was fake? That she was dead (that's really how she turned out). "She made herself into the blonde who looks dumb. So she was complicit in her own fate, I'm afraid," Oates sorrowfully observes. Although Oates seems to be suggesting that there is a difference between how Monroe looked and who she was (she only "looks dumb"), at the same time she offers this appearance as an explanation for Marilyn's fate: because she allowed herself to look dumb, she also asked to be treated as dumb—which, apparently, for Oates, was a dumb thing to do. What Oates *doesn't* explain is why looking blonde means looking dumb—or why how you look becomes how you "turn out."

The idea that becoming blonde signifies an "ontological anxiety," as Oates actually argues (let it not be forgotten that Oates is brunette, and perhaps I should mention here that I'm blonde), is hardly unique to her; it's fairy-tale logic again. The exterior seeps in and infects the interior: the metaphor kills the self.

Blondeness is also a fairy-tale symbol in its own right, of course, invested with the same associations of purity, goodness and wealth with which Christian metaphysics associates light. But lightness also symbolizes triviality, frivolity and even light-headedness, which seems to relate back to the association of dumbness with blondeness (opinions vary as to when the phrase "dumb blonde" first entered the language; Anita Loos has taken credit for inventing the first dumb blonde in Lorelei Lee, the antiheroine of *Gentlemen Prefer Blondes,* which first appeared in the magazine *Harper's Bazaar* in 1925). As Marina Warner notes in *From the Beast to the Blonde,* her study of the symbolism of fairy tales, blondeness is associated with "beauty, with love and nubility, with erotic attraction, with value and fertility."[87] As others have pointed out, "gold" hair also symbolizes wealth by association. Blondeness has been seen as the deracinated ideal of a racist society: "Blondeness is the ultimate sign of whiteness: the blonde woman is offered as the prize possession of the white man, the most desired of women, the most 'feminine' of women" and "it was also, to many, an image of the white race that excludes all other races."[88] Warner notes that blondeness's "tradition enfolds femininity, and its conventional link with youth and beauty, as well as with privacy, modesty and an interior life in both senses—indoor pursuits and affective experience. For blonde hair implies pale skin, which in turn entails lack of exposure, again on a doubled level, either to the rays of the sun in outdoor work, or to the gaze of others."[89] But a bleached blonde, as Zolotow is at pains to emphasize, and as Oates implies, signals pretense and complicity in selling oneself: it doubles back against its connotation of lack of exposure and becomes a sign of overexposure. Marilyn Monroe's blondeness functions as a metaphor, as Oates reveals, of an actress "selling herself." It is a sign of being not the real thing, but a manufactured commodity. It is a sign of being unnatural.

SPLIT IDENTITY

For all their individual variation, these accounts unite over their feeling that changing from Norma Jeane into Marilyn Monroe is related to her destruction: it may have been cause, and it may have been effect, but it was not insignificant, as a title like Lucy Freeman's *Why Norma Jean Killed Marilyn Monroe: A Psychological Portrait* demonstrates. Similarly, Mellen declares that "there were two selves [. . .] the conscious and the unconscious, the willed and the real."[90] The splitting is always antagonistic: the story becomes Norma Jean versus Marilyn, a pathologically divisive self-hatred that these narratives discover is the true story. Thus although Freeman will declare that Norma Jean killed Marilyn Monroe, George Barris will assert (more typically) that "her biggest enemy was Marilyn Monroe. Her true self was little Norma Jeane."[91] In the end it doesn't matter whether Norma Jean killed Marilyn or Marilyn killed Norma Jeane: it's the split itself that is fatal. So much for postmodern conceptions of identity as protean and shifting: the bildungsroman is alive and well in biography.

In fact, identity is seen as so necessarily stable that change itself becomes pathological. The more literal the difference between the two, the more lethal it grows: one recent film version, HBO's *Marilyn/Norma Jeane,* went so far as to cast two different actors to play the same woman: Ashley Judd played Norma Jeane, while Mira Sorvino played Marilyn Monroe. The split between the two was not, however, merely temporal: the film continued to place them together in scenes that depicted dialogues, arguments and fights between them. Norma Jeane remained symbolically "inside" Marilyn Monroe throughout the film, but in actuality physically *outside* Marilyn Monroe— because she was an entirely different person. Ultimately the film suggested that this split identity was the cause of Marilyn Monroe's death, which it wrote as deliberate and unproblematic suicide; Marilyn screams at Norma Jeane (tritely reflected in the mirror): "I know how to make you shut up" and (they both) proceed(s) to swallow several bottles of pills. Writers insist that Norma Jeane is inside, but they keep putting her outside.

This faux-psychology permeates not only popular accounts, but

supposedly "scholarly" ones as well. Louise J. Kaplan condemns
Marilyn Monroe as a manufactured commodity fetish that destroyed
Norma Jeane: "Marilyn Monroe is the cultural commodity. But
where is Norma Jeane? The virtual annihilation of the abandoned
and abused child who was Norma Jeane is 'a prerequisite' for the
manufacturing of the sex goddess who is Marilyn Monroe."[92] Anything manufactured becomes by definition pathological in narratives
that sentimentalize a "real," but always already lost (that is, abandoned) identity. This is also a preindustrial ideal, part of our suspicion
of the commodity. Monroe's value should reside in her humanity; if
she is made, she is assumed to be worthless (despite the fact that a
cut diamond is worth rather more than an unrefined nugget).
Whether Norma Jeane killed Marilyn Monroe or Marilyn Monroe
"annihilated" Norma Jeane doesn't matter in part because either way,
Marilyn Monroe is guilty of killing Marilyn Monroe: the metaphor of
self-division masquerades as an explanation for Monroe's death,
when in fact it only redescribes it.

This helps explain why in so many accounts "the real self" is *also*
inadequate, pathetic. As I have said, Steinem diagnoses Marilyn
Monroe as a prime example of the "lost inner child," who is called
Norma Jeane. Mailer declares that she was always "living with the
full equivalent of two people within her," which is why "so many of
her affections are replaced by hate." One part of herself is a "female
Napoleon," whereas the other is "sick, weak, wounded, miserable,
stunned, and near to used up."[93] (Conversely, he grants that Arthur
Miller, of whom he is usually contemptuous, is "too complex a man
to remain in one consistent piece."[94]) Mellen begins to confuse
Marilyn's selves such that it becomes impossible to tell which one is
really "inside," making the decisions: "The person Norma Jean was so
long abandoned by the exigencies of being 'Marilyn' that the fear of
allowing 'the mouse' to emerge drove Marilyn Monroe deeper into
pills and alcohol. At the same time, she felt pride in the body that had
at least created a Marilyn Monroe behind whom the shy, frightened
Norma Jean could hide."[95] Norma Jeane is usually abject, somehow
left "unfinished," as in Spoto's rendition: "although Hollywood's
Marilyn Monroe was indeed a part of her real self, there was [. . .] a
deeper self, however unformed."[96] The relationship between Norma

Jeane and Marilyn is represented in terms that suggest, implicitly or explicitly, parts and wholes, but wholeness is never granted either one of them.

However obviously symbolic all this rhetoric about the dangers of transformation may seem, it is unique to Marilyn Monroe: a moment of reflection reveals that being renamed by a film studio does not always equate to self-destruction even in our cultural myths, much less in reality. If renaming symbolized tragically early death, one would also see titles like *Why Harlean Carpenter Killed Jean Harlow*. Admittedly, although Harlow died young, she didn't self-destruct in the same way as Monroe (her appendix burst). But why not *Why Frances Gumm Killed Judy Garland*? Judy Garland was similarly addicted to drugs and is popularly held to have been "destroyed" by Hollywood, but "Judy Garland" as a persona is not perceived to be pathologically false, however much Judy Garland the person may have been self-destructive; nor is the real Judy Garland supposed to be particularly hard to find; nor, indeed, does anyone lament: "Good-bye Frances Gumm."

Marilyn's story is not just about the difference between public performance and private self. Many other Hollywood stars accepted—or courted—public roles that were at odds with their private lives. So for that matter do all public figures in an age of mass media who wish either to protect or to hide their private lives. Thus, for example, Rock Hudson played the public role of a heterosexual, and John F. Kennedy played the public role of a faithful husband. It is common knowledge that the Hollywood studio system sanitized the stories it told about its stars in order to package and sell them as commodities more successfully, and persistent rumors about the sexuality of certain Hollywood stars today suggest the degree to which most of us assume knowingly that secrets are still kept and that the "truth" continues to be fictionalized for public consumption. But for Marilyn Monroe, becoming "a fiction" is held to have killed her—despite the fact that her early years are much more of a fiction than her later ones.

GOODBYE NORMA JEANE

Norma Jeane is a ghost, associated with memory and loss: in 1969, Guiles wrote that Marilyn was haunted by "the intrusive past, the ghost of Norma Jean." "As you read and think about Marilyn," Steinem admonishes the reader, "remember Norma Jeane."[97] "Good-bye Norma Jean," says Mailer at the end of *Marilyn* in 1973, the same year that Elton John would use the phrase in "Candle in the Wind." Norma Jeane is remembered so that our culture can say goodbye to her.

Like paradise, Norma Jeane was invented in order to be lost. The idea of Norma Jeane sentimentalizes reality, identity and *normality*, the ordinary, as something absent, lamented, and beautiful—when it is found in Marilyn Monroe. It is something the rest of us have in (over-)abundance: Marilyn seems interesting because she appears to have shed that ordinariness, but didn't really (as will become clear when she dies). The reality that Norma Jeane represents is profoundly fictional: it is textual, inconsistent, even incoherent. It is an invention, the result of contentious biographical interpretation. For all that Norma Jeane is invoked as the stable, interior, original truth, and Marilyn Monroe dismissed as the unstable fraud, the stories about Norma Jeane create a notion of "reality" that is precarious, rootless, and lost. Norma Jeane, the abandoned child, is supposed to be the antithesis of Marilyn Monroe, the "most desired woman in the world," but they are both fragmented and sick.

In describing Marilyn Monroe's death, Summers declares that "there was irony in the fact that the death certificate, in 1962, would refer only to the passing of a Hollywood invention called Marilyn Monroe. For it was Norma Jeane that died."[98] Although the apocrypha declares Norma Jeane the real woman who must be saved from the grotesque artificiality of Marilyn, they see Norma Jeane as hidden, partial, childlike, suicidal, and dead. Norma Jeane is the retrospective fiction. Marilyn Monroe was a real person in every way recognized by our culture—except in her own biographies. She lived with and answered to the name Marilyn Monroe, other people could recognize and name her as Marilyn Monroe, professionally she was

Marilyn Monroe, legally she was Marilyn Monroe, financially she was Marilyn Monroe. Ironically, only the "true stories" about her life declare her a fiction and Norma Jeane a real person, but it is Norma Jeane who is the fiction, the cultural figment, the ghost of the real invoked as a death sentence.

Marilyn Monroe at Tobay Beach, New York, 1949. PHOTOGRAPH BY ANDRÉ DE DIENES.

4

"THE NAKED TRUTH," 1946–1952

They ask you questions like "What do you wear to bed?
Do you wear pajama tops, the bottom of pajamas,
or a nightgown?" So I said, "Chanel No. 5," cause it's
the truth. And yet, I don't want to say,
"Nude," you know? But it's the truth.

—MARILYN ON MARILYN,
BBC documentary

The back cover of the paperback edition of Summers's *Goddess: The Secret Lives of Marilyn Monroe* promises its reader "the whole naked, deeply moving truth about the all-too-beautiful, talented, and tormented woman who played a role in public and private that was too much for flesh and spirit to survive." If *Goddess* provides "the naked truth," the cover of Eunice Murray's *Marilyn: The Last Months* maintains that from its pages "Marilyn emerges as a real, flesh and blood woman." Peter Brown and Patte Barham's *Marilyn: The Last Take* offers a striptease—it will "strip away the lies to bring Marilyn Monroe back as she beautifully and tragically was"—and Zolotow's *Marilyn Monroe* touts "La Monroe Desnuda! Marilyn Monroe unveiled."

When Norma Jeane becomes Marilyn Monroe, all that the iconic Marilyn symbolizes comes rushing into the story. Seeking the truth behind the image of Marilyn, the apocrypha locates that truth in her body. If Marilyn represents cheerful female sexuality permanently on offer, the biographies will seek not to dispute the centrality of sexuality and nudity to Marilyn Monroe's life, but rather to pathologize it. Marilyn is cynical sexual manipulator to Norma Jeane's innocent sexual victim, but sexual attitudes remain Marilyn Monroe's defining feature. In the end, innocence will be reclaimed: the tale returns full circle to the real Norma Jeane who will be left dead in Crypt 33 in the Los Angeles County Morgue, abandoned and anonymous.

The premise that Marilyn Monroe is made up enables biographers to expose "shocking revelations" of the reality behind the façade, a reality that they give different names: Norma Jeane, pain, loss, sex, the naked body. The jacket copy for Summers's self-styled exposé indicates the movement between public and private, performance and reality, that will characterize the biographical writing about Marilyn Monroe, the movie star, whose life is understood as a struggle between these extremes. Public/private, artifice/reality, fantasy/truth are presented as dichotomies, a terminal either/or in which she is trapped, neither one nor the other. This trap will kill her flesh *and* her spirit, as in Summers's book-jacket bromide, but both will be found in the naked truth that is Marilyn Monroe's body. What is actually a tension in the interpretation of Marilyn becomes, in the apocrypha, the solution to the mystery: she will be destroyed by the struggle between innocence and cynicism, love and sex, light and dark, Norma Jeane and Marilyn, that animates the tale.

The convenient thing about such simplistic dichotomies is that they provide biographers with a ready-made discovery: all one has to do is invert the cliché, and—voilà!—"revelation." In public, Marilyn Monroe's beautiful body is understood to have been for sale and was supposed to be the reason for her phenomenal success. Biographies just keep inverting this truism to create surprising "secrets" about Marilyn: her body was for sale in private, too; it was not really beautiful; and it was not really successful or desirable, but in fact scarred by falsity, suffering, and the signs of an always impending death. Whatever her image seems, in all its supposedly contradictory inconstancy, will be a lie; anything opposed to the image will be deemed true. She seems successful; she was a failure. She seems desirable; she was discarded. She seems innocent; she was shameful. She seems glamorous; she was ordinary. Mostly the lives want to show that she seems to have it all, but in reality she had nothing, not even herself. Having abandoned Norma Jeane, Marilyn Monroe will forever be understood as a lost soul in search of a real identity. Her supposedly lost self prompts, and legitimates, the biographer's own search for her, in what film critic Mary Ann Doane has called the "hide and seek game associated with vision" that prompts the urge to investigate, an investigation usually sexual in nature.[1]

Despite the intense media surveillance of her life and, indeed, of her afterlife, fierce controversies persist even in the stories about the years of Marilyn Monroe's stardom, which are the subject of the next two chapters. Surveillance itself, as philosopher Michel Foucault has influentially argued, is a sovereign form of power: to see without being seen, to regulate and judge, to scrutinize and examine, is to control. By no coincidence, surveillance is also one of the hallmarks of literary realism, in which "everyone is either a performer or a spectator, an inspector or a specimen."[2] It follows that surveillance provides biography with a substantial, and influential, series of rhetorical figures associated with the procedures of inspection. To inspect Marilyn Monroe, to diagnose, to dissect her—all of these metaphors suggest the power of the biographer over her. But they also suggest that truth is located in her body. In particular, worries about acting and performance seep into the story as soon as artificial Marilyn makes her entrance, and become questions about truth, falsity and madness. How do we know we're not being deceived by her crazy feminine mind? Because of the inescapable truths of her body.

BODY OF EVIDENCE

A sex symbol is by definition a tease. As an image, it is infinitely consumable, can be owned by everyone and anyone, but the person is not there. A symbol of sex is the abstract representation of an experience that we regard as irreducibly real, the most human because the most physical. Descriptions of Marilyn Monroe's body and sexuality are always paradoxical not because she herself was more paradoxical than most people, but because culturally she represents both the real and the symbol. Phrases such as "the naked truth" or "Marilyn unveiled" move her from the figurative to the literal: nakedness is already a dead metaphor for truth, and in Marilyn's case, stories about her naked body are treated as literal truth, fact incarnate. The apocrypha's prime "body of evidence" consists in stories about Marilyn Monroe's body, stories that will be held to represent reality in terms of sex, desire and, most of all, pain.

Her body becomes a polygraph in these stories; "body language" is the unconscious betrayer of truth:

> That her body was her emotional spine, so to speak, can clearly be seen in the way she walks in all her films. It is a walk that tells the world, I am my body, love it, love me. If you do not love my body, I am as nothing. I might as well die.[3]

If her body speaks the truth, her words, however, are suspect, potentially an act or a scripted performance—one of many ways in which writers suggest that her body is more genuine than her mind. When writing about his discussions with her of her childhood, photographer George Barris writes: "Did Marilyn always tell me the truth? I believe so, even though, being an accomplished actress, she may have dramatized some events and added a bit of color to them—still the facts were there. Her eyes would tell me she was truthful."[4] Summers's account of Ben Hecht's "reading" of Monroe's body language during the composition of *My Story* similarly sees it as inherently truthful, despite her propensity to deceive: "Hecht found himself struggling to interpret Marilyn's 'odd little physical body language, to read when she was going into something fictional or when she was leveling.'"[5] Her body becomes the ultimate arbiter, because she is unreliable, because she is a fantasy. The fantasies that Marilyn represents are as threatening as they are desirable:

> The facts about Marilyn's life for the most part are well-known. But, ah, the fantasies. It is the fantasies that can kill us if they become too intense, too terrifying. As they killed Marilyn.[6]

The responsibility for the fantasies seems to shift: are they our fantasies about Marilyn, or her own fantasies? No matter; for Freeman, whether homicidal or suicidal, fantasies are fatal. Summers is less ambivalent; he knows that Marilyn is to blame for our fantasies about her:

Marilyn, an international fantasy figure, constructed her image, both public and private, from a blend of fact and self-serving fantasy. She exercised to excess a common human license. Fantasy was part of this creature, and part of the challenge is to discover the woman who sheltered behind it. [. . .] Norma Jeane had begun weaving her web of delusion before the break with Jim Dougherty and along with the fantasies there was some outright deceit. Only when that is dealt with can we move along to the actress called Marilyn Monroe.[7]

"Fantasy" soon becomes delusion, demonstrating how writers project their fantasies about Marilyn back onto her. If she looks like a fantasy—she is the one who must be fantasizing, not us. And soon all these fantasies become delusion (madness) and lies, a dark perversion of Monroe's skill as an actress. The possibility that she's acting makes her audience nervous: she is in the business of deception, and gifted with a fatal, feminine talent for duplicity.

For example, all the major biographies at some point expose one of her best-kept secrets: it turns out that Marilyn Monroe wasn't really that great-looking. Her appearance is only an image, her face a façade. In fact, declares the apocrypha triumphantly, Marilyn's appearance of beauty is the result of feminine wiles and trickery. Guiles provides a version of the often-repeated allegation: "she was not naturally beautiful, her face being disproportionately large above a body that ranged during her lifetime from magnificent to stout."[8] Joan Mellen writes that "Norma Jean transformed herself into Marilyn Monroe, accentuating through make-up and dress the physical attributes of an otherwise ordinary girl."[9] Declaring on two separate occasions that it was her "will to be beautiful" that enabled Marilyn to fool everyone into thinking she was gorgeous, Guiles adds that she "was not endowed by nature with great beauty—the tip of her nose, quite unlike her mother's, was too fleshy, her chin too weak—but when she began to take on a few contours, she exercised some of the will to be beautiful that was to lead to the Marilyn she conjured up in later years, who certainly seemed to be a great beauty."[10]

Would that it were so easy. The wellspring of the Marilyn legend is our lingering sense that there *was* something unique about her. In her last interview Monroe commented on attempts to manufacture another Marilyn: "These girls who try to be me—I guess the studios put them up to it, or they get the ideas themselves. But gee, they haven't—you can make a lot of gags about it—like they haven't got the foreground or else they haven't got the background. But I mean the middle, where you live." The charisma that made her a star simply could not be transferred to any of the other bleached blondes who were offered to the public in Monroe's place: Jayne Mansfield, Sheree North, Diana Dors and Mamie Van Doren all enjoyed a moment or two of fleeting popularity, but none of them had anything like the impact of Marilyn Monroe. Maybe they just lacked sufficient will.

Not that there haven't always been those who don't find Marilyn especially appealing; but that is not what these writers are saying. They all assume that she seems beautiful to everyone, and want to reveal that she wasn't really.

Knowing the secret that Marilyn Monroe wasn't beautiful after all, biographers can distinguish themselves from the rest of us, who continue to be taken in by her. Both Spoto and Summers quote Monroe's longtime makeup artist and friend Whitey Snyder, asserting that her beauty was manufactured: "she knew every trick of the makeup trade. [. . .] She looked fantastic, of course, but it was all an illusion."[11] In other words, she looked fantastic, but she didn't really look fantastic? That phrase "trick of the trade" was repeated often in accounts of Monroe's appearance: Milton Greene said something very similar: "You don't just wake up in the morning and wash your face and comb your hair and go out in the morning and look like Marilyn Monroe. She knows every trick of the beauty trade. She knows what has to be done to make her look the way she wants to look."[12] The rhetoric emphasizes deceit—trickery, conjuring—and how made-up her appearance is, how artificial. McCann notes that "'cosmetic' became, for critics, synonymous with superfluity,"[13] but in Marilyn's case it also became synonymous with fictionality. Not merely uncovering the falseness of the Marilyn persona, these stories find the grotesque lurking in the Nietzschean will to beauty of a self-made woman. Mailer invokes this threat when he imagines Monroe excitedly realizing that "one could paint oneself into an instrument of one's will!"[14] There's more than a hint of Frankenstein's monster about these stories, a suggestion that her power—her beauty—was not only false, but grotesque.

Although she wasn't really beautiful, most of her biographers think that Monroe really was narcissistic. Narcissism locates responsibility for voyeurism in the object of the gaze: she invites us to watch her, she likes it, she wants it. The double entendres in such phrases—she wants it—are no accident: she encourages us to want her body because she wants her own body. For Freud, the narcissist is her own object of desire. Accusations of narcissism let the viewer off the hook. In the apocrypha, Marilyn will always be at fault: what will be exposed are failings. Thus her perceived successes are a lie, and her perceived failures are true. Narcissism also transforms desire into derision: we can be contemptuous of her even as we watch, blaming her for our own voyeurism.

Marilyn's relationship to the mirror is thus symbolic in more than one regard: it suggests her self-division, it suggests her self-love, and it suggests self-commodification. Writers emphasize Monroe's relationship with her mirror, dwelling on stories that claim she would spend whole days gazing into them, contemplating her face for hours at a time. Marilyn is held to reflect the desires of her audience: for example, Weatherby wrote that "she had an ability, unique in my experience, to appear to be what you wanted her to be and therefore the real person remained elusive."[15] Guiles agrees that "Marilyn was a kind of living abstraction. She was what you believed her to be."[16] Our projection becomes her projection: she is naturally a fantasy. She belongs in front of the mirror, because in her, as Mailer maintains, "we can see the magnified mirror of ourselves."[17] She is both viewer and viewed, her narcissism inextricable from her desirability. She watches her own performance in the mirror, "on her knees before her own beauty," as Arthur Miller declares in *Timebends*. As we shall see in a moment, being on her knees in Marilyn's case is also an image of prostitution, of sexual commodification.

Hidden in the accounts of those who believed her to be narcissistic is another explanation, as in dress designer Billy Travilla's assessment:

She was totally narcissistic. She adored her own face, constantly wanted to make it better and different. Everything she did in that regard, by the way, was right at the time. She once told me, "I can make my face do anything, same as you can take a white board and build from that and make a painting."[18]

Monroe's account would seem to be less about self-love than about artistry: her body was her work of art. She knew it was her instrument (likening it once to a violin), but if she was at once artist and work of art, she lived in a world that could only let the beautiful woman be picture, not painter; object, not subject. Which might help explain why Travilla goes on to add: "If ever there was a prick-teaser, it was Marilyn."

For Spoto, her reliance upon the mirror is "not simply the sign of an actress's narcissism," but of "ruthless assessment" that led to "refashioning and recreating," because she was perpetually "dissatisfied" with her image, trying to finish an "unrealized image of an unfinished self."[19] It seems clear that Monroe did spend hours in front of mirrors, but she also said that it was work, and a "strain":

> Marilyn Monroe has to look a certain way—be *beautiful*—and act a certain way, be talented. [. . .] But we actors and actresses are such worriers, such—what is your word?—Narcissus types. I sit in front of the mirror for hours looking for signs of age. Yet I like old people; they have great qualities younger people don't have. I want to grow old without face-lifts. They take the life out of a face, the character. I want to have the courage to be loyal to the face I've made.[20]

When she accepts the label "Narcissus type," it is out of anxiety, not self-love; she struggles toward a sense of self as evolution. What others see as narcissism Monroe saw as work: it was part of her attempt to control how she was seen, and thus, what she was worth. Although her image "became a burden, a—what do you call it?—an albatross,"[21] it was also part of her "business," as she knew:

> When the photographers come, it's like looking in a mirror. They think they arrange me to suit themselves, but I use them to put

over myself. [. . .] I felt occasionally that I was killing the truth when I killed the ones that were bad for my public image. Here is Marilyn Monroe with egg on her face. I used to feel as tied to the beauty business as an addict to his drugs.[22]

Monroe was an object of surveillance: she sought to control her image precisely because it was difficult for others to separate her image from her self. But it is obvious from this passage that Monroe could distinguish between her self and her "public image"; she was simply trying to avoid being shamed, being shown with egg on her face. Humiliation underlies the story of Marilyn Monroe's life, a humiliation that relates to exposure.

One of the passages from *My Story* most frequently quoted in the Monroe apocrypha concerns a fantasy the narrator reports having had as a child of taking off her clothes in church:

> I wanted desperately to stand up naked for God and everyone else to see. I had to clench my teeth and sit on my hands to keep myself from undressing. Sometimes I had to pray hard and beg God to stop me from taking my clothes off.
>
> I even had dreams about it. In the dream I entered the church wearing a hoop skirt with nothing under it. The people would be lying on their backs in the church aisle, and I would step over them, and they would look up at me.
>
> My impulse to appear naked and my dreams about it had no shame or sense of sin in them. Dreaming of people looking at me made me feel less lonely. I think I wanted them to see me naked because I was ashamed of the clothes I wore—the never changing faded blue dress of poverty. Naked, I was like other girls and not someone in an orphan's uniform.[23]

This symbolic story—it is a dream, after all—appears repeatedly in the stories of Marilyn Monroe's life, usually as literal evidence of her pathological exhibitionism, as in Freeman's account, which simply accepts the story as an unvarying fact about Monroe's character and psyche and uses it to diagnose her. The judgmentalism of Freeman's tone exemplifies the censure with which writers treat Monroe's naked body:

> Marilyn never achieved womanhood. She lived like an adoles-
> cent. She did not possess the mature mind needed for a lasting
> marriage. Her body was her whole reason for being. She hated
> underwear, wanted to be a nude child, loved for her body. She
> later said that she often had the desire, when her mother occa-
> sionally took her to church, to take off all her clothes, stand in the
> nude. As though it were the only way she could arouse love and
> caring.[24]

Quite apart from the way in which Freeman misrepresents what *My Story* says, there's also the question of whether Monroe actually said it, or dreamed it, in the first place. This might well be a fictionalized passage from this most corrupted of texts. If it is a fiction, it suggests again the way in which the Marilyn apocrypha makes her the natural embodiment of a fantasy its authors have projected onto her. And it shows how little respect these books have for their subject—and for the body they claim to adore.

But the story could be true. Certainly many of the people with whom Monroe lived—her acting coach Natasha Lytess, her friends John and Lucille Caroll, her maid Lena Pepitone, among others—report that Monroe liked to be naked when she was at home. There are stories of her embarrassing Joe DiMaggio, and also Frank Sina-tra, with whom she was later involved, by wandering into the room nude when they had guests. Although the *My Story* passage insists that nudity was not shameful—indeed, that it was a correc-tive to the embarrassment of poor clothes—Natasha Lytess's account shows that stories about Monroe's nudity will be used to denigrate her:

> She'd come wandering naked from her bedroom into the bath-
> room at 11 A.M. and mid-day. It took her at least an hour to bathe.
> Then—still without a stitch on—Marilyn would drift in a sort of

dreamy, sleep-walking daze into the kitchen. [. . .] When she became a famous star [. . .] still she ambled unconcerned, completely naked, around her bungalow, among wardrobe women, makeup girls, hairdressers.

Being naked seems to soothe her—almost hypnotize her.

If she caught sight of herself in a full-length mirror, she'd sit down—or just stand there—with her lips hanging slack and eyes droopily half shut like a cat being tickled, absorbed in the mirror's reflection of herself.[25]

Words like *narcissism* and *exhibitionism* suggest that a predilection for nakedness, and self-absorption, were not just blameworthy, but a problem, even a disease. Summers calls it "compulsive nudity," in which she couldn't stop herself from "parading naked" in front of people because of her traumatic childhood. This kind of faux diagnosis punishes Monroe for precisely those aspects about Marilyn that supposedly the culture celebrates—like her free and open sexuality.

The idea that Marilyn cannot be understood in terms other than the sexual is diagnosed as a psychological truth of her existence, in literal interpretations of her figure:

Sex was as essential to her as eating. Sex was food for the fantasies that threatened to overwhelm her, would send her to a madhouse, as they did her mother. Unless someone loved her, she would feel a "nobody" (no body), so she made her body the most alluring in the world. If men found her sexually desirable she would not go crazy as her mother did after she could not find a permanent man though she searched eight years.[26]

Freeman's account is the most egregious example of the apocrypha's tendency to explain Monroe by means of literalism: if Marilyn is symbolic, then the literal can look like truth. In the example from Freeman, Monroe's body and mind are not organically linked, but rather pathologically split; nonetheless, her desirable body is connected to madness in the space of a few sentences. If Marilyn was supposed to be desirable because she made sex innocent, the lurking guarantee of madness and death—both twinned with sex in Monroe's story—brings punishment back into the tale. Sex is consistently a sign of her pathological psyche even as it also symbolizes the truth of her body:

> When Marilyn told a friend, as she married Arthur Miller, "now I won't have to suck cock any more," she referred to a sexual practice more akin to feeding at the breast than an expression of mature love. [. . .] When Marilyn was a novice she used sex to get parts in films. [. . .] She saw sex, as many women do, not only as a way of unconsciously still trying to get a mother's love but for the release of a hidden rage.[27]

Freeman's mishmash of watered-down Freudian psychology is, on the one hand, stupid to the point of incomprehensibility; on the other hand, it also represents a trend in the apocrypha to seek out spurious psychological explanations for perfectly normal feelings, which have the effect of reinforcing Marilyn's extraordinariness (when positive), or pathology (when negative). The assumptions informing Freeman's account—that fellatio is immature, that women have sex with men because they want to be loved by their mothers—show that sex remains something many in our culture can't quite take for granted. Monroe becomes the repository of all this ambivalence; our mixed feelings are translated into her confusions. The solution for such ambivalence is the pathology of the literal.

ON HER KNEES: FELLATIO AND THE WORK ETHIC

Four years would elapse after she first signed a contract with 20th Century-Fox in 1946 before Marilyn Monroe's "will to be beautiful" and determination to be a star paid off and brought her to the notice of the movie-going public. During those four years she worked as a model and struggled, like many aspiring actresses, to get noticed in bit parts and insignificant films, hanging out at Schwab's drugstore with the other Hollywood hopefuls. Because she would become our most famous sex symbol, and according to many the most desired woman in the world, most biographers ask the "obvious" question about a woman whose career overlaps with sex: Did she sleep her way to the top? This question already assumes that Marilyn's body was not only her greatest asset, but a commodity she was willing to exploit. Like the implication that Monroe was courting rape as an adolescent, and like the diagnosis of narcissism, the allegation of prostitution says she asked for it.

Writing about the years during which Monroe was trying to break into Hollywood, biographers repeatedly return to the question of how she succeeded. Nearly all writers quote Emmeline Snively, who ran the Blue Book modeling agency and who gave Monroe her professional start. She once said: "Girls ask me all the time how they can be like Marilyn Monroe. And I tell them, if they showed one tenth of the hard work and gumption that that girl had, they'd be on their way. But there will never be another like her."[28] But most writers are at pains to show that Monroe was on the make; associating her with prostitution, in various manifestations, they try to determine whether, or how much, Marilyn Monroe traded on sex rather than work. Summers asks in the very first pages of *Goddess* how much of Monroe's success was attributable to the "carefully chosen embraces of powerful males."[29] Despite their repeated insistence upon Monroe's fictions, in the end biographers want to believe that her image reflected a reality, that a sex symbol can really be reduced to sex.

Monroe did quite well as a model for men's magazines, but the story goes that during her neglected childhood, when she was often sent to the movies by foster families that couldn't be bothered to care for her, she had stared at the silver figures on the screen and dreamed of being a movie star. The pop-psychological consensus is that the film studios came to represent a form of identity and belonging for her: success, love, understanding and protection would all be found if she became a movie star, and the studio would provide at once parent, home, profession and self. Less frequently noted is the fact that little Norma Jeane was dreaming her dreams in the heart of the

Depression, and that her dream was not unique. It was the American Dream, and she was determined to live it. The fact that she did just gives biographers more tension with which to play between fantasy and sordid reality.

Monroe's determination was quite active: she met everyone she could, had her picture taken everywhere. Most writers agree that while she was a starlet, she made herself available to the Hollywood publicity machinery, and according to many that was when she learned how to handle the press with the skill she would show in later years. From the beginning she was also determined to improve herself, taking classes in acting, modeling and literature, and talking to photographers about what made a good model, a good photograph. There are conflicting stories about her chronic unpunctuality: some say that in these early years she was always on time, professional and ready to work; others that her inability to memorize her lines or be anywhere less than an hour or two late had always characterized her. Her lateness was so extreme, and so unvarying, that it would become part of the story. Newspaperman Erskine Johnson memorably quipped:

> Newsmen have waited for Marilyn to come out of airplanes. Airplanes have waited for Marilyn. Newsmen have waited for Marilyn to come out of trains. Trains have waited for Marilyn. Movie producers, husband Arthur Miller, clothes designers have waited for Marilyn. Waiters have waited for Marilyn.[30]

Monroe responded: "It's not really me that's late. It's the others who are in such a hurry."[31] In any event, she was not seen as promising in her early years by anyone in the Hollywood studio system: her first brief contracts at 20th Century-Fox and Columbia were both unceremoniously dropped; the powerful men in Hollywood who encountered her during these years generally reported later that she had seemed unmemorable.

It was at this time, while struggling to make ends meet in 1949, that Monroe posed nude in the pictures that would cause an international scandal three years later. As we saw, the pictures earned millions for Hugh Hefner, who bought the negatives for $500, whereas

Monroe would only earn the $50 she was initially paid. (This pattern of exploitative economic inequality would continue throughout Monroe's career: for her last, unfinished film, Dean Martin had been hired as her costar at a reported five times her salary.) We will look at the calendar scandal in greater detail at the end of this chapter, but for now it is just worth mentioning that posing for this picture meant that from the beginning, for many observers, Marilyn would always be defined as "cheesecake," as sex on display, and as sex for sale.

In 1949 Monroe acquired an extremely powerful ally in agent Johnny Hyde, one of the most influential men in Hollywood. The story goes that Hyde was the first person in the industry to believe in Monroe's potential for stardom, although many at the time considered him deluded by his own passion for her. Hyde was by all accounts intensely in love with Monroe and repeatedly asked her to marry him. He was generally held to have tried to persuade her on pragmatic grounds: he was very rich, and unlikely to live long. Monroe consistently refused, saying that she wasn't in love with him.

Norman Mailer, charitable as ever, considers her refusal to marry Hyde "one of the mysteries of motivation in her life,"[32] but the explanation seems simple enough: she didn't see marriage as a business transaction. There's no reason to doubt that Monroe married for love when she married DiMaggio and Miller, although just as likely her definition of love was complicated (as it is for everyone) by conflicting needs, desires and fears, but it seems clear that she would only marry for emotional, not financial, security. Mailer finds that mysterious presumably because he has already decided that she was defined by cupidity. Leaming considers Monroe's sexual opportunism so fundamental that it allows her to slip from a speculative mood ("Marilyn must have been nervous" as a starlet at a Hollywood party) into mind-reading: "she knew people were saying that she had been foolish to have repeatedly turned down Johnny Hyde's proposals of marriage; [. . .] it crossed her mind that perhaps they were right."[33] Spoto is the only investigative biographer to attribute Monroe's refusal not only to her disinclination to enter a marriage of convenience, but to calculation as well—she realized that if she married a man "known to be gravely ill" she would be called a "gold digger"—attributing self-interest even to an episode that clearly demarcates the limits of Monroe's opportunism: she *did* turn Hyde down.[34] These stories disagree about almost everything, but they stand united in their defiance of the principle of Occam's razor.

The earliest accounts, such as Zolotow's, maintain the truth of Marilyn's iconic innocence, denying that Monroe was sexually opportunistic on the grounds that she was too naïve to "submit" to sexual advances even if they could help her career; Zolotow concludes by anonymously quoting a producer who says: "Marilyn never slept with a man who could do her any good."[35] In 1969, Guiles says the same thing in a more specific context, discussing Monroe's relationship in her early years with powerful Hollywood mogul Joseph M. Schenck, whose "friend" Monroe was known to have been: "it is unlikely that Joe was in any sense Marilyn's sponsor," Guiles declares, but this is the first the reader has heard that he might have been.[36] Indeed, he goes further and insists that an affectionate kiss in greeting "was as close as she would ever come to fulfilling the charge that she was mistress to this man nearing his seventieth year."[37] Even in these earliest versions, which want to believe that the innocent image unproblematically reflects the natural Monroe, the specter of prostitution is always there; sexual exploitation is fundamental to the myth of Hollywood, and the female body on (visual) offer is Marilyn's stock in trade.

Unlike the fictional writing about Monroe, which imagines scenes of exploitative anal sex, the biographical writing about Monroe emphasizes oral sex. When Guiles revised his biography in 1984, he abruptly changed his tune, reporting rumors of Schenck's predilection for "the act of fellatio" and the assumption that Marilyn was his "sexual partner in this and other variations." But then he adds:

> it is the considered opinion of most who knew Marilyn well that if she slept with Joe Schenck it was not to advance her career or open any doors. At every opportunity where Marilyn could advance herself by means of the "casting couch," she turned it down. If anything, she hurt her career at Fox by the liaison with Schenck, since [studio head Darryl F.] Zanuck assumed that she was "putting out" for his fairly powerless senior partner; as a

consequence, Zanuck despised her and consistently refused to take any personal interest in her career.[38]

The story is gradually evolving; Guiles draws on Zolotow, opening the door wider to the possibility that Monroe might have tried to use sex to advance her career. In these early accounts, though, she's still too ingenuous to work the system successfully: she sleeps with the *wrong* men. Such naïve ineptitude is vital to the Marilyn persona: it is Sugar Kane in *Some Like It Hot* explaining that she always falls for the wrong guy because she's "not very bright." Although Guiles has gone further toward admitting the image of the casting couch into the story, his interpretation still maintains Marilyn's fundamental innocence and endearing artlessness.

In attributing Zanuck's famous contempt for Monroe to Zanuck's (mistaken) assumption that she was trying to use sex to advance her career, Guiles also assigns moralistic prudery to a rather unlikely person: Zanuck's reputation in many accounts of his tenure at 20th Century-Fox places him on an extremely well-worn casting couch. Zanuck's personal dislike for Monroe is not much disputed, although whether he was subsequently "disinterested" in her career is; many writers claim that his eventual recognition of Monroe's box office value far outweighed his personal antipathy to her. Despite the well-known antagonism between them (or perhaps because of it), many writers, such as Oates, assume that Monroe must have slept with Zanuck as well. But when Zanuck's biographer Mel Gussow asked him in 1971 whether the casting-couch stories were true, Zanuck categorically denied them, adding: "Not even Marilyn Monroe. I hated her. I wouldn't have slept with her if she'd paid me."[39] Presumably she didn't; and although he might simply be an artful dodger of the awkward question, it doesn't really sound as if Zanuck were (re-)paying her for sexual favors, either.

Paralipsis—introducing an idea through its denial—enables writers to emphasize the sexual commerce from which they pretend to be averting their eyes. Thus, although Mailer's 1973 life is not noteworthy for its squeamishness, he only brings fellatio into the story through paralipsis (and his is the first mainstream text to mention it). While affecting not to, Mailer nonetheless implies that Monroe assumed the position: "Hollywood had long sustained the obscene myth of the big producer installed in his private office, welcoming the little starlet in the middle of business hours, then locking the door, unzipping his fly—we can skip the moment when she goes to her knees."[40] Only we haven't skipped it: Mailer has put her on her knees and left her there, all the while saying he won't.

By the mid-1980s, the presumption had become that Monroe must have used sex to get parts, and the male biographers are all, to a man, quite clear that oral sex is at issue. The story no doubt became more accepted as we began to congratulate ourselves on our sexual liberation; at the same time repetition granted it the status of fact. While acknowledging that Monroe "flatly denied ever having had sex with Joseph Schenck," Summers then quotes several assertions to the contrary, including Amy Greene's, who says Monroe told her: "I spent a great deal of time on my knees" and that she had the "impression [Monroe] slept her way to her start."[41] (However, Rollyson claims that Monroe was careful about taking Amy Greene into her confidence, considering her opportunistic and untrustworthy.[42]) Spoto also reports the sexual liaison with Schenck as fact, and like Guiles makes it clear that oral sex was involved: Monroe, he says, told "a few" "confidantes" that her relationship with Schenck was the "first of many times she had to kneel before an executive, a position not assumed in prayerful supplication. She wanted desperately to work, to succeed as a movie star."[43]

The prurience of all this almost goes without saying: biographers are certainly enjoying the salacious image of Marilyn Monroe at the service of studio moguls. But they are also enjoying the spectacle of her submission, of a powerful woman brought to her knees. If the novels that reconceive Monroe's life accentuate their fantasy of exploitation by figuring it as (imaginary) forced anal sex with studio executives, the biographies have Monroe acquiesce to the powers that be. Anal sex, according to the fictions, is something Marilyn "doesn't do," whereas fellatio is automatically enough associated with her that Kate Millett assumes its presence: "it is the mouth Warhol goes for, multiples over and over, playing upon the implications of fellatio in this opened and ecstatic orifice," she declares, despite the fact that Warhol manifestly reproduces the whole face (and her mouth is barely open). We have struck the limits of representation: fellatio is everywhere, but anal sex must be licensed by fiction. In both fantasies, Marilyn's job is to give pleasure, not to receive it. She will be on her knees, but she will not be flat on her back. Submissive, but not inert, Marilyn is still working at making men happy.

In the biographical version Monroe becomes more culpable for her own abuse. But then again, these tales grant Monroe more choice and self-determination than do the outright fictions: the composite biographical view sees Monroe less as passive victim, more as the active architect of her own career. Capitulation is a choice: it implies the possibility of refusal. The story is thus also paradoxically about keeping Marilyn pure. In Hyatt's graphic novel, when the studio mogul wants to "butt fuck" Marilyn and she refuses, he retorts, "It can't be worse than sucking Joe's dick," declaring that Schenck is tired of her, and that he is prepared to do her favors if she's nice to him—at which point Hyatt's Marilyn smacks him in the face and stalks out of the room. This is the adult version of *My Story*, in which Norma Jeane throws the nickel in Mr. Kimmel's face in outraged innocence.[44] Although she symbolizes the "shame" of sex, her innocence must also be reclaimed. When she dies, however, the biographies will also manage to bring Monroe's anus back into the tale, having their cake and eating it, too.

As did Spoto above, Guiles, Rollyson, Steinem and Oates all justify what they consider Monroe's prostitution or sexual self-exploitation in terms of the work ethic. Steinem goes even further than Spoto in her defense: "Marilyn supplied sex so that she would be allowed to work, but not so that she wouldn't have to work."[45] That is, in these accounts, prostitution is justifiable if it doesn't substitute for labor, and is only used to make "real" work possible. If sex is not exchanged directly or explicitly for money, prostitution can, apparently, be excused: "She didn't want money, she wanted work."[46] Rollyson describes the sex Monroe may have had with producers as a thank-you, a motive implicitly more acceptable than calling it a payment, although in fact the distinction is only semantic.[47] Guiles makes an even finer distinction, between being paid *for* sex and paying *with* sex, when he assures the reader that "if she paid for a few dinners with a 'thank you' in the bedroom, she made no serious compromises."[48] All of these writers take a very knowing attitude toward the sexual politics of Hollywood, assuming that success depends upon the exploitation of a woman's body (whether by herself or others). But where Steinem can't decide whether such utilitarianism is selling out or an example of enterprising American get-up-and-go, Guiles doesn't consider it serious business in the first place.

None of these arguments allows that sex for money is labor; prostitutes are apparently not actually working, and sex for work is implicitly more acceptable than sex for money, although the end result will be the same: sex earns money. The unspoken assumption seems to be the idea that sex is pleasure rather than work, although whether sex is pleasure or work presumably depends upon the feelings of the people involved.

If this is figurative prostitution, Summers and Spoto agree that Monroe also "literally" (in Summers's words) prostituted herself; once, according to Summers, for fifteen dollars to a man on the street the summer after she left Jim Dougherty. Both Summers and Spoto also believe another anecdote, which appeared in a biography of her teacher Lee Strasberg, who told his biographer repeatedly ("three times, on tape") that Monroe informed him she had worked as a call-girl at conventions.[49] Both of these writers believe the "evidence" given by Strasberg, although Summers for one doesn't credit Monroe's own claims to have been raped. Only Steinem points out that "no independent evidence" supports the stories that she was a call girl (although she doesn't point out that the number of times Strasberg repeated the story is no index of its veracity), and that it is equally possible that Monroe dramatized her hard-luck tale of enforced prostitution as that she fabricated childhood stories of rape.

Leaming is the only female chronicler who assumes that Monroe was "doing the rounds" of Hollywood; she tells the story matter-of-factly. Unlike the male biographers, she never bothers to specify which sexual acts she presumes to have taken place; instead the description is psychologized, laden with conjecture about what Monroe felt and why:

When Marilyn attended Uncle Joe's parties, or accompanied him to Palm Springs for the weekend, he was happy to pass her around to friends. There were plenty of men willing to take Marilyn upstairs for half an hour, but no one seemed even remotely interested in casting her in a film. [. . .] Though Marilyn did her best to play the happy girl, the party circuit was a brutal, degrading, sometimes dangerous business. At times, the men became violent. On one occasion, Marilyn found herself in a bedroom, with two holding her down while a third tried to rape her. Somehow, she managed to break free, but the incident recalled the sexual assaults she had endured as a child, when Grace [McKee] taught her to believe that somehow she had provoked the violence. Marilyn had come to these parties seeking help and attention. She had no illusions about what most of the guests expected from her and the other girls. [. . .] So on one level Marilyn believed she had brought the incident on herself. But on another level she knew better, and she was filled with rage at the men who had done this to her.[50]

Leaming accepts that Marilyn was the victim of numerous sexual assaults throughout her life, but this claim provokes Summers, for one, to outright derision: "Was Marilyn a freak case in assault statistics?"[51] Arthur Miller also strongly implied his skepticism toward the story in *Timebends*: "she might tell about being held down at a party by two of the guests in a rape attempt from which she said she had escaped, but the truth of the account was far less important than its strange remoteness from her personality."[52] This is not to imply that Summers and Miller must be right; on the contrary, it seems more likely than not that a woman on the Hollywood party circuit would have been assaulted. But that is conjecture, nothing more. The more important point is that Leaming neglects to mention the contempt with which these stories of assault have been greeted by the men who knew, or would like to have known, Marilyn. Instead of confronting the ridicule with which Marilyn's claims are greeted, Leaming ends by condescendingly "explaining" Monroe's confusion of guilt and rage, emotions she has presumed in the first place.

When she spoke about her early sexual experiences in Hollywood, Monroe was considerably more pragmatic than even Leaming suggests. Monroe is directly quoted on the subject by two different journalists who knew her, Weatherby and Jaik Rosenstein. Here is what she said to Rosenstein:

> You know that when a producer calls an actress into his office to discuss a script that isn't all he has in mind. And a part in a picture, or any kind of a little stock contract is the most important thing in the world to the girl, more than eating. She can go hungry, and she might have to sleep in her car, but she doesn't mind that a bit—if she can only get the part. I know, because I've done both, lots of times. And I've slept with producers. I'd be a liar if I said I didn't.[53]

Monroe's version highlights her own resemblance to all the other girls with similar ambitions and dealing with similar pressures. It doesn't sound especially guilty, or enraged. In Weatherby's *Conversations,* Monroe spoke a bit more psychologically of a person growing, changing her mind, and reevaluating past experiences in the light of later experience:

> Sometimes I've got such lousy taste in men. There was a whole period when I felt flattered if a man took an interest in me—any man! I believed too easily in people, and then I went on believing in them even after they disappointed me over and over again. I must have been very stupid in those days. I guess I'm capable of doing it again with some guy, only he'd have to be someone more outstanding than a heel. Not that I didn't pay for it all—all I've ever done. There were times when I'd be with one of my husbands and I'd run into one of these Hollywood heels at a party and they'd paw me cheaply in front of everybody as if they were saying, *Oh, we had her.* I guess it's the classic situation of an ex-whore, though I was never a whore in that sense. I was never kept; I always kept myself. But there was a period when I responded too much to flattery and slept around too much, thinking it would

help my career, though I always liked the guy at the time. They were always so full of self-confidence and I had none at all and they made me feel better. But you don't get self-confidence that way. You have to get it by earning respect.[54]

If we accept the premise that these two renditions more or less accurately convey Monroe's own words, what they suggest is the failure of the apocrypha to take Monroe's perfectly normal feelings into account.

She might have been using sex in part strategically, seeking professional advancement, but is it so hard to believe that she also convinced herself, at least in some cases, that these men might genuinely care about her? For stories that are so certain that Marilyn's need for love determined all her future decisions and behaviors, they are curiously unwilling to consider the possibility that Monroe might have been like the rest of us, prey to a confused mixture of infatuation, bad judgment, romantic hope and insecure longing for affirmation by an object of desire—all of which may create ruefulness when one is older and wiser. If these accounts are accurate, then Monroe's early relationships were as aspirational as they were opportunistic: just because she's a sex symbol doesn't mean she was immune to the cultural stories that affect the rest of us. The pragmatic and optimistic tenor of these two accounts is lost in the censoriousness of the biographers, all of whom apparently find it difficult to consider being sympathetic to Monroe were they to conclude that she might have engaged in the power struggles, and felt the conflicting emotions, that sexual relationships so often create.

Fairness can be as easily lost in efforts to purify or save Marilyn as in the stories that sneer at her. Insisting on Monroe's victimization, Oates denies the persistent stories that Monroe "slept her way to the top" as "false rumors" whose "cruel tenacity was an ominous sign" of malicious misogyny, ignoring the fact that Monroe admitted to having slept with producers.[55] The flawed logic that appeared in the accounts of Monroe's childhood rape recurs: just because the source of the rumor is suspect does not mean the rumor is false. The assumption that Monroe *must* have slept her way to the top is indeed (profoundly) misogynistic, but this doesn't mean that Monroe didn't engage in the sexual realpolitik of the Hollywood studio system. These writers seem to prefer a Marilyn made "safe," because victimized and powerless. This response on the part of some women to Marilyn goes at least as far back as Ayn Rand's declaration when Monroe died in August 1962 that "if ever there was a victim of society, Marilyn Monroe was that victim."[56]

Monroe was a real woman who made difficult choices; they may not all have been exemplary; they may not all have been consistent. The inability to categorize or determine her motives is not a sign of her abnormality—it is a sign of her normality. Monroe was *not* a fictional character, and thus to judge her on the basis of whether her actions were always ideal effaces an important truth about the way in which women have always had to strike difficult bargains with patriarchy, and measures her by anachronistic and rigid standards.

Moreover, the equation of morality and sexuality has been one of the prime mechanisms by which society historically has controlled women's bodies. To counteract the misogyny of the studio system, Oates and Steinem keep their Marilyn morally pure, but ironically this stratagem only maintains her in the misogynistic dichotomy of madonna/whore, a framework in which the number of sexual partners a woman has determines her moral, social, and also her economic value. Arthur Miller gets caught in the same trap in *After the Fall*, when his alter ego, Quentin, wails that "she was chewed and spat out by a long line of grinning men!" However contemptible the grinning men may be, she is the exhausted commodity. The feminist view of Steinem and Oates is not, in the end, very far from the arguably misogynist portrait by Miller. Even more ironically, Steinem and Oates are at pains to maintain the same innocence that was a key element in the false persona of childish femininity that they hold to have been foisted upon Monroe by a society of men interested only in "little girls." Most ironically of all, any apologia on the basis of the work ethic ignores that ethic's own ideological role in maintaining and justifying the monopoly capitalism that consistently exploited Monroe both financially *and* sexually throughout her life.

These writers' emphasis upon the morality of sex obscures a more tacit, but no less important, theme in these stories: the morality of

labor. The question of how hard Marilyn Monroe worked for her success—whether she *deserved* it—is crucial to every account. Did she
achieve success too easily, or even pleasurably? Did she mix commercial business with sexual pleasure in a way that transgressed the
meritocratic, Puritanical boundaries between work and play? As long
as she didn't enjoy it, writers will excuse what they see as breaking
the rules, but they will also insist that such sex was not work—
although surely doing something that one does not enjoy for money
is a good definition of work. Only within the framework of coercion
and violation can we understand her (apparent) complicity in (apparently) exploitative sexual situations: although sex in these cases is not
labor, being victimized is, and means she paid for her success.

Marilyn was only ever given such "backhanded" recognition for
her success. This was true not only figuratively, but literally: when
she did finally get discovered, most of the focus was from the rear,
watching Marilyn from behind as she walked away, and the compli-
ments she received were backhanded indeed. Her big break was
in *Love Happy,* a forgettable Marx brothers film in which she had a
brief walk-on, in which she saunters away from Groucho. She later
reported that Groucho told her she had the "prettiest ass in the business." Another frequently quoted line is reporter James Bacon's
observation that "her derriere looked like two puppies fighting under
a silk sheet"; photographer Philippe Halsman said that "with every
step her derriere seemed to wink at the viewer." Actress Constance
Bennett was, however, the most prescient: she described Marilyn as
a "broad with her future behind her," which would become all too
ironically true in the many conspiracy theories about Monroe's death
that give enemas a prominent role, as the specter of anal penetration
returns to conclude the tale.

HYSTERIA

Throughout the early years of Monroe's career, from 1949 to 1956,
there are also repeated stories of bisexuality, which primarily focus
upon Monroe's relationship with her acting coach, Natasha Lytess.
In 1948, Monroe was hired for a six-month contract by Columbia
Studios, where she met Lytess; Monroe would insist on Lytess being

her coach for the next seven years and twenty-two films, up to and including *The Seven Year Itch*, until she was replaced by Paula Strasberg.

Lytess was "Marilyn's teacher, cheerleader, psychiatrist, best friend, handmaiden, slavedriver, and whipping boy, all rolled into one," as Leaming puts it.[57] Leaming's comprehensive list doesn't include lover, but in discussing Lytess's relationship with Monroe, all of the other biographers address the persistent rumor that the two women had a sexual relationship. Guiles explains that "some of Marilyn's colleagues," whom he doesn't name, believed the coupling was sexual, but Guiles feels that if Monroe did sleep with Lytess it was because Marilyn was so abundantly, naturally sexual that she had no inhibitions. Summers quotes former maid Lena Pepitone's tell-all memoir, in which she reports that Marilyn told her she slept with Lytess to placate the older woman, and later regretted it. He adds for good measure that Skolsky (who was certainly a close friend of Monroe's) also believed the women were lovers, before censoriously quoting Monroe's psychiatrist at the end of her life as saying she was homophobic. Steinem, too, tells the Pepitone story, but explains Monroe's supposed willingness to sleep with Lytess in terms of her need for a surrogate mother.[58] For conservative Spoto as well, Lytess was surrogate mother and only aspired to be Monroe's lover: Spoto's Marilyn exploited the older woman's desire, but successfully deflected it. If she was bisexual, that is, it's only because she was so excessively sexual or because she was once again using sex opportunistically. The chance that she might have actually desired or even enjoyed sex with women is neither admitted nor discussed: biographers toy with the prospect of her bisexuality without bringing it into serious consideration. Bisexuality will only be understood as excess heterosexuality, with which her cup runneth over.

In 1976, Weatherby reports that he discussed the rumors of her bisexuality with Monroe. Her response to the rumors, according to Weatherby, was:

> I was remembering Monty Clift. People who aren't fit to open the door for him sneer at his homosexuality. What do they know about it? Labels—people love putting labels on each other. Then they

feel safe. People tried to make me into a lesbian. I laughed. No sex is wrong if there's love in it. But too often people act like it's gymnasium work, mechanical. They'd be as satisfied with a machine from a drugstore as with another human being. I sometimes felt they were trying to make me into a machine.[59]

Here Monroe displays considerably more psychological acuity than any of her major biographers, all of whom fail to pick up on the implication of this quotation: labels make people feel safe, they make the world seem predictable and controlled. But most people's desires don't fit into our neat prearranged categories.

Although her major biographers leave the possibility of Monroe's bisexuality a very open question, it has nonetheless become fact in some circles. In a scholarly article about fandom, cultural critic John Fiske uses Monroe as an example of the way in which some groups define themselves in terms of knowledge about celebrities: "the gay community, for instance, circulates the knowledge of which apparently straight stars are actually gay, and thus knew, long before the general public, for instance, that Rock Hudson was gay and Marilyn Monroe was bisexual."[60] But in the case of Marilyn, this is not knowledge, it is ideology. The need to define ourselves through sexual categories is itself already an ideological (and arbitrary) decision, as Monroe observed. This seems another example of the transformation of familiarity into truth: hear that she is bisexual often enough and it becomes fact. And it shows the way that belief becomes "knowledge": believing firmly enough that Marilyn was bisexual translates into knowing that she was.

There are some other rumored stories of bisexuality, including Brigitte Bardot's reputed claim to have had sex with Marilyn in the ladies' room at a reception for Queen Elizabeth in 1956. Some writers offer a bisexual twist on the incident that became known in the press as "The Wrong Door Raid": soon after Monroe separated from Joe DiMaggio, he and Frank Sinatra burst through the door of an apartment in which they expected to catch her in flagrante with her (male) voice coach but broke into the wrong apartment. In the bisexual variant, the secret "truth" is that they expected to find her with a woman.

The most persistent rumors apart from Lytess, however, are that Monroe's famous, public disputes with Joan Crawford were caused by a private sexual rebuff. Guiles reports in 1984 that Crawford publicly criticized Monroe because Monroe had rejected her sexually; some ancillary versions report that the two had an affair. This story has apparently been "confirmed" recently in some editions of Matthew Smith's *Victim: The Secret Tapes of Marilyn Monroe*. The South African *Sunday Times* reported that the book "lifts the lid on [Marilyn's] lesbian affair with the fading film star Joan Crawford." Its review quotes a passage from the "transcripts," in which Marilyn supposedly tells her psychiatrist (as one would):

> "Oh, yes, Crawford. We went to her house from a cocktail party, feeling no pain. We went to the bedroom and went down on each other. Crawford had a gigantic orgasm and shrieked like a maniac.
>
> "Next time I saw her she wanted another round. I told her straight out I didn't enjoy it much, doing it with a woman. After I turned her down she became spiteful."[61]

The U.K. edition is evidently censored, as it only paraphrases the story:*

> For those who have wondered about Marilyn's sexuality, another question was settled in her tapes. She described an intimate moment in some detail and how she and Joan Crawford had sex. Crawford, she said, wanted this relationship to continue, but Marilyn decidedly didn't.
> *I told her straight out I didn't much enjoy doing it with a woman. After I turned her down she became spiteful.*[62]

To my knowledge, there are no rumors about Marilyn having sex with a woman after 1956, however; it is as if the year Lytess leaves the story and Arthur Miller enters it (along with Monroe's well-documented

---

*Smith explains delicately in his preface that "some references have been omitted to preserve decorum. Had I published those portions of the tapes in question, Marilyn would have been embarrassed and, no doubt, my readers would have been embarrassed for her" (Smith, xvi).

"hysterical" desire to have a baby) bisexuality leaves the story too, and Monroe becomes firmly defined by an equally hysterical heterosexuality. Like her supposed artificiality, which can be associated with almost any aspect of her character, hysteria too will be conserved by the narrative, but floats, so to speak, from bisexuality to miscarriage to suicide. This is an appropriate symbolic journey for hysteria to take, given that its name derives from the ancient belief that women's mysterious physical disorders were caused by the womb becoming detached and subsequently floating erratically around the body, causing paralysis wherever it happened to alight. Monroe's symbolic hysteria, like her artifice, functions in exactly the same way, and her womb will be held to determine much of her behavior in later years, as we shall see. One could go so far as to characterize these as entirely "hysterical" narratives all about the suffering of the womb (which appropriately symbolizes the suffering of Marilyn-as-eternal-Woman).

As Showalter explained in *The Female Malady*: "By the end of the [nineteenth] century, 'hysterical' had become almost interchangeable with 'feminine' in literature, where it stood for all extremes of emotionality. [...] [Hysteria's] vast, unstable repertoire of emotional and physical symptoms—fits, fainting, vomiting, choking, sobbing, laughing, paralysis—and the rapid passage from one to another suggested the lability and capriciousness traditionally associated with the feminine nature."[63] All these "maladies" share simultaneous associations with sexuality, promiscuity, and with pathology, which together comprise what psychiatry used to call "nymphomania." Bisexuality seems to operate in the Marilyn apocrypha as a contemporary form of nymphomania, a mark of excessive sexuality. But biographers don't take it seriously: in a woman, episodic bisexuality is cute, even titillating.

There is a related story here, which is about discipline. Just as the question of work underwrites discussions of Monroe's prostitution, so is discipline shored against considerations of her hysteria. Hysteria is censured as immoderate, extravagant. Monroe is always understood to be undisciplined, disordered—which is not just a fault, but a reason, and one that again conforms to the Puritan work ethic. If she had just worked harder, this line of reasoning implies, she might have survived. Truman Capote, who knew Monroe, reports that acting teacher and grande dame Constance Collier associated Monroe's lack of discipline with a prediction of early death, sometime between 1950 and 1955, saying (in Capote's rendering): "Of course, Greta [Garbo] is a consummate artist, an artist of the utmost control. This beautiful child [Monroe] is without any concept of discipline or sacrifice. Somehow I don't she'll [sic] make old bones. Absurd of me to say, but somehow I feel she'll go young. I hope, I really pray, that she survives long enough to free the strange lovely talent that's wandering through her like a jailed spirit."[64] All of the stories of Monroe's "unbridled" sexuality are laden with the same foreboding that her liberation will unravel into disarray; this leitmotif disregards the ambition, hard work and perseverance that most who knew her say characterized her approach to her profession (her increasingly severe behavioral problems notwithstanding).

After a year of dedicatedly promoting Monroe's career, including paying for minor plastic surgery on her chin (and perhaps her nose, although Summers disputes this), Johnny Hyde died suddenly of a heart attack in 1950. At the funeral a grief-stricken Monroe is said by most writers to have thrown herself "hysterically" over his coffin and to have repeatedly screamed his name (Hyde's son is usually cited as the source of this story). Only Spoto declares that, "contrary to the established account," she was "the picture of dignified grief."[65] For all the other writers, she was the picture of hysteria: sobbing and shrieking in a frenzy of suffering.

According to Lytess, Monroe tried to kill herself soon afterward: Lytess said she found Monroe asleep with gelatin capsules softening in her mouth, scooped them out, and rushed Monroe to the hospital. Most biographers report this story as fact. Summers chooses to believe not only Lytess, but also what Summers refers to as Monroe's "own account" of two other early suicide attempts: "if we accept her own account of two suicide attempts before she was nineteen, this [after Hyde's death] was the third."[66] Summers is, in fact, the only biographer to claim that she told Hecht when they were working on *My Story* that she had tried to kill herself as an adolescent with gas and with sleeping pills, but that Hecht left it out of *My Story*.[67] In other words, this is not Monroe's own account at all, but Hecht's. Moreover, at other points in his story Summers dismisses Monroe's words as fantasy, hyperbole and fabrication ("we must treat what she tells us with informed skepticism"),[68] but here he decides to promote her "own account."* Spoto, however, utterly rejects Lytess's report of the 1950 suicide attempt:

> Without a drink of water, Marilyn explained, she had tried to take a single pill and had then fallen asleep while it slowly dissolved in her mouth. "Natasha often accused me of overreacting," Marilyn later told Milton Greene. "But this time she took the prize. I never went along with all that romantic stuff about following your loved one into the grave. I remember that when Johnny died I felt miserable, I felt guilty, and I had a lot of feelings to sort through—but oh, baby, I sure didn't want to die." And then she added with a radiant, grateful smile, "The fact is, he had made certain that I had nothing to die for." And much to live for, she might have added.[69]

Spoto's source for this story is the "Milton Greene papers": although he gives box and file number, he does not explain in what kind of paper (diary? letter?) this quotation is found, or who wrote it down. Marilyn? Milton Greene? If it was Greene, when did he write it down? As she said it, or many years later?

The other writers, all of whom accept the story of the attempted suicide, recount it in accents of deep foreboding, as the sign of what will come. Guiles offers a nicely tautological account that echoes his confused language about the Norma Jeane/Marilyn split: "This is

---

*Summers's citation for this assertion gives almost no detail or context, reading, in its entirety: "Suicide: *New York Post* Aug. 7, 1962" (Summers, 475). Although he disbelieves *My Story* when it reports childhood rape, he believes an incident *not* in *My Story* reporting adolescent suicide, although it would not be cited by a newspaper until two days after she died a "probable suicide."

the first recorded instance when someone close to Marilyn had to maintain a vigil until Marilyn was herself again."[70] But implicitly not the last. It is also the "first recorded instance" in which Marilyn tried to die for love, which the apocrypha confirms as the ultimate, mythical reason for her untimely death. Spoto is the only non-conspiracy-theorist who also denies that Monroe died by her own hand; his rejection of this story is thus consistent with his conclusion. It is hard to know which is the chicken, which the egg: Does Spoto have trouble believing that she killed herself in the end partly because he "knows" that she didn't try to kill herself in 1950? Or does he have trouble believing that she tried to kill herself in 1950 because he "knows" that she didn't kill herself in 1962? The internal coherence in all of these accounts is itself suspect, quite apart from the fact that they all tell different stories. Most lives are inconsistent, and many suicides do not leave a trail of breadcrumbs behind them.

As usual, Spoto is alone in his interpretation, but despite these questions about the source of the story, it is not without persuasiveness: Monroe *did* have much to look forward to, although perhaps only hindsight tells us so. Certainly Monroe's career took off in the months immediately following Hyde's death. In March 1951 she was a presenter at the Academy Awards, and she got a new, seven-year contract from Fox on May 11, 1951, which guaranteed a steady income, whether actually working on a film or not, with incremental pay raises starting at $500 per week and increasing to $3,500 per week in the seventh and final year. It was a standard studio contract, which carried the following riders: every year the studio had the right to renew or drop her contract; she could not work for another studio unless Fox loaned her out, in which case she would receive her usual salary and Fox any differential profits; she was not permitted to earn money from any other source without Fox's permission; and if she refused to accept a role she would be suspended without pay; the time of the suspension would be added to the length of the contract when she returned to work. In September 1951 she was the subject of her first full-length feature in a national magazine, *Collier's*. She had roles in three B-grade films in 1951 (*As Young As You Feel*, *Love Nest* and *Let's Make It Legal*) and another in 1952 (*We're Not Married*).

According to many ancillary accounts, and Wolfe's, Monroe embarked on her legendary affair with John F. Kennedy during this time, in 1951; the story goes that she met him on the Hollywood party circuit. But Summers, Spoto and Leaming all place the beginning of the affair with Kennedy in 1961. In 1951 Monroe did meet Arthur Miller, who was in Hollywood in hopes of a selling a screenplay; their mutual attraction was, it is agreed, immediate and powerful, but most biographers believe that they did not become sexually involved until Monroe moved to New York in 1955.

CHARACTER REFERENCES

Two major events in Monroe's life happened within days of each other in March 1952, which together catapulted her into national view. She revealed that she was the nude model in the underground calendar, and she went on her first date with Joe DiMaggio. For the three principal male biographers, the timing is a coincidence, but Barbara Leaming claims that Monroe first accepted a date with DiMaggio two days after the nude calendar story broke in order to manage the scandal, using DiMaggio as a national "character reference" while keeping her name in the papers.[71] Certainly if the timing is a coincidence it's a remarkable one, given Monroe's lack of interest in baseball before she met DiMaggio, and given the symbolic tension that would quickly develop between the notorious nude calendar model and the wife of conservative Joe DiMaggio, national sports hero. Biographers have given conflicting accounts of how the nude calendar story broke: these disputes typify the question of Monroe's power, and the way it is defined in relation to the studio system. In one version she is the vixen who wraps powerful men around her little finger, and in the other the little girl at their mercy.

The officially accepted story of the scandal was repeated without much variation from the time the story broke until Summers offered a new interpretation thirty-five years later. The long-running, standard version was that studio executives were informed by an anonymous blackmailer that rising star Marilyn Monroe was also the model for a nude calendar that was displayed in factories, garages and truck stops across the nation. It was, in other words, always a story inflected by class anxieties: the problem was not only the notorious grip that prudery had upon 1950s American culture, but also the vulgarity of being sexually exposed in such working-class venues. The received history had it that Monroe was hauled, stammering and terrified, onto the studio carpet, where she was excoriated: "What kind of woman are you?" one of the executives was supposed to have yelled. She wept and apologized, wringing her hands, and asking what to do. The studio insisted that Monroe deny that it was she; she panicked, says the story, and went to Sidney Skolsky, her gossip-columnist friend, who cannily advised her to admit the truth and throw herself upon the mercy of the American public. She did, and her international fame was secured. Class remained an important, if tacit, part of how the story was managed, because Monroe defended her nudity as a gesture of populist solidarity: "I don't want to be just for the few, I want to be for the many, the kind of people I come from. I want a man to come home after a hard day's work, look at this picture and feel inspired to say 'Wow!' "[72]

In 1985 Summers argued, however, that in truth Monroe was far from a manipulated victim, but herself the canny stage-manager of her own performance, who arranged to have herself interviewed and then further arranged to have the reporter "tipped off" to ask her about the nude calendar. Monroe played on the female reporter's sympathies, and a compassionate account appeared in the national papers the next day. In 1992, Brown and Barham's *Marilyn: The Last Take* attributes the same story of manipulation of the press to the person they consider the "architect" of Monroe's career, Harry Brand, head of publicity at Fox. Finally, Spoto returns to a portrait of Marilyn in charge of her own destiny, but less manipulative than Summers's Marilyn, at once more heroic and more pragmatic: although terrified when the story breaks, only she has the courage and common sense to realize that the truth is her best defense.

All of these stories revolve once again around the question of whether Monroe was author of her own fate or a studio puppet, and these doubts reflect the central anxiety in Marilyn's story: Was she natural or manufactured? Scripted or real? The nude calendar story helps clarify the stakes of such a question: a woman's sexual commodification carries with it a host of associated anxieties about power and control, cheapness and ready availability versus the unique, inaccessible woman or object. It also shows that nudity is a barometer of Marilyn's power: when she posed nude her threatening power was affirmed, a double-edged power that prompts writers like Mailer to shame Monroe back into submission (as submissiveness). The biographies respond on the whole by vitiating her power: she is trembling target of studio head wrath; passive beneficiary of the counsel offered by older, wiser, male heads; or a coy manipulator who exploits female sympathies.

"SHE BELONGED TO ALL MEN"

In essence, the anxieties about Marilyn Monroe's body all relate to the problem of ownership. Who owned Marilyn Monroe's body, who controlled it, who gained access to it? Who possessed her? It is no accident that to "have" or "possess" a woman is a euphemism for having sex with her (and that it is *not* a euphemism for having sex with a man). Those writing about Marilyn always want to know who owns her, and they insist that she can be owned. "The Most Advertised Girl in the World" in 1945 became the first centerfold of *Playboy* in 1953; now her image adorns hundreds of millions of commodities. The question is not just whether Marilyn was literally for sale, as well as figuratively; it is whether she could be *had*. Postulating self-possession, as self-respect, is an alien concept to the Marilyn myth.

Zolotow quotes Norman Mailer declaring that he did not think Monroe should be married because "she belonged to all men," implying that she was a shared cultural commodity, that she was, as Elton John knew, "our Marilyn Monroe."[73] But such a statement also means that she belongs to no man, if ownership, by definition, is exclusive. More important, it implies that she belongs to—or could belong to—every man, like Arthur Miller's "long line of grinning men." When photographer Bert Stern first met Monroe, he wrote:

> Sometimes when something is perfect in every detail, it's not beautiful anymore. It's impressive, it's even slightly intimidating, but you find yourself thinking, "Who could possess that?" Marilyn

was *possessable*. Who cared if her lips weren't perfect? They were made for kissing.[74]

Condescension and belittlement are linked to ownership: to own is to master, whereas perfection is intimidating and unpossessable. Commodification and commercialism are understood, conversely, not only as prostitution, but as vulgar and crass.

Feminist film theorist Mary Ann Doane has persuasively argued that the figure of the prostitute does not merely commodify the human body: she humanizes the commodity, which is, Doane argues,

> a way of selling the commodity form of culture itself. In the pros-
> titute, sexuality and exchange value coincide most explicitly. But
> she is not an isolated case—to be confined within the walls of the
> bordello. One could plausibly argue that the prostitute in the late
> nineteenth and early twentieth centuries [. . .] exemplifies or
> embodies what becomes *the* task of characterization in the twen-
> tieth century—particularly in the cinema—the humanization of
> the commodity. [. . .] The process of characterization now
> endows the commodity with speech, with emotions, with a moral
> psychology.[75]

Doane goes on to suggest that psychobiography, with its investment in the revelation of character, accelerates and augments this process. Making character a commodity, sex the secret, and prostitution the answer creates an equivalency among work, sex and character. All of this is about value: What is Marilyn Monroe really *worth*?

Implicated in all of these interpretations, a symptom of our anxi-eties about sex and work, Monroe herself was always trying to be obtainable without being cheap, consumable without being used up. In her last interview, Monroe acknowledged that her audience was uncertain "if [she] were real," an uncertainty that she related both to commodification and to evaluation: "Sometimes it makes you a little bit sad because you'd like to meet somebody kind of on face value . . . I don't look at myself as a commodity, but I'm sure a lot of people have." At the end of this interview, Marilyn Monroe ran after

Richard Meryman as he was leaving and said: "Please don't make me a joke." She knew better than anyone the double binds in which she was caught. Made up in the minds of others, she was blamed for being a fiction; derogated as cheap, she was also accused of overrating herself: "People you run into feel that, well, who is she—who does she think she is, Marilyn Monroe?"

The wedding of Marilyn Monroe and Joe DiMaggio, January 14, 1954.

Marilyn Monroe and Arthur Miller in New York City, 1956. PHOTOGRAPH BY SAM SHAW.

5

"FEMALE TROUBLE," 1952–1961

"I intend to remain in pictures," Marilyn told
reporters [when she married DiMaggio]. "But I'm
looking forward to being a housewife, too."

—FRED LAWRENCE GUILES,
Norma Jeane: The Life and Death of Marilyn Monroe

"Movies are my business," she said, "but Arthur is
my life. Wherever he is, I want to be. When we're
in New York Arthur is the boss."

—ANTHONY SUMMERS,
Goddess: The Secret Lives of Marilyn Monroe

Fred Lawrence Guiles opens his revised *Norma Jeane: The Life and Death of Marilyn Monroe* with a description of the house Marilyn Monroe bought in February 1962, six months before she died. She bought it, says Guiles, because she failed to conceive a child with Arthur Miller, and had just learned that he and his new wife, Inge Morath, were expecting a baby. As a consequence, she retreated to a "womblike environment," which Guiles calls "an extension of herself"—and which, he adds, was empty, unfurnished, cramped, with no place to conceal anything, and on a dead end.[1]

Miller told Guiles in an interview that he did not consider Inge's pregnancy a motive for Monroe's suicide because Monroe already knew that there "wasn't anything wrong" with Miller that had kept the couple from conceiving. The fact that she died a full six months after learning of the pregnancy would seem a more compelling reason to discount it as a motive for her alleged suicide, but Guiles nonetheless concludes that Monroe was in despair because "she knew that *she* was the reason they never had any children together. Inge Miller was the whole woman she could never be."[2]

Despite the fact that Marilyn Monroe was, and remains, one of the biggest and most popular movie stars of all time, the stories about her years of stardom focus not upon professional success, but upon personal failure. Both Monroe's marriages, and her career, will be undermined by her failure to be a "whole woman." In particular, as Guiles's portrait demonstrates, her defects will continually be associated (whether directly or indirectly) with sexual or gynecological problems. Steinem concludes that Monroe's alleged sexual problems demonstrate her "incompleteness":

> [Psychiatrist] Dr. Greenson's notes conclude that Marilyn "found it difficult to sustain a series of orgasms with the same individual." That incompleteness could have been the reason why Greenson believed that Marilyn feared and yet was drawn into "situations with homosexual coloring." Perhaps. But by her own testimony, she didn't find sexual satisfaction in affairs with either men or women.[3]

Steinem's equation of orgasm with completeness returns sexuality to the center of Monroe's identity; according to Guiles the partial woman moves into an unfinished house, a symbolic womb, to compensate for the failures of her real womb, which was as empty as the house, and in which she would die.

And all of this happens on the first page of Guiles's biography. None of the major biographies begins with Marilyn Monroe triumphing: they start with death, madness, childlessness. Peter Brown and Patte Barham similarly open *Marilyn: The Last Take* with an account of Monroe "fleeing" to this suburban house that Guiles finds so deficient, but for Brown and Barham she is in flight to domesticity from her professional failure, her fear "of the camera, of the front office, of her acting coaches, and of her directors."[4] Because of these fears, and her long battles with the studio, Brown and Barham explain, "Norma Jean Baker was fully prepared to 'murder Marilyn

Monroe.' [. . .] Monroe no longer wanted to be a movie star at Twentieth Century-Fox."⁵ Their reason? "If Twentieth Century-Fox had once been a shabby surrogate family for Monroe, it was now the hated authority figure, resented by the rebellious child within her." If not mother manquée, then she will once again be Norma Jean(e), lost murderous child. Either way, her "truths" will always be located in the domestic sphere of sexuality and family, rather than on the public stage because that is just an image.

This chapter is about the relationship between Monroe's career and her marriages, during the years of her greatest stardom, 1952 to 1961. Monroe's courtships with two men who were symbolic in their own right coincided exactly with her years of success: she began dating DiMaggio in 1952, the year she became an indisputable star, and divorced Miller at the beginning of 1961, the year that whispers became open discussion of a star "on the wane," and after she had finished her last completed film. For all that she is sex symbol par excellence, and for all these stories' insistence upon the threatening and/or liberating nature of her sexual persona, it remains the case that for most of her career, Marilyn's sexuality was also contained within the safe domesticity of marriage to equally symbolic men. The literalism, and determinism, of the Marilyn myth means that her problems will be understood to be individual and aberrant, but in fact the conflict Monroe faced between career and marriage is another of the many ways in which Marilyn reflects the larger cultural dilemma of postwar femininity. Monroe's spectacular failure to have it all becomes at once lament and cautionary tale.

Although the effect that her marriages had on her career, and that her career had on her marriages, has been cataloged in detailed individual anecdotes, what gets left out is the way in which the larger arcs of her marriages and her career coincided: "as her marriage [to DiMaggio] touched bottom," writes Guiles, "Marilyn's romance with the world was about to peak."⁶ Each stage of their relationship was not merely recorded in the media; it coincided with a pivotal moment in her career. Marilyn's story becomes even more laden with mythical overtones as her feminine "conflict" between mind and body first encounters male body in DiMaggio and then masculine mind in

Miller: as Mailer writes of the Monroe-Miller union, "the Great American Brain is marrying the Great American Body."[7] The tension between her marriages and her career centers on the question of where a woman belongs, and how her power will be construed—and contained.

WORKING WIFE

After the nude calendar scandal in 1952, it became clear to Darryl Zanuck that Monroe was a "property" worth developing. He assigned her to the role of Rose Loomis, a wife conspiring with her lover to murder her shell-shocked husband, in *Niagara*. The film garnered a great deal of publicity for a portrayal of female sexuality that was considered quite threateningly explicit (and explicitly threatening), despite the fact that the femme fatale would meet poetic justice and be killed by the very husband whose death she was plotting. Monroe was dating DiMaggio throughout the filming, and her performance in the film continues to elicit condemnations of vulgar exhibitionism and self-exploitation from her biographers, reproaches that seem markedly similar to the attitudes famously held by DiMaggio, who resented Monroe's willingness to capitalize on her sexuality.

The ambivalence that Monroe's allure has always provoked, not just during her lifetime but in the biographical retellings, is captured well in the stories about one of her appearances to publicize *Niagara*, at an awards ceremony given by *Photoplay* magazine in 1952, at which she appeared in a now-famous gold lamé dress into which she reputedly had to be sewn. Monroe arrived an hour late, drunk in some accounts; her dress hobbled her, forcing her to take little mincing steps through the room to her table. Her appearance prompted comedian Jerry Lewis to leap onto a table on all fours and begin pawing it. Rollyson's account, in which his tone swings unstably between defense and reproof of Monroe's show-stopping appearance, is representative of the tone biographers take toward Monroe's "displays" of sexuality:

Publicity for *Niagara* demanded that its female star engage in crude exploitation of her sexuality, and Monroe obliged by appear-

ing at public gatherings in skin tight costumes from her movie wardrobe. DiMaggio refused to accompany her on such occasions and bitterly protested the show she was making of herself. Hollywood columnists played up her exhibitionism, and soon newspapers and fan magazines were receiving letters criticizing her vulgar behavior. Monroe created such a sensation at a *Photoplay* Awards dinner that Joan Crawford publicly condemned her for conduct unbecoming an actress and a lady.[8]

Rollyson seems to share DiMaggio's and Crawford's qualms that Monroe was lowering herself by indulging in such "vulgar behavior." (Only Spoto mentions that Crawford's high-minded shock sits uneasily with her own alleged start as a naked dancer in speakeasies; Guiles claims that it was spite, because she had gotten drunk and made a pass at Monroe, and been rejected.)[9] Summers offers DiMaggio's reaction as the only standard by which to judge Monroe, as if he were an interpretive touchstone. DiMaggio, writes Summers, "was not amused by Marilyn's flaunting of her body. She said she was trying to moderate her style, but the exhibitionist in her was stronger [. . .] she wore a ludicrous dress cut almost to the navel. DiMaggio was said to be hurt and embarrassed."[10] Leaming, one of the writers who says Monroe was drunk, concludes that her appearance showed she was "hell-bent on self-destruction"—rather than on the more obvious goal of self-promotion.[11] From Guiles in 1969 to Leaming in 1998, both male and female commentators are united in their contempt for this woman's "vulgar" display of sexuality, a sexuality for which they elsewhere claim to love her. And Monroe's commercial sexual display was always denounced as much on the grounds that it was low-class, as that it was immoral. If the last fifty years are anything to go by, we can look forward to Marilyn being judged by Victorian standards of female decorum until the end of time: cultural attitudes to women's sexuality may have evolved, but the apocryphal Marilyn has been fossilized.

When Crawford attacked Marilyn's "vulgarity" in the press, Monroe offered interviews and wrote in her own defense to the newspapers, some of which Rollyson quotes: "besides adopting her familiar guise of injured innocence," he says, Monroe also explained the decisions behind her characterization of Rose Loomis in terms of her profession of acting, demonstrating a precision and thoughtfulness about her performance that maintained the distance between the performer and the role: "the uninhibited deportment in the motel room and the walk seemed normal facets of such a character's portrayal. I honestly believe such a girl would behave in that manner."[12]

In fact, Monroe justified her behavior in several ways, and this episode is also representative of her tactics. She would defend her performances on the grounds of acting, but she also used humor consistently as a shield against criticism. More flippantly, she is said to have remarked about the fuss over the gold lamé dress: "You would think all the other women kept their bodies in vaults." Spoto and Leaming both quote from another of Monroe's rebuttals, in which she appealed to sentiment: she told Skolsky that she was hurt by Crawford particularly because she had always admired Crawford for taking in "motherless" orphans like herself. Guiles calls it a cynical, "hypocritical" story that probably arose from rumors already in circulation about Crawford's being a bad mother.[13] If it was a barbed rejoinder, however, we might admire her spirit instead of deploring her cynicism. "With that response," Leaming concludes, "Marilyn did her best to repair some of the damage she herself had done" at the awards (when, Leaming comments severely, "the laughter she provoked was that of a group of men smoking cigars as they watched a dirty movie"). Spoto, always more sympathetic than most, quotes her director in *Niagara*, Henry Hathaway, as saying that Monroe was

> marvelous to work with, very easy to direct and terrifically ambitious to do better. And *bright,* really bright. She may not have had an education, but she was just naturally bright. But always being trampled on by bums. I don't think anyone ever treated her on her own level. To most men she was something that they were a little bit ashamed of—even Joe DiMaggio.[14]

It was during the filming of *Niagara* in 1952 that one of the most controversial stories in the Monroe apocrypha is alleged to have taken place. In 1975 Robert Slatzer published *The Life and Curious Death of Marilyn Monroe,* in which he claimed to have been married for three days to Monroe in October 1952. Biographers have been divided over the claim: Guiles and Leaming ignore it, Summers and Wolfe accept it, and Spoto disputes it. In *Goddess,* Summers treats Slatzer as a key witness, explaining that although Slatzer's claim had initially "aroused skepticism," his story "remained consistent through-out a series of intensive interviews, and a number of compelling wit-nesses corroborate the closeness of his relationship with Marilyn."[15] The "compelling witnesses" Summers names as corroboration prove to be rather minor figures in Marilyn Monroe's life, however, includ-ing Slatzer's own dentist. Summers uses Slatzer's reminiscences as key testimony about Monroe's experiences, especially the controver-sies about her relationship with Robert Kennedy and her death. In 1986, Rollyson too would accept the story of Slatzer, arguing that Monroe used the marriage as a "dress rehearsal" for a wedding with DiMaggio that she both desired and feared. "Whatever her motiva-tions in pursuing Slatzer," Rollyson concludes, "Monroe's behavior reflects a divided and confused mind bordering on an hysteria that left her susceptible to engaging in conflicting and contradictory actions."[16] Apparently it is easier for Rollyson to believe that Monroe was confused, hysterical and unstable, than that Slatzer might be lying for profit.

Certainly Spoto excoriates Slatzer as a witness in 1993; in an enraged pages-long footnote and then in an afterword entitled "The Great Deception," Spoto says Slatzer was a "deranged" fan who met Marilyn Monroe once at Niagara Falls and parlayed posed snapshots and "importuned autographs" into a cottage industry of conspiracy theory for commercial gain. Spoto protests:

> There is no convincing evidence that Marilyn Monroe and Robert Slatzer ever met again, and there are neither letters, additional photos, nor any documentation of a relationship between them [. . .] not one of Marilyn's friends, relatives, business associates, colleagues, spouses or lovers could ever recall meeting him (much less Marilyn ever mentioning him) [. . .] not one of her intimates ever heard of Robert Slatzer during her lifetime or after her death.[17]

Most damningly, Spoto cites a canceled check written by Monroe in Los Angeles on the day that Slatzer claims to have been marrying her in Mexico. But Spoto also seems to have omitted—or missed—a few facts. Slatzer's book opens with a testimonial by Monroe's longtime friend and makeup artist Whitey Snyder, which affirms the friendship, if not the marriage.[18] In addition, George Carpozi, Jr.'s biography of Marilyn, published in 1961, before Monroe died, calls Slatzer an "old friend" of Monroe's (Carpozi also calls him "the noted literary critic from Columbus, Ohio") with whom she became reacquainted on the set of *Niagara* and remained close friends;[19] Spoto never refers to this independent corroboration. Quoting from Slatzer early in his book, Wolfe observes in a footnote that "Spoto accused Slatzer of being merely a fan who once met Marilyn during the filming of *Niagara*. However, evidence and statements made by numerous individuals who knew Slatzer and Marilyn during the decades of their friendship clearly establish their enduring relationship."[20] But the note ends there, Wolfe never identifying these "numerous individuals."

Slatzer is a crucial witness because a great many of the stories about Robert F. Kennedy hinge on his claims to have known Monroe well. Most of the conspiracy theories quote Slatzer at length, often opening with an effusive acknowledgment of his assistance in sharing the "Slatzer Archives"; the unversed reader will no doubt take his relationship with Monroe at face value. The latest Monroe biography, Smith's *Victim: The Secret Tapes of Marilyn Monroe*, opens with a Slatzer preface and relies heavily upon him; by no coincidence, Smith believes that Monroe was murdered. Slatzer's presence or absence in a Marilyn life indicates from the outset the shape that the story will take. In particular, whither Robert Slatzer goes in the Monroe apocrypha, so goes Robert F. Kennedy.

STAGE FRIGHT

During these same years Monroe began to develop a reputation for being difficult on film sets. She would report to work hours late, or not at all; when she did appear on set she would not know her lines, or burst into tears before or after takes; there are reports of her vomiting before going on set. She always demanded scores of retakes because she could "do it better"; although commentators differ as to the source of these problems, the three most commonly cited causes are some combination of stage fright, perfectionism and pills. Guiles alone dismisses all of the psychological reasons as "beside the point" and makes her difficulties instinctive: "Marilyn moved through her day running on some interior clock quite different from everyone else's. Insist that she alter it and she might scoot away, not to be seen again."[21] But for the most part, biographers agree that she felt a tremendous pressure to succeed, and was a marked perfectionist. There is very little argument about this: Summers says that she was professional and hardworking at the beginning of her career, and only began to behave provokingly later, when the combined pressures of drugs, trying to escape the confines of being a sex symbol, and others' exploitation of her made her terrified to appear; most other writers say that she was always afraid. Costars such as Richard Widmark, who made *Don't Bother to Knock* with Monroe in 1951, and Lauren Bacall, who was in *How to Marry a Millionaire* in 1953, tell myriad stories of Monroe failing to emerge from her dressing room. Bacall said: "She was always late, but I think it was in terror. She couldn't face doing what she was called upon to do; she couldn't cope."[22] Speaking of the filming of *Gentlemen Prefer Blondes* in the same year, Jane Russell said: "She would come in way before me, and she'd have rehearsed. She'd be all ready, but too nervous to go out on set. So I'd arrange with Whitey that when it was time to go I'd come and get her, and we'd walk out there together."[23] Leaming, on the other hand, says that Monroe was never able to remember her lines, and had been chronically unprepared from the start of her career.

Biographers locate the beginnings of Monroe's drug use during the same years. Drugs circulated freely not only in Hollywood, where studios by all accounts handed them out, but also in New York, where Benzedrine in particular was enjoying immense popularity with many writers, artists and musicians. Milton Greene, Monroe's partner for three years, was also reputedly addicted to pills, and several stories identify him as one of Monroe's chief procurers. According to Spoto, Greene not only shared Marilyn's liking for barbiturates, but was himself sampling amphetamines and even taking Dilantin, an antiepileptic medication popularly credited with "increasing the brain's electrical impulses," to counteract the effect of barbiturates. Spoto leaves the speed-taking to Milton, insisting (unconvincingly, given the preponderance of assertions to the contrary) that Marilyn "never took amphetamines, marijuana, or intravenous drugs." Summers, on the other hand, has Milton accusing Marilyn of having used Dexamyl, "the fashionable 'upper' of the period," long before they met.[24]

Monroe certainly suffered from chronic, debilitating insomnia through much of her adult life; she was often not only exhausted as a consequence, but anxious about appearing fatigued, especially as she grew older. While some writers argue over which specific drugs Marilyn was taking at any given time, the significance—and gravity—of her chemical addictions is beyond question. By the time of the production of *The Misfits,* in the summer of 1960, there is little reason to doubt the stories that many days Marilyn could not be roused from her barbiturate stupor; often Whitey Snyder would make her up while she was still unconscious. Her drug-taking was recklessly uncontrolled, and a habit of many years' standing. Summers quotes a woman who worked with Monroe at Fox in the early fifties: "she used to come to the dressing room and put down a plastic bag; and you never saw so many pills in one bag. There would be uppers, downers, vitamins and God knows what."[25] Spoto places the beginning of Monroe's drug-taking earliest, saying that Skolsky first gave her sleeping pills in 1950, but that they did not begin to affect her behavior professionally until *Show Business* in 1954. Rollyson concurs, saying that reports of Monroe's "excessive drinking, addiction to sleeping pills and amphetamines, and her need to consult a psychiatrist first surfaced" during the filming of *Show Business,* although he is careful to acknowledge that not all of the rumors are verifiable.[26] While acknowledging that Amy Greene said Marilyn was "a baby when she started taking pills, just seventeen or eighteen," Summers says her serious drug use probably began under the auspices of her friendship with Charlie Chaplin, Jr., and Eddie Robinson, Jr., in 1953.[27] In Truman Capote's reminiscence, she was habitually popping pills by 1955. Guiles doesn't mention them until 1956; Leaming only discusses them in the context of suicide attempts and overdoses, never mentioning her ongoing use of sleeping pills and uppers. Neither fixes a starting point, but simply observes that Monroe was taking drugs. Wolfe similarly explains that, like many in Hollywood and in the New York theater world, she had begun relying upon barbiturates and amphetamines to get her through the day "early in her career," but he argues that it was only with her marriage to Miller and subsequent unhappiness with his coldness, indifference and disapproval that her "slide into drug dependency became a life-threatening problem."[28]

In 1953, while still dating Joe DiMaggio, Monroe became a superstar through the creation of two of her most iconic roles: Lorelei Lee in *Gentlemen Prefer Blondes* and Pola Debevoise in *How to Marry a Millionaire;* both films were enormous critical and commercial successes, and she played gold diggers in both. Although the films did very well, Monroe was already growing frustrated at the limitations of the image she was creating, and beginning to balk at the roles Fox was assigning her. Spoto quotes her as saying later:

> I had to get out, I just had to. The danger was, I began to believe this was all I could do—all I was—all any woman was. Natasha and everybody else was talking about how convincing, how much of me must have been in this role [Lorelei Lee], or how much of the role was in me. I knew there was more I could do, and more that I was. Nobody was listening to me.[29]

Whether Monroe was motivated by money, power, or the need for respect as she began her long battle with 20th Century-Fox for control over her career becomes an important question at this point. When shooting finished on *The River of No Return,* she refused to make her next assigned film, *The Girl in Pink Tights.* "Neither Joe nor Marilyn liked the script," writes Wolfe, as "Marilyn thought her role stupid and ill-motivated, and Joe thought her part risqué,"[30] but Spoto says that the role itself was only "one of the last several straws in the burden of Marilyn's resentment against Fox," adding that she was "not mollified" to learn that her costar, Frank Sinatra, was contracted at $5,000 a week, four times her salary of $1,250 a week.[31] Leaming argues that money was not initially important to Monroe, and that she feared being suspended by the studio because "constantly being passed from one foster home to another had taught her to dread being cast out and abandoned"—rather than because she didn't want to jeopardize her newfound enormous professional success.[32] In Leaming's version it is DiMaggio who teaches her that "money and respect might be linked. For Joe, money was a sign of respect. [. . .] It was only a matter of time before Marilyn—vulnerable as she was to Joe's approval—began to see things Joe's way."[33] Monroe's value always registers economically, but here her triviality is associated less with cheapness than with professional incompetence: although she is willing to prostitute herself, she is too stupid to realize that money relates to power.

Instead of reporting to the set of *Pink Tights,* Marilyn married DiMaggio, on January 14, 1954, in a private ceremony in San Francisco. As a "wedding present," Fox lifted her suspension and asked her to return to work. She chose rather to go with DiMaggio on a baseball tour to Japan. While there she was invited to perform for the American GIs stationed in Korea. Under the auspices of the USO she reportedly entertained some sixty to seventy thousand men over the next four days, singing songs from her films and cracking jokes. The performances were an enormous success; Monroe often referred later to that experience as the happiest of her life, adding fuel to the fire of interpreters like Summers, who are convinced she was nothing but an "exhibitionist": "film of the concerts shows a Marilyn high on her own gyrations, visibly reveling in the excitement of a uniformed multitude."[34]

Monroe resolved the dispute with Fox through compromise: she agreed to make an Irving Berlin musical, *There's No Business Like Show Business,* in exchange for the starring role in the film adaptation of George Axelrod's stage hit *The Seven Year Itch.*

THE SEVEN YEAR ITCH

In 1954, Marilyn Monroe played "The Girl" in *The Seven Year Itch,* probably her most iconic role, and certainly the source of her most famous photographs, in which she stands on a subway grating in a white dress, displaying her ostensible pleasure in her own body for the watching crowds. The famous skirt-blowing scene was shot in New York in September 1954, in a publicity stunt that thousands gathered to see, including DiMaggio, enraged at what he considered his wife's indecent exhibition. Guiles declares that within "hours after the famous scene was shot," "the marriage was over."[35]

Most biographies report stories of an altercation ("shouts and screams," according to Spoto) between Monroe and DiMaggio that night, from which they conclude that he beat her up.[36] Summers says that "the cameraman on *Itch*, Milton Krasner, heard shouts of anger through the wall. Though one must ever be alert for fantasizing on Marilyn's part, the accounts that follow are hard to dismiss."[37] Summers seems to give it his best effort, though: How could Marilyn's fantasizing be responsible for the shouts of anger heard by another hotel guest through the adjoining wall? He remarks elsewhere that witnesses saw her a few weeks earlier with a black-and-blue arm, which she explained by saying she had "bitten herself in her sleep," and adds that later "she would claim that DiMaggio had beaten her," a turn of phrase which certainly suggests doubt on Summers's part.[38] Guiles and Spoto both believe that the relationship with DiMaggio was always a violent one; when Monroe arrived at the airport en route to Tokyo on their honeymoon, she had a broken thumb, and Spoto, for one, implies clearly that DiMaggio was the cause: "the union had a dark side. Signs of violence would surface with alarming frequency during the next eight months."[39] Guiles names two "witnesses to DiMaggio's violence around Marilyn," one of whom describes him "slapping her around," and the other of whom says he was "vicious."[40] Having apparently established DiMaggio's violence, Guiles then extenuates it in a footnote, explaining that "there is no evidence Marilyn was ever really injured in a fight with DiMaggio," and attributing her fear of "any suggestion of violence" to a violent foster home—as if only a woman traumatized as a child fears being beaten up by her husband. Nonetheless, the stories remain unproven: Leaming acknowledges in 1998 that "only DiMaggio knows" whether he had beaten Marilyn. These tales of DiMaggio's violence do also carry a symbolic charge, however, given that the Monroe-DiMaggio union represented a meeting of bodies, rather than of minds; the question of DiMaggio's alleged beatings manifests in very real terms the struggle for power—sexual, economic, domestic—over Monroe's body that so characterizes the apocrypha.

In October 1954, Marilyn Monroe separated from Joe DiMaggio. Most versions represent her as genuinely distressed at the end of her marriage, but Leaming describes Marilyn stage-managing and acting her way through the press conference in which she announced their divorce: "She had publicly humiliated him in New York; his upset over the skirt-blowing scene had been widely reported. America's sympathies were likely to be with Joe. [. . . Therefore] she must appear to be as devastated as Joe. There was to be no trace of her steely determination to get rid of him."[41] For Guiles, on the other hand, the "true heartbreak of the situation" was that "for the first time, Marilyn had attempted to summon up the passions and concerns of an ordinary, loving woman, and her efforts had ended in mutual frustration and, finally, failure."[42] Either way, although both these biographers believe that DiMaggio beat Monroe, the failure of the marriage becomes her fault. Summers reports that Monroe had a "more immediate reason for weeping," however: as she got into the car after the press conference, she was handed an envelope by someone in the crowd. Inside was the word *whore,* written in "fecal matter," as Summers's source delicately puts it.[43]

DiMaggio's jealousy of Monroe is usually construed as sexual jealousy, but in Marilyn's case this overlaps with questions of professionalism. It isn't simply that DiMaggio worried about Monroe's marital fidelity, although most accounts do stress his possessiveness. In particular there is the much-recycled incident that became known as "The Wrong Door Raid," in which DiMaggio enlisted his friend Frank Sinatra's assistance in catching Monroe in bed with another man—usually named as her voice coach, Hal Schaefer—after the separation, and burst into the wrong apartment (a variation of this story, discussed in chapter four, holds that they really expected to find Monroe in bed with a woman). But apart from DiMaggio's quite public displays of sexual jealousy (Sinatra had to appear in court; the story made headlines and humiliated both men), DiMaggio seemed to resent even more that sexuality was Marilyn's job, that what was conventionally private, and thus "his" once he married her, she was willing to make public, and to sell. Monroe wrote about the reason for their split, apparently in a letter in Milton Greene's papers, from which Spoto quotes:

> He didn't like the actors kissing me, and he didn't like my costumes. He didn't like anything about my movies, and he hated all my clothes. When I told him I had to dress the way I did, that it was part of my job, he said I should quit that job. But who did he think he was marrying when he was marrying me?[44]

Monroe herself is blurring the boundaries, first explaining that being a sex symbol is just her job, but then also claiming that job as her "self." But more than one writer adds that DiMaggio seemed jealous of another aspect of her career, her popularity per se: they all report an anecdote in which Marilyn returned from entertaining the troops in a glow, telling DiMaggio that he'd never heard anything like the cheering from seventy thousand fans. To which the baseball star is supposed to have replied: "Yes I have," and walked away.

There is another explanation for the end of their marriage, which is that DiMaggio spent most of his days sitting in front of the television and hardly ever spoke to her: "filled with resentment, he'd retreat behind a wall of silence. Sometimes he didn't utter a word to Marilyn for days at a time. [. . .] On the rare occasions when the couple dined out, they ate in grim silence."[45] This hostile silence is the flip side of his famous refusal after Monroe's death to speak of her at all: he was the only person intimately connected with Marilyn who neither spoke of her publicly nor profited from their relationship after her death.

"WILL ACTING SPOIL MARILYN MONROE?"

In December 1954, Monroe bought a plane ticket under the name "Zelda Zonk" and abruptly abandoned Hollywood for New York. She had hatched a plan with photographer Milton Greene, who had ambitions to become a producer: he promised her more creative control and more money if she set up her own production company with him. So she left Fox, where she felt unappreciated, and Los Angeles, which according to Truman Capote she described as "one big varicose vein," and moved in with Greene and his wife, Amy, in Connecticut. Soon she had installed herself in an apartment in New York, as well, and would spend 1955 fighting 20th Century-Fox to break or renegotiate her contract, setting up her production company, and studying the Method at the Actors Studio in New York. It was a year of striving for self-improvement, of fierce battles for power and legitimacy. "In 1955," writes Spoto, "she set herself several tasks—producer, acting student, analyst—that suggested her desire to try a very different persona than 'Marilyn Monroe', whom she all but abandoned that year."[46] The business side of her relations with Fox and with Greene are the focus of much of Leaming's research; she is extremely persuasive about the miscalculations and misjudgments made by Greene and Monroe because of inexperience and competing interests in Monroe's profitability, problems that would result in the company's effective dissolution after only two years. It was during 1955 as well that Monroe encountered Arthur Miller again, and their affair began in earnest. According to Spoto, Marilyn also had an affair with Milton Greene over 1954 and 1955, although this was disputed by his wife, Amy; none of the other principal biographers concurs.[47]

When it became known that Monroe had joined the Actors Studio, she was attacked in the press for what was considered her ridiculous pretension. Given that until that point she had been castigated for being a bad actress, this seems a little unfair. Journalist Pete Martin conducted a series of interviews with Monroe during this year for the *Saturday Evening Post,* interviews he would then publish in book form under the title *Will Acting Spoil Marilyn Monroe?* That question says it all: no one, including perhaps Monroe herself, believed that she was acting already. As Diana Trilling asked when Marilyn died: "How mean-spirited can we be, to have denied her whatever might have added to her confidence that she was really a solid person and not just an uninhabited body?"[48] It wasn't just mean-spiritedness, but also a need to believe that she was what she appeared to be: not a deceptive actress, but a "natural" self, not a mind, but a body, not an active person, but a passive receptacle. Her role as The Girl affirmed a cultural fantasy; her efforts to become someone else not only undermined it, but suggested that it was insufficient, openly challenged what Trilling aptly identified as "the prized illusion that enough sexual possibility is enough everything."

This resentment was displayed by playwright George Axelrod, who graciously followed up the success of Monroe's performance in the film version of his play *The Seven Year Itch* by lampooning her in *Will Success Spoil Rock Hunter?*, which starred Marilyn-imitator Jayne Mansfield and satirized the idea of a screen goddess named Rita Marlowe who tries to form her own production company. (Monroe attended a performance, and understandably is not held to have found it funny, apparently telling Axelrod only: "I saw your play.")[49] Like most satires, Axelrod's play was exerting social control, using mockery and humiliation to punish Monroe's transgression in taking herself too seriously, her rebellion against the comedy of her stereotype. Marilyn was trying to emerge from the double bind of being ridiculed for the sexuality her audience claimed to love—"Everyone's just laughing at me. I hate it. Big breasts, big ass, big deal. Can't I be anything else?"—and the response was to laugh even harder. Accused of pretension, Monroe responded with one of her trademark self-deprecating quips: "They've said I want to direct pictures. I couldn't direct traffic."

Despite the country's snickering, Monroe's stratagem worked: Fox capitulated, and agreed to a new contract that guaranteed her script and director approval, and $100,000 per film; it also allowed her to make films with her own production company, the first of which would be *The Prince and the Showgirl.* On March 12, 1956, she legally changed her name to Marilyn Monroe—and according to many had been instrumental in breaking the back of the Hollywood studio system.

HEAD GAMES

As Monroe began studying at the Actors Studio, she developed a close relationship with its then director, Lee Strasberg, and his wife, Paula; the Strasbergs are understood to have become another set of surrogate parents, offering Marilyn not only affirmation of her talent, but the dignity of being a "serious" actress. She also hired Paula Strasberg as an acting coach and insisted upon bringing her onto the set of all the films she made after 1956. Strasberg provided emotional support, but was also extremely well paid (she reportedly made $50,000 for her services on the set of *Some Like It Hot* in 1958); writers argue over whether she was a sycophantic, self-serving charlatan, or a well-meaning woman trapped between a diva's vanity and insecurity and a director's resentment at being undermined. In her review of Leaming's biography, Molly Haskell characterized Strasberg and Natasha Lytess as "female monsters" who formed "a grotesque parody of a woman's support group";[50] but John Huston reportedly said that Paula Strasberg might have been holding the production of *The Misfits* together. Similarly Lee Strasberg's motives are questioned: Leaming in particular blames him for being entirely self-seeking and manipulative in his exploitation of Monroe's bankability, and charges him with having harmed her, professionally and psychologically. But most observers agree that her acting did improve under Lee's tutelage, and clearly both Strasbergs gave her some much-needed confidence.*

The Method claims to be an intellectual acting technique; it emphasizes the use of one's mind; it is interior, and psychological. Those

---

*Lee Strasberg was the major beneficiary of Monroe's estate; estimates of its value at her death vary, but most recent valuations place it around $1 million. (It is often reported as approximately $100,000, but that was apparently its cash value; she also had real estate, personal property including jewelry, her interest in Marilyn Monroe Productions, and 10 percent profit share of *Some Like It Hot*, *The Prince and the Showgirl* and *The Misfits*.) Monroe left small bequests to friends such as the Rostens and her secretary May Reis; established a trust fund for the care of her mother; and left 25 percent of the value of her estate after these bequests to psychiatrist Marianne Kris "to be used by her for the furtherance of the work of such psychiatric institutions or groups as she shall elect." The bulk of the remaining estate (75 percent), including Monroe's personal effects, was left to Lee Strasberg; the will instructed that he should distribute her personal belongings "among my friends, colleagues, and those to whom I am devoted." Because of legal wrangling and disputes over taxes, no beneficiaries were paid until 1971. Paula Strasberg had died in 1966, and Lee married Anna Mizrahi, a woman whom Monroe had never met, in 1968. After Lee Strasberg's death in 1982, Anna Strasberg inherited the income from Monroe's estate, including the vast amount of money generated by licensing fees for Monroe's name and likeness. Lee Strasberg had never distributed Monroe's personal effects as instructed; in 1999, Anna Strasberg had Christie's auction them off, for a reported gain of approximately $14 million. The estate was put in order by attorney Roger Richman in 1982; it is now represented by CMG (Curtis Management Group Worldwide), which is reportedly trying to "ban any reference to Marilyn's marriages and divorces, her physical problems, and 'alleged chemical dependencies,' and of course, the circumstances of her death." The Richman agency trademarked the names "Marilyn," "Marilyn Monroe," and "Norma Jeane," with the result, as Adam Victor observes, that it is technically "a breach of copyright to even write this movie star's name."[51]

who admire Marilyn appreciate either her body or her "instinctive" genius, as in director Billy Wilder's assessment of her talent: "God gave her everything. The first day a photographer took a picture of her she was a genius."[52] Although many who knew her considered Monroe smart, they also qualified her intelligence as "street smart," "shrewd," or "native intelligence," all of which distinguish her intelligence from intellection. No one regards Marilyn as cerebral (including Monroe herself, who told *Life* magazine in 1959: "I don't consider myself an intellectual. And this is not one of my aims. But I admire intellectual people"[53]). In other words, she remains in these interpretations more body than mind, intuitive rather than rational; and this stress on intuition, of course, further reinforces her "femininity." When Marilyn sought out the "intellectual" arena of the Method, and began to undergo the psychoanalysis that Strasberg always recommended for his students, she was thus not only deemed to be doing something inappropriate to her talents. For many observers, then and now, psychological or intellectual efforts were an active danger to her. Her body, her instincts, her intuition were her "natural" strengths, whereas her mind was a weakness. Ultimately Marilyn's craziness is not unrelated to her stereotypical dumbness.

In part because it so identified itself as a cerebral technique, for many the Method was also pretentious; as historians of the theater have noted, it seemed to become popular in America precisely at the time when the American theater was looking for cultural and professional legitimation. It is perhaps not surprising that a woman like Monroe, insecure about her lack of education and seeking confirmation of her intellectual and personal worth, would be drawn to it. The Method itself linked the identity of the performer with the role, blurring the boundaries between actor and performance, and making it all seem more real; this also would make the actor associated with the Method all the more serious. It isn't just the case that Marlon Brando played serious roles; Marlon Brando was a serious actor. Whereas for many writers Marilyn's supposed lack of identity is precisely what made her a good actress: "Norma Jeane seems to have been a naturally gifted actress because, perhaps, she so lacked an inner core of identity," opined Oates in an interview.[54]

For someone like Marilyn, who is not supposed to have known

who she was, a Method that insisted she delve into her own psyche not only wouldn't work, according to the apocrypha; it would become fatal, as it would reveal to her for the first time the hollowness of her own mind. If her lack of self, finally, is supposed to be what destroyed her, then it is the Method and psychoanalysis that exposed that lack to her. In particular, there is a persistent strand of the myth that holds psychoanalysis itself to blame for her fate. The effort to root Monroe's problems in psychoanalysis itself goes back to Guiles, but Spoto is its major proponent:

> Notwithstanding the insights provided by Freudian principles, their wholesale application to someone like Norma Jeane Mortensen/ Marilyn Monroe was futile. Excessive introspection exacerbated her lack of self-confidence. Intuition suffered at the expense of a forced, conscious intellectualism that paralyzed her and pushed her further back into herself. There was, therefore, a confusion of realms and realities here.[55]

Spoto hardly ever uses the split name "Norma Jeane/Marilyn," but in a discussion of her lack of identity, that becomes the obvious way to represent her. Spoto blames "pop-Freudian" psychoanalysis, and thus, indirectly the teacher and Method that took her to it, for encouraging her faith in ersatz father figures whose failures would accelerate her emotional disintegration: "instead of freeing her, it froze her."[56] Certainly Monroe's relationship with both the Strasbergs and with her psychiatrist Dr. Greenson (as we shall see) was a familial one; most biographers agree that she was always seeking a substitute father figure, and that psychoanalysis only served to make conscious what until then had been an unconscious desire. But Spoto's distrust of psychoanalysis in general seems not unrelated to his accusations about her psychoanalyst in particular: if he says psychoanalysis was destroying her, Spoto is also the one who argues that her psychoanalyst killed her. The two belief structures thus go hand in hand, and one narrative paves the way for the other. These accounts are also united in feeling that Marilyn was better off being unconscious, instinctive—natural, rather than skilled. At best, she was a gifted child; at worst, an idiot savant, or madwoman.

Although Spoto feels that Monroe's psychological problems were greatly exacerbated (if not produced) by psychoanalysis, most writers prefer the borrowed authority of a psychiatric diagnosis. The most egregious example of the problems with such "psychobiography" is undoubtedly Freeman's *Why Norma Jeane Killed Marilyn Monroe.* Freeman diagnoses everything about Monroe, even her humor. She quotes Monroe saying: "Was it Milton who wrote: 'The happy ones were never born'? I know at least two psychiatrists who are looking for a more positive approach." Freeman helpfully (and literal-mindedly) interprets this remark for the reader: "In quoting this thought of Milton's, she reveals the wish she had never been born."[57] Freeman recycles the opinion offered by Dr. Greenson, which appeared both in Steinem and in Summers, that Marilyn "found it difficult to sustain a series of orgasms with the same individual." For Steinem, as we saw, this "difficulty" is a result of Monroe's incompleteness; for Summers, as we are about to see, it is because Marilyn believed "she was frigid." But Freeman takes the opportunity to offer a literal "psychoanalytical" explanation: this "difficulty"

> could be attributed to the guilt that followed her fantasy that each man was her elusive father. To have sex with one's father is forbidden, a sign of "craziness." The fantasy often remains, however, [*sic*] it may become the eternal plight of a woman who emotionally still remains a child seeking in vain to work through the oedipal rivalry, a natural part of maturing.
>
> Marilyn was never able to face this fantasy.[58]

Of course, neither is Freeman ever able to prove this fantasy, in part because of its utter circularity. Nonetheless, she has associated Monroe with fantasy, craziness, frigidity and an unresolved oedipal complex that kept her from maturing, all of which locate aberrant sexuality and the need for a father at the center of Monroe's identity.

Summers and Leaming seem the writers most convinced that Monroe was clinically insane. Most of the lives say that Monroe first began analysis in New York in 1955, but Summers remarks ominously that "Marilyn was no stranger to the psychiatrist's office" even before she left Hollywood. As evidence that she definitely "needed psychiatric help," however, the first person Summers quotes is her gynecologist, who called her insecure, frightened, "a very disturbed young woman." Then Summers quotes, in order: her male physician (not psychiatrist); her former friend, partner, alleged addict and perhaps ex-lover Milton Greene, who says sympathetically that he considered Monroe "schizo"; her ex-husband Miller, who says psychiatry helped her; and director Billy Wilder, who said: "It is better for Monroe not to be straightened out. The charm of her is her two left feet."[59] In a sense, Wilder is right: clearly part of Marilyn's appeal in these stories is her reassuring inability to cope, which mitigates the threat of this most sexually powerful of women.

Guiles voices his suspicion of psychoanalysis in the context of Monroe's drug-taking, as a sign of her self-destruction. His first reference to her drug abuse comes in 1956, during the filming of *The Prince and the Showgirl*; Guiles then turns to the beginnings of Monroe's psychoanalysis, and, mentioning drugs for only the second time in his narrative, suggests that "in the interaction of patient and actress may lie the key to Marilyn's destruction." "To kill the pain" of her effort "to relate to others in meaningful ways" "she was now pricking her barbiturates with a straight pin to make them work faster." Guiles reports Miller on Monroe's attempted suicide in 1957 (some will say it is one among many during the marriage) before asking:

> Was there some residue of despair over losing her baby earlier that autumn? Or was the spark the work [*The Misfits*] that was going on in Miller's study—and her growing realization that Miller was sharing his intimate knowledge of her with the world? Did she think she could *abort* this literary image of herself through her own death? [. . .] It is also possible that her despair may have been triggered by her inability to unlock certain doors to Norma Jeane's past and to come to terms finally with her origins—those unstable Monroes.[60]

In emphasizing the word *abort*, Guiles makes a gynecological metaphor the key to Monroe's psyche, and seems to imply that the metaphor should be taken literally. Madness, sex and death begin to converge: the veil of innocence has been lifted, and the "truth," in all its monstrosity, is about to be exposed. This exposure will prompt Marilyn to kill herself—and it is the motive force of the biography.

Popular Freudianism was, of course, enjoying a heyday in the 1950s. In its most simplified and banal forms, Freudianism is held to reduce all identity to the sexual, and to see sex everywhere it looks. Marilyn's own status as sex symbol par excellence gives her association with Freudianism a peculiar magnetism, as if in Marilyn the theory finally met the patient of its dreams. If, for Freud, sex is supposed to explain everything, then Marilyn provides at once the question and the answer, the unconscious anxiety and the conscious explanation. Pop psychology, and in particular watered-down Freudian theory, seems to tend toward extreme literalism when it is "applied" in this way, when symptoms are confused with diagnosis. But Freud said in *Beyond the Pleasure Principle* that psychoanalysis should be considered a kind of figurative language; it is symbolic, metaphorical. Psychoanalysis interprets dreams, the unconscious, the instinctive, all of which reveal themselves through figurative means. The psychological literalism of writers like Guiles and particularly Freeman, whose literalist approach to psychoanalysis is so extreme that it is absurd, may cling to Monroe so tenaciously because as a figure, she herself so often enacts the tension between the literal and the figurative. Interpreting her literally makes her seem real, and it begins, almost ritually, to prepare her for death.

WORKING HUSBAND

Where Monroe's relationship with DiMaggio was fought over the private bounds of sexuality, her relationship with Miller was fought at least in part over the public ground of politics and professionalism. She had first met Miller in Hollywood in January 1951 while he was still married to his first wife (and while she was apparently having an affair with his close friend, writer-director Elia Kazan), but they did not begin a serious relationship until she moved to New York in 1955. At that time, Miller was being investigated by the House

Un-American Activities Committee (HUAC), which was focusing its search for "subversive activities" on Hollywood and the New York theater world. Miller refused to be a friendly witness for the Committee—unlike Kazan, who notoriously cooperated with the HUAC in 1952, prompting a rift with Miller that would only be resolved when they worked together on *After the Fall* in 1964.

Monroe's relationship with Miller began publicly on a political footing and was always represented partly in terms of intellectualism manqué. It was at the press conference he held announcing he would refuse to cooperate with the HUAC that Miller announced he and Monroe would be marrying and traveling to London: her marriage to Miller was interpreted as an attempt to assert not only her intellectual viability, but also political worth. The standard version is that Monroe "stood by her man," throwing the weight of her considerable popular support behind him as he resisted the pressures of the HUAC. Most commentators agree that championing Miller so publicly was quite a brave move, given the power of the Committee in 1956, and the real effect of the blacklists it caused. Leaming argues further that Monroe carefully stage-managed the episode to help Miller through it, using her experience with the press to gain popular support. Miller is also understood to have shown courage and integrity in the face of enormous pressure as he was faced with the choice between betraying his colleagues and his principles, and a jail sentence.

Many writers report a story that Congressman Frances E. Walter said the hearing would be dropped if Monroe agreed to have her photo taken with him, and that Miller angrily refused and "denounced" the suggestion.[61] Miller also refused to plead the Fifth Amendment, which protects a witness from self-incrimination, and insisted upon the more principled stand of taking the First Amendment, which protects freedom of speech. Taking the First meant that Miller risked being cited for contempt of court, which is precisely what happened. Monroe later commented: "Some of those bastards in Hollywood wanted me to drop Arthur. Said it would ruin my career. They're born cowards and want you to be like them."[62] She added that one of the reasons she wanted to see Kennedy win in his presidential bid was because Nixon was associated with the HUAC, which he had chaired before Joseph McCarthy took it over.

However, Spoto says that Miller cynically exploited his relationship with Monroe to protect himself: he claims that she said Miller never proposed to her, and that she found the public nature of the proposal coercive, commenting sarcastically to friends, "It was awfully nice of him to let me know his plans."[63] Leaming says she felt precisely the opposite, and basked in the affirmation: " 'He announced it before the whole world!' Marilyn exulted. 'He told the whole world he was marrying Marilyn Monroe. Me! Can you believe it?' " Leaming reports that the Rostens "wondered whether Arthur wasn't simply using Marilyn 'to get off the hook,' " but in Leaming's account a more naïve Monroe has no such dark suspicions.[64]

That summer Monroe returned to Hollywood to film *Bus Stop* with director Joshua Logan, her first film under her new contract with Fox, and received her first respectful reviews: even *The New York Times* declared that she had at last proved she could act (although it did so in terms of what director Logan "got her to do"). She and Miller married in June 1956 (Monroe converted to Judaism for the ceremony), and flew to England on their honeymoon. Their wedding was announced with the notorious headline EGGHEAD WEDS HOURGLASS; mind met body in a monstrous union that would manifest itself in stories of miscarriage, hysteria, suicide and madness. Only when the union ended could her mind return to the story, albeit destroyed by the "death" of her marriage: Summers entitles his chapter about the end of the Miller marriage "Broken Marriage, Broken Mind."

Monroe's political interests have not been absorbed into her public persona, but her principal lives concur on her strong political sensibility; even Summers, hardly Monroe's most generous biographer, maintains that by 1960 she was "more politically sophisticated than has ever been acknowledged."[65] Although it has latterly been erased from the Marilyn myth, Monroe's political consciousness did register with her contemporaries. (Sylvia Plath, for example, noted in her journal that Monroe and Miller were important to her precisely *for* their resistance to the HUAC.) Spoto says that Monroe's political conscience was responsible for the real end of the marriage with Miller, when he "broke ranks" with a Writers Guild strike in order to get paid for doctoring the script of *Let's Make Love* in 1960. Spoto quotes costar Yves Montand on the situation: "Miller 'came running [back from Ireland, where he was working on *The Misfits* with John Huston] to rewrite some scenes, pocketed a check [from Fox] and complained about prostituting his art.'" Spoto adds that Miller made himself unpopular by commenting "imperiously" about the film and "generally playing the experienced playwright who was slumming in Hollywood—an attitude that had caused problems on *Some Like It Hot*. Nonetheless, his fee of several thousand dollars for his contributions must have alleviated whatever agony he felt."[66] For Monroe, Spoto says, this was the end of her faith in his character: "Violating his own ethics, Arthur forever lost Marilyn's confidence: the man whose courage and moral outrage a few years earlier had won her admiration had betrayed his own ideals. 'That was the moment I knew it was over,'" a friend quotes her as saying.[67]

Miller's relationship to Monroe's films is a crucial aspect of the story that all the biographies tell, but they offer diametrically opposed accounts of that relationship. One strand of the story, which has a source in *After the Fall,* has Miller the heroically suffering silent man who is vampirically destroyed by Marilyn's neediness, which affects his own ability to work ("Miller had for the most part stopped writing. He had made what was to become a critical mistake in looking after her nearly full time").[68] This is primarily the version of Guiles, Summers and Oates, with Mailer weighing in ambivalently, half-enjoying the downfall of his imaginary rival for Marilyn's affections ("he is now doing less writing than ever. He is her god, her guard, her attendant, and her flunky")[69] and taking the opportunities to express his artistic superiority over Miller ("He is also ambitious, limited, and small-minded, an intellectual who is often scorned by critics outside the theater for his intellectual lacks").[70] Steinem feels that, although it is true that Miller allowed himself to serve Marilyn, he was just "paying the price" for being the product of a culture that teaches men to find "extreme dependency extremely appealing."[71]

The other story is that Miller was a pious prig who exploited Monroe's popularity and used her illnesses to account for his own artistic failures: this is the interpretation of Spoto, Wolfe and Leaming.

Leaming considers Miller pompous and self-righteous; Spoto writes acidly that he was "a world famous but curiously inert playwright," who "used her fragility as the excuse for his own literary setbacks."[72] Mailer certainly remarks upon Miller's lack of productivity during these years, although the sexual and professional rivalry that undercuts his interpretation of Miller cannot be ignored: "fair to wonder if Miller is still full of love, or whether rage at her habits is now begun with him as well. He is a most ambitious man. In his own way, he is as ambitious as she is."[73] Leaming argues that Miller "needed Marilyn's prestige to get *The Misfits* made. Whatever his intentions, there was at least the appearance that an ambitious husband was using a movie-star wife to cash in."[74] She quickly relates this to Marilyn's

> self-loathing explanation for why he remained after her failure to give him a child. [. . .] Arthur's screenplay, begun as an attempt to make Marilyn feel better about herself, soon appeared to have very much the opposite effect. It seemed only to confirm that, childless, she was no longer of interest as a wife.[75]

Most writers, however, identify rather more with Miller than with Monroe, as if sympathizing with a fellow writer (or perhaps because a world-renowned author's opinions must be authoritative). Oates takes this the furthest, abruptly abandoning Monroe's viewpoint, which has dominated *Blonde,* when "The Playwright" comes on the scene, and narrating the story of their marriage sympathetically from his perspective. When husbands enter the story, writers transform Monroe into a wife, not just in terms of her name (although Guiles does entitle one chapter "Marilyn Miller") but conceptually, such that she becomes defined in relation to the husband's attitudes. We saw this previously, when Summers offers DiMaggio's feelings about Monroe's "exhibitionism" as the norm. Similarly, in his discussion of the Monroe-Miller relationship, Summers likens Monroe to Vivien Leigh, who was married to Laurence Olivier at the time of *The Prince and the Showgirl* and was undergoing a manic-depressive breakdown. He declares that "Arthur Miller and Sir Laurence Olivier found common ground in the ordeal of dealing with their women."[76] Wolfe, always indebted to Summers (and misinformed about Olivier's rank),

defines Marilyn in similarly relational terms: "Arthur Miller soon discovered that the Marxist boy from Brooklyn and the Earl of Notley
had something in common—difficult wives [. . .] there were days
when Olivier would brace himself with a stiff drink in his Pinewood
dressing room before going home, and Arthur Miller would join him
for commiseration and a bracer."[77] The commiseration becomes collective, spreading from husband to biographer, all of whom sympa-
thize with the ordeal of a "difficult wife." In a biography of Miller,
such an attitude would be much less remarkable (if no less disagree-
able), but the shifts out of Marilyn's vantage point and into her husbands' contribute to the sense that this sex object cannot even be the
subject of her own biography.

"BE SEXY, DEAR MARILYN"

Although it started out with high hopes on everyone's part, the only
independent film made by Marilyn Monroe Productions,* *The
Prince and the Showgirl,* was fraught with trouble. The problems are
variously ascribed to Olivier's condescension and Monroe's difficulties, which are in turn attributed to drugs, narcissism, miscarriages
and hysteria. Monroe's own accounts of the production, however,
hinge on the question of respect, and what Rollyson calls her "powerful ability to be disappointed," which is a backhanded way of
acknowledging her aspirationalism.[78]

   One much-recycled incident concerns a press conference held to
publicize the film, during which Olivier slowly repeated questions for
Monroe's benefit, and sometimes answered them on her behalf. All
the biographers, including those who elsewhere insist upon her intelligence and wit, seem to feel that Monroe must have been grateful
for this "assistance." Even Rollyson, who notes that Olivier's behavior may have irritated Monroe, also feels compelled to attribute

---

*Marilyn Monroe Productions had also coproduced *Bus Stop* with Fox, and was coproducing the unfinished *Something's Got to Give* when Monroe died; these were the only three films in which the company
was involved.

thankfulness to her for what he construes as Olivier's protectiveness, and to pathologize any resentment of it:

> presumably one part of Monroe drew sustenance from following Olivier's lead, but another part of her may already have been storing up resentment at his preemption of her replies. He was gallant in his protection of her, but she was capable of twisting his gentlemanly behavior into the schizoid's dread of being disrupted and divided from others.[79]

However, Olivier's description in his memoir of the incident emphasizes that he was "more embarrassed" than he'd ever been by the fact that she kept him and the press corps waiting for an over an hour; he then comments ruefully that she won the offended reporters over the instant she arrived, and in the process gave him an "object lesson in charm, and in no time at all she had got this vast ballroomful of people nestling cosily in the hollow of her hand."[80] Olivier's immediate response, he tells us in his very next sentence, was to "give her a chance" to come up with her answers by "repeating each question" for her. Even as late as 1986, Rollyson will not acknowledge that Olivier's condescension might have been punitive, and will insist that Olivier was a gallant gentleman in protecting her and Monroe was crazy for resenting it.

When production commenced, Monroe began her "usual tricks"—unpunctuality, absence, apparent drug use. One observer, according to Rollyson, ascribed her failure to complete takes under Olivier's direction to her being simply "'too dumb and uncultured and obsessed with herself' to be able to cooperate with Olivier." Rollyson, however, concurs with another observer that she had a "quite unconscious but basic resistance to acting."[81] Or perhaps she had a quite conscious but basic resistance to cooperating with someone who was patronizing her.

Olivier famously told Monroe in the first week of filming: "All you have to do is be sexy, dear Marilyn."[82] Every biographer repeats this comment, and most of them feel compelled to explain, mitigate or emotionalize her subsequent anger. Guiles evidently predicts readers will have trouble understanding it, because he instructs his audience: "Imagine if you can a child—who has learned to use his innate wisdom and intuition to make others relate to him and react to him—suddenly walking into a salon of bewigged aristocrats. [. . .] Such was Marilyn's reaction to Olivier's direction."[83] That is, Monroe's rage is infantile and instinctive; she deserves sympathy because she *was* a child, not because she was a twenty-nine-year-old woman at the pinnacle of her profession being treated as one. Mailer notes that Olivier had "revealed his secret contempt for her," so, in order to do "justice to her wrath, now Olivier will get *her* treatment."[84] Even Rollyson, the most sympathetic to Monroe's professional difficulties, wants to downplay the legitimacy of her anger: "Much has been made of Monroe's outraged reaction to Olivier's direction: 'Be sexy.' [. . .] He found her strangely lacking in humor."[85] Summers emphasizes not Monroe's talent but her obstructiveness: while poor Olivier was in for "professional hell," Monroe was spending her time "lapping up" Paula Strasberg's flattery. Despite Joshua Logan's warning that Monroe didn't need intrusive direction and indeed reacted badly to it, Summers censures Monroe for taking offense at what he too depicts as Olivier's supportiveness: "Olivier tried to help. [. . .] He suggested she sit still, count up to three, then speak the line. When this failed, he burst out, 'Can't you count either?' "[86] With help like that, who needs criticism? According to Monroe's maid, Lena Pepitone, she said later:

> I think Olivier hated me. He gave me the dirtiest looks, even when he was smiling. I was sick half the time but he didn't believe me, or else he didn't care. He looked at me like he had just smelled a pile of dead fish. Like I was a leper or something as awful. I felt like a little fool the whole time.[87]

All biographers report that Arthur Miller kept a notebook in England, which he left lying on a table open at a page that she read, on which he complained (she said) about the difference between his vision of Monroe as an "angel" and the reality, which was that she seemed to be a "troublesome bitch." Later, according to Guiles and Mailer, she would report that he had called her a "whore."[88] (A different version of this story also appears in *After the Fall,* as discussed in chapter two.) Spoto says she eventually concluded that Miller "likes dumb blondes. [. . .] Some help he was." But according to Spoto she was pregnant in August, and although some of "those close to the situation" always "doubted the pregnancy," "two London doctors" confirmed the condition and that she lost the baby in September, implying that her heavy drinking at the time might have been implicated.[89] Olivier, who was not informed of the pregnancy, "was allowed to believe that Marilyn was simply being moody and intransigent."[90] Although this is sympathetic, it does suggest that Monroe should be forgiven professional misconduct because of personal problems, implying that her rage is domestic, personal, chemical and hormonal; her problems are either psychological or gynecological.

Monroe's response to being insulted by a director she had hired for a film that her company was producing was apparently not at all unconscious, although it may have been instinctive. Weatherby quotes her own description of her response to Olivier:

> "he came on like someone slumming. He upset me a lot by telling me to"—and here she imitated his voice—" 'Look sexy, Marilyn.' It sounded condescending to me [. . .] I started being bad with him, being late, and he hated it. But if you don't respect your artists, they can't work well. Respect is what you have to fight for."[91]

Summers repeats this quotation, but neither grants her the right to fight for respect, nor even acknowledges the consciousness of her knowledge that her lateness was a punishment and an attempt to exert (passive) control over a situation in which she felt disempowered (whereas Olivier always insisted that he was "helping" her and treating her well). Summers instead continues the tradition of paternal responses to Monroe, censuring her conduct: "It was Marilyn who failed to give respect," he adds severely, "to Olivier and everyone else, in big and little things."[92]

For many viewers, Monroe's acting in the film is considerably more accomplished, subtle and funnier than Olivier's. For some, however, including Olivier, this remains an irony; he would later characterize her as a "glorious amateur, an untrained, probably untrainable artist of instinct."[93] Summers remarks that Olivier "would write wearily in his memoirs that people thought 'I was as good as could be, and Marilyn! Marilyn was quite wonderful, the best of all. So. What do you know?' "[94] In fact, Olivier's memoirs tell the story not wearily, but rather in the context of a joke:

> Two years or so ago, a couple of my Hollywood friends, as a sort of joke after a dinner-party, ran this twenty-five-year-old picture for me on their library projection machine. I was a bit embarrassed as I didn't know how long it might be before the joke would begin to get a bit tired; however, the picture ran through, much to my surprise. At the finish everyone was clamorous in their praises; how such enchantment could have been poorly received defied imagination; I was as good as could be, and Marilyn! Marilyn was quite wonderful, the best of all. So. What do you know?[95]

The joke in question was still, twenty-five years later, supposed to be on her but, to his surprise, turned out to be on him.

SOME LIKE IT HOT

Monroe took almost a year off before beginning work on her next film, *Some Like It Hot.* During that year she lived with Miller in Amagansett, Long Island, and had a well-publicized miscarriage, after which she returned to work (reportedly with Miller's encouragement). Filming lasted three months, from August 4 to November 6, 1958, and the difficulty of the production would become legendary, even for a Monroe picture. The film was written by Billy Wilder, who had worked with Monroe on *The Seven Year Itch,* and so thought he was prepared for her stage fright, her chronic lateness, her demands for retakes, and her failure to remember the simplest lines, but he was provoked to the point of violence by Monroe's obstructiveness, later declaring that it was months before he could look at his wife without wanting to hit her because she was a woman.[96] Similarly, costar Tony Curtis famously remarked that kissing Marilyn was "like kissing Hitler." Both comments suggest not only exasperation at Monroe's misbehavior, but resentment of her power; one man responds to it by wanting to beat her into submission, the other by saying it made her a monster, but both associate it with physical violence.

Two other stories that emerged from this production are repeated regularly: that it took Monroe between thirty and eighty takes (depending on the source) to say "Where's that bourbon?" even coherently, instead of "Where's the bonbon?" or "Where's the whisky?" The clear implication is that her drug use was spiraling out of control.* The second story is that Monroe was called on set by an assistant director, who discovered her reading Thomas Paine's *The Rights of Man* ("of all things," Guiles adds); without glancing up from her reading, she told the man to go fuck himself. Although Guiles explains in 1969 that Billy Wilder, for one, attributed her profanity to her "adamant refusal to be caught up in the studio pressure surrounding any film production,"[97] by 1984 this acknowledgment will have dropped out of his account—and then out of many subsequent ones. Instead of seeing her anger as at least partially resistant, Guiles now feels that "such arrogance requires some reflection. Was she, as Olivier believed, truly schizoid? Was this mean woman tossing obscenities at quiet young men part of a split personality? Very possibly, and the nasty Marilyn would get worse."[98] Or, possibly, "nasty Marilyn" didn't become more of a (different) person, but Marilyn Monroe became nastier as she grew more frustrated, more raging, more anxious, and more addicted to the chemicals that were making her moods even more volatile. For all that biography is supposed to reveal the woman behind the performance, the difference between Marilyn's performance of cheerful sexiness and the reality of her frustration and rage can only be attributed to dissociated personalities—not acting. The effect of this is to deny the reality of her arrogance, to refuse her the dignity of her own rage. Would a biographer ask the same question about a male actor who told a director to go fuck himself? Frank Sinatra evidently said it all the time, and no one calls him schizoid, just arrogant. End of story.

Mailer likes the anecdote well enough to include it on his third

---

*Less frequently noted is that Monroe speaks the line while rifling through a drawer, with her back to the camera. There was no reason why Wilder couldn't have rerecorded the dialogue and looped it in during postproduction; his insistence on take after take until she got the line right suggests that they were engaged in an overt power struggle—indeed, in a pissing contest.

page of text, implying its prominence in any assessment of Monroe's character:

> "Go fuck yourself," she said. Did she anticipate how a future gen-
> eration of women would evaluate the rights of men? Even so con-
> summate a wit as Billy Wilder would yet describe her as the
> meanest woman in Hollywood, a remark of no spectacular humor
> that was offered nonetheless in an interview four years after her
> death, as though to suggest that even remembering Marilyn across
> the void was still sufficiently irritating to strip his wit.[99]

Or maybe Monroe anticipated how a future generation of women would evaluate the rights of women. Certainly Mailer sees this episode as an unwarranted eruption of feminism from his "sweet angel of sex," holding her anger against her. In any event, it seems clear that the world's most famous dumb blonde had no trouble grasping the gist of Paine's message. Joyce Carol Oates, by contrast, seems (inexplicably) to miss the joke: she tells the story in *Blonde,* but has Marilyn Monroe reading *The Origin of Species* when she tells famous director "W" to fuck himself.[100]

Although Mailer's sympathy for Monroe is uncertain at the best of times, he later unexpectedly generates a moment of insight when he notes that her problems on set suggest her barely suppressed rage at the men around her (although this sudden perceptiveness is almost certainly derived from Zolotow's 1960 intuition that her lateness was to punish those around her). Even her most loyal friends, according to Spoto, had to admit "at such times Marilyn was trouble itself, a difficult woman who brought along the entire baggage of her emo-tional insecurities."[101] Apparently none of them had to admit that many of the men around her were not at all easy to get along with, either. John Huston had drinking and gambling problems; Howard Hawks used machismo to bully those who were not part of his inner circle; Billy Wilder was considered a "monster" and a "sadist" on the set by some who knew him; and Arthur Miller was deemed pompous, arrogant and unhelpful, even by close friends like Norman Rosten, who once suggested Miller was more interested in people as a con-cept than in real persons.[102]

Wolfe is the only biographer who suggests that Monroe might have forced take after take in order to control the interpretation of her character, that it was the only way to fight Wilder's direction. In another famous story, Wilder grew infuriated as Monroe was "unable" to register surprise in a shot where Sugar Kane accidentally drops her flask; Monroe reportedly argued that in the given situation Sugar would be afraid, not surprised, but Wilder insisted on the broad reaction of farce. Those around her concluded that she *couldn't* show surprise, but obviously she was quite capable of it (her character in *How to Marry a Millionaire*, for instance, is permanently surprised). No one seems to have concluded that she *wouldn't* show surprise. Her tactic seems obvious in retrospect: the only time she said "Where's that bourbon?" coherently, she also delivered the line the way she wanted to; that take made it into the final film. The irony is how "amazed" they all continued to be at how good her final performance was, including Wilder. Wolfe observes that: "Wilder, of course, knew what she was doing, but didn't believe she was right [in her interpretation]. She knew she was right and believed that a star of her stature had the prerogative of playing a scene the way she felt it."[103] She wouldn't take direction—but she would take suggestions. Costar Jack Lemmon complained that she had no sense of professional commitment to the film, but Wolfe persuasively argues that she had a different commitment—to Sugar Kane. Similarly, Oates suggests that the few times when Monroe completed an entire scene in one take during filming—which she famously did during the "Pullman" scene, much to the amazement of all—she did so to make a point: "she'd played the scene brilliantly in a single take simply to demonstrate that yes, she could do it. When she wished."[104]

But then having understood all this, Oates cuts to a memory of Marilyn's traumatic miscarriage of "Baby," while Wolfe explains that her difficulty arose from an interior, psychologized struggle with Norma Jeane and role-playing instead of an exterior, political struggle with her director: "not everybody who worked with Marilyn knew the private ordeal she went through to make the metamorphosis from Norma Jeane to Marilyn Monroe to Sugar Kane. It was a transcendental trick that didn't happen instantaneously."[105] But Wilder wasn't the only one who knew what she was doing; so did Monroe, as is evident from her admission that she was "bad" with Olivier because he didn't respect her. She was resisting—and punishing—them all, and she knew it. As a producer on her last, unfinished film is reported to have said: "Marilyn doesn't need script approval. If she doesn't like something, she just doesn't show up."[106]

Wolfe ends his account with the story of Monroe's miscarriage after the film's ending. In his rendering, she was confronted in the newspapers with Wilder's gibe that working with her had made him sick, and demanded that Miller do something to defend her. Miller, who had already tried to protect her against Wilder in a famous exchange of telegrams and had emerged looking like a fool, refused. So, Wolfe says, she overdosed. Norman Rosten visited her in the hospital and she told him: "Cruel, all of them *cruel,* all those bastards. Oh Jesus . . ."[107] (Summers, however, locates that quotation after her *first* miscarriage, in the summer of 1957 in Amagansett.) For Summers, the miscarriage after *Some Like It Hot* provokes the following symmetrical observation: "The movie star had made her film and lost another baby."[108] Guiles claims she may have got pregnant that summer in order to give herself an escape clause from the film, although he also says that "Marilyn's career could never be everything to her."[109] Leaming goes the furthest to suggest that she used threats of pregnancy as leverage in battles with the studio.[110] All of these accounts share the feeling that pregnancy is somehow inextricable from a woman's artistry, that creation and procreation will mirror and reflect each other.

THE MISFITS

In 1960, Monroe made *Let's Make Love,* during which she had an affair, widely reported at the time, with her costar, Yves Montand. Monroe was publicly humiliated when Montand told an interviewer that Monroe took a trivial affair seriously, because she was so naïve: "Had Marilyn been sophisticated, none of this would have happened," he remarked, ascribing the affair to his desire to make his performance as her lover in the film as believable as he could.[111] Brown and Barham relate that Monroe's publicist, Rupert Allan, tried to convince her to fight back in the press: "he used her shame-lessly [. . .] there was a lot Marilyn could have said and done, and I advised her to go public with her side [. . .] in the end, she was just too kind."[112] The film failed commercially, and Hollywood whispered that Monroe was on the skids.

Her marriage with Miller was ending, too. They had already con-tracted to make *The Misfits,* a film based on a short story Miller had written early in their marriage, about a woman whose tender heart binds together a group of male "misfits" and convinces them, through her own vulnerability, to stop preying on the wild horses they hunt. Conceived as a "valentine" to Monroe, the film costarred Clark Gable, Montgomery Clift and Eli Wallach, and was directed by John Huston. But Miller's supposed tribute to Marilyn involved an already obviously fragile Monroe exposing herself and her own anxieties on-screen: the male characters speak lines that mirror other words Miller published about her, while she plays a woman called Roslyn and alludes to scenes that recognizably parallel her own life and unhappy past. Wolfe sets out the tensions well:

> Rupert Allan commented that Marilyn was "desperately unhappy at having to read lines written by Miller that were obviously doc-umenting the real-life Marilyn." Though Roslyn was supposed to be based on Marilyn, and much of the dialogue and situations had been drawn from the Millers' life together, Marilyn felt that the character of Roslyn had inconsistencies—she was too passive, voiced platitudes, and needed to be humanized. Marilyn had never been satisfied with the script [. . .] Miller was still making revisions on the screenplay he had been working on for over three years. When production finally started she found herself faced with playing the most difficult role of her career—a misconstrued concept of herself.[113]

Roslyn is imagined as a spirit of pure femininity: sexual, giving, natu-ral, instinctive, emotional, irrational: in fact, most of the characteris-tics of the Marilyn persona that Monroe had been struggling to escape. Steinem quotes from maid Lena Pepitone's account, in which Marilyn describes the scene in which Roslyn convinces the cowboys not to kill the wild horses they have caught: "I convince them by throwing a fit, not by explaining anything. So I have a fit. A screaming crazy fit . . . And to think, *Arthur* did this to me . . . If that's what he thinks of me, well, then I'm not for him and he's not for me."[114]

Leaming argues that Monroe's disappointment was not just at the way in which Roslyn is herself a cliché, a trite version of femininity on permanent offer, but that Miller had "sentimentalized" Roslyn's past, whereas Monroe wanted to give her "the ugly backstory Miller had left out" and that this was more than an artistic problem: "Marilyn felt betrayed because Arthur seemed unable to acknowledge her past. From the first, the whole point of marriage was to be accepted by such a man. She needed Arthur to love her in spite of all the shameful things she had done."[115]

Wolfe takes the most critical approach to Miller, quoting the passages from *Timebends* in which Miller reveals that he felt he was making a sacrifice in lowering himself to write a screenplay for her (despite the fact that he had not finished a new play for five years), and that he was "constructing a gift for her" in the part of Roslyn. Wolfe notes caustically that Miller received $250,000 from Marilyn Monroe Productions for this "gift."[116] Spoto argues that it "asked everything of her except what she was most equipped to give—her unique, highly imaginative talent and a special gift for subtle and sophisticated comedy."[117] *The Misfits* was Monroe's first noncomedic role since she became a star in 1953; as the film shifts into tragedy, so does her story. But that story will still, inexorably, hinge on the relationship between her performance and herself. In the case of this film, so late in Monroe's career and written by her playwright husband, such an interpretation is not a cultural fantasy but the result of the film's own deliberate blurring of performer and character. Summers reports that Huston "accurately" explained that she had not been acting in the role of Roslyn: "she had no techniques. It was all the truth, it was only Marilyn. But it was Marilyn, plus. She found things, found things about womankind in herself."[118]

In the rather less mythologizing account of Rupert Allan, her publicist: "Just when she might have expected some support, she was miserable. She felt she had never had a success. She felt lonely, isolated, abandoned, worthless, that she had nothing more to offer but this naked, wounded self."[119] The Marilyn apocrypha will concur with this assessment, as it spins into the circular stories of her "decline" and death.

On the set of *The Misfits,* she was first introduced to British journalist W. J. Weatherby. They met off and on again in New York during the winter of 1960–61, usually in a bar; these conversations formed the basis of Weatherby's memoir, *Conversations with Marilyn.* Rollyson offers a nice précis of Weatherby's sense of Marilyn in these months, as her marriage to Miller ended and she searched for her next project, her next goal:

> In a series of intermittent discussions with W. J. Weatherby in New York from late 1960 to some time in January 1961, Monroe latched onto his phrase, a "pattern of selves," to argue against the idea of a single self persisting through an entire lifetime and in favor of "fragmentary, changing natures." In his presence, her moods changed quickly. Her contradictoriness and fatiguing awareness of deeply divided feelings were driving her toward collapse and hospitalization. Weatherby sensed she was struggling for control of herself.[120]

ABORTIVE VENTURES

After *The Misfits* wrapped at the end of 1960, Monroe did not embark upon a new film for another year. The reason? According to Freeman, *cherchez la* womb:

> Marilyn did not make one film in 1961. She suffered frequent abnormal bleeding from her uterus and had an ulcerated colon. Twice that summer she found herself in a hospital. In May she underwent a gynecological operation in Los Angeles. On signing in, Marilyn used the name her mother gave her, Norma Jean, not her screen name, as though wishing her mother were there to

comfort her through this serious operation, one that would place another slash on her once-perfect body.

Doctors discovered that her Fallopian tubes were blocked as a result of inept surgery following an abortion—Marilyn once said she had undergone fourteen abortions. The guilt over this act ran high in this era and Marilyn no doubt thought of herself as a murderer, as most women did after an abortion. In society, at this time, Marilyn would thus be considered a murderer fourteen times over.[121]

It's a wonder they didn't give her the chair. But it's also worth remembering that this long litany of gynecological and psychological disasters is offered as an explanation for why Monroe made no films.

Beneath the surface of the biographical writing about Monroe's career, as we have seen, runs the theme of her "hysterical" need to be a mother. Pregnancies, miscarriages and abortions play throughout Marilyn's many lives like a perverse obbligato, grounding her life in a series of defeated attempts at domesticity. Unless one believes her former maid, Lena Pepitone, that Marilyn Monroe had a child as a teenager with Doc Goddard and gave it up for adoption, then she had no children. She did, however, have a highly disputed number of abortions, miscarriages and "hysterical pregnancies," all of which combine to suggest not only the excess and confusion that always characterize her myth, but also the idea of failure. Marilyn's neediness is so fundamental that even her womb reflects it—and her body will always be her truest self:

Marilyn's badly scarred body betrayed her again. One painful ectopic pregnancy had to be ended surgically. A second pregnancy ended in miscarriage. In spite of undergoing a gynecological operation at the age of thirty-three to aid her conceiving, her last rumored pregnancy came too late for the marriage to Miller that she hoped would be completed by a child. It was a pregnancy by a lover, not a husband, and ended in abortion. Her body had conceived only when she herself needed mothering too much to become a mother, or when she would have had to bear a child as fatherless as she herself had been.[122]

Steinem's sympathetic tone notwithstanding, there is much in this passage to dispute, including both the idea that Monroe's body was "badly scarred" and even the truth of that "last rumored pregnancy" itself, which is far from established fact. The language of the passage hammers home the theme of suffering and defeat, both physical and psychic. As important, perhaps, is that Steinem's account makes Marilyn's body the agent in her story: it is her body that betrays her, and conceives despite her (psychic) inabilities. Steinem's final sentence implies that, had Monroe given birth, only her body would have been a parent: her mind was fatally childish, and apparently incapable of making decisions. Indeed Marilyn's mind is remarkably absent from Steinem's (*soi-disant* "feminist") description of her desire to become a mother.

In part, Marilyn's sexuality remained a fantasy precisely because it never was compromised by maternity. Because she never became a mother herself, Monroe remained by definition more childlike and thus more attractive. She stayed innocent Norma Jeane, virgin, not whore. In this sense, the "failures" of her womb are both part of her malady and part of her appeal: "her stomach, untrammeled by girdles or sheaths, popped forward in a full woman's belly, inelegant as hell, an avowal of a womb fairly salivating in seed—that belly which was never to have a child—and her breasts popped buds and burgeons of flesh over many a questing sweating moviegoer's face. She was a cornucopia."[123]

Although there are some ancillary stories that claim she never intended to allow children to interfere with her professional ambitions (Jim Dougherty is quoted in several places as believing she never intended to become a mother), Monroe's principal biographers agree that she genuinely wanted children. Many repeat the dramatic story of her appendectomy in 1952, in which she taped a note to her abdomen for the surgeon to find, which read, in part:

Cut as little as possible. I know it seems vain but that doesn't really enter into it. The fact that I'm a woman is important and means much to me. Save please (I can't ask you enough) what you can—I'm in your hands. You have children and you must know

<u>what</u> it means—<u>please Doctor</u>—I know somehow you will! thank you—thank you—for Gods sake dear Doctor <u>No ovaries</u> removed—please again do whatever you can to prevent large <u>scars</u>. Thanking you with all my <u>heart</u>. Marilyn Monroe.[124]

Spoto writes of Monroe's "terror of infertility"; Summers describes this note as part of her "long quest to bear children."[125] Other writers, such as Leaming, understand her desire for children more as part of her determination to be a perfect wife. But Spoto argues that such attempts to fulfill the role of supportive helpmate, while "touching," were "unnatural for her," a helpless fallback after the failure of her production company, when she was "desperately assuming a socially acceptable but disastrous role for herself."[126] However, she was unable to bear children with Miller, and the cause of this inability is variously attributed to gynecological problems, drug problems and her disputed "history" of a vast number of abortions.

Given that abortions are by definition private and by convention secret, they highlight the question of whom—and what—a biographer chooses to believe about his subject. Summers selects among his sources for "perhaps" the "most reliable," Amy Greene, who "says Marilyn made the horrendous admission that she had had twelve abortions."[127] Next, "in 1955, Marilyn told Amy Greene that she had had yet another abortion. It brought the total to thirteen at this point [. . .] if Marilyn's own account to Amy Greene is correct."[128] In this case we are apparently not to be skeptical of Marilyn Monroe's own account. But this is not Monroe's own account in any event: it is Summers's version of what Amy Greene told him Monroe told her (and as we saw in chapter four, Rollyson argues that Monroe considered Amy Greene untrustworthy). At the story's end, we are told that Marilyn Monroe looked "poorly" during the filming of *Something's Got to Give* in the last summer of her life "because she had just had an abortion."[129] Summers neglects to keep score at this point, but that would bring the count to fourteen. Then Summers spends pages outlining doubts about the final rumored pregnancy. Here are the possibilities he offers, in order: she had an abortion; she had a miscarriage (these take him to her autopsy, which unfortunately can't settle the question); she fantasized a miscarriage; she had "gynecological problems" that resulted in skipped periods; or the pregnancy was one among many of her various drug- and alcohol-induced fantasies. The one possibility Summers doesn't seriously entertain is that the uncertainty might derive from the story's unreliability, rather than from Marilyn's.

Spoto, in contrast, eschews the intimacy of girlish confessions in favor of the authority of masculine medical science. He quotes Monroe's gynecologist, who declares that she never had any abortions: "'And the rumors of her multiple abortions are ridiculous. She never had even one. Later there were two miscarriages and an ectopic pregnancy requiring emergency termination, but no abortion.'"[130] Brown and Barham claim that coroner Thomas T. Noguchi found evidence of "multiple abortions" during the autopsy, but offer no citation for this assertion, and in fact neither Noguchi's book (*Coroner to the Stars*) nor the full autopsy report cites any such evidence.[131] Having simply asserted that Monroe had "multiple abortions," Brown and Barham struggle to determine in particular whether she became pregnant with and aborted a child conceived with one of the Kennedy brothers. Beginning with "clues," they reprint "reports" from various people who claim that Monroe told them she was pregnant, though these reports differ on which of the brothers was meant to be the father. After outlining these "clues"—five named "witnesses," Monroe's "wanness" when she reported to work, and a vial of morphine capsules—Brown and Barham write in their next paragraph: "When Monroe fearfully called Bobby [Kennedy] at Hickory Hill, she must have told him that she had just endured another abortion."[132] Within the space of a page, this speculative allegation assumes the status of confirmed fact: "Monroe's aborted pregnancy [. . .] caused great consternation in the offices of the posh Arthur Jacobs Public Relations Company."[133]

Marilyn Monroe's reputed abortions also apparently caused great consternation in the offices of her biographers. Freeman, who does believe Lena Pepitone's story of a child given up for adoption in Marilyn's teens, offers her usual literal interpretation of what all these alleged abortions reveal about Marilyn's psyche. Like Steinem,

Freeman links Monroe's physical difficulties in bringing pregnancies to term with her psychic insufficiencies, repulsions and fears:

> The aim of Norma Jean's dreams was to replace the child she had lost in her teens. Judging by at least fourteen abortions, we can assume Marilyn was repulsed at the thought of bearing a child, believing it would end what, to her, was her most precious possession—her career. She also unconsciously feared she would be unable to bring up a child as her mother and father had proved themselves unable to do with her.
>
> Marilyn's repeated abortions were a vital force in fighting Norma Jean, the innocent within, who finally fought back at the price of Marilyn's life. How many abortions could one woman stand? This was a gruesome way to punish the self.[134]

Freeman also accepts the story of the abortion at Cedars of Lebanon, writing that this alleged abortion occurred "fourteen days before she would take her own life. A death for a death, so to speak."[135]

The womb's symbolic association with death becomes manifest in Summers's account of the coroner's report, from which, he tells us, we can learn salient truths about Monroe's body. But those truths are instantly and reductively sexual, as the only direct quotation Summers offers from Noguchi's report is what seems a routine acknowledgment that the body he was examining was biologically female:

> We are told [Summers says] that "distribution of the pubic hair is of female pattern. The uterus is of the usual size." We learn of the scars the photographer's airbrush had hidden so efficiently, of the appendectomy, of the gall-bladder removed. We learn that, for all the storied excess, the living Monroe had been in fairly good shape.[136]

Behind the deceptive airbrushing of her public image, "we learn," by means of dissection, that the truth of Monroe's body is located in her pubic hair, her uterus, and her (two) scars. This account leaves the reader with the impression of death in the shape of female genitalia, scars and surgeries—not with the impression of an otherwise healthy young woman who happened to die young. Summers acknowledges that the excess is "storied" (and is contrary to the fact of her relative health). What he doesn't acknowledge is that this belief in her "storied" excess comes from stories precisely like his. The autopsy report says that Monroe's body was normal and healthy, but the apocrypha keeps looking for the scars.

Monroe suffered from endometriosis, a condition in which the lining of the uterine wall is found outside the uterus, and for which no medical cause has been established; it produces the intense pain that so tormented Monroe that she had a clause in her contract protecting her from working when she was menstruating. But rather than treat endometriosis as a medical condition (and therefore presumably morally neutral), biographers read it as a gauge of character. For example, Freeman interprets Monroe's severe menstrual cramps as a sign of her hatred of her own sex, and her need for a mother:

> She confessed she became depressed when she menstruated, a time she always suffered acute cramps. The latter occur in women who resent the monthly period, dislike being women, rebel against what they call the "curse" that reveals what they consider their frailties. Marilyn was reported at times walking around with monthly bloodstains showing through the back of her dress, as though she were a little girl waiting for her mother to "clean" her up, lessen the pain of an unwanted flow of blood.[137]

Are there any women who *like* "the monthly period"? Or who wouldn't find a monthly onslaught of "acute cramps" depressing? This passage was published in 1992, showing if nothing else that, if Marilyn Monroe seems a cultural throwback, this is due in no small part to the regressive attitudes our culture expresses about her.

Summers introduces the topic of Monroe's difficult periods via his discussion of abortions, as if to suggest that the two were related, writing, "Marilyn's poor battlefield of a womb had been a torment since adolescence, even before those surgical invasions."[138] Immediately following this statement is a paragraph describing Monroe's history of menstrual problems, all of which occurs within the first few chapters of Summers's biography. In order to know Monroe, we must first understand the (failed) functions of her uterus: miscarriages, abortions and menstruation all make it into the first twenty-five pages of Summers's life, just as pregnancy, infertility and the womb feature on the first page of Guiles's. When *Vanity Fair* published the only excerpt from Mailer's play *Strawhead* that has been made publicly available, it chose a two-page scene from act one that squeezes Marilyn's periods, abortions and pregnancies into the space of thirteen lines. Marilyn Monroe, the "most womanly of all women" according to the piece Arthur Miller wrote for *Life* in 1958, and the "All-Girl Girl" according to the jacket notes of Zolotow's biography, suffered in appropriate excess from what is sometimes referred to as "female trouble."

Endometriosis can cause complications with pregnancy, and is particularly correlated with ectopic (tubular) pregnancies, of which Monroe reportedly had several. Spoto reports that she miscarried several times during her marriage to Miller, including on the set of *The Prince and the Showgirl* in 1956, during the summer of 1957, on Long Island, and while filming *Some Like It Hot* in 1958. Like abortions, miscarriages will be read as symbolic omens, harbingers of Monroe's own death. For example, Monroe had a tubular pregnancy that ended in miscarriage on August 1, 1957, which prompts Summers to observe that "Marilyn was to die, five years later, on the anniversary of this miscarriage."[139] Mailer isn't even willing to believe that the pregnancy was tubular, suggesting it might have been "hysterical." And as usual, it will be her fantasy, not his:

the question remains whether her pregnancies were tubular or hysterical. [Milton] Greene claims she once had a fearful abortion that made it impossible for her to be pregnant. Miller, in an interview, said she could not, but later in the same interview thought she did have a tubular pregnancy. It is a confusion that she may even have disseminated herself and it persists. What may be the best explanation, from a friend who knew Marilyn well, is that she had had many abortions, perhaps so many as twelve! And in cheap places—for a number of these abortions came in the years she was modeling or a bit player on seven-year contracts— thus her gynecological insides were unspeakably scarred, and her propensity for tubular pregnancy was increased.[140]

Again, though, we should bear in mind that the autopsy report says nothing about her "unspeakably scarred" "gynecological insides." The hypothesis that Marilyn was just fantasizing her pregnancies allows Mailer to confirm Zanuck's alleged diagnosis that she was "a sexual freak."[141] Summers reports a friend who also claims that throughout Monroe's life, "every two or three months, she'd gain, maybe fourteen or fifteen pounds. She was forever having false pregnancies."[142] Here are the two usual explanations: she is failure, or she is fake.

For Oates, Marilyn's need to be a mother is so fundamental that two terminated pregnancies cause her total disintegration. The first is an early abortion that Oates attributes to her need to protect her career: the father is either one of the two "Gemini" twins with whom Oates imagines her Marilyn having a ten-year ménage à trois. Marilyn is so devastated over the abortion that she barely recovers her sanity. When she miscarries during her marriage to The Playwright, she attempts suicide and then falls apart altogether in the space of a page, which Oates represents as a total breakdown in her thought process. Oates's Marilyn is demonstrably mad once she loses her baby.

It is hard not to see lurking in these accounts, especially given the medical and psychiatric language and authority assumed by all of these writers, an older history of medical corrective efforts to "discipline" the oversexed woman. The rhetorical emphasis on abortions, painful menstruation, ectopic pregnancies and miscarriages is more than a little punitive. In fact, it recalls figuratively the actual medical treatment inflicted upon women in the nineteenth century who were judged by (male) doctors to be sexually "abnormal"; such abnormalities took various forms, including hysteria, masturbation, neurasthenia, lack of desire for sex with men or "frigidity," and nymphomania. Ironically enough, Summers accuses Monroe of both: he has her having affairs with countless (unnamed) men throughout both of her marriages ("Marilyn had for some time ceased to be wholly faithful. 'She had this terrible neediness,' says [a] friend, 'she went with other men simply for something to hold on to'"[143]), but he also recycles that favorite anecdote from the indiscreet Dr. Greenson, who told colleagues, according to Summers,

> that he thought the Miller marriage had collapsed "to a consider- able degree" on sexual grounds. Marilyn, he observed, felt she was frigid. She "found it difficult to sustain a series of orgasms with the same individual."
>
> Greenson would also report that, pathetically, this sexually dis- satisfied woman "gloried and revelled in her personal appearance, feeling that she was an extremely beautiful woman, perhaps the most beautiful woman in the world."[144]

Surely biographies' interest in the function of Marilyn Monroe's actual sexual organs is the vestigial trace of the fear and loathing women's bodies elicited from their culture as much as it is a mis- placed faith in the empirical. Showalter's account in *The Female Mal- ady* of such nineteenth-century medical and psychiatric practices is a not inapt description of Monroe's treatment at the hands of many of her biographers. Showalter distinguishes between the women patients in insane asylums and the women forced to undergo "corrective" gynecological surgeries, but contends that both practices were meant to regulate women's minds and bodies. Both psychiatry and medi- cine, she argues, expressed the power of male doctors "over defini- tions of femininity and insanity"; where medicine preferred "the surgical knife," psychiatry relied upon "moral management" through "domestic routine."[145] The failures of domestic routine and moral management will similarly determine the apocrypha's diagnosis of Marilyn: what ails her is a combination of

> all that oncoming accumulation of ills she has postponed from the past, all that sexual congress with men she has not loved, and all those unfinished hours with men she has loved, all the lies she has told, all the lies told about her, all unavenged humiliations sleeping like unfed scorpions in the unsettled flesh. Worse!—all

unfinished family insanity, plus her own abused nerves. Plus the need to come to rest in some final identity.[146]

Mailer's catalog of the myriad ways in which Marilyn is annulled and undone (there are twelve negatives or pejoratives in three sentences) makes clear that she suffers especially from being unfinished. The only way that Marilyn Monroe can come to rest in a final identity is when she comes to an identity in her final rest, as the most famous dead woman in the twentieth century.

6

FEMME FATALE, 1961–1962

Marilyn died, really, on a Saturday night. The girl
whose translucent beauty had made her the "love
object" of millions of unknown lonely or unsatisfied
males had no date that evening.

—CLARE BOOTHE LUCE,
"What Really Killed Marilyn," *Life,* August 7, 1964

From the very first of her many lives, Marilyn Monroe has been
defined as out of the ordinary: in 1960, Zolotow declared that once
she became an unnatural creation, she could no longer "*be* ordinary."[1]
When she does try to be ordinary, to be real, such endeavors bring
defeat: "For the first time, Marilyn had attempted to summon up the
passions and concerns of an ordinary, loving woman, and her efforts
had ended in mutual frustration and, finally, failure."[2] For Marilyn
Monroe, to be ordinary is not only a failure, it is to be sexually
exhausted and dead. Mailer declares that in *Let's Make Love,* among
Monroe's least successful films:

> She has never made a movie where she is so agreeable to the direc-
> tor. She has also never made a movie where she is so ordinary. A
> sad truth is before us again. Art and sex are no more compatible than
> they care to be. She is wan in the film and dull. Hollywood looks
> at *Let's Make Love.* Hollywood offers the verdict: "Fucked-out."[3]

Marilyn Monroe at the Last Sitting, 1962. PHOTOGRAPH BY BERT STERN.

An ordinary Marilyn is a tired Marilyn. No longer desirable, she is either exhausted (fucked-out) or pathological (fucked-up). In 1964, Clare Boothe Luce wrote in *Life* magazine that "what really killed Marilyn" was the most ordinary of fates, finding herself dateless on a Saturday night: "Marilyn died, really, on a Saturday night. The girl whose translucent beauty had made her the 'love object' of millions of unknown lonely or unsatisfied males had no date that evening." Confronted with the possibility of losing her "extraordinary power to project sex," Marilyn "despaired," in Luce's portrait, at the onset of ordinariness. Summers similarly implies, repeatedly, that age made it harder to fight ordinariness, or reality: in March 1962, he writes, she "spent hours dressing, turning the aging Norma Jeane into 'Marilyn.'"[4] She was not yet thirty-six.

As Marilyn Monroe's story nears its end, her audience begins to interpret her image as already damaged and dying. The photograph that opens this chapter was taken during the Last Sitting with Bert Stern; it shows a woman arguably more attractive (at least by today's standards of beauty) than Monroe had ever been before. Nonetheless, accusing Marilyn of having "indulged her exhibitionism one last time" in this session, Summers implies that this photograph, which he does not reproduce, reveals the truth of her imminent death (despite the fact that the deluded photographer was misled by her glamour): "She was photographed completely naked. The camera saw the weariness, the slash in the belly—a legacy of the gall bladder operation—but the cameraman saw some sort of immortality."[5] In 1962, Diana Trilling also saw death lurking in these pictures:

> The photographs leave, however, a record only of wasted beauty, at least of the famous body—while Marilyn Monroe's face is lovely as ever, apparently unscarred by her intense suffering, her body looked ravaged and ill, already drained of life. [. . .] At the last, the nude Marilyn Monroe could excite no decent viewer to anything but the gentlest pity, and much fear.[6]

Writers have a habit of searching out Monroe's scars and seeing them as cryptic indications that she's about to die. Trilling pities her and Summers despises her, but they both look down on her from a great height. And they both make the scar the whole picture.

Describing Monroe's state in her last summer, Brown and Barham declare that the photos George Barris took "showed a rail-thin Monroe leaning lifelessly against a balcony with the sea behind her—the very portrait of a middle-aged anorexic," as if that were a diagnostic category.[7] Would Marilyn Monroe look "lifeless" if she hadn't died soon after? She was certainly thin that summer, but she had also been relentlessly criticized in the press for her heaviness in her recent films, and was trying to make a comeback. Her slimness was supposed to be a sign of renewed youth and vitality; because she died, her weight loss becomes "anorexia." At this point in the tale, any sign of illness, decay or physical mortality will become a symptom of fatality. Summers captions a photograph with Monroe's remark that "gravity catches up with all of us"; the photograph shows only laugh lines by Monroe's eyes (and the light fuzz on her cheeks that Summers associated with aging in a bizarre early footnote).* Similarly, Paige Baty writes that in the film of Monroe's birthday tribute to John F. Kennedy "she seems already disappearing, gone the way of the vampire, dead yet immortal, a memento mori of herself."[9]

Her imminent death makes Marilyn Monroe a corpse waiting to happen. Summers declares that "Marilyn had begun to die" in 1957, five years before she completed dying.[10] Richard Meryman, who conducted Monroe's last interview for *Life,* calls her lifeless—twice:

> I was struck by how pasty her skin was—pasty and lifeless-looking. There was not much health in that skin. [. . .] It was a little bit coarse, lifeless. It looked like skin that had had makeup on it for a long, long time. She looked terrific, but when you really studied that face, it was kind of cardboardy.[11]

---

*In the text, Summers describes Monroe's habit in her early years of smearing Vaseline on her face in order to "keep her skin young," and reports that she was advised that "it would simply encourage the growth of unwanted hair." He then appends a footnote that adds an I-told-you-so: "As photographs taken in her thirties show, Marilyn did later grow facial hair on her cheeks."[8]

Like Guiles and Whitey Snyder discussing her fraudulent beauty, Meryman distinguishes between "looking terrific" and *really* looking terrific. Her death is written on her very skin, and comes from being too "made-up." Artificiality is closing in on her.

In February 1961, Monroe's New York–based psychoanalyst, Marianne Kris, became alarmed by what she considered Monroe's suicidal behavior, and persuaded her to enter the Payne-Whitney psychiatric clinic. Monroe entered willingly, signing in as "Faye Miller," but was terrified to be treated as a disturbed patient, locked in a padded cell, and threatened with a straitjacket when she screamed to be released. "There is no partition to the john," writes Mailer.

> Which nurse, intern, resident, visiting doctor or hospital attendant will fail to take a good look? Soon gossip is blazing like brush fire. She has whipped off her clothes, goes the gossip, she has . . . one can fill in any obscene gesture if one wants to hear the gossip.[12]

She spent three days there, during which by most accounts she was hysterical ("so they'll really have something to stare at," Guiles says she declared,[13] although Spoto has her "rationally" riposting a doctor's query as to why she thought she was so unhappy: "I've been paying the best doctors a fortune to find out why, and you're asking *me*?"[14]), before she was able to reach Joe DiMaggio, who flew instantly to New York and insisted that she be released. Many stories have him threatening to dismantle the building "brick by brick" if they tried to keep him out. He arranged for Monroe to be admitted to a private room at the Columbia University Medical Center, where she stayed until early March, recovering. In early October, she attended a dinner party at Peter Lawford's home, where she met Robert Kennedy for the first time; in November she went to the Lawfords with President Kennedy.

In early 1962, Monroe began work on *Something's Got to Give*. In May, after another bout of absenteeism (which Monroe ascribed to the flu, some biographers say was sinusitis, others insist was drugs and depression, and many observers assumed was business as usual), she defied studio orders and appeared at Madison Square Garden to sing "Happy Birthday" to the president. Arthur Schlesinger, Jr., admiringly described her appearance as "skin and beads," but most of her biographers seem to find this now legendary display of glittering sexuality slightly pathetic, indeed shameful. Female writers are particularly censorious: "Marilyn's appearance at the birthday gala was, in short, vulgar," Sandra Shevey declares severely in *The Marilyn Scandal.* "Her outfit was wrong: the wig was awful (it didn't seem to fit right) and the dress was too revealing (her body had, after all, matured)."[15] Even Marilyn's quondam sexiness only shows suffering: Steinem calls her performance a "great embarrassment. Marilyn's very fear and doped slowness created long sexy pauses."[16] Like Mrs. Clark complaining of Marilyn's "fat derrière," these female biographers find a woman displaying her "mature" body a "great embarrassment." She returned to Hollywood, and to the set. Her thirty-sixth birthday, June 1, was her last day at work at Fox; after calling in sick six more days, and having worked a total of thirteen out of thirty production days, she was fired on June 7 and sued for breach of contract.

Dismissed from the studio she had triumphed over only six years before, Monroe went to work on her publicity. She began granting interviews (it was at this time that she held the two taped interviews with Richard Meryman and Georges Belmont that are used in the film *Marilyn on Marilyn*), offering her side of the story and showing her fitness for work. She also participated in her first photo sessions in some time, including the ones with George Barris on Malibu beach (in which she wore the handmade brown Mexican cardigan that Christie's sold at auction for $167,500 in 1999), and the Last Sitting for *Vogue* with Bert Stern.

SOMETHING'S GOT TO GIVE

The stories about Monroe's end do not begin to diverge on the day that she died; the whole of her last summer gives rise to conflicting interpretations that lay the foundation for the different conclusions of each tale. All of the standard controversies of her lives—the condition of her body and her mind, the quality of her acting pitted against the opposition of a male director, and questions of her current sexual involvements—come to a head in the final days of her story.

The first scriptwriter of *Something's Got to Give,* which would become Monroe's final, unfinished film, was Nunnally Johnson. Johnson had been vocal in his dislike of Monroe early in her career, describing her in terms of overt contempt:

> Marilyn's a phenomenon of nature, like Niagara Falls or the Grand Canyon. You can't talk to it. It can't talk to you. All you can do is stand back and be awed by it. She's got no charm, delicacy, or taste. Nobody will ever call her America's Sweetheart. She's just an arrogant little tailswitcher. She's learned how to throw sex in your face.[17]

But in working on *Something's Got to Give,* according to Rollyson, Johnson changed his mind. Monroe was

> stimulated by Johnson's assurance that he had chosen to write the screenplay rather than accept other projects offered to him. When she realized he was not talking to her merely out of a sense of obligation, she became enthusiastic about the film, exploring questions of casting and plot development. He was so taken with her sharp perceptions that he regretted every harsh word he ever said against her and became her unabashed admirer.[18]

However, as Rollyson also notes, the film's director, George Cukor, was less of a fan, admitting to Johnson that he "loathed" Monroe. Monroe feared that Cukor would deliberately sabotage her part, and became so controlling and sensitive of changes to her role and to the script that some observers—and Leaming, for one, gives them the last word—considered her literally paranoid, and insane.

According to Guiles, Monroe was in despair during her last summer for two reasons: the end of her career and the end of a romance. Although in discussion with Fox to resume work on *Something's Got to Give,* and developing a few other film projects outside the studio, she nonetheless felt "close to defeat" and was "courting annihilation." He alleges that extant footage from *Something's Got to Give* demonstrates her disintegration: Cukor considered her "quite mad" and the film itself showed her "vacant or disconnected; vague or not relating to other characters."[19] Summers says Monroe was in a "narcotic nose-dive" all summer long, and "thinking about death." He claims that the summer was punctuated by several overdoses during which she nearly died, partly because she had been fired. Although there were negotiations to reinstate her at Fox, they were leading nowhere and she was desperate at finding that "there was no more work."[20] Cukor was "shaken" at her appearance on the film, as she seemed to be in sedated "slow motion."[21]

Brown and Barham base their revisionist account upon the "rediscovery" of the footage of *Something's Got to Give* in the Fox archives in 1988. "Hollywood history," they write, "and forty-two biographers, have depicted Marilyn Monroe as a stumbling, pill-ridden wreck on the set" of her last film, but the unearthed footage shows "an actress remarkably in control despite take after difficult take."[22] They explain that Henry Schipper, a Fox News producer, released a forty-seven-minute documentary in 1990, in which he revealed that the studio deliberately set out to smear Monroe to cover for their own financial problems. Brown and Barham contend that Fox had in fact rehired Monroe:

> the studio offered to radically renegotiate her contract into a $1-million deal: $500,000 for *Something's Got to Give* and an additional $500,000 or more for a new musical called *What a Way to Go,* which, not so coincidentally, was to be produced by Monroe's chief publicist, Arthur P. Jacobs. The discovery of this new contract in the Fox archives invalidates most accounts of the star's final dealings with Twentieth Century-Fox.[23]

They claim to have seen a copy of the contract. Spoto tells the same story a year later: Fox could not afford to lose Marilyn, still one of the world's biggest stars, and was wooing her back. Cukor had been fired and replaced by Jean Negulesco, who had successfully directed her in *How to Marry a Millionaire*; Nunnally Johnson was to rewrite a script that Monroe had felt was seriously damaged in last-minute rewrites. Spoto also insists that the extant footage of *Something's Got to Give* shows not a drugged ruin, but a consummate professional at the height of her genius: "The Marilyn Monroe of this film is wholly unlike that of *All About Eve* or *Niagara,* of *Gentlemen Prefer Blondes* or *The Seven Year Itch.* She is mature, serene, fragile—but graceful and resplendent too. The outtakes," he concludes, "remain among the indisputable examples of her greatly underestimated talent."[24]

Schipper's documentary has now been released on DVD and videotape as *Something's Got to Give.* Schipper does claim that, having been traduced in order to save the studio's face, Monroe had been secretly rehired at two and a half times her original salary. Certainly the footage the documentary includes does not show a deranged or detached woman wandering around in a narcotic fog: she knows her lines, is in character, and trying out different interpretations. Arguably she appears slightly unfocused in certain scenes, but wide-eyed incognizance is also part of the Marilyn persona, which she is resurrecting after several films away from it. We find ourselves back at the inescapable question: is Monroe acting, or are we seeing the "real" Marilyn?

Wolfe concurs that Fox deliberately defamed Marilyn; he finds this "incongruous attempt by a major studio to destroy its own star" to be "incomprehensible," despite the fact that everyone agrees on Fox's financial motives. For Wolfe, the explanation is *cherchez l'homme*: Bobby Kennedy was "behind Marilyn's dismissal and the ruthless campaign to discredit her in order to ensure her silence."[25] But Leaming's version is different yet again: although Marilyn was in negotiation with Fox to resume the picture, which it was in their best financial interest to complete, the studio was also determined to bring "a recalcitrant star to her knees" by inflicting stringent and humiliating conditions on her: she had to relinquish any say about director, cameraman, costars or script; she was forbidden to request additional takes or to view the daily rushes; an acting coach or "other helpers" were banned from the set without the director's permission; and finally she had to apologize publicly.[26] Leaming thus reconciles Monroe's rehiring with the suicidal depression from which she is convinced Monroe was suffering.

In 2001, Fox released another documentary, entitled *Marilyn Monroe: The Final Days.* This documentary moves in detail through the filming of *Something's Got to Give,* interviewing producers, screenwriters and costar Cyd Charisse, as well as showing much of the footage. The documentary ends with a restored and reconstructed "film" of *Something's Got to Give.* This documentary asserts that not only was Monroe rehired, but that she triumphed:

> Fox did an amazing about-face and told Marilyn that they wanted her back. Trade-offs were negotiated, and concessions were made on both sides. Marilyn agreed to give up having Paula Strasberg on the set, and in return director George Cukor would be replaced with Jean Negulesco. On August 1st, Marilyn signed a one-million-dollar, two-picture contract with Fox, and plans were made to resume shooting *Something's Got to Give* as soon as possible. [. . .] Marilyn had scored a major victory with Fox.[27]

DRAMATIS PERSONAE

Other inconsistencies in the various stories about Monroe's death derive from conflicting opinions about some of the "witnesses" to Monroe's last months. Monroe moved into her house on Fifth Helena Drive in February 1962, at the advice of Dr. Greenson, whom she saw daily for intense consultations. Greenson invited Monroe to dine with his family, introduced her to his children, and encouraged her to become friends with them; he consistently explained this deviation from standard therapeutic practice as a result of his conviction that Monroe was in such dire need that drastic, and unorthodox, measures were required.

But the biographical language describing Greenson's attachment to Monroe stresses his inability to resist her feminine charm. Guiles concludes that Greenson abandoned "necessary precautions" because he was "seduced by her air of helplessness" and "lost all perspective where Marilyn was concerned."[28] Summers, too, defends Greenson on the basis of Marilyn's childlike appeal: he was "genuinely touched by this thirty-five-year-old waif."[29] Brown and Barham consider Greenson harmful and domineering, and they don't look far for a motive, reporting that Whitey Snyder was convinced Greenson was driven by "money, money, money."[30] For Spoto, Greenson is a poisonous "Svengali," who sought not to make Monroe more independent, as he claimed, but rather to transfer her dependence onto himself. Spoto accuses Greenson of collaborating with her general practitioner, Hyman Engelberg, in continuing to keep her dependent on drugs, and even of providing her with them.[31] Leaming, who is very severe with the other men she felt exploited Monroe (namely Arthur Miller and Lee Strasberg), deems Greenson "decent, compassionate," someone who "sincerely wanted to help"; he admitted that he had a "weakness for damsels in distress," but was helpless in the face of Monroe's self-destructive behavior.[32] Finally, Wolfe claims that Greenson always disguised the true reasons for his decision to "sacrifice the basic tenets of his profession," which were neither personal nor financial, but political: Greenson, says Wolfe, was an agent of the Comintern, assigned to spy on Monroe. Wolfe's source is Frank A. Capell's 1964 *The Strange Death of Marilyn Monroe,* which is suspect for greater reasons than Capell's fanatical right-wing bias, as we shall see.[33]

It was also Greenson who advised Monroe to hire Eunice Murray. As the only other person definitely in the house when Monroe died, she would become the pivotal—and problematic—witness in the story of Marilyn's death. Most agree that Mrs. Murray was a casual friend of Greenson's who had some experience (although no formal education or training) in acting as "factotum and hand-holder," in Guiles's phrase, for psychiatric patients.[34] Spoto is the only biographer to argue that Monroe came seriously to resent Murray's presence as Greenson's "spy" in her house; the rest seem to feel she accepted the help Greenson and Murray were providing. Wolfe comments that the Murray-Greenson "friendship" (his scare quotes) is shrouded in mystery (not mentioning that Summers and Spoto both explain that she sold her house to Greenson and offered to work for him then), and asks whether the sinister explanation might not be that Murray's husband was also an agent for the Comintern.[35] Murray's character is consequential only if one believes in the homicide; if Monroe killed herself, then what Murray was like is irrelevant: Leaming doesn't bother to characterize her.

There are a few other disputed witnesses. Robert Slatzer, whose contested claim to have married Monroe in 1952 and been her life-long friend was discussed in chapter five, starts cropping up all over the conspiracy versions, claiming to have known about her affair with Robert Kennedy and to have evidence that she was assassinated. But those who discount Slatzer's story (notably Spoto and Leaming) don't mention him at all in their versions of Monroe's last days. The other significant, and unauthenticated, witness is a woman named Jeanne Carmen, who, like Slatzer, claims to have been a good friend of Monroe's, to have known all about Monroe's relationship with Robert Kennedy, and to have spoken with her on her last day alive; much of the conspiracy version hangs upon her statements. Summers, Brown and Barham, Wolfe, and now Smith, rely upon her; Guiles and Leaming don't mention her; Spoto discredits her as a former "bit-part actress" who claimed to have been Monroe's roommate in their early days in Hollywood. Just like Slatzer, says Spoto, Jeanne Carmen

> emerged from obscurity many years [after Monroe's death] to transmute her geographic proximity to Marilyn Monroe into something of a career. Claiming that she knew Monroe intimately, she began, in the 1980s, to describe a fantastic series of scurrilous tales for which there is simply no basis in fact. [...] Like that of Slatzer, however, Carmen's name is nowhere to be found in Marilyn's address books, nor did anyone who knew Marilyn ever hear of or see (much less meet or know) her.[36]

But Spoto's confirmation that Monroe had no significant relationship with Carmen comes from a woman named Betsy Duncan Hammes—whom none of the other lives even mentions.

Joe DiMaggio had resurfaced after the Payne-Whitney episode, escorting Monroe to Florida for recuperation, and, according to some writers, asking her to remarry him. Only Spoto asserts that there had been a rapprochement and definite plans to remarry.[37] Guiles writes that although there were rumors of a reconciliation, and even of plans to marry again, "no one ever heard Marilyn concede that she might."[38] For Summers, only DiMaggio sought a reconciliation; Marilyn was friendly, but in a tailspin and too involved with her relationships with the Kennedys and the Rat Pack to take him seriously. Wolfe quotes Lena Pepitone claiming that they loved each other, but that DiMaggio knew better than to try to reunite with her while her career remained of paramount importance.[39] But Leaming cites a different story from the same source: she writes that Pepitone asked him if remarriage was a possibility, and that in response he "clutched his stomach as though in excruciating pain. He said he loved Marilyn. He would always be there for her. But he could not live with the woman without quarreling."[40]

The biggest biographical dispute of that summer, however, is whether—and if so, to what extent—Monroe was involved romantically with Robert F. Kennedy. No one contests anymore that she had a sexual relationship of some kind with his brother, then president, although Spoto insists that it consisted only of a few brief encounters. "No serious biographer," opines Spoto, "can identify Monroe and [John F.] Kennedy as partners in a love affair," if that phrase denotes "a protracted intimacy sustained by some degree of frequency."[41] Guiles and Leaming also both accept only a handful of intermittent liaisons, beginning in December 1961, and Brown and Barham write that "JFK had bedded Monroe half a dozen times" before tiring of her.[42] But Summers and Wolfe both believe in a prolonged affair; Summers fixes its probable beginning in 1954, while Wolfe calls it "a unique relationship that ultimately endured for over a decade," enjoying a "longevity" not shared by Jack's other more "casual" affairs.[43]

The alleged affair with Robert is far more problematic. Rumors about Marilyn and Bobby go all the way back to Capell's *The Strange Death of Marilyn Monroe*. Guiles was the first biographer to mention, in 1969, the possibility of a romance with the attorney general, but only referred to him anonymously as the "Easterner," a well-known public servant. In 1973, Mailer would name names, and tell of the rumors that Marilyn and Bobby Kennedy had been lovers; characteristically, however, he would only do so paraliptically, relishing the prurient details before concluding that it was "only a flirtation."[44] Brown and Barham report that an investigative biographer named Tony Sciacca published a book called *Who Killed Marilyn Monroe?* in

1976, which purports to reproduce a "secret statement" by the attorney general about his relationship with Marilyn—a secret statement that was first "stumbled upon" by none other than Robert Slatzer, whose claims Brown and Barham credit.[45] The documents released on the Internet by the FBI under the Freedom of Information Act (FOIA) also reveal that these rumors were circulating as far back as 1964, although the documents in no way affirm their truth.

After Robert Kennedy's name had entered the story, the question of an affair with him became fundamental to the apocrypha. Summers quotes several people who confirm the relationship; the controversial Slatzer and Carmen figure prominently, but Summers's other witnesses are more persuasive, including the historian Arthur Schlesinger, Jr., who knew the Kennedys well, two of Peter Lawford's ex-wives, Senator George Smathers, who was a friend of John Kennedy's, and Dean Martin's ex-wife, whom Summers quotes making one of the fairer statements that ever finds its way into a life of Marilyn: Jeanne Martin "became 'quite sure' Marilyn was involved sexually with both Kennedy brothers but says, 'Unless you're in the bedroom, it's unfair to presume.' "[46] Immediately following this eminently reasonable conclusion, Summers dispenses with its logic: "on the basis of the assembled information," he declares, Monroe's affair with both Kennedy brothers "must now be considered beyond presumption."[47]

For Spoto, the rumors of an affair with Robert Kennedy are "unfounded and scurrilous accounts," based on four meetings between the two, who "never shared a bed."[48] Spoto quotes one, Pulitzer Prize–winning, witness, Edwin Guthman, as demonstrating that "their respective whereabouts" made the possibility of an affair impossible, although Spoto's one witness denying the affair does not necessarily stack well against Summers's six and more (some of whom also won prizes) affirming it. Spoto argues that the stories that Kennedy was in Los Angeles the last weekend of Marilyn's life are "the most outrageous assertions"—which would be "hilarious" were they not so "injurious"—given that the AP wire service and the *Los Angeles Times* both announced his arrival in San Francisco on Friday, and that the family with whom he stayed (the Bateses) all confirm his presence with them the entire day leading up to Monroe's death; they even played the inevitable Kennedy game of touch football.[49] Certainly Spoto's faith in the truth of the journalistic record seems dubious; Kennedy could easily, as Summers and Wolfe both maintain he did, have flown from San Francisco to Los Angeles without alerting the newspapers. Whether the Bateses would lie to protect him is also impossible to know.

Maintaining that Spoto was driven by a need to maintain the purity of the Kennedys at all costs, Wolfe alleges that Spoto relied on the "systematic elimination of witnesses' statements and established facts," including

> [Eunice] Murray's statements to the BBC, 20/20, and *The New York Post*; Marilyn's phone records; Jean Kennedy Smith's note to Marilyn; the helicopter logs; Dr. Robert Litman's notes regarding Marilyn and the Kennedys; Senator George Smathers's statements; [former L.A Police Chief] Daryl Gates's confirmation that Robert Kennedy was in Los Angeles on August 4, 1962; Mayor Sam Yorty's disclosures [that Kennedy was in Los Angeles]; and [private detective] Fred Otash's statements to *The Los Angeles Times*.
>
> Rather than refute evidence proffered by investigative journalists, Spoto elected to assassinate the character of those bearing ill news of Camelot.[50]

Wolfe then hotly defends Summers from Spoto's accusations of misrepresentation, and cites the settled lawsuit Summers brought against Spoto for defamation. However, Wolfe is not entirely accurate in this representation. Spoto does report the "ill news of Camelot" that Jack Kennedy and Monroe appear to have had a sexual relationship; it is the relationship with Bobby he denies.* Spoto's arguably nostalgic idolatry of the Kennedy brothers is offset by Summers's worship of their transcendent sexual blessings: he declares

---

*Wolfe also misrepresents Spoto's theory of the cause of Marilyn's death, writing that Spoto "accused Dr. Ralph Greenson and Eunice Murray of murdering Monroe by administering a fatal barbiturate-laced enema. The reader was informed that Greenson and Murray's motive was that they had been fired."[51] In fact, Spoto says repeatedly that he believes it to have been an accident, not murder, so the triviality of the "motive" is not at issue.

that they "led sex lives that were, in ordinary mortals' terms, outside the ordinary."[52]

Brown and Barham write that Marilyn's long-distance relationship with Bobby Kennedy "was both more intense and more likely than her lusty, tempestuous affair with the President. Bobby and Monroe were soulmates."[53] But Leaming, although relating the handful of times when they met in public, and acknowledging that Marilyn phoned Bobby "a good deal" after the president "cut her off," states that she did so only as "a way of maintaining a Kennedy connection."[54] Incredibly, Leaming never refers to the thirty years of rumors of an affair between the two at all.

THE CAL-NEVA WEEKEND

The turning point between suicide and homicide comes in the rendering of the controversial stories about a weekend Monroe spent shortly before she died at the Cal-Neva Lodge. Cal-Neva was a resort in Lake Tahoe, on the California-Nevada border, in part owned by Frank Sinatra, with whom Monroe had been friends, and occasionally involved romantically, for some years. Reports vary as to who his partners were, but there seems little doubt that it was a Mafia-financed operation, in which Sam Giancana, a Chicago gangster who had been Al Capone's driver, had invested. Also included in the arrangement was Milton (Mickey) Rudin, who was Sinatra's attorney as well as Marilyn Monroe's; he was, in addition, the brother-in-law of Dr. Greenson. Cal-Neva was managed by Paul "Skinny" D'Amato, who has been implicated in the alleged fixing of the West Virginia primary that helped elect Jack Kennedy. The close familial, political and financial connections of all of these people have been seen as cause for suspicion by many—but these close connections may well have helped *prompt* the conspiracy theories.

Events surrounding the Cal-Neva weekend are highly disputed. Guiles says Monroe was never there at all; it was a "cover story" to mask a stay at Cedars of Lebanon hospital, which she entered under an alias on July 20. He reports rumors that she was there to have an abortion, before adding à la Mailer that "it would be easy to assume that the aborted child was a Kennedy," although she was seeing other

men as well that spring and summer, and he hasn't actually established that she had an abortion in the first place.[55] For Summers,
Cal-Neva was a catastrophically damaging weekend that pushed
Monroe over the "brink" on which she was already teetering. Peter
Lawford, a friend of both Monroe's and Sinatra's, and a Kennedy
brother-in-law, said Monroe was his guest at Cal-Neva three weeks
before her death (which would, as in Guiles's account, have been
July 20), when Sinatra was performing there. She spent the weekend
in a barbiturate haze (thus Summers) before she overdosed and
nearly died; she was then "whisked" back to Los Angeles on Sinatra's
private plane.[56] An anonymous film processor alleges that he developed photographs taken by Sinatra that weekend that show "Marilyn
in utter disarray."[57] Meanwhile, says Summers, DiMaggio, who was
"trying to help Marilyn," arrived at Tahoe but stayed elsewhere,
"because there was a feud between him and Sinatra at the time"; he
wanted to remarry Monroe, but whether Monroe agreed Summers
leaves open to question.[58] For Summers "the real trigger for this week
of Marilyn's despair" was that "she was pregnant again."[59]

Spoto, however, claims that Monroe entered Cedars of Lebanon
on July 20 to have a scheduled surgery to solve her chronic gynecological problems, asserting that her gynecologist's records "leave no
doubt that the later rumors of an abortion are sheer fiction."[60] He
says the trip to Cal-Neva occurred over the weekend of July 28 and
29, and that, contrary to "scurrilous and unfounded rumors" of overdose or sexual involvement with "various figures from the criminal
underworld," she spent a quiet weekend with Joe DiMaggio and
agreed to remarry him. Spoto also names some witnesses who were
at Cal-Neva that weekend, who knew Giancana and other Mafia figures; they attest that the gangsters alleged to have been at the resort
that weekend were nowhere to be seen (although Spoto does not
acknowledge that Mob "witnesses" have been known on occasion to
be less than reliable).[61] Brown and Barham went even further than
Spoto, dismissing the entire story as a belated invention by Peter
Lawford to "bolster" his story that Monroe had been suicidal all
along, a story invented ex post facto to cover for the Kennedys' having killed her.[62]

Wolfe says that on July 28 and 29, Monroe was invited to the lodge under the pretense of seeing Sinatra perform, but in truth to persuade her "not to go to the press" about her liaison with Robert Kennedy.[63] According to Wolfe, not only was Giancana definitely there, but he was also identified by the Nevada Gaming Commission, which led to Sinatra losing his gambling license. DiMaggio was unexpectedly there, too, but couldn't find Monroe (who was under an assumed name), and was barred from the hotel on Sinatra's orders.[64] While there, according to two witnesses Wolfe quotes, Monroe was drugged and then photographed "being sexually abused in the presence of Sam Giancana and Sinatra."[65] These would seem to be the pictures of "Marilyn in utter disarray" to which Summers euphemistically referred. Both Summers and Wolfe report that these incriminating photos were destroyed.

Leaming, whose Marilyn deliberately killed herself, never mentions the weekend at all.

THE LAST DAY

Saturday, August 4, 1962, was the last day of Marilyn Monroe's life. The events of the morning are not much disputed, but Monroe's mood and temperament are. She had invited her press agent, Patricia Newcomb, to stay overnight on Friday. Newcomb claims that Marilyn awoke in a bad temper, irritated by Newcomb's ability to sleep until noon when she herself suffered from her chronic insomnia. During the morning she met with photographer Lawrence Schiller, who was discussing with her the possibility of a *Playboy* spread using nude photos of Marilyn in a pool on the set of *Something's Got to Give*. The pictures had knocked Elizabeth Taylor off the front pages for the first time since the beginning of *Cleopatra* and her sensational affair with costar Richard Burton, as well as giving Monroe her first *Life* cover in two years. (Thus Monroe's career ended, ironically enough, where it began, with nude pictures and *Playboy*.) Greenson came to consult with Monroe at some point during the afternoon and stayed at least until early evening. Two other key assertions are each made by only one biographer: Spoto claims that the day Monroe died was supposed to be the last day at work for Eunice Murray, as she had been fired for insolence, and because Marilyn had realized that Murray was spying on her for Dr. Greenson. Wolfe claims that Robert Kennedy visited Marilyn in the early afternoon on the day she died. Finally, there are disputes about a beach party at Peter Lawford's nearby house in Malibu, which Monroe may or may not have attended, and a dinner party later that night, to which she was invited.

SUICIDE

Guiles and Leaming are the two primary proponents of the theory that Monroe killed herself more or less deliberately on the evening of August 4. Although there are slight variations (Guiles's version of Monroe's last day is far more detailed), there are no serious disagreements in the basic outline they provide of the events that took place that Saturday. For Guiles, Monroe may have resented Newcomb's long sleep, but nonetheless spent part of the afternoon sunbathing with her by the pool; she wrote on the back of the nude photographs she discussed with Schiller, "these should go to *Playboy*," which Guiles likens to the distribution of personal property by someone gathering her effects together. Leaming says that Monroe was "enraged" by Newcomb's late morning, yet another in a long line of "irrational" angers to which she was subject that summer.[66]

Guiles reports that Marilyn received calls from friends congratulating her on the interview that had just appeared in *Life,* calls that "seemed to lift her spirits a bit."[67] Dr. Greenson arrived at four-thirty, say both Guiles and Leaming, finding Monroe "despondent." He stayed until early evening and asked Newcomb to leave "in the interest of peace,"[68] arranging for Mrs. Murray to stay overnight instead, although she usually went home at night. Marilyn's masseur and close friend, Ralph Roberts, phoned around 5:30 or 6 P.M., to be told by Greenson that she wasn't in, a "polite lie" that Guiles finds not at all sinister; rather, Greenson was either in the middle of a session, or had just given her a tranquilizer.[69] Leaming makes no mention of the phone call or of Greenson tranquilizing Monroe, saying only that she seemed better when Greenson departed at 7 P.M. for a dinner party.

As Leaming never mentions even the possibility of an affair with Robert Kennedy, she tells the reader only that Marilyn had been invited to a party at Peter Lawford's, but was in "no shape to attend."[70] Guiles, however, relates a rather more complicated story: Robert Kennedy was going to be at the Lawfords', "and it is almost certain that the purpose of his coming was to end his relationship with Marilyn. In all probability, it was fear of this final confrontation—at the Lawford beach house—that triggered her compulsion toward oblivion."[71] She received a phone call some time before 8 P.M. from her former stepson, Joe DiMaggio, Jr., announcing that he had ended an engagement of which Monroe disapproved; she phoned Greenson at 7:40, jubilant, to report the news, says Leaming.[72] Around 8 P.M., she called the Lawfords, says Guiles, not to decline the invitation to their house, but for some "more urgent" reason that so alarmed Lawford that his first impulse was to go to Monroe's house. But then he decided to behave more circumspectly and phoned his manager, who tried to reach Marilyn's doctors or attorney.[73] Leaming tells it the other way around: Lawford called Marilyn, asking where she was, and was alarmed when she said to him: "Say goodbye to Pat [Lawford]. Say goodbye to Jack [Kennedy]. And say goodbye to yourself because you're a nice guy."[74] This quotation, often represented as Marilyn Monroe's last words, appears in virtually every account. Like Guiles, Leaming reports that Lawford called his manager, who called Mickey Rudin, Monroe's attorney. Rudin called the Monroe house around 9 P.M.; Mrs. Murray answered and reported that all was well, which both Guiles and Leaming accept she said in good faith, as someone with no reason to believe that Marilyn was dying behind her bedroom door.

At this point, however, their versions diverge significantly. Guiles tells two different stories in 1969 and in 1984, although he remains convinced that Marilyn died by her own hand; the 1984 account does not allude to the fact that some arguably essential details have altered since his first telling. His first version was that Dr. Greenson called later to check on Marilyn; Mrs. Murray answered the phone, and without knocking on the door, saw the light under it and told him that Marilyn was fine. She then awoke before 3 A.M. "with an uneasy feeling," hurried to Monroe's room, and saw the light still on under the door. Worried, she tried the door, and found it locked; she called

Marilyn's name, and went outside and peered through the windows. She thought Monroe looked " 'peculiar' " as "one arm was stretched across her bed and a hand hung limp on one of her telephones." So she called Dr. Greenson, who arrived "within minutes" and broke a windowpane with a poker to enter the room. Although he knew she was dead, he called Dr. Engelberg, Monroe's general practitioner, who arrived at 3:30 A.M., to confirm it. The police were phoned shortly after 4 A.M. Although the coroner's report determined "probable suicide," according to Guiles, "very few of those who knew her well believed that it was an intentional act. They saw her death as a terrible accident."[75]

But by 1984, Guiles had decided the suicide was intentional. Now he reports that Mrs. Murray saw (at some unspecified time) not a light under the door, but rather that the cord of Marilyn's private phone was under the closed door of the bedroom, although she couldn't hear Marilyn speaking to anyone. This seemed "unusual," so she used the second, house line, to phone Dr. Greenson. He told her to check on Marilyn, at which point she tried the door, but found it locked. Mrs Murray ran outside to look in the window, but because of curtains and iron grilles, had to get a poker to push the curtains back. She "sensed that Marilyn was dead" because although the night was cool, Monroe was "uncovered." She then called both Greenson and Dr. Engelberg. Greenson broke into the window and told Mrs. Murray: "We've lost her."[76] Leaming tells the same story, returning to the original version that Mrs. Murray awakened at 3 A.M. with a "sixth sense" that something was wrong; this sense of foreboding sent her to Monroe's door to discover the phone line.

The rest of Leaming's story follows Guiles's without comment, a remarkable decision in light of the thirty years of rumor, contradiction and reinterpretation that intervened (rumors that had presumably influenced Guiles's decision to revise his biography in the first place). Only one paragraph even alludes to these controversies at all: she explains that it is "natural" for the friends and family of a suicide to go into denial, even to suspect "foul play," but that "everything pointed to the conclusion that Marilyn had killed herself."[77] Whereas Guiles has Marilyn kill herself in despair over being abandoned by Robert Kennedy, Leaming's Marilyn killed herself to fulfill "her mother's judgment. On the night of August 4, she finished what she believed Gladys had set out to do when she tried to kill her baby daughter."[78] What Leaming fails to acknowledge is that *not* everything pointed to the conclusion of suicide, and that the discrepancies in the stories told of Monroe's last hours had been apparent for twenty-five years by the time she wrote her version.

A COMPENDIUM OF LIES

Mailer was the first major author to reveal the inconsistencies in the version favored by Guiles (and later by Leaming). Mailer disagrees with Guiles about the death but absolves him for his errors because his story "may be no more than a compendium of the lies he was told."[79] Admitting that "there seems next to nothing of such evidence" as would prove murder, nonetheless Mailer introduces the rumors into the narrative of Marilyn's death.

Mailer does raise for the first time some apparently pertinent questions that will preoccupy subsequent biographers. He explains that Monroe, always battling insomnia, had stapled her curtains down to keep out the light, begging the question of how Mrs. Murray saw her dead body through the window in the first place.[80] "Nor are one's questions reduced," he adds, "by the fact that Mrs. Murray will go off on a six-month tour of Europe in the next few days, and Pat Newcomb, who is naturally hysterical in the aftermath, will be flown to Hyannisport," the summer home of the Kennedys. He reports an anonymous claim that earlier in the evening there was a "quiet party at Marilyn's house which is attended by Peter Lawford, Bobby, Pat Newcomb, and Mrs. Murray." When Kennedy left with the rest, "a little later Marilyn begins to call, and keeps phoning him."[81] He also cites "another version" with "Natalie Wood and Warren Beatty" at a party thrown by Lawford, which *Marilyn* leaves. "One way or another, she seems to have had some disagreement with Kennedy," Mailer concludes. By means of this rhetorical sleight of hand Mailer implies that the difference is only over *which* party she attended with Kennedy, rather than over *whether* she attended a party with him. ·

After being relatively scrupulous, Mailer then heads down a trail of conjecture, granting himself permission to speculate freely: "Why not assume," he suggests, that a puerile Robert Kennedy began to mature "in the reckoning he took of himself on the escape from Los Angeles in the dead morning hours after Marilyn was gone." Again Mailer uses a secondary assumption (that Kennedy matured that night) in order to deflect attention away from a primary assumption (that he was in Los Angeles and "escaped" after Monroe's death). Then "if we are to grant this much," he asks, reasoning backward from these first assumptions, "why not assume even more and see her death as the seed of assassinations to follow. For who is the first to be certain it was of no interest to the CIA, or to the FBI, or to the Mafia, and half the secret police of the world, that the brother of the president was reputed to be having an affair with a movie star who had once been married to a playwright denied a passport for 'supporting Communist movements.' "[82] In the end, Mailer concludes:

> Political stakes were riding on her life, and even more on her death. If she could be murdered in such a way as to appear a suicide in despair at the turn of her love, what a point of pressure could be maintained afterward against the Kennedys. So one may be entitled to speak of a motive for murder. Of course, it is another matter to find that that evidence exists.
>
> There seems next to nothing of such evidence, and we have all the counterproof of Marilyn's instability, and all the real likelihood that she had taken too many barbiturates and was labored over for hours by frantic medicos trying to save her life, which certainly accounts more simply for many of the curious discrepancies. [. . .] In all this discussion of the details of her dying, we have lost the pain of her death. Marilyn is gone.[83]

This pious conclusion seems all the more ersatz when one adds the salient fact that Mailer was interviewed by Mike Wallace on *60 Minutes* in 1973 and under pressure conceded that it was, in his opinion, "ten to one" that Monroe died "an accidental suicide." When asked to explain his motives in speculating about Kennedy's involvement in Monroe's death, he answered: "I needed money very badly."[84] Accident, apparently, does not pay: the market demands that the lady die for love.

CORONER TO THE STARS

In 1983, Thomas T. Noguchi published *Coroner to the Stars,* in which he detailed the forensic evidence derived from Monroe's autopsy, among others (as Los Angeles County coroner, Noguchi's famous corpses also included Robert F. Kennedy, Janis Joplin, John Belushi and Natalie Wood). Noguchi's controversial evidence and the even more contentious interpretations of it have been used to bolster conspiracy theories ever since. Noguchi's book may have been partly in response to the fact that in 1982 the Los Angeles Board of Supervisors asked the district attorney's office to review the case of Monroe's death, particularly because of the allegations of a former coroner's aide named Lionel Grandison that key evidence had been destroyed and disregarded. The assistant district attorney's report "did not find Grandison credible" and officially concluded from "the information available [that] no further criminal investigation appears required into Miss Monroe's death."[85]

When Monroe died, the autopsy found 8 mg of chloral hydrate and 4.5 mg of pentobarbital (Nembutal) in her blood, and 13 mg of pentobarbital in her liver, all of which Noguchi says indicate a "massive" dose of barbiturates, enough to kill anyone many times over. Her stomach was empty, its lining showed congestion and hemorrhaging, and her colon showed "marked congestion and purplish discoloration."[86] Furthermore, Noguchi found no injection mark; he explains that he would later be questioned about this absence, because it is known that Monroe was given a routine injection by her doctor the day before she died; he says that only very recent needle marks are customarily visible. He sent specimens of blood, the stomach and its contents, intestines and other organs including the liver to toxicologists for further tests, but only received reports on the blood and the liver, which Noguchi explains was an odd failure on the part of the lab; it has certainly been interpreted as sinister by many people, who claim that the specimens were deliberately destroyed.

The controversies center around claims that the autopsy reveals that the overdose could not have been orally ingested (which seriously undermines the suicide theory). Noguchi says that the hemorrhaging of her stomach lining was consistent with oral ingestion of a drug overdose; he also explicitly answers questions as to why no pill residue was found in her empty stomach if she swallowed a large number of pills, explaining that he would expect the system of an addict like Monroe to absorb drugs much faster than most. He then says that those who claim there should have been traces of the yellow dye from the capsules in her esophagus or throat are misinformed, that Nembutal does not customarily leave traces of its dye. Although he noted a small bruise on her lower back, he believes that it may well have indicated violent contact with a piece of furniture while falling, and that at the time of the examination he considered it too "slight" and in the wrong location to be associated with the death.[87] Noguchi concludes that on the basis of his "own involvement with the case" he "would call Monroe's suicide '*very* probable.'" On the other hand, some of the reasons he reports for believing this have been seriously disputed, including the proposition that her room was locked on the inside and had to be broken into, as we shall see in a moment.[88]

Biographers after Noguchi (notably Summers, Spoto and Wolfe) spend pages delineating and then interpreting this evidence—differently—for their readers. Summers sensibly seeks corroboration for Noguchi's claims, consulting "Medical Examiners from six American cities, two British pathologists, two toxicologists, and a gastroenterologist" to help interpret the information from the autopsy, and then tells us that *they* had conflicting interpretations. Spoto flatly informs the reader of what the evidence means, as does Wolfe; but their interpretations contradict each other. The state of her colon, according to both Summers and Spoto, is consistent with a drug having been administered by enema; both also add that she was in the habit of taking enemas for weight loss. But Wolfe says she had colitis and an ulcerated colon, which accounts for the bruising and discoloration.[89] The fact that these interpretations of physical evidence are incompatible and contradictory gives rise, in turn, to further narratives explaining away, resolving the inconsistencies.

However, it is not only the questions raised by the physical evidence that have prompted doubts about the suicide theory. There were discrepancies pronounced enough in the various stories told by Murray, Greenson, Lawford and the other key witnesses to Monroe's last hours to prompt questions—and, perhaps, paranoia—among the biographers, questions that have spawned and supported the notorious conspiracy theories about the death of Marilyn Monroe.

HOMICIDE

Morning

According to both Summers and Wolfe, Marilyn was in a bad temper that Saturday morning not simply because Pat Newcomb had slept well. Summers reports that Jeanne Carmen says she was awakened at dawn by a distraught Marilyn, who had been receiving harassing phone calls telling her to "leave Bobby alone" and who requested Carmen to bring her a "bag of pills" later that night.[90] Brown and Barham say that she told Carmen she didn't think the calls were from Ethel Kennedy (Robert Kennedy's wife) but that she thought Ethel "had something to do with it."[91] In Wolfe's account, Carmen wonders of her own accord whether the calls were from Ethel Kennedy.[92] Brown and Barham say that Marilyn and Pat "patched up their quarrel," only to fight again when Marilyn received two phone calls, which were "undoubtedly from Lawford and Bobby Kennedy, in that order—with Kennedy strongly fighting against a trip to Los Angeles."[93] This made her "angry, tired, and vengeful" that morning, "a woman not to be trifled with."[94] No one else reports these calls.

Summers relates that Norman "Jeffries" [*sic*], a relation of Mrs. Murray's, who was working on the house, said that he'd never seen Monroe look as "sick" as she did that morning: "she must have taken a lot of dope or maybe she was scared out of her mind."[95] Wolfe also reports this claim, adding that "Jefferies" [*sic*] confided that Monroe resented Newcomb (as he learned from "a loud, vitriolic confrontation") for Newcomb's "loyalty to the Kennedys"[96] of whom she was a family friend (according to Wolfe it was Newcomb who looked after Bobby Kennedy's children when he went to Dallas at the assassination of his older brother[97]). Summers interjects a further motive for Monroe's irritation at Newcomb: Pat was "deeply in love" with Bobby Kennedy, according to one friend, a story that returns Marilyn's fundamental motivation to sexual jealousy.[98]

Summers adds a detail not found in other versions: Monroe

received a stuffed toy tiger in the mail in the late morning, which her hairdresser reports made her seem "terribly, terribly depressed."[99] Summers asks whether "some devastating note" had arrived with the tiger, or whether indeed ("curious thought," Summers interpolates) the tiger itself was a coded message. Summers is certain the tiger is significant, although he's not sure *what* it signifies; but whatever it indicates makes Marilyn "lose control." At some point during the day—perhaps in the form of the ominous stuffed tiger—Marilyn learned that she would not be seeing Bobby that night at the Lawfords': "that, on the evidence," writes Summers, "triggered her final despair."[100] Part of the putative "evidence" is a photograph of a stuffed animal on the lawn in front of Monroe's house—evidence that the toy was there (though not when it arrived), but certainly not evidence that it made Monroe suicidal.

Spoto paints a completely different picture: Marilyn was arranging for home repairs and a new couturier gown in the following week, during which she planned to be in New York, where she was expected by the Strasbergs.[101] He depicts a sunny domestic morning on her last day that was "hardly dramatic": Marilyn sipped grapefruit juice before signing for deliveries, speaking with friends on the phone (including arranging a barbecue for Sunday with Ralph Roberts), and meeting with photographer Schiller, who told Spoto she seemed "fresh and alert, 'seemingly without a care.' "[102] At noon, Newcomb awoke to find Monroe "surly," not only because Pat had slept so long while Monroe had suffered from her persistent insomnia all night, but also because of the "awkward atmosphere" attending what Spoto alone says was to be Eunice Murray's last day at work; Monroe had fired her out of irritation over her insolence. She was anxious because eager for Joe DiMaggio's imminent arrival, and because of her usual nerves about professional projects, however eagerly anticipated.[103]

Afternoon

Summers uses Greenson as his key witness for the events of Monroe's last afternoon, explaining that although Mrs. Murray's statements are "dubious," Greenson is credible enough to be the main source for Summers's account:

research for this book, including interviews with Dr. Greenson's family and colleagues, and his contemporary correspondence, satisfies this author that Marilyn's psychiatrist was honest about this weekend. It is he who takes up the story of that Saturday afternoon.[104]

Other writers, notably Spoto, are considerably less satisfied as to Greenson's honesty, but Greenson's version, via Summers, is that when he arrived around 4:30 he found Marilyn depressed and somewhat drugged. She was in a rage over Newcomb's ability to sleep, and he spent two and a half hours calming her down. Greenson also adds that Marilyn was distressed at being the most beautiful woman in the world but dateless on a Saturday night; she had been expecting to meet someone "very important" and was feeling "rejected."[105]

Spoto says that Greenson arrived three hours earlier, shortly after 1 P.M., and stayed with Monroe until 7 P.M., except for an "interval" between three and four-thirty, when he told Mrs. Murray to take Monroe for a walk on the beach. Greenson went home, and Murray drove Marilyn to Lawford's house, returning for her an hour later. Friends of Lawford's remembered seeing Marilyn at Lawford's house that afternoon; "by the time she arrived at the beach she was drugged."[106] She had been sedated while with Greenson, whether by his hand or her own. At 4:30 Greenson returned to resume therapy, which is the time when most biographers claim he first visited the house. Spoto quotes from Greenson's letters, in which he admits that Marilyn was "annoyed" with him; Spoto feels the "likelihood" is that they discussed terminating her therapy.[107] (Leaming agrees that Monroe was angry at Greenson in her last days, but attributes this to her irrational rages and fears of abandonment.) At about 5 P.M., Marilyn took a call from Lawford, inviting her to a casual dinner party that he was spontaneously assembling; she declined but he said he would call again to persuade her. Ralph Roberts called, somewhat earlier than the 6:30 time given by other accounts, and was dismayed at the abrupt rudeness of Greenson, who said, "Not here" and hung up. At around 7 P.M., "Greenson claimed," says Spoto, he departed.

Although admitting that "the story of Monroe's last afternoon has come down to us in a series of glimpses, fragments of conversation, murky, unreliable confessions, and inept police work," Brown and Barham nonetheless assert that one thing "seems certain": Bobby Kennedy, with or without Lawford, drove to Monroe's house "to quash the impending scandal" of a news conference she was planning, in which she would divulge her affair with both Kennedys, and the many political secrets they had let slip, while she was riding around on Air Force One with them.[108] Wolfe reports a publicist at Fox who contends that Robert Kennedy arrived suddenly in Los Angeles early Saturday afternoon by helicopter (although Wolfe does not address Kennedy's reasons for landing at Fox Studios). In addition, he cites former Los Angeles chief of police Daryl Gates confirming Kennedy's presence in L.A. that day (Wolfe's source is Gates's 1992 autobiography), former Los Angeles mayor Sam Yorty, who also confirmed it (Wolfe's sources are Summers and Brown and Barham), and Eunice Murray, who "finally" admitted Kennedy's presence in a 1985 interview with the BBC. Whether her thirty-year delay in placing Kennedy at the scene fortifies or undermines Murray's credibility is open to question, of course.

Between 3 and 4 P.M. on Saturday, according to Wolfe, via Jefferies, Robert Kennedy and Peter Lawford arrived at Monroe's house and told Jefferies and Murray to leave. They were gone about an hour; when they returned, Jefferies says, " 'Marilyn was hysterical and looked awful. Something terrible had happened—she was scared out of her mind [. . .] and at the same time she was terribly angry.' "[109] Wolfe also quotes Monroe's hairdresser, Sidney Guilaroff, who Summers said had refused to speak about his knowledge of Monroe's last days. Wolfe says Guilaroff admitted in 1995 that he found out on Saturday for the first time that Monroe had been seeing Bobby as well as Jack, and that she had been threatened that afternoon and "felt she was in terrible danger."[110] They eventually left, and Greenson arrived between 4:30 and 5 P.M., found Monroe "despondent, angry, and afraid," did what he could to calm her, and departed at 7, leaving Murray and Jefferies to watch over her.[111]

Evening

The events of the evening are reconstructed within two accepted temporal boundaries: Joe DiMaggio, Jr.'s call to Marilyn some time before 8 P.M., and the notification of the Los Angeles Police Department at 4:25 A.M.

The most important discrepancy, acknowledged by everyone except Guiles and Leaming, is that although Mrs. Murray would later claim to have awakened at 3:30 A.M. with a "sixth sense" that something was wrong, the first press reports on August 5 and the initial police officer on the scene, Sergeant Jack Clemmons (who will shortly become a controversial figure), both reveal that she first claimed she awakened at midnight and saw a light on under the door. When it was later pointed out to her that the carpeting was too thick to admit light, she changed her story to seeing a phone cord.[112] Summers and Spoto agree that Marilyn feared locked doors and prohibited them in her house.

Peter Lawford always professed to have spoken to Monroe early Saturday night (around 8:30 or 9), and that she told him "goodbye," at which point he called his friend and manager Milton Ebbins, who persuaded him that rushing to her house could implicate him in scandal and that they should call Monroe's lawyer, Milton (Mickey) Rudin, who phoned the house to be told that all was well. According to Spoto, Rudin received a call sometime between 10:30 and midnight from his brother-in-law, Greenson, who said he was at the house and Marilyn was dead. Summers and Spoto both agree that Monroe's publicist, Arthur Jacobs, received a call around 10:30 P.M. at a concert he was attending, telling him that Monroe was dead. When the police asked why it took four hours to notify them, Summers maintains that Greenson said they were waiting for permission from Fox Studios. Spoto, however, neglects this detail, simply saying that Murray changed her testimony about the timing the next day, because "she soon must have realized" the discrepancy; he never acknowledges that the police should have realized the discrepancy rather sooner than that, and that everyone else maintains they did.

The police become another vexed question. As already noted, Summers and Wolfe claim that both the Los Angeles mayor and the chief of police later "admitted" that Robert Kennedy was in Los Angeles the day Marilyn Monroe died. A great many of the conspiracy theories also hinge upon the presumably disinterested testimony of the first officer to arrive on the scene, Sergeant Jack Clemmons. Everyone concurs that Clemmons considered it "odd" that Mrs. Murray was doing the laundry when he arrived (though no one reports him to have considered her to be tampering with a death scene); Brown and Barham report, from his point of view, that he had a terrible "sixth sense" (it seems to have been in the air that night) that something was wrong. In particular, they say, he explained that Monroe's body was placed unnaturally, facedown with legs and arms straight down behind her; he is quoted in many of the books as having found the scene suspicious in general, although his suspicions do seem to have increased as these accounts evolve.

Spoto tells a different story. In his long afterword, "The Great Deception," he explicitly takes on the conspiracy theories and points out some arguably pertinent details. Spoto tells a story about the development of the Kennedy rumor: the day before Monroe died, gossip columnist Dorothy Kilgallen wrote a teaser that alleged Monroe was "vastly alluring to a handsome gentleman who is a bigger name than Joe DiMaggio." This could well have been John F. Kennedy, rather than Robert, however; insinuations of their affair had famously been made by columnist Art Buchwald in a satirical piece in November 1960 entitled "Let's Be Firm on the Monroe Doctrine." Kilgallen's teaser was taken up by Walter Winchell, a friend of DiMaggio's and no friend of Marilyn's. Winchell has been well established historically as a Red-baiter, and he was "following a lead," says Spoto, that was planted by right-wing conspiracy theorist Frank A. Capell. Both Wolfe, and now Matthew Smith, rely quite heavily upon Capell; although noting that he was right-wing, Wolfe seems not to feel that this necessarily compromises Capell's information (and who's to say that it does?). Smith goes further, defending "the soundness and excellence of Capell's work" against charges of having been "spoilt by what appeared to be his compelling motive for writing his book," namely, that "he was an avid right-winger, and was seeking to discredit Robert Kennedy."[113]

Rather more dubious is the fact that in Capell's pamphlet, *The Strange Death of Marilyn Monroe*, which was published by his own imprint in 1964, he quoted Winchell as his main source; but because

Winchell was quoting Capell, as Spoto points out, in the end Capell was simply quoting himself. Brown and Barham argue that, although he may seem an unreliable source, nonetheless Capell's pamphlet is "remarkable for the amount of inside data Capell was able to uncover."[114] "Secret results" from official Los Angeles police probes to hotel bills to doctors' bills "fill page after page."

According to Spoto, Capell happened to be a "buddy" of none other than Sergeant Jack Clemmons, who was himself associated with a right-wing group called the Police and Fire Research Organization, whose mission was to expose "subversive activities which threaten our American way of life."[115] Such groups had been sending J. Edgar Hoover letters exposing Marilyn Monroe and Robert Kennedy, separately and together, as enemies of the state, for some years, as even the heavily censored documents from Marilyn Monroe's file that the FBI has released on the Internet demonstrate.* Spoto explains that Capell, Clemmons and another associate of theirs were indicted in February 1965 by a California grand jury for conspiracy to libel a U.S. senator; they had planned to produce a false affidavit that he had "a homosexual encounter in the back of a car."[116] Spoto alleges that Clemmons was dismissed from the police force as a result of this indictment for conspiracy to commit perjury. Whether this leaves him a credible witness—if one believes Spoto—is up to the reader to judge; certainly Summers, Brown and Barham, and Wolfe make no mention of any of this as they repeat the "testimony" of "the first officer on the scene."

Summers spends more than fifty pages exhaustively and intricately outlining the controversy and dispute about Monroe's last hours, shifting back and forth between Mrs. Murray's changing stories and the conflicting testimony of Peter Lawford. He invokes dizzying numbers of "expert witnesses" in the shape of doctors, policemen, officials, detectives, ambulance drivers and former federal agents, not to mention countless friends who claim to have knowledge of

---

*Available at http://foia.fbi.gov/monroe.htm. "This file," says the first page, "contains accounts of publicity about Miss Monroe's alleged affairs and speculation about the circumstances surrounding her death."

Marilyn's last days. The cumulative force of all of this detail is over-whelming, but none of it actually proves anything. He also spends pages discussing allegations that Monroe's telephone records for that day had "disappeared." He concludes that the FBI removed them, primarily from the "significant testimony" of an anonymous former agent, who claims that any orders to remove her phone records had to have come from "either the Attorney General or the President. I know that from my knowledge of the structure of the FBI, the way things were handled in those days."[117] In other words, this anony-mous former agent knows what happened because he knows what he knows. Having convinced us with this tautology, and having also quoted an ambulance driver who contends that Monroe was taken to the hospital while still alive in the early morning hours of August 5, Summers then pronounces: "Taking all the evidence into account, we can build a scenario for the last days and hours of Marilyn's life." It goes like this:

Marilyn had been in a "narcotic nosedive" for months; she was disintegrating, hysterical and psychotic. She had been involved with both Kennedys for some time; Jack treated it with his usual insou-ciance, but the more serious Bobby fell for Marilyn, until he realized that she "should have been institutionalized," in the words of Dr. Greenson. Marilyn was so delusional she hoped to marry either brother, not particularly caring which one. When Bobby tried to leave her, she threatened exposure; Lawford was enlisted to ensure her silence, inviting her to Cal-Neva, where she spent her last week-end "floundering in drink and drugs." On her last day alive, Bobby responded to her escalating pleas with a hurried, secret trip to L.A., tried to calm her, and left. "In anguish," Marilyn called Dr. Greenson, who also tried to calm her, and also left. Abandoned and desperate, Monroe "made a series of calls for help," but it does not seem that she deliberately intended to kill herself. At 10 P.M. she called the Lawford home; either Bobby or Lawford arrived to find her "coma-tose, but not yet dead." They called an ambulance, but she died en route to the hospital; because any connection to her death might prove ruinous to the attorney general, he had her body returned to her home and engineered a cover-up. Lawford "destroyed some com-promising document" and then was ordered to hire a private detective (Fred Otash) to "sweep dust" over any remaining tracks. J. Edgar Hoover was then ordered to remove Monroe's phone records, which would show she had called the Kennedys.[118]

That is, in the end Summers believes that Marilyn died of an accidental overdose. All of the long discussion of murder becomes a paralipsis, like Mailer's, in which the writer indulges in conspiracy theory as long as possible, before concluding (reluctantly?) that Monroe actually died by her own hand. The entire Kennedy narrative turns out to be incidental, as well as speculative.

Brown and Barham also offer a capsule reconstruction, which they, like Summers (and unlike Wolfe, who presents his story as a series of assertions of fact), admit is hypothetical. Realizing that Marilyn was ready to go public with their affair, and fearful of her "vindictive spirit" and "angry new determination," Bobby Kennedy "probably" promised to come to Los Angeles on Saturday. "We also believe," they say, "that Monroe threatened to hold a press conference about both of her affairs, and that she might have been willing to publicize excerpts from the notebooks she had filled with details of the romances, which provided a record of sorts of everything her political lovers had told her over the previous year or so." Kennedy held a "strategy session" at the Lawford mansion; "we believe he made another call to Monroe, who by then was hysterical and told him to get out of her life."[119] Kennedy brought a doctor to Monroe's house about 6:30 P.M., who sedated her; when he returned at 7 P.M., she was on the phone, raging.[120] Dutiful son that he was, Kennedy called not only the president but his mother for advice; "some time between 6:30 and 9 P.M., someone entered Monroe's house and administered a potent shot of Nembutal in her rectum or under her armpit. An injection in either of these places would not be detected during an autopsy that missed evidence of the shots she had received in the preceding two days."[121] This final statement disregards, of course, Noguchi's explanation that only very recent puncture marks are visible (though to be sure one must accept his authority).

For Brown and Barham, the cover-up was assisted by 20th Century-Fox and Monroe's publicity agents. They place this cover-up within

the context of other notorious efforts by Hollywood to protect its
stars' reputations, including the deaths of William Desmond Taylor
and Thelma Todd in the 1920s.

> Early on the morning of August 5, 1962, two uniformed security
> guards from Twentieth Century-Fox stationed themselves at the
> front and back entrances to Monroe's house. An hour later,
> another studio guard took up a post at the enormous gates at the
> front of the estate.
>
> Their faces were impassive, but their fingers lingered on their
> service revolvers, reminding everyone that serious Hollywood
> business was transpiring behind the thick adobe walls.
>
> The press was kept at bay while Frank Neill, Arthur Jacobs,
> Eunice Murray and, at one point, Peter Lawford rifled through
> the disarray left behind by the world's most enigmatic film star.
>
> Publicists, studio policemen and members of Monroe's per-
> sonal staff, particularly Murray and Monroe's business manager,
> Inez Melson, poured thousands of prescription drugs down the
> toilet, removed the star's contracts and memos, and carted off
> armloads of personal belongings.[122]

Why no one noticed this, Brown and Barham do not explain. They
rely heavily upon Clemmons's testimony, and claim that the major
forensic reason for doubting Monroe's suicide is that the amount of
barbiturates in her system equates to approximately seventy pills,
and that no one could swallow that many without passing out first.
Although Marilyn was accustomed to dissolving her pills in champagne to make them work faster (all the lives report this), no glass
was found in her room (they don't mention that it might well have
been removed during all the sanitizing that clearly was going on
before the police arrived on the scene). They also feel that she had
no reason to kill herself, as she was so upbeat about resuming her
career. The only other possible explanation, apparently, is that Robert
Kennedy had her assassinated. Like Summers, Brown and Barham
hold that Greenson was merely a dupe of the machinations of others,
and that he informed the police that the delay in their notification
was due to waiting for representatives of Fox to come to the house.

*   *   *

Like Summers, Spoto outlines the forensic evidence before offering his version of the events of Monroe's last night. He says that the lack of pill residue in her stomach and the ratio of Nembutal in the blood to that found in her liver means that she was swallowing pills gradually over the course of the day—hardly a method of premeditated suicide. He rules out injection because of these blood levels and the lack of a puncture wound, leading to his conclusion that only an enema could have administered the fatal dose.[123] He repeats the disclosure that Monroe regularly took enemas for "dietetic purposes" and then concludes, even more firmly than Summers: "The exact circumstances of Marilyn Monroe's sad and unnecessary death can, in the light of all this evidence, at last be established."[124] This is Spoto's version:

Monroe was happier than she had been for some time, upbeat about her career and looking forward to her forthcoming wedding to Joe DiMaggio. On Saturday her sudden bad temper came partly from insomnia, and partly from her frustration with what she considered Greenson's recent betrayals,* and his efforts to remove Joe DiMaggio from her life. To make her manageable, Greenson decided to administer chloral hydrate in the form of a sedative enema, without ascertaining that she had already taken Nembutal.† Only Eunice Murray could have delivered the fatal enema, unless Greenson never actually left the house. Regardless, he was there "before the small hours" of Sunday morning, when they realized that Marilyn was comatose and

---

*Greenson had indisputably involved himself in Monroe's negotiations with Fox Studios, offering them a guarantee that he could get her on the set. For some writers, this is a misguided but well-meaning effort to help her get her career on track, by assuring the studio of her fitness for work. For Spoto and others, it is an arrogant, boastful insistence upon his own power, and an effort at ingratiating himself with Hollywood powers that be, which infuriated Monroe, who felt betrayed when he went behind her back to the studio and intruded into her professional affairs.

†In Fox's 2001 documentary *Marilyn: The Final Days,* Monroe's general practitioner Hyman Engelberg enters into a major, albeit tacit, argument with Spoto. Engelberg says that he gave Monroe a prescription of twenty-four Nembutals before she died—"which was a good dose," he admits. He explains she was intended to take only a few, every night, but, he adds,

> even if she took it all at once, it's problematic that that was a fatal dose. We try to keep it down, and give her the Nembutal more frequently, in smaller amounts. [. . .] I believe she was in a manic phase [the night she died], and that something happened to suddenly depress her, and she grabbed pills

failed to resuscitate her. Marilyn's death was thus a terrible, but care-
less, accident, and the subsequent "cover-up" and its inconsistencies
were the frantic efforts of two ordinary citizens to erase the evidence
of the crime they unwittingly committed, and to concoct a story that
would account for her death. Before the police arrived, Murray and
Greenson set the scene to corroborate their story of Murray awaken-
ing inexplicably and finding Monroe dead, including breaking the
bedroom window, and "destroying evidence" of the enema, which
must have been expelled after death, by washing the sheets.[126]

Wolfe believes that Dr. Greenson, Dr. Engelberg and perhaps Mrs.
Murray's husband were all agents of the Comintern. He relies heavily upon newly augmented claims by Norman Jefferies, who is suddenly willing to tell more of the story than ever before, and upon the

---

there. She had plenty of pills at the bedside. I think she was suddenly depressed, and in that sense, it
was intentional. Then, I think she thought better of it, when she felt herself going under, because she
called Peter Lawford. So, while it was intentional at the time, I do believe she changed her mind. [. . .]
At the side of her bed there was a *lot* of Seconal, which I had *never* given her; also the autopsy showed
that her liver had a *lot* of chloral hydrate. I never gave her chloral hydrate and I don't think any doctor
in the United States gave it to her. She must have bought it in Tijuana.

Spoto, however, had earlier accused both Engelberg and Greenson of extreme negligence in their han-
dling of Monroe's drug addiction (an accusation that, unsurprisingly, Engelberg doesn't acknowledge in
his interview):

She had received several injections [. . .] from Hyman Engelberg—"vitamin shots," as Eunice
Murray euphemistically called them, but clearly more potent combinations of drugs. Among them
were Nembutal, Seconal and phenobarbital (all dangerous and habituating barbiturates) and, for
quick sleep, chloral hydrate (the so-called Mickey Finn knockout drops). These drugs, also provided
for Marilyn in capsule form by prescription, were not so strictly controlled by the government then as
they were later.

As the noted pathologist Dr. Arnold Abrams observed later, "It was irresponsible to provide this
sort of thing in the amounts Marilyn Monroe received them, even in 1962." [. . .] To make matters
worse, Greenson, too, began to provide heavier doses of sleeping pills; only later did he and Engelberg
try to coordinate their prescriptions, with completely ineffectual results. [. . .]

That same year, as was subsequently documented in her divorce petition, Engelberg's wife was
maintained by him on appallingly massive doses of barbiturates and hypnotics—ostensibly to keep her
calm during the trauma of the termination of their thirty-year marriage. But the result of this prodigal
administration of dangerous drugs was very nearly disastrous.

Spoto concludes by quoting three of Monroe's closest associates—Ralph Roberts, Allan "Whitey" Snyder
and Pat Newcomb—all of whom remember Greenson providing Monroe with drugs, rather than attempting to get her off them. He quotes Snyder saying that he never trusted Greenson, believing there was
something "phony" in his relationship with her, and ending, "when he got himself on the Fox payroll, I was
certain of it."[125]

allegations of Lionel Grandison, who worked in the coroner's office in 1962. Wolfe fails to admit the presumably inconvenient fact that Grandison's accusations (stories that Wolfe repeats as fact) had been deemed "not credible" by the Los Angeles District Attorney's Office's 1982 review of Monroe's death.[127] Wolfe also relies heavily upon other controversial witnesses, namely Jeanne Carmen, Jack Clemmons and Robert Slatzer.

Wolfe depends more than anyone upon the putative significance of the forensic evidence for his interpretation. He says that barbiturate overdose victims vomit, and that the lack of vomit shows Marilyn didn't overdose; but Summers said his experts agree this isn't necessarily the case.[128] Wolfe concludes that because of the high level of barbiturates in her blood and lack of trace in her stomach, the dose could only have been administered by injection; he admits that Noguchi found no injection mark, but maintains that fresh needle marks are hard to find, contradicting Noguchi's assertion that only very recent puncture wounds are visible. Wolfe also declares flatly that "bruised areas are an indication of violence, and the fact that obvious bruises weren't questioned, and that minor ones weren't even noted, is a disturbing omission."[129] But Noguchi says that he did consider the bruise a result of violence (which is, after all, the only possible cause of bruises), but not related to the death. Wolfe states confidently that there should have been yellow dye in her system, but Noguchi negates this assertion, a fact that Wolfe doesn't mention. Wolfe pronounces that "it is now known that Marilyn Monroe died at approximately 10:30 P.M. Saturday," but this is not known at all; it is postulated.[130] Part of Wolfe's reasoning about her murder involves the "fact" of her earlier suicide attempts, including the one in 1950 reported by Natasha Lytess, but Spoto explicitly denies that this happened. Most important, most of Wolfe's allegations about the autopsy depend upon the claims of Grandison.

Wolfe's reconstruction of Monroe's last hours goes like this: shortly after dusk, one of Monroe's neighbors was playing bridge, and saw Robert Kennedy, accompanied by two other men, walk up the drive to her house. They ordered Norman Jefferies and Eunice Murray from the house, who waited nervously for an hour at an unidentified neighbor's house. (Wolfe can determine that it was *not* one couple, who were out until after 11 P.M., but perhaps Jefferies was "referring to the nearby home of Hanna Fenichel on Fifth Helena Drive"? Or perhaps not. At any rate, Wolfe doesn't substantiate the speculation.) At 10:30, from the unidentified neighbor's window, Jefferies watched Kennedy and the two men depart, and hurried back to Monroe's house, where they found her in the guestroom, "unclothed, lying across the daybed," comatose, but alive. They immediately called an ambulance and then Greenson, who arrived shortly afterward, and tried desperately to resuscitate Monroe with adrenaline to the heart, but his efforts failed, hitting a rib, and she died in the house. " 'After that, all hell broke loose,' " says Jefferies. " 'There were police cars, fire trucks, more ambulances—you name it! A police helicopter landed at the golf course and soon they were all over the place.' "

Just before midnight a dark speeding Mercedes was pulled over on the highway: Peter Lawford was driving, with Robert Kennedy, and a man the officer later identified as Ralph Greenson, in the passenger seats. They claimed to be on official business and Officer Franklin "waved them on."[131] Although this passage quotes Monroe's neighbors and Officer Franklin, there are no notes for it; Wolfe's last citations end just before it begins. It is rendered in italics, which presumably represent some kind of acknowledged reconstruction or fictionalizing, but precisely how fictional it is, Wolfe leaves entirely to the reader to judge. This is made even more uncertain by the fact that Wolfe told exactly the same story on the fourth page of his book in roman type, very much as "fact"; again, however, there are no citations offered to corroborate it.

In 2000, Joyce Carol Oates writes a story in which Marilyn Monroe is murdered by a "Sharpshooter" who has been tracking her, at the behest of the "Agency" and an "informer" known as R.F. Although Oates's Marilyn has been disintegrating in despair over the miscarriage of "Baby" and the end of her marriage to "The Playwright," and seems to share Summers's sense of a woman in a narcotic nosedive, nonetheless, like Summers, Oates will write a story in which Marilyn is suicidal and yet murdered by someone else. Oates's Sharpshooter is a self-styled American "patriot," an enemy of the Communist conspiracy, who is willing to murder Marilyn because of her left-leaning sympathies (including a rumored liaison with President Sukarno of Indonesia in April 1956, which the Sharpshooter believes took place). There are several ironies in this plot: first, Oates's "Sharpshooter" kills Monroe by lethal injection, rather than by shooting her. Her decision to name him "Sharpshooter" suggests that he is a character straying into Monroe's story from the Kennedy conspiracies. But although it is the Sharpshooter who "tails" Marilyn, only when she has sex with Jack Kennedy and he hurts her does Oates reveal that her Marilyn feels she is always under surveillance. The final irony is the way in which this story treats the "leftist" Kennedys and the far-right anti-Communists as interchangeable. Oates's plot was first authored by Capell, whose right-wing "patriotism" made him finger the Kennedys as Monroe's killers; in Oates's version the killer is a far-right "patriot" himself. Marilyn can be the victim of any political system one cares to name because the tales' interest in politics is cursory at best. The politicians and conspirators at the finale of Marilyn's story work in the same symbolic way as the studio system at the beginning. She will be watched, she will be fucked, and finally male power, in the form of one lethal injection or another, will finish her off.

CASE NO. 81128

When Monroe died, her body was left unclaimed for several hours in the morgue. Few biographers miss the opportunity to comment; the humiliations of Monroe's dead body become part of the story. Each writer uses the same rhetorical blueprint:

> At nine o'clock an ambulance delivered Marilyn's body to the coroner's office. After the autopsy at 10:30 A.M., it lay unclaimed on a slab in the storage vault there, as Coroner's Case No. 81128. Marilyn dead had no one to claim her, her life ending as it had begun.[132]

The body desired by millions belonged to no one: on Monday
morning, August 6, Marilyn Monroe's remains still lay unclaimed
at the Los Angeles County Morgue.[133]

Marilyn had become a statistic—Coroner's Case No. 81128.[134]

For Wolfe, the phrase "Marilyn Monroe became Coroner's Case
#81128"[135] occurs in a chapter also called "Case #81128"; the dra-
matic use of statistics will be echoed a hundred pages later in a flash-
back to the child abandoned at the orphanage: she was "registered as
the three thousand four hundred and sixty-third child to be admitted
to the Los Angeles Orphans' Home. Ten years later number 3,463
would become Marilyn Monroe."[136] Who would become Coroner's
Case #81128. Summers declares that "there was irony in the fact
that the death certificate, in 1962, would refer only to the passing of
a Hollywood invention called Marilyn Monroe. For it was Norma
Jeane that died," returning the death to the realm of ordinary, poor
little, abandoned Norma Jeane.[137] If no one wants Marilyn, she
ceases to exist.

The coroner's man who collected the body from the house said:
"She didn't look good, not like Marilyn Monroe. She looked just like
a poor little girl that had died, no makeup, fuzzy unmade hair, a tired
body. To some degree or other, we all come to that."[138] When Noguchi
described performing Monroe's autopsy, he explained that he was
immensely shocked to be confronted with "the *real* Marilyn Monroe"
on the table.[139] Death becomes both test and proof of reality—because
only real people die.

The *real* Marilyn Monroe appeared in Summers's *Goddess* as a
photograph of the corpse photographed after Noguchi's autopsy. It is
a shocking photograph for many reasons, not least the simple, obvious fact that most of us are not accustomed to viewing the dead. We
consider it morbid, or disrespectful, to view the dead except when
protected by appropriate interpretive rituals. Or perhaps we are just
afraid. Certainly to *publish* death in quite this way, and to profit from
its shock value, seems transgressive. Whether out of civility or fear,
however, one certainly wishes to avert one's eyes from this spectacle,
an aversion that makes this photograph simultaneously the *real*

Marilyn and the *anti*-Marilyn.* This picture is particularly shocking for its implicit contrast with the still-circulating glamorous images of the "living" Monroe.

The reprinting of this photograph in *Goddess* has occasioned quite a bit of commentary, nearly all of it critical. McCann complains not only of the trespass, but of its cynicism:

> Summers, a "trained investigative journalist," cannot resist trying to "find Marilyn"—even to the extent of entering the morgue. It is a particularly great misfortune that Summers should find it necessary for his narrative to include a photograph of Monroe's corpse. It is not so much what she looks like that appalls, but rather the feeling that this is the ultimate intrusion, on our part as well as on the author's. It is a needless gesture from the author, a cynical sign, one which reflects very badly on his profession.[140]

But it is *precisely* what she looks like that appalls. McCann's response is probably human (as opposed to academic), but it seems self-deluding. In declaring that it is not what she looks like that appalls, McCann disavows her appearance, in the same way that Marilyn Monroe's audience always declares her beauty artificial. She has never looked like what she is, until now, when the reality and the image violently collide into each other, and the "tricks of her trade" can no longer avail her.

In interpreting this frightening photograph, Baty implicitly disagrees with McCann, arguing:

> Marilyn the pinup queen is reduced to "a picture retrieved from police files." The once beautiful face is now "sagging, bloated"; the hair is limp, the facial muscles severed, the brain removed . . . Summers is dismembering, and thereby introducing, the "hag" Marilyn Monroe. The hag replaces the beautiful living woman by

---

*This photograph has also been published on the Web. Although there is an argument to be made for reprinting it, given that it has become part of the Marilyn apocrypha, such reproduction also risks continuing to exploit the shock value of death, and in the end seems supererogatory, since it is in circulation anyway. There are many sites that reproduce it, such as http://www.pharo.com/intelligence/marilyn_monroe/articles/ifmm_102_death.asp.

surviving as a postmortem photograph democratically numbered and labeled.[141]

Baty crucially returns our attention to Monroe's appearance, but she seems to overlook the fact that this picture of the corpse, although it surfaced in a best-selling biography, is never reprinted, even by the texts that discuss it. It has not entered mainstream culture; until it began to appear on the Internet it was not available outside of Summers's text. Even if circulating more widely now than when Baty wrote, it still most certainly has not *replaced* the pictures of the beautiful living woman. The photograph of the corpse, a memento mori, a death's head, is discussed but rarely seen. Its existence in all of the texts about Marilyn Monroe but Summers's is, as far as I can ascertain, purely referential. This is not the hag Marilyn, but the *real* Marilyn, whose artificiality, glamour and deception have been stripped away to reveal the ordinary, weary, dying person we've been trying (not) to see all along. This is the payoff of biography, the scar, the dirty secret behind the glamour. This is what death actually looks like, and—to coin a phrase—it isn't pretty.

The real Marilyn Monroe is a corpse: pure body, and utterly powerless. The focus on her naked sexual body has shifted, and we are left gazing upon her dissected dead body. Both bodies are figures for reality, and for truth. In *Over Her Dead Body: Death, Femininity, and the Aesthetic*, Elisabeth Bronfen has argued that because death is by definition beyond anyone's experience, in narrative it can only be a metaphor. Furthermore, if death is a metaphor, it is a paradoxical one, for it stands as the mark of ultimate certainty, but represents the final uncertainty: a measure of the real, death is itself unmeasurable. In this way, Bronfen suggests, it functions metaphorically like the female body, which is also coded as "site of an original, prenatal dwelling place, as site of fantasies of desire and otherness, and as site of an anticipated final resting place."[142] Death and Marilyn Monroe mirror each other: she, too, as we have seen, was always a metaphor for certainty and uncertainty, for reality and for the unknowable. The emphasis in these stories on the symbolic impact of her dwelling places, as we saw in chapter five, always relates her home to her womb. The story of Marilyn Monroe embodies, quite literally, the mythical journey from womb to tomb.

In fact, Marilyn Monroe's dead body metaphorically transforms womb *into* tomb, which is the conventional representation of the spinster. The woman who promised plenitude has proved to be barren; her redemptive femininity has not, in fact, brought us deliverance, but her death. The apocrypha explains Marilyn's death through variations on the theme of spinsterhood, the woman alone who might as well die. The spinster is nothingness: barren, alone, the solitary female is supposed to kill herself, registering her nullity through the only means left to her, her futile, abortive body. The spinster is the dead, negative flip side of the Virgin, and she is associated with a failure of home, a failure of fertility, with emptiness and with death. Unmarried, childless, a professional success, she will still be branded a personal failure. The prospect of the most desirable woman in the world becoming a spinster is finally what will kill her. She will die when the men have left the tale. She will die because she was a woman alone on a Saturday night—a fate worse than death.

In almost every biography (Spoto is the only exception), Marilyn Monroe died for love. She was rejected sexually, and died. This story has several implications, not least of which is that she continues to be defined in relationship to men, to sex and to men's desire. Marilyn has no reason to exist apart from the men who want her, and if they don't want her, she shrivels up and dies. The fact that two such radically different explanations for her death—homicide and suicide— share a belief that Monroe had been rejected by Robert Kennedy shows how powerful this narrative is. Why would a woman die *other* than for love? What possible other reason could a woman have for suffering? Moreover, Bobby's own symbolism as perfect husband and father seems part of the reason for his resonance in Marilyn's story—isn't he the happy ending, the perfect marriage, without which her life, and her lives, are incomplete? Bobby is cast as a potential Prince Charming, in a way that Jack Kennedy never could be once his sexual callousness had been revealed. Her affair with Jack will simply reinforce her spinsterhood, as in Oates's account of their first sexual encounter: "[. . .] settled myself on top of him, fitted myself to him, my slightly sore vagina, my empty womb this man might fill."[143]

Oates uses this story as a way of suggesting Marilyn's extreme gullibility, trying to cast Jack Kennedy as her "Prince," despite his manifest exploitation of her. Oates's Marilyn has an affair with the president, but not with Robert Kennedy. Marilyn remains a victim, convinced that she is in love with a man who is clearly toying with her: in a chapter called "The Beggar Maid in Love," Oates imagines Marilyn waiting and waiting for the phone to ring, for "her Prince" to call, making her "happy, joyous, smiling, singing and dancing all day." Not only is Oates's (and Summers's) Marilyn a victim of the Kennedys' manipulation of her: she is a dimwit. This is the stereotype, of course, seeping into the life: she is innocent, sentimental, sweet, and so could only have an affair with the president if she were in love with him. The idea that Marilyn Monroe, who had grown up in an orphanage in the Depression and fought her way tooth and nail through Hollywood to become the most desired woman in the world, might get a charge out of knowing that she was sleeping with the president of the United States, the most powerful man in the world— that she might have been "using" him, as knowingly as he was using her—is not part of the myth.* Summers believes that she was sufficiently unsentimental about sex to be able to prostitute herself, but not that she could have sex with the president without being in love with him. That she could have been a "woman of the world" is only seen as an irony, but that is exactly what she was. Why not believe that she went into the affair with her eyes open—she was thirty-six years old, thrice divorced—knew what it was and wanted no more?

CONSPIRACY THEORIES

Although there are many variants of the conspiracy theories, they reduce to a few standard structural components. Confronted with

---

*Spoto quotes Monroe's friend Susan Strasberg, who had no doubt about Marilyn's attitude toward Kennedy: "Not in her worst nightmares [. . .] would Marilyn have wanted to be with JFK on any permanent basis [. . .] he certainly wasn't the kind of man she wanted for life, and she was very clear to us about this."[144]

the self-contradictory and dubious nature of much of the testimony surrounding Monroe's last hours, the conspiracy theories look for a "compelling" explanation for these discrepancies, a neat solution for the narrative incompatibilities. Of course, it is only narrative that promises a *reason* for early death; reality offers no such assurance. But if one believes that Monroe was involved with—or better, in love with—either or both of the Kennedy brothers, then many explanations, and hence many plots, arrive prêt-à-porter. Involved as they were in expedient politics and internecine battles, the Kennedys had many enemies: organized crime, on which Robert Kennedy had publicly declared war (and which encompassed not only Mafia figures like Sam Giancana, but also allegations against the likes of Teamsters leader Jimmy Hoffa); right-wing nationalists disturbed by the Kennedys' espousal of liberal tenets; and any professed enemy of the nation for which the Kennedys were now figureheads, including Fidel Castro and Nikita Khrushchev.

The Kennedys' alleged sexual liaison with Marilyn is thus presented as a political liability, whether because she herself was threatening to blow the whistle, or because someone else was. In these stories she is either assassinated by an enemy of the Kennedys to incriminate them, or she is assassinated by the Kennedys or their associates in order to protect their secrets.

In particular, accounts that believe the Kennedys were implicated in Monroe's death use the alleged bugging of her house to help lay the groundwork for the story they intend to tell. Again quasi-forensic "evidence" is invoked as if readers can see, or hear, it for themselves, when in fact the supposed wiretaps become just another part of the text, no easier for the average reader to confirm than any other. The most persistent story is that both the Mafia and Teamsters leader Jimmy Hoffa were attempting to get hard evidence to incriminate, or blackmail, the Kennedys. Monroe's house is supposed to have been tapped "in strategic locations" by Bernard Spindel, Hoffa's personal wiretapper. Spindel claimed to have tapes of Monroe with both Jack and Bobby Kennedy, although these tapes have subsequently been lost. Spindel's house in New York was raided by the police in 1966; his widow apparently attempted unsuccessfully to sue for return of the alleged tapes and other confidential documentation. None of this material has ever been produced, but many stories rely upon testimonials by sources who claim to have heard them.

Summers, Brown and Barham, Wolfe, and now Smith list all sorts and conditions of private detectives, Secret Service agents, former government employees, CIA and FBI operatives, some named, some unnamed, who reveal in various ways that Bobby Kennedy feared Marilyn would "blow the whistle" on his sexual or political secrets— or both. Summers did much of the investigative research into phone records and wiretaps upon which others rely, and which they arguably embellish. For example, Wolfe repeats Summers's allegation that private detective Fred Otash had been hired to bug Monroe's house, and that he told ABC's *20/20* (in an interview allegedly suppressed by then head of news Roone Arledge, a Kennedy in-law); Wolfe adds that in the tapes one could hear Lawford and Kennedy screaming: "Where is it? Where the fuck is it?" and Monroe screaming back and ordering them out of her house.[145] Smith tells the same story in *The Men Who Murdered Marilyn* and now in *Victim*; it has found its way into Kennedy biographies as well, but their source is Summers's *Goddess*, leaving the tale entirely circular. In the end whether one believes in the wiretaps comes down to what one believes, because all that we have in the way of evidence is the "testimony" of various people reported in various biographies who claim to have heard them.

Each of these tales, however, concludes with a different "villain." In Capell, Slatzer, and Brown and Barham, the culprit is Robert F. Kennedy himself; in James Haspiel's *Marilyn: The Ultimate Look at the Legend,* Kennedy smothers her with a pillow. Private detective Milo Speriglio, who was hired by Slatzer to investigate Monroe's death, has accused Jimmy Hoffa and Sam Giancana, working together, of killing Marilyn; Giancana's brother and godson similarly gave him "credit" for Monroe's death in their "tell-all." Speriglio later expanded his story: the villain was actually Joseph Kennedy, who hired Giancana to kill Monroe because she was pregnant with Bobby's child. Several authors, including Matthew Smith and Joyce Carol Oates, blame the CIA, who used Marilyn's death to get even with the Kennedys for the Bay of Pigs fiasco. Tony Sciacca's *Who Killed Marilyn* offers two solutions to the mystery: it might have been the CIA, or it might have been Castro, who was growing weary of the Kennedys' attempts to assassinate him.

The conspiracy theories' favorite methods of assassination are the lethal injection and the enema. While the lethal injection goes to Marilyn's heart, the enema goes to her behind. The two modes are often associated with each other: Oates's Sharpshooter tails Marilyn and will kill her by lethal injection, having entered her house "from the rear." Both methods sexualize Marilyn's death, making sure she is fatally penetrated; but it is also the perverse penetration appropriate to the rattling womb of the spinster. While the lethal injection allows for a sanitized—even "sentimental"—death, the enema does the opposite. It means that the story ends explicitly with expulsion, with shit, with the evacuation of all the shame the stories have forced into Marilyn's figure. It ends with Mrs. Murray washing the sheets.[146] The fatal enema would seem to bring us full circle back to the anal rape stories: or rather, since the rumors about enemas came first, they would seem to explain the anal rape stories, creating a symmetrical story of victimization and shame. Marilyn's creation will be associated with anal rape, and her destruction with anal suppositories, and her behind remains at the forefront of the tale.

Cause and effect can similarly be reversed: if Monroe died for sleeping with a Kennedy, there are those who believe that John Kennedy was killed for sleeping with Monroe (in one version, he was killed by "Italian friends" of Joe DiMaggio, who was outraged by Kennedy's cavalier treatment of her). One sweeping theory on the Internet attributes Monroe's death to all of the most popular conspiracies simultaneously: she knew too much about the Bay of Pigs, the Cuban Missile Crisis, and the UFOs that crashed at Roswell, New Mexico, in 1947, as well as the dead bodies found there (the story I saw is not clear, however, about who precisely needed to protect this delicate information so ruthlessly). One survey of popular conspiracy theories makes the assertion that "one thing that almost all those who believe Monroe was murdered agree on, is that if she was killed, it was probably done whilst she was held down with pillows and injected in the foot with barbiturates."[147] However, this theory does not appear in *any* of the principal lives, some of which do believe she was murdered.

Marilyn Monroe's death was contemporaneous with the rise of conspiracy theories per se in American culture: she died in 1962, and John F. Kennedy in 1963. A year later, in 1964, historian Richard Hofstadter published an essay called "The Paranoid Style in American Politics," which remains one of the most influential, if heavily disputed, theses about conspiracy theorists. According to Hofstadter, the conspiracy theorist projects onto the imaginary enemy his own anxieties and desires: certainly this would seem an accurate description of the chronicles of Marilyn Monroe's life.

Conspiracy theories, as scholars like Mark Fenster and Robert Alan Goldberg have argued, though extant for centuries (one need only think of the Illuminati and the Freemasons), have flourished in our postwar age because global mass media promises a kind of populism that it never delivers: conspiracy theories are the ordinary response of people seeking narratives to organize and interpret the information that is thrown at them.

There is something else all of the conspiracy theories have in common: the idea that Monroe was killed to silence her. She was going to talk, or hold a press conference, or publish her "little book" of secrets. She was silenced in order to keep her from revealing secrets, which, ironically, is what the conspiracy theorists promise to do. The entire story of Marilyn Monroe reflects the ways in which we create secrets in order to uncover them: she is our invented secret, and we reveal what was there all along. Marilyn's dead body is what is exposed, instead of the secrets: her silence is a figure for death itself, and for the helplessness of her corpse.

Conspiracy theory is always associated with political power, particularly of the nation-state, and economic power: "conspiracy theory perceives the power of the ruling individual, group, or coalition to be thoroughly instrumental, controlling virtually all aspects of social life, politics and economics."[148] Certainly the conspiracies surrounding Monroe's death are *always* about the intersection of her story with politics. There are not similarly powerful theories surrounding the untimely death of any other celebrity except Diana, Princess of Wales, whose life intersected much more obviously (if no less sexually) than

Monroe's with international politics, and whose death has already generated more than thirty thousand Web sites devoted to conspiracy theories.[149] The theories about other cult figures like Elvis Presley or Jim Morrison are less conspiracy theories explaining their deaths than disavowals of those deaths in stories about their survival in darkest Africa (or Tennessee). Those stories don't seek to explain what seems inexplicable: they simply deny it. One of the things the conspiracy stories disclose is how very political the figure of Marilyn actually is, the ways in which sexual politics have transmuted into governmental politics—and vice versa.

Our most powerful secrets are the political and the sexual, and thus our most compelling stories are those that blend the two: the Profumo scandal, the Lewinsky-Clinton affair, Clarence Thomas and Anita Hill, the death of Princess Diana, and Marilyn Monroe and the Kennedy brothers. These are the stories that preoccupy us because secrecy *is* power, it is the mastery of unshared knowledge. The secret proves Marilyn's singularity: she was special, she was different, she was important. Thus she was not ordinary after all; she rewards the attention and care we have given her; it was "worth" buying a biography and reading four hundred pages about the life of a woman who became an actress and died. Now we, too, are in the know; now we, too, share in the power. The closing words of Leaming's biography reinforce this notion that Monroe's appeal derives from the revelation of secrets: "As a symbol, she promises us that sex can be innocent, without danger. That, indeed, may not be the truth, but it continues to be what we wish. And that is why Marilyn remains, even now, the symbol of our secret desires."[150] This explanation is as typical as it is inaccurate: what on earth is secret about the desires Monroe represents, except the tautological desire *for* secrets, and the paradoxical desire for secrets revealed?

Conspiracy comes to seem the biographical impulse writ large, the search for meanings that organize random events, the projection of fantasies and desires onto public figures. Most biographies of Marilyn Monroe are not classical conspiracy narratives. Rather, they are hybrids that borrow from conspiracy theories their philosophies, their perspective and their conclusions. Oates's *Blonde* is one of the most gratuitously conspiratorial of all the Monroe texts, positing as it does a voyeuristic sniper/spy/spook who is at once an aberrant acting alone and the puppet of a governmental plot: the more fictional the tale, the more it can toy with the pleasures of conspiratorial "solutions" to the mystery.

Monroe is a perfect figure to associate with conspiracy theories: her life and death almost demand them. Her story was always about the intersection of desire and power, about individual agency and the sense of a secret, manipulative authority—whether Monroe herself, the Studio, patriarchy, or political power in the form of the Kennedys (or the Mob/the CIA/the FBI/the KGB), the story is consistent. There is an author, someone is in charge, and in most of these stories it is not Monroe. Rather she is a character in her own life story, one being authored by other powerful people, who themselves are authored by the biographer. The knowledgeable biographer, ferreting out and revealing secrets not just about sex but about political power, turns out to be the most powerful figure of all.

At the end of his text Summers writes over uncertainty by invoking civic rights: "the Marilyn Monroe case may serve a purpose more important than her dying. May it move people to insist, urgently, on their right to know."[151] But Summers neither explains why it is so urgent for people to know, nor, perhaps more crucially, *what* they have a right to know. How Marilyn Monroe died? Why she died? Whom she had sex with? How many abortions she had? The sense of urgency may arise partly from Summers's own need to know Marilyn, a knowledge, as Baty suggests, that is biblical in nature and related to the desire to "author" her. But the audience's urgent need to know more certainly seems an urgent need to resolve their anxiety, a lingering romantic compulsion to believe that there is a reason for everything, even death. The need to know is the effect of the need to believe.

The drive to know prompts several writers, Matthew Smith included, to demand that Monroe's corpse be exhumed and dissected again. Dissection is itself a mechanism for knowledge: autopsy means auto-optic, to see for oneself. The claim is that new scientific techniques would reveal more evidence about whether Monroe was lethally injected or not. In practice, the serial calls made by the conspiracy theories to dissect Marilyn's corpse again—which, if anything, have proliferated over time—are more than a little obscene. They are the desire to know, and to manage, death. While couched as a desire for knowledge (even, in Smith's *Victim,* as a desire to defend Marilyn's reputation against the smirch of wrongful accusations of suicide), this urge to dissect Marilyn seems also to express an urge to do violence, to take her apart, to destroy the corpse. The discomfort such a suggestion provokes is not simply pious, but also a recognition of the unconscious sadism being expressed. Dissecting Marilyn again would be the most literal, and punitive, version of the biographical desire: it is an explicit display of the figurative knowledge, mastery, power and authorship these stories seek.

OVER HER DEAD BODY

Suicide, like homicide, presumes agency: accidental death, as Mailer knew, won't make money, because it is anticlimactic, unsatisfying. We want there to have been a decision, a purpose, so that we can blame, and understand, and feel certain. Although the suicide story seems the most reasonable, the least fictionalized, it too conforms to narrative patterns in which suicidal women die for love, or to pop-Freudian patterns in which they die to rejoin their mother (Leaming) or father (Oates), like Sylvia Plath dying to join hers. Suicide, too, is interpreted as an utterance: Monroe died not because she was going to speak but instead of speaking, in order to speak; it was a cry for help. It is also the flip side of self-love, poetic justice waiting to happen as a punishment for narcissism. Suicide is seen as a performance, as a work of art in which a body and a mind that have been perceived to have been at odds are reconciled at last: so the body becomes autobiography, the statement to the world that it was always supposed to be.

Baty argues that the transgression of suicide elicits containment and punishment: "as [Marilyn's] suicide strained against 'normal' cultural behavior, so the culture in turn attempts to direct its 'expert' authority in naming and mapping her actions post facto," because "suicide is a particularly threatening and contaminating force."[152] Baty then lists some of the traditional ways in which cultures have sought to sanitize, contain and punish suicides, including burying them at crossroads to confuse the spirit and keep it from returning to the community: "the community, then, acted to reassert its power over the corpse in response to the insurgence the suicide had exercised in taking of her life."[153]

Academics writing about Monroe assume that she killed herself: good intellectual skepticism does not admit taking conspiracy theories seriously, and suicide is in keeping with the humanist tradition of locating agency in the subject. Baty's index identifies "suicide and agency" as a named subtext: words like *renegade* and *insurgent* reinforce the implication that suicide is not only an act of decisive (ultimate) self-will, but that it is resistant, rebellious, powerful. In *Over Her Dead Body*, her study of representations of dead women, Bronfen makes the similar argument that suicide "involves the conscious and explicit choice of death as a strategy for lending authority to the woman's version of her story."[154]

Well, maybe. But suicide is also an absolute relinquishment of authority and agency. Associating suicide with such politically powerful words as *agency, authority, rebellion* and *resistance* implies that suicide is an insurrectionary act. Eldridge Cleaver once said the same thing of rape, and it is not clear that self-victimization is particularly more salutary than victimization at the hands of another, although it is certainly more complicated. But if a society wants to eradicate resistance, what could be more convenient, or accommodating, than the voluntary suicide of a "renegade" subject? It may be tempting to conclude that Monroe's suicide—if suicide it was—was an act of desperate, last-ditch resistance to determination by others, but to debate the agency of suicide seems perilously close to implying that suicide is a feminist gesture, a suggestion that in real terms is asinine.

Suicide certainly troubles our comfortable assumptions about the necessary benignity of agency and choice, which is where I part company from Baty and Bronfen. Suicide begs the question of what happens when we choose—or claim—pain or self-destruction, but it does not answer the question. Bronfen argues that "suicide implies an authorship with one's own life."[155] In theory this may be true, but in practice Marilyn Monroe's suicide hardly released her from the determination of others; it fixed her forever within their interpretations. She became not author, but character, much more surely than while she lived, when she could attempt, with however limited an effect, to resist the interpretations of others.

But whether one tries to recuperate it or merely laments it, suicide still presumes agency, and it is this agency that seems to me profoundly absent at the end of Monroe's story. Each version gives death a name, a face and a reason, but that is precisely what the few certain facts do not offer. And there is something resonant in this loss of agency, given the ways in which biographies have staged a battle between subject and object, author and protagonist, star and studio (or director), wife and husband: Monroe's story always places her on the cusp of power and inadequacy; it is about the precarious moment of losing control. If we see Marilyn eternally poised between power and its loss, then we might be able to conceive of her outside of debates about victimization and blame. If we see her death as a contingent accident, caused by an overdose unintentionally swallowed by someone in the habit of taking too many pills too often, we might be able to imagine her life as something other than a tragic myth, preordained and foreclosed.

However, that is not the way the story is going. If the latest entry into the lists is anything to judge by, the story is heading further into apocrypha.

Matthew Smith's 2003 *Victim: The Secret Tapes of Marilyn Monroe* is based upon a series of "transcripts" purportedly of tapes made by Monroe in the last days of her life, which she supposedly gave to Dr. Greenson the day she died. The "transcripts" (which Smith refers to repeatedly as "tapes," although he has neither seen nor heard the original "recordings") display remarkable prescience, and helpfulness, on the part of Marilyn. Apparently, in her last days, she decided—as part of her therapy, an exercise in free association, not because she had any premonition that she was about to be assassinated—to share with Dr. Greenson her thoughts about many of the most controversial aspects of her story. Smith bestows them upon the world for the first time, although, having read them in their entirety himself, he has too much tact not to edit them for our delicate sensibilities. He scrupulously preserves us, and Monroe, from embarrassment—and also from the effort of having to make up our own minds. Smith's biography provides the following substantiation for his story:

a "select" bibliography; fifty-nine photographs (including such vital evidence as an autographed studio portrait of Robert Mitchum; half a dozen public images of the Kennedys; another half dozen of Monroe's house, etc.); seven reproduced quasi-official "records" (such as a grocery bill from the night before Monroe died, Pat Newcomb's application for federal employment, and the certificate of death), most of which come directly from Capell's 1964 pamphlet; and eight "footnotes" that give book titles but no page numbers. Other than that, Smith proceeds without doubt or documentation.

His story is that on Wednesday, August 8, 1962, John Miner, deputy district attorney of Los Angeles when Monroe died, and present at the autopsy, was sent to interview Dr. Greenson, who told Miner that Monroe had not committed suicide. He played for Miner the tapes Monroe had made for him, and allowed Miner to make a transcript of them. He swore Miner to secrecy, and Miner

kept his promise until, more than 20 years after Greenson's death [in 1979], and after seeing the doctor maligned as a murderer while Marilyn's memory continued to be tainted with the stigma of suicide, he was finally released from his promise by Hildi, Greenson's widow. Miner spoke out on Greenson's behalf when the psychiatrist was attacked by authors such as Donald Spoto. [. . .] He quoted sparingly from the transcript he had of the tapes and released only a small segment of the contents until now, when he agreed to let them be featured in this book in their entirety.

There are the strongest reasons for accepting that the tapes were recorded by Marilyn very shortly before she died, and they survived only because she passed them to Dr. Greenson, probably on the very day she died. Here then is the voice of Marilyn. This is the only surviving contribution made by the star herself, in which she tells of her disposition at the time she died. Among other things she talks about what was happening to her, about Jack and Robert Kennedy, about her marriages and why they failed, about her friends—Clark Gable, Frank Sinatra, Joan Crawford, Laurence Olivier and others—about her sexual deficiencies, the book she was reading, experiments in lesbianism and, most important of all, her plans for the future.[156]

Even if we accept that Miner waited twenty years and then suddenly changed his mind, and that he equally arbitrarily and suddenly decided to entrust the precious documents to Smith, there are still some niggling questions. What are those "strongest reasons for accepting that the tapes were recorded by Marilyn"? Smith doesn't offer them. And of course the reader is not given tapes, or the voice of Marilyn. The reader is given "edited" italic passages in Smith's book, which he claims are from transcripts that he claims John Miner claimed to have written from tapes he claimed to have heard from Dr. Greenson, who he claims obtained them from Marilyn.

And of course it was thoughtful of Marilyn to dispose of so many of our questions about her life just before she died, and to offer summary versions of *all* her most famous relationships to the psychiatrist she'd been seeing daily for two years:

> *Joe has an image in his stubborn Italian head of a traditional Italian wife. [. . .] There was no way I could stop being Marilyn Monroe and become someone else to save our marriage. It didn't take too long before we both realized that and ended our marriage. But we didn't end our love for each other. Any time I need him, Joe is there. I couldn't have a better friend.*[157]

In fact, the "secret tapes"—or, rather, italic passages—"by Marilyn Monroe" comprise less than twenty pages of a 310-page book. Most of the book rehashes the conspiracy "evidence," largely via Summers and Wolfe, for believing that if Monroe didn't deliberately kill herself, she must have been assassinated by a political operative. Smith does offer a different plot: the CIA killed Marilyn in order to get revenge on the Kennedys for the Bay of Pigs disaster. They intended to implicate both brothers in her death, but inexplicably failed to do so. They made up for their lapse, however, as they were subsequently responsible not only for both John F. Kennedy's and Robert F. Kennedy's assassinations, but also—in some entirely unexplained way—for Ted Kennedy's decision to get drunk and drive Mary Jo Kopechne off the bridge at Chappaquiddick and to flee the scene.

Ours is a world poised always on the brink between public and private, ready to hear that truth is not stranger than fiction, but reflects it: hence our penchant for hybrid genres that combine fact and fiction, such as reality TV, talk shows, biography, fictional memoir, true crime, historical fiction, the tell-all memoir, the docudrama. A famous woman who really died young and beautiful at the hands of powerful men who will themselves be destroyed by hubris leaves our voyeuristic gaze resting upon tragic archetype, satisfying many expectations at once. And Marilyn Monroe is invented at precisely the moment when this intense media surveillance began, she is the ultimate icon in an age of advertising, the perfect image for blending fact and fiction, story and reality until—to our delight and sublime terror—we can no longer distinguish between them.

Necrophilia is, of course, the end of the story. Marilyn Monroe is far more desirable now that she is dead. Our culture's oldest stories associate dead women with glamour and sex appeal. Snow White and Sleeping Beauty are most desirable when most nearly dead, and we especially love to tell stories about women who die for love— Cleopatra, Dido, Hero, Ariadne, Phaedra, Semele, Semiramis, Isolde, to name just a few. It's so familiar a story that we might better ask which beautiful women *don't* die at the end of the tale. The textures of these stories have altered with time, but our predilection for stories about women who die young has never faltered, from classical myth to medieval saints' lives to modern biography. The dead woman is a favorite novelistic, dramatic and operatic subject: Clarissa Harlowe, Anna Karenina, Emma Bovary, Catherine Earnshaw, Mimi, Camille, Tosca, Violetta, Carmen, Lily Bart, Catherine Barkley . . . the list of women whose death provides the romantic (heterosexual) love story with its symbolic climax goes on and on. To mourn a beautiful woman clearly pleases us: in 1846 Edgar Allan Poe said that "the most poetical topic in the world" is the death of a beautiful woman, and it would seem that our culture continues to agree with him. "Death" is the key: the most poetical topic is not a dead beautiful woman, but rather her death. It's the process we enjoy, the journey from power to punishment, from beauty to fatality.

The link between beauty and death is loss, which is related to desire. We cannot desire what we possess; we are more likely to desire what we have lost. The beautiful woman is already a symbol of desire in stories that exalt heterosexual consummation, in a world structured by the power of the male. The link between sex and death is instinctive—one doesn't need Freud to tell us that, knowledge of French will do. *La petite mort,* the little death, suggests a larger death. The loss of the beautiful woman is unconsciously linked to desire for the beautiful woman—and to fulfillment of that desire. A particular poignancy—even gratification—results when reality seems to correspond to these ancient erotic models.

Although the story insisted that Marilyn was Cinderella, she was always much closer to Snow White, down to the iconography of her look: skin as white as snow, lips as red as cherries, eyebrows black as ebony. First childishly innocent, then terrified, fleeing victim, then beautiful corpse encased in a coffin made of glass: the myth of Marilyn Monroe makes her both wicked queen and persecuted hero-ine: the tale is one of self-division. The story opens with a mirror, and the fatal need for sexual perfection. The conflict in the mirror is between mother and daughter, and between self and image: as the clever, skilled, deceptive performer grows older, she fears the waning of her desirability. This fear leads her to kill the beautiful young daughter, an image of her own lost perfection. In the traditional ver-sion, the aging woman tries to kill the beautiful imago by means of old-fashioned accessories to female beauty: lacing her stays too tight, a poisoned comb, and finally the apple of temptation itself, the eat-ing of which brings not just knowledge and sex, but labor, pain and death. Snow White is there to be looked at, trapped behind glass, entombed in passivity. The wily, self-absorbed manipulative brain is eradicated, and the beautiful corpse remains in a state of perfect nul-lity, most herself when most nearly dead.

But the tale is unfinished, for our heroine is not reborn at the end of the tale. That will be left for the next biography: to bring her back to life in order to enjoy the serial pleasure of killing her off once again.

Marilyn Monroe, c. 1956. PHOTOGRAPH BY ELLIOTT ERWITT.

AFTERWORD: MY MARILYN

I said well, she's a little bit like you, she wears her heart
on her sleeve and talks salty and Marilyn said fuck you
and said well, if somebody asked me what Marilyn Monroe
was like, what was Marilyn Monroe *really* like, what
would I say, and I said I'd have to think about that.

—TRUMAN CAPOTE,
"A Beautiful Child"

At its best portraiture remains one of our finest arts. In Marilyn Monroe's case, however, it is at its best only sporadically, so colored is her portrait by fantasies, fallacies and falsehoods. Marilyn stands as a prime example of the seductions of biography—the temptation to substitute belief for knowledge, prejudice for thinking. Biography can be the generous act of imaginative empathy, or it can be an obliterative slide from identification into colonization. I would not argue that all biographies are autobiographies, but there is no avoiding the fact that Marilyn is par excellence a screen for cultural projection. Scientists call it experimental bias: finding what you were looking for.

In this afterword, then, is the Marilyn I have tried to keep to the margins of the book, the Marilyn I was looking for, "my Marilyn." It's a deliberately amorphous picture, but I have tried not to treat selectivity as a license to choose only my favorite moments. It is certainly *not* the real, true or private woman—nor is it intended as an alternative, or even a corrective Marilyn. It's just a personal one, still drawn exclusively from the extant, public sources, but turning now more toward memoir, where public and private blend in provocative ways.

I first recognized "my" Marilyn in a story that Truman Capote tells in his idiosyncratic reminiscence, "A Beautiful Child." He reports a conversation with Marilyn in which she asked him what Elizabeth Taylor was really like. He responded (he says): "Well, she's a little bit like you, she wears her heart on her sleeve and talks salty." To which Marilyn said, "Fuck you," and then asked what he would say if asked the same question about her: what would he say Marilyn was *really* like? And he said he'd have to think about that. But he'd already answered the question, a little: the Marilyn he knew talked salty and wore her heart on her sleeve.

Suddenly Capote's Marilyn came alive for me—and eventually I realized, with some wryness, why that was. Now I hear those phrases of his whenever someone asks me what I think Marilyn was *really* like. My public answer is usually, "I'd have to think about that." But in private, I am hearing him say to me, "Well, she's a little bit like you, she wears her heart on her sleeve and talks salty."

Let her subjectivity remain her own: what follows is a biographical sketch of Marilyn Monroe as a kind of kaleidoscopic, sideways self-portrait. If Marilyn is a screen for our desires and our fears, here are some of mine. Just to keep things fair.

"A Beautiful Child" describes a conversation Capote claims to have had with Monroe at the funeral of their mutual friend, actress and teacher Constance Collier, in April 1955, when Marilyn had surprised the world by moving to New York and going into hiding at the very height of her fame.

Marilyn is late for the funeral, because she "got all made up," and then worried that false eyelashes and lipstick would be disrespectful, and so washed it all off. She shows up with her face scrubbed clean, her hair in a black chiffon scarf, dressed "like the abbess of a nunnery in private audience with the Pope" (bar the "vaguely erotic black high-heeled shoes"). She immediately asks Capote if she can run to the bathroom; he accuses her of wanting to pop pills, and makes her wait through the service. After the funeral ends, she enlists his aid in avoiding the paparazzi, confiding that she hadn't had time to get her hair colored.

Capote remarks flippantly: "Poor innocent me. And all this time I thought you were a bona fide blonde." To which Marilyn retorts: "I am. But nobody's *that* natural. And incidentally, fuck you."

That's my Marilyn. Humorous but prickly, witty and with a sharp tongue, she took no grief and no prisoners. My Marilyn would always have a rejoinder, and she would give as good as she got. Often self-deprecating, she was also aware how disarming it was; my Marilyn wouldn't willingly let others get the best of her. The woman talking in Capote's reminiscence could have survived for years on the fringe of a predatory world like Hollywood in the 1940s: this is no breathy wide-eyed innocent aghast at having Mr. Z insert his "Thing" into her rectum. My Marilyn would tell absurd, raunchy stories like Capote's:

> Did I ever tell you about the time I saw Errol Flynn whip out his prick and play the piano with it? Oh well, it was a hundred years ago, I'd just got into modeling, and I went to this half-ass party, and Errol Flynn, so pleased with himself, he was there and he took out his prick and played the piano with it. Thumped the keys. He played *You Are My Sunshine*. Christ! Everybody says Milton Berle has the biggest schlong in Hollywood. But who *cares*?[1]

Marilyn had seen it all; she would not have been easy to shock, and even harder to impress. But once she was impressed, she threw herself into the enterprise. Her tough-talking was the voice of experience, her cynicism that of a frustrated romantic who's dying to be proved wrong. She was born an idealist; it was life that made a realist out of her.

She was, to use her own description of Roslyn Taber, the character she played in *The Misfits*, "a girl who knows what life can be."[2] Far from unconscious, my Marilyn enjoyed her own slyness—just watch the scene in *The Seven Year Itch* when The Girl pries open the stairs to Sherman's apartment, announces with bright insouciance: "We can do this all summer!" and then gives Sherman a knowing look that would have made Mae West proud. Another moment she appears on film comes in *Bus Stop*, when Cherie finds herself entrapped by the cowboy pestering her with unwanted attentions. He has hoisted her onto his shoulders, when she sees her friend Vera in the crowd below her and engages in a sign-language conversation to explain that she thinks Bo is crazy and that she's trying to run away. That exchange shows my Marilyn at her best: funny, pragmatic, trying to contend with life's vagaries, but a bit bemused by them all the same.

My Marilyn was a grown-up, and she was nobody's fool. Which

doesn't mean she couldn't have been "immature" in the ways that so many writers are quick to point out. She was clearly insecure, needy, easily wounded. Prone to self-pity, my Marilyn had the thin skin of someone who felt life had rubbed her raw, and resented it. But constant friction made her calloused in some ways as well. "Marilyn was a gambler," said Lucy Freeman, in the one sentence in her book that I think gets Monroe right.[3] My Marilyn had nerve. When Mrs. Murray suggested that her dress for the JFK birthday gala at Madison Square Garden was too revealing, Marilyn is said to have counseled gaily, "Be brave, Mrs. Murray! Be brave!"

She was not only daring, but determined to win. She was ambitious, competitive, and worked tremendously hard to achieve her success. Emmeline Snively, her first mentor, said:

> She was a clean-cut, American, wholesome girl—too plump, but beautiful in a way. We tried to teach her how to pose, how to handle her body. She always tried to lower her smile because she smiled too high, and it made her nose look a little long. At first she knew nothing about carriage, posture, walking, sitting, or posing. She started out with less than any girl I ever knew, but she worked the hardest. . . . She wanted to learn, wanted to be somebody, more than anybody I ever saw before in my life.[4]

Her intensity and force of will were widely acknowledged: "steel" and "iron" come up frequently in assessments of Monroe's character. She was both irresistible force and immovable object. Sidney Skolsky wrote: "She appeared kind and soft and helpless. Almost everybody wanted to help her. Marilyn's supposed helplessness was her greatest strength."[5] Her longtime publicist Rupert Allan declared, "Under all the frailty was a will of steel."[6] Allan's replacement, Pat Newcomb, said: "At the core of her, she was really strong [. . .] and that was something we tended to forget, because she seemed so vulnerable, and one always felt it necessary to watch out for her."[7] Paula Strasberg, so reviled in the lives, offered a vivid image: "Marilyn has the fragility of a female but the constitution of an ox. She is a beautiful hummingbird made of iron."[8] Ezra Goodman, who interviewed her for

Time in 1956, remarked: "If, as a Hollywood medical friend of mine maintains, 'all actresses are made of steel,' Monroe was cast in an even mightier mold than most of them."[9]

She was accused of being ruthless, of abandoning those who had outlived their usefulness. "Never forget," Amy Greene cautioned, "that Marilyn wanted above all to be a *great* movie star. She would do anything, give up anyone, to move on up."[10] But *ruthless* is the wrong word for my Marilyn; she was not without remorse. She could be relentless, however—which is different. She was uncompromising. When Weatherby mentioned to Marilyn her reputation for dropping people easily, she frowned, and answered:

> I've never dropped anyone I believed in. My trouble is, I trust people too much. I believe in them too much and I go on believing in them when the signs are already there. You get a lot of disappointments.[11]

She couldn't operate in moderation; she had no ability to back off, no innate caution. Her only defenses were aggression or total withdrawal. She was either in or she was out, all or nothing. She would rather work herself up, be in a rage or on a high, than ever be "bland and just shrug everything off, the way so many people do."[12] She was not ever going to be overlooked.

Colin Clark worked as an assistant on the set of *The Prince and the Showgirl* and published an amusing and perceptive "diary" of the production, *The Prince, the Showgirl, and Me*, in 1996. Clark recognized the power plays underlying Marilyn's notorious "bad behavior," and also the probable cost to her of her own enormous energies:

> This plump, blonde (?) young lady with the big eyes is certainly very hard to control. Right now, she is almost too much for a young, smart producer (Milton), a top playwright and intellectual (AM), America's foremost dramatic coaching couple (the Strasbergs) and England's best actor/director (SLO). MM is just a force of nature. This is sort of wonderful for us, to watch and be associated with, but it must be very uncomfortable for her.[13]

He also understood that her defiance might have been a defensive reaction against feeling besieged. He tells a story about accidentally coming in on Monroe nude in her dressing room. Monroe cracked a joke at his being flustered by her nudity ("Oh Colin, and you an old Etonian!"), which prompted Clark to wonder:

> How did she stay so cool? And how did she know which school I had gone to and what it meant?
>   When I managed to get out of the room and pull myself together, I realized that behind the fog MM could be a bit brighter than we all think. How much of the MM image is contrived? Acting dumb is a good way to make other people make fools of themselves. What fun it might be to make a movie with MM when she felt everyone around was her friend.
>   Dream on, Colin.[14]

Her successes may have made her expectations outsized; certainly she behaved like a diva in some ways, demanding unreserved loyalty and instant attendance to her whims. She was impatient, and she didn't suffer fools. My Marilyn knew her own worth, but still required constant reassurance that others recognized it (the many people who remember her "lapping up" Paula Strasberg's sycophantic flattery are no doubt not exaggerating the case). If she flaunted her power, or tested it, she was trying to convince herself as much as anyone. When Weatherby recommended Mailer's *The Deer Park* to her she reported back that she hadn't cared for it because "he's too impressed by power, in my opinion. [. . .] You can't fool me about that. [. . .] I've felt that way myself—scared of being a loser."[15] Aspirational, a perfectionist, she expected as much of others as of herself. As Rollyson observed, she had an enormous capacity to be disappointed.

Her idealism was reflected in her serious love affairs. If she could be accused of marrying "trophy husbands," her spoils represented what she valued: strength, intelligence, success. She selected men who might affirm her own worth, to be sure, but let he who is entirely without narcissism cast the first stone. What lover doesn't hope in part to be confirmed by the other's desire? Marilyn chose popular "heroes" to marry (as an adult); she was misled by both men's air of authority. What she thought was moral rigor turned out to be rigidity; she took their self-importance for confidence. If she chose badly, she chose for good reason. It wasn't her fault that the men she fell in love with needed her to be less than they—and less than she was. She idealized the men she married, but they certainly demanded a fantasy from her, too. "You wanted a happy whore, right?" Miller's Maggie demands in *After the Fall*. So much illusion could create only disillusionment: she hated feeling like a disappointment as much as she hated being disappointed. She was terribly sensitive to being unappreciated, and her capacity for hope was commensurate to her capacity for frustration.

I do not doubt the rage in her: it fueled her ambition, propelled her forward and accelerated her success. Many self-styled "victims" (which Marilyn certainly was; she played the victim card with brio) should in fact not be tangled with. Natasha Lytess wrote after Marilyn dropped her that whenever Monroe "explained something, her right hand darted forward, weaving to the left and right like a serpent. It was a gesture of evasiveness and survival through expediency." Whatever else she was, Lytess complained, Monroe was "most definitely not a child. [. . .] A child is naïve and open and trusting. But Marilyn is shrewd. I wish I had one-tenth of her ability for business, of her clever knack of promoting what is right for her and discarding what is not."[16] And later, not long before she died, Lytess repeated the charge in slightly different language: "I wish I had one-tenth of Marilyn's cleverness. The truth is, my life and my feelings were very much in her hands. I was the older, the teacher, but she knew the depth of my attachment to her, and she exploited those feelings as only a beautiful younger person can. She said she was the needy one. Alas, it was the reverse."[17]

"She could certainly be a bitch," said Weatherby. "A lady with a bad temper."[18] I am quite sure that Miller nails her rage in some of the fight scenes in *After the Fall*. These battles for supremacy have the ineffable ring of the real, as when Maggie fires an underling for laughing at her:

Maggie, *furiously*: She didn't cough, she laughed! And you stand
   there going ho-ho-ho to her high-class jokes! Christ sake, just

because she played in a symphony? [. . .] I'm not finishing this
tape if she's in that band tomorrow! I'm entitled to my conditions,
Quentin! *Commanding*: And I don't have to plead with anybody!
I want her out!

When he defends the girl, Maggie spits out:

> All you care about is money! Don't shit me!
> Quentin, *quelling a fury—his voice very level*: Maggie, don't use that
> language with me, will you?
> Maggie: Calling me vulgar, that I talk like a truck driver! Well, that's
> where I come from. I'm for Negroes and Puerto Ricans and truck
> drivers!
> Quentin: Then why do you fire people so easily?
> Maggie—*her eyes narrowing, she is seeing him anew*: Look. You don't
> want me. What the hell are you doing here?[19]

That's my Marilyn, too. Always poised on the knife-edge of rejection,
she thought she would only be redeemed by unconditional love.
When she was scared or angry, her reprisals were vicious; she could
be "the meanest woman in Hollywood," as Wilder said: "slashing, out
to destroy" when in a rage, according to Miller. Guiles notes that "she
was never to be patronized—or criticized."[20] My Marilyn was volatile,
and could be dangerous; she relished being someone of whom others
said, "hmm—she's to be dealt with."[21] Her friend photographer Sam
Shaw commented:

> She laid the laws down. She became a tough, tough tomato. A
> tough tomato. She became a tyrant as a producer, a big tycoon try-
> ing to lay the law down to the Hollywood bigshots. And she nearly
> beat them. In today's atmosphere, with women all over demand-
> ing more rights, she would have won hands down.[22]

Marilyn took life seriously, and she took things hard: she wore her
heart on her sleeve, as Capote said. Living in a state of relentless self-
appraisal left her tremendously exposed. She suffered not only her own
pain, but also the pain of others, which, Miller wrote, could make her

"frantic."[23] *The Misfits* first developed out of a story called "Please Don't Kill Anything," which represented Marilyn's devastation when she saw any living thing dying or killed: it could make her "cry as if she were wounded" to see flowers dying; she paid boys trapping pigeons in the park to release them; she threw fish back into the sea after they had been left by fishermen. Miller wrote in his story, with typical condescension: "while part of his heart worshipped her fierce tenderness toward all that lived, another part knew that she must come to understand that she did not die with the moths and the spiders and the fledgling birds."[24] Marilyn understood this just fine by the time she finished filming the movie he based on this story. "I had to use my wits," she said of the battles she fought on set, "or else I'd have been sunk."[25] She knew how tough she had to be to survive. "For a long time I was scared I'd find out I was like my mother," she told Weatherby.

> I wonder when I break down if I'm not tough enough—like her. But I'm hoping to get stronger. [...] I ask myself what am I afraid of. I know I have talent. I know I can act. Well, get on with it, Marilyn. I feel I still try to ingratiate myself with people, try to tell them what they want to hear. That's fear, too. We should all start to live before we get too old. Fear is stupid. So are regrets.[26]

She was determined not to let fear rule her life. When she made mistakes, she tried always to make new ones. My Marilyn was an object lesson in self-determination, in the unique human ability to reinvent oneself, to make oneself, as Mailer said, an instrument of one's will. She tried to be the product of her own volition—which doesn't make her pathological. On the contrary: my Marilyn was trying to learn to judge for herself, and to become someone she respected. She fought to take responsibility for her own life, to be accountable. The fact that she often failed—that she descended into self-pity, into helplessness, carelessness, recklessness—just means she was human.

I think of Marilyn, above all, as a fighter. When Weatherby described an afternoon spent at Schwab's drugstore rubbing elbows with the "would-be's," Marilyn laughed and told him: "Now you've graduated. [...] You've seen where we come from and what we have to fight and what happens to some of us."[27] She knew the risks, was opportunistic, and seized her day: "Don't hold the future like a vase," Maggie counsels Quentin when they marry. The probability that Marilyn died by her own hand (and yes, for the record, like Mailer I would say ten to one she was an accidental overdose) doesn't mean that she wasn't a fighter. If Marilyn Monroe was "doomed" to lose her fight, well, so are we all. We're all dying, and death is also always in some sense an accident.

The fact that she died hardly lessens the degree to which she was a life force. At her best, her magnetism is overwhelming: in an otherwise forgettable film like *The Prince and the Showgirl* a magic charisma really does emanate from her, and she makes everyone else on the screen look wooden and dead. In *The Misfits,* Eli Wallach's character, Guido, tells her she has a "gift for life," while "the rest of us, we're just looking for a place to hide and watch it all go by." "Here's to your life, Roslyn, I hope it goes on forever," he concludes. Perhaps we should stop holding the fact that it didn't against her.

Marilyn's stardom was her life's triumph. And if she exploited people, they exploited her, too. After all, maybe that's just what people do: whose relationships are entirely self-sacrificing? For my Marilyn also, as Capote said, "labors like a field hand to please everybody."[28]

Or anyway, that's what Ernest Cunningham, compiling a list of Marilyn characteristics for *The Ultimate Marilyn,* quotes Capote as saying. Cunningham also remarks that, to him, Capote's account in "A Beautiful Child" "sounds misremembered or manufactured."[29] In *Victim,* Matthew Smith reports a story that *he* finds completely unbelievable, concerning Monroe's recuperation after her gall bladder surgery:

> Suffering a great deal of pain, she worried the operation would leave a scar, and became very depressed. It was at times like this when she particularly suffered from not having a family looking in, helping her out and talking about things. For a while she was said to have become an unpleasant character, foul mouthed [sic]

and unkempt. The very idea of it is so uncharacteristic as to be mind-boggling.[30]

Well, that depends on what you believe. Many witnesses report that Monroe—whether because of depression or drugs—was often bedraggled and stained. As she left New York to film *The Misfits*, a fan reports seeing her with "bags under her eyes and a period stain across the back of her skirt. I didn't want to see her like that, and I turned away."[31] A reporter, sent to interview her in 1953, wrote that he was shocked at her appearance: "Her hair was in tangles. [...] She had cold cream all over her face, and her eyebrows were smeared. She was the same old Marilyn in spirit, but on the outside she was Dracula's daughter. I couldn't get out of there fast enough."[31] All of these reports emphasize what they want to believe, what they want to see—and what they don't want to see. They don't want to see what Marilyn, with typical self-blame, called "the monster" inside her, the ugliness that most people, if they're honest, know they have lurking inside them.

Director John Huston gives me one of my glimpses of Marilyn, in a reminiscence at once candid and refreshingly fair-minded:

> People say Hollywood broke her heart but that is rubbish—she was observant and tough-minded and appealing but she adored all the wrong people and she was recklessly willful. . . . You couldn't get at her. She was tremendously pretentious (she'd done a lot of shit-arsed studying in New York) but she acted as if she never understood why she was funny and that was precisely what made her so funny. . . . In certain ways she was very shrewd. [. . .] If she was a victim, it was only of her own friends.[33]

I like this passage because it gives her credit, and makes her take responsibility. And because it acknowledges the complex negotiations between self and other, between Marilyn and her friends, between Marilyn and her audience, that defined her, define us all. That's what definition means, after all: ascertaining limits. The disquiet her story still has the power to provoke is surely as much about limits as it is about anything. The extremity of her unraveling, and the discomfort one feels participating vicariously in it, registers the limits of self-determination, the margins of love, it reveals the barrier of consciousness that separates all of us from each other. "It's nice to be included in people's fantasies," she said to Richard Meryman in her last interview, "but you also like to be accepted for your own sake." Everyone wants to be seen plain by someone, but this usually leaves us seeking out ourselves in other people—which doesn't necessarily do them any favors, either.

Marilyn's fortune was exceptional, for good as well as bad, and no doubt she made many of her own circumstances. Capote also said that "there was something exceptional about Marilyn Monroe. Sometimes she could be ethereal and sometimes like a waitress in a coffee shop."[34] (Or, as Lauren Bacall's character is told in *How to Marry a Millionaire,* "The trouble with you is, you're strictly a hamburger with onions dame and won't admit it.") Marilyn was uncommon, but she was not inhuman. All of us are more protean than we care to admit; few of us wholly know ourselves, let alone truly knowing an other. Marilyn was rather more mindful than most of her own status as a work of art: self-aware and self-conscious, she could also, when she hit the limits of her ability to reinvent herself, be self-destructive. "You mean I'm really no different from anyone else," she joked with Weatherby. "And there I was thinking I was special!'

Most writers succumb to lamentation at the end of Marilyn's story, and Capote is no exception: he leaves his bawdy, laughing Marilyn behind, so that he can stare out at the sky and enjoy grieving for this "beautiful child": "I wanted to lift my voice louder than the seagulls' cries and call her back: Marilyn! Marilyn, why did everything have to turn out the way it did?" But at least Capote quickly descends from this lofty plain and adds, "Why does life have to be so fucking rotten?" The myth usually ends more like Baty, who shows off her learning as she sighs in closing, "Ah, Marilyn. Ah, humanity." And maybe Capote's entire portrait is as counterfeit as Cunningham thinks. But we all believe in the Marilyn we choose, make up the Marilyn we require. We desire the Marilyn we want to have, or think we deserve; we identify with the Marilyn we think we are, or want to be.

So mine wears her heart on her sleeve and talks salty. And in the end, my Marilyn knows that nobody's *that* natural.

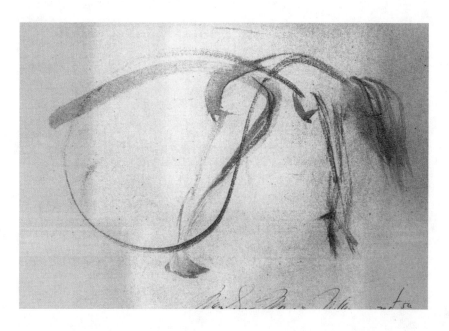

Self-portrait in charcoal by Marilyn Monroe, signed "Marilyn Monroe Miller, Sept. 56."

NOTES

INTRODUCTION

1 Mailer, *Marilyn*, 18.
2 Morin, 53.
3 Victor, 36.

1 PRODUCING THE IMAGE, 1946–1962

1 Gates, 56.
2 Guiles (1969), 143.
3 Mellen, 22.
4 Summers, 4.
5 McCann, 169.
6 Spoto, 548.
7 Oates, 619.
8 Johnson, n.pag.
9 Baty, 69.
10 Cunningham, 30.
11 Summers, 176.
12 Riese and Hitchens, ix.
13 Mailer, *Marilyn*, 15.
14 Victor, 270.
15 Millett, 80.
16 Mailer, *Marilyn*, 15.
17 Victor, 267.
18 Rollyson, 55.
19 Dyer, *Heavenly Bodies*, 36.
20 Quoted in Cunningham, 38.
21 Haskell, *From Reverence*, 254.
22 Haskell, *From Reverence*, 254–5.
23 McCann, 33.
24 Baty, 24, original emphasis.
25 Gates, 56.
26 Mailer, *Marilyn*, 16–17.
27 Zolotow (1961), 311.
28 De Beauvoir, 229.
29 Victor, 40.
30 Zolotow (1961), 313.
31 Baty, 23.
32 Victor, 267.
33 "To Aristophanes," 80.
34 Quoted in Zolotow (1961), 194.
35 Quoted in Victor, 267.
36 O'Hagan, 6.
37 Ochs, 52.
38 Martin, 32.
39 Meryman, 36.
40 Steinem, 17.
41 Gates, 56.
42 Banner, 284.

43 Piercy, 105.
44 Carpozi, 105–6.
45 Buskin, 229
46 Leaming, 322.
47 Miller, *After the Fall,* 77.
48 Dyer, *Stars,* 31.
49 Baty, 57–8.
50 Piercy, 103.
51 Piercy, 107.
52 Victor, 6.
53 Victor, 6.
54 "Marilyn Monroe," 88.
55 Dyer, *Heavenly Bodies,* 20.
56 Benzel, 4.
57 See, for example: Benzel, Dyer, Lesser, McCann.
58 "What Makes Marilyn?," 17.
59 "What Makes Marilyn?," 17.
60 Byer, 21.
61 "Marilyn Monroe," 88.
62 "Marilyn Monroe: The Talk of Hollywood," 104.
63 "To Aristophanes," 74.
64 Goodman, 240.
65 McCann, 77.
66 Cunningham, 245.
67 Arnold, 10.
68 Benzel, 14.
69 Cunningham, 231.
70 Arnold, 25–6.
71 Arnold, 27.
72 Benzel, 3.
73 Greene, 21.
74 Stern, 17.
75 Stern, 28, original emphasis.
76 Barton, 138.
77 Cunningham, 45.
78 Quoted in Summers, 204.
79 Rollyson, 38.
80 Arnold, 17.
81 Rollyson, 59.
82 Buskin, 104.
83 Buskin, 126.
84 Rollyson, 67.
85 Miller, *Timebends,* 303.

86 Buskin, 145.
87 Leaming, 76.
88 McCann, 87.
89 Barton, 126.
90 Rollyson, 76.
91 Solomon, 183.
92 Dyer, *Stars,* 11.
93 "To Aristophanes," 80–1.
94 Rollyson, 87–8.
95 Rollyson, 89.
96 Rollyson, 127.
97 Rollyson, 127.
98 Buskin, 199.
99 Buskin, 10.
100 Buskin, 203.
101 Buskin, 9.
102 McCann, 104.
103 Shaw, 98.
104 *Some Like It Hot,* United Artists, dir: Billy Wilder, 1959.
105 Rollyson, 155; McCann, 107.
106 Buskin, 218.
107 "Powerful Stars," 68.
108 Buskin, 229.
109 Wolfe, 431.
110 Rollyson, 200–1.
111 Barton, 127.

2 PRODUCING THE LIFE, 1946–2003

1 O'Hagan, 6.
2 Spoto, 503.
3 McCann, 22.
4 Spoto, 330.
5 Rev. of Zolotow, 174.
6 Zolotow (1961), 50.
7 Cunningham, 285.
8 Guiles (1969), 77, original emphasis.
9 Guiles (1969), 333.
10 Gosling, 21.
11 Mailer, *Marilyn,* 257.
12 Mailer, *Marilyn,* 20, original emphasis.

13 Ratcliffe, 16.
14 Mailer, *Marilyn,* 15.
15 James, 44.
16 Corliss, n.pag.; Merkin, 72.
17 Victor, 260.
18 Speriglio, *Conspiracy,* 20.
19 Corliss, n.pag.
20 Riese and Hitchens, 302.
21 Guiles (1984), 60.
22 Mailer, "Strawhead," 63.
23 Riese and Hitchens, 504.
24 McCann, 8.
25 Summers, 4.
26 Zolotow (1990), 4.
27 Kennicott, n.pag.
28 Kakutani, "Commodified Blonde," C17.
29 O'Hagan, 7.
30 Johnson, n.pag.
31 Johnson, n.pag.
32 Smith (1996), 73.
33 Smith, *Victim,* 41.
34 Wolfe, 122–3.
35 Guiles (1984), 37.
36 Miller, *Timebends,* 370.
37 Cunningham, 241.
38 "Monroe," *My Story,* 108.
39 Spoto, 331.
40 Steinem, 12.
41 Quoted in Steinem, 87.
42 Cunningham, 30.
43 Summers, 9–10.
44 Mailer, *Marilyn,* 18.
45 Miller, *After the Fall,* 5.
46 Miller, *After the Fall,* 80.
47 Miller, *After the Fall,* 61.
48 Miller, *After the Fall,* 76–7; original ellipses.
49 Miller, *After the Fall,* 106.
50 Miller, *After the Fall,* 113.
51 Miller, *After the Fall,* 119.
52 Miller, *After the Fall,* 120.
53 Miller, *After the Fall,* 120.
54 Miller, *After the Fall,* 161.
55 Miller, *After the Fall,* 121.

56 Miller, *After the Fall,* 121.
57 Miller, *After the Fall,* 122–3.
58 Miller, *Timebends,* 527.
59 Miller, *Timebends,* 533.
60 Miller, *Timebends,* 534.
61 Miller, *Timebends,* 380.
62 Miller, *Timebends,* 242, 369.
63 Miller, *Timebends,* 242.
64 Miller, *Timebends,* 359.
65 Miller, *Timebends,* 483, original emphasis.
66 Miller, *Timebends,* 484–5.
67 Miller, *Timebends,* 307.
68 Quoted in Summers, 161–2.
69 Miller, *Timebends,* 436.
70 McCann, 159.
71 Mailer, *Marilyn,* 18.
72 Johnson, n.pag.
73 Mailer, *Marilyn,* 19.
74 Baty, 98.
75 Mailer, *Marilyn,* 46.
76 Mailer, *Marilyn,* 25, 28, 32, 39.
77 Oates, iv.
78 Johnson, n.pag.
79 Kakutani, "Darkening," 45.
80 Siegel, n.pag.
81 Quoted in Summers, 96.
82 Oates, 407–8.
83 Mailer, *Marilyn,* 92, original emphasis.
84 Hyatt, 153–4.
85 Hyatt, 46, original emphasis.
86 Oates, 268–9.
87 Guiles (1984), 19.
88 Summers, 107.
89 Mailer, *Marilyn,* 78.
90 Oates, 901–2
91 Oates, 269.

3 "GOODBYE NORMA JEANE," 1926–1946

1 Goldstein, n.pag.
2 Steinem, 54.
3 Kobal, 9.

4 Rooks-Denes, 10.
5 Morley and Leon, 1.
6 Guiles (1984), x.
7 Spoto, 17.
8 Summers, 5–6.
9 Spoto, 16.
10 Summers, 70.
11 Spoto, 16.
12 Victor, 25–6.
13 Shevey, 51.
14 Spoto, 16, original emphases.
15 Summers, 5.
16 Mailer, *Marilyn,* 248.
17 Oates, 939
18 Summers, 10.
19 Summers, 402.
20 Baty, 33.
21 Baty, 33.
22 Showalter, 204.
23 Summers, 8.
24 Summers, 8.
25 Summers, 169.
26 Leaming, 397.
27 Guiles (1984), 6–7.
28 Leaming, 51.
29 Wolfe, 129.
30 Summers, 7.
31 Guiles (1984), 9.
32 Spoto, 39.
33 Steinem, 218.
34 Steinem, 159.
35 Steinem, 12.
36 "Monroe," *My Story,* 23.
37 Guiles (1984), 4.
38 Steinem, 82.
39 Guiles (1984), 37; Summers, 8;
   Spoto, 18–68; Leaming, 11.
40 Spoto, 235–6.
41 Guiles (1984), 23.
42 Summers, 20.
43 Spoto, 68.
44 Summers, 28.
45 Guiles (1984), 37.
46 Guiles (1984), 38.

47 Summers, 21.
48 Rollyson, 13.
49 Steinem, 65–6.
50 Mailer, *Marilyn,* 42.
51 Spoto, 68.
52 Spoto, 60.
53 Wolfe, 144–5.
54 Wolfe, 146, original emphases.
55 Spoto, 34.
56 Leaming, 12.
57 Pepitone, 86.
58 Summers, 26.
59 Guiles (1984), 50.
60 Guiles (1984), 43.
61 Mailer, *Marilyn,* 44.
62 Mailer, *Marilyn,* 46.
63 Mailer, *Marilyn,* 48.
64 Summers, 24.
65 Quoted in Spoto, 90.
66 Spoto, 99.
67 Spoto, 99.
68 Oates, 180–1.
69 Spoto, 118.
70 "Monroe," *My Story,* 47.
71 "Monroe," *My Story,* 48.
72 Summers, 15.
73 Wolfe, 237.
74 Guiles (1984), 69.
75 Guiles (1984), 73.
76 Guiles (1984), 73.
77 Guiles (1984), 73.
78 Guiles (1984), 65–6.
79 Spoto, 139–41.
80 Wolfe, 234.
81 Steinem, 49.
82 Freeman, 119.
83 Rollyson, 24.
84 Zolotow (1961), 55–6, original
   emphasis.
85 Mailer, *Marilyn,* 63.
86 Wolfe, 222–3.
87 Warner, 366–7.
88 McCann, 20, 94.
89 Warner, 368.

90 Mellen, 42.
91 Barris, 12.
92 Kaplan, 462.
93 Mailer, *Marilyn,* 226.
94 Mailer, *Marilyn,* 160.
95 Mellen, 28.
96 Spoto, 548.
97 Steinem, 79.
98 Summers, 15.

**4 "THE NAKED TRUTH,"
1946–1952**

1 Doane, 255.
2 Kaplan, 7.
3 Freeman, 11.
4 Barris, 4.
5 Summers, 9–10.
6 Freeman, 125.
7 Summers, 10, 15.
8 Guiles (1984), 55.
9 Mellen, 26.
10 Guiles (1984), 34.
11 Quoted in Spoto, 246.
12 Quoted in Zolotow (1961), 228.
13 McCann, 66.
14 Mailer, *Marilyn,* 39.
15 Weatherby, 4.
16 Guiles (1969), 140.
17 Mailer, *Marilyn,* 17.
18 Summers, 95.
19 Spoto, 370.
20 Weatherby, 147.
21 Weatherby, 146.
22 Weatherby, 154.
23 "Monroe," *My Story,* 21–2.
24 Freeman, 101.
25 Guiles (1984), 97.
26 Freeman, 36.
27 Freeman, 47–8.
28 Quoted in McCann, 76; Victor, 279; Mailer, *Marilyn,* 53.
29 Summers, 4.
30 Victor, 163–4.
31 Kidder, 131.
32 Mailer, *Marilyn,* 84.
33 Leaming, 10.
34 Spoto, 179.
35 Zolotow (1961), 66.
36 Guiles (1969), 78.
37 Guiles (1969), 79.
38 Guiles (1984), 76–7.
39 Gussow, 173.
40 Mailer, *Marilyn,* 68.
41 Summers, 43.
42 Rollyson, 96.
43 Spoto, 163.
44 Hyatt, 46.
45 Steinem, 90.
46 Oates, 285.
47 Rollyson, 27.
48 Guiles (1984), 83.
49 Summers, 19; Spoto, 156.
50 Leaming, 16.
51 Summers, 38.
52 Miller, *Timebends,* 359.
53 Summers, 39–40.
54 Quoted in Weatherby, 144.
55 Oates, 281.
56 Rand, 158.
57 Leaming, 31.
58 Steinem, 113.
59 Weatherby, 146.
60 Fiske, 42.
61 "Monroe's Secret Lesbian Fling," n.pag.
62 Smith, 201.
63 Showalter, 129.
64 Capote, 208.
65 Spoto, 216.
66 Summers, 56.
67 Summers, 27.
68 Summers, 10.
69 Spoto, 217.
70 Guiles (1984), 120.
71 Leaming, 42.
72 Quoted in Spoto, 261.
73 Quoted in Zolotow (1961), 311.

74 Stern, 42, original emphasis.
75 Doane, 265.

5 "FEMALE TROUBLE,"
  1952–1961

1 Guiles (1984), 4.
2 Guiles (1984), 4, original
  emphasis.
3 Steinem, 156.
4 Brown and Barham, 12–13.
5 Brown and Barham, 14.
6 Guiles (1984), 175.
7 Mailer, *Marilyn,* 157.
8 Rollyson, 69.
9 Guiles (1984), 142, 155.
10 Summers, 81–2.
11 Leaming, 72.
12 Rollyson, 69.
13 Guiles (1984), 155.
14 Spoto, 272.
15 Summers, 29.
16 Rollyson, 67.
17 Spoto, 279–81.
18 Snyder, xvii–xviii.
19 Carpozi, 99.
20 Wolfe, xi, 13.
21 Guiles (1984), 158.
22 Guiles (1984), 158.
23 Summers, 93.
24 Spoto, 471, 404; Summers, 98.
25 Summers, 98.
26 Rollyson, 85.
27 Summers, 98, 97.
28 Wolfe, 318, 384.
29 Spoto, 284.
30 Wolfe, 295.
31 Spoto, 312.
32 Leaming, 90.
33 Leaming, 94.
34 Summers, 110.
35 Guiles (1984), 178.
36 Spoto, 349.
37 Summers, 118.
38 Summers, 116–7.
39 Spoto, 322.
40 Guiles (1984), 177.
41 Leaming, 131.
42 Guiles (1984), 181.
43 Summers, 120.
44 Spoto, 359.
45 Leaming, 123.
46 Spoto, 369.
47 Spoto, 377.
48 Trilling, 241.
49 Spoto, 416.
50 Haskell, "Engineering," 8.
51 Victor, 93.
52 Riese and Hitchens, 549.
53 "Walk Like This," 104.
54 Johnson, n.pag.
55 Spoto, 475.
56 Spoto, 678.
57 Freeman, 6.
58 Freeman, 47.
59 Summers, 169.
60 Guiles (1984), 243–4; original
   emphasis.
61 Spoto, 445.
62 Weatherby, 74.
63 Spoto, 445.
64 Leaming, 234.
65 Summers, 247.
66 Spoto, 510.
67 Spoto, 511.
68 Guiles (1984), 264.
69 Mailer, *Marilyn,* 163.
70 Mailer, *Marilyn,* 171.
71 Steinem, 153.
72 Spoto, 468, 503.
73 Mailer, *Marilyn,* 163.
74 Leaming, 289.
75 Leaming, 289.
76 Summers, 191.
77 Wolfe, 365.
78 Rollyson, 190.
79 Rollyson, 143.
80 Olivier, 170.
81 Rollyson, 148.

82 Wolfe, 361–2.
83 Guiles (1984), 228.
84 Mailer, *Marilyn,* 163.
85 Rollyson, 146.
86 Summers, 163.
87 Freeman, 56.
88 Mailer, *Marilyn,* 164.
89 Spoto, 461.
90 Spoto, 462.
91 Weatherby, 84.
92 Summers, 163.
93 Summers, 187.
94 Summers, 188–9.
95 Olivier, 176.
96 Summers, 203.
97 Guiles (1969), 241–2.
98 Guiles (1984), 254.
99 Mailer, *Marilyn,* 17.
100 Oates, 91.
101 Spoto, 493.
102 Spoto, 475.
103 Wolfe, 395.
104 Oates, 798.
105 Wolfe, 396.
106 Guiles (1984), 311.
107 Wolfe, 399.
108 Summers, 206.
109 Guiles (1984), 248.
110 Leaming, 113.
111 Leaming, 372.
112 Brown and Barham, 312–3.
113 Wolfe, 431.
114 Steinem, 102.
115 Leaming, 367.
116 Wolfe, 401.
117 Spoto, 529.
118 Summers, 224.
119 Spoto, 533.
120 Rollyson, 219.
121 Freeman, 7.
122 Steinem, 190–1.
123 Mailer, *Marilyn,* 16.
124 Spoto, 268; Summers, 71.
125 Spoto, 268; Summers, 71.
126 Spoto, 469.

127 Summers, 26.
128 Summers, 170.
129 Summers, 325.
130 Spoto, 179.
131 Brown and Barham, 307.
132 Brown and Barham, 306.
133 Brown and Barham, 307.
134 Freeman, 102.
135 Freeman, 144.
136 Summers, 363.
137 Freeman, 36.
138 Summers, 26.
139 Summers, 197.
140 Mailer, *Marilyn,* 171.
141 Mailer, *Marilyn,* 173.
142 Summers, 26.
143 Summers, 212.
144 Summers, 216.
145 Showalter, 78.
146 Mailer, *Marilyn,* 167.

6 FEMME FATALE, 1961–1962

1 Zolotow (1961), 55, original emphasis.
2 Guiles (1984), 181.
3 Mailer, *Marilyn,* 184.
4 Summers, 295.
5 Summers, 314.
6 Trilling, 239.
7 Brown and Barham, 296.
8 Summers, 92.
9 Baty, 35.
10 Summers, 201.
11 Quoted in Summers, 315.
12 Mailer, *Marilyn,* 213, original ellipsis.
13 Guiles (1984), 299.
14 Spoto, 561.
15 Shevey, 21.
16 Steinem, 169.
17 Quoted in Zolotow (1961), 177.
18 Rollyson, 229.

19 Guiles (1969), 311, 317.
20 Summers, 317.
21 Summers, 313.
22 Brown and Barham, 6.
23 Brown and Barham, 266.
24 Spoto, 626, 644.
25 Wolfe, 526.
26 Leaming, 418.
27 *Marilyn Monroe: The Final Days,* 20th Century-Fox, 2001.
28 Guiles (1969), 306.
29 Summers, 234.
30 Brown and Barham, 300.
31 Spoto, 611.
32 Leaming, 391–2.
33 Wolfe, 474.
34 Guiles (1984), 307.
35 Wolfe, 213–5.
36 Spoto, 580.
37 Spoto, 674.
38 Guiles (1969), 318.
39 Wolfe, 446.
40 Leaming, 384.
41 Spoto, 597.
42 Brown and Barham, 179.
43 Summers, 245; Wolfe, 402.
44 Mailer, *Marilyn,* 232.
45 Brown and Barham, 375.
46 Summers, 243.
47 Summers, 243.
48 Spoto, 600–1.
49 Spoto, 689–91.
50 Wolfe, 122.
51 Wolfe, 99.
52 Summers, 240.
53 Brown and Barham, 270–1.
54 Leaming, 421.
55 Guiles (1969), 320.
56 Summers, 324.
57 Summers, 336.
58 Summers, 336–7.
59 Summers, 324.
60 Spoto, 666.
61 Spoto, 674.
62 Brown and Barham, 360.
63 Wolfe, 543–4.
64 Wolfe, 546.
65 Wolfe, 547.
66 Leaming, 423.
67 Guiles (1969), 322.
68 Leaming, 423.
69 Guiles (1969), 322.
70 Leaming, 423.
71 Guiles (1969), 324.
72 Leaming, 423.
73 Guiles (1969), 324.
74 Leaming, 425.
75 Guiles (1969), 324–7.
76 Guiles (1984), 325–6.
77 Leaming, 427.
78 Leaming, 425–6.
79 Mailer, *Marilyn,* 237.
80 Mailer, *Marilyn,* 241.
81 Mailer, *Marilyn,* 237.
82 Mailer, *Marilyn,* 242.
83 Mailer, *Marilyn,* 243–4.
84 Spoto, 741.
85 Summers, 375.
86 Noguchi, 74.
87 Noguchi, 68.
88 Noguchi, 81, original emphasis.
89 Wolfe, 562.
90 Summers, 348.
91 Brown and Barham, 332.
92 Wolfe, 561.
93 Brown and Barham, 332.
94 Brown and Barham, 332.
95 Summers, 349.
96 Wolfe, 563.
97 Wolfe, 79.
98 Summers, 351.
99 Summers, 350.
100 Summers, 352.
101 Spoto, 693.
102 Spoto, 695.
103 Spoto, 697.
104 Summers, 350.
105 Summers, 351.
106 Spoto, 696.
107 Spoto, 697.

108 Brown and Barham, 333.

109 Wolfe, 566.

110 Wolfe, 567.

111 Wolfe, 569.

112 Summers, 378; Spoto, 706.

113 Smith, 158.

114 Brown and Barham, 365.

115 Spoto, 737.

116 Spoto, 739.

117 Summers, 382.

118 Summers, 402–5.

119 Brown and Barham, 382.

120 Brown and Barham, 382.

121 Brown and Barham, 382.

122 Brown and Barham, 367.

123 Spoto, 717–8.

124 Spoto, 718.

125 Spoto, 610–1.

126 Spoto, 718–23.

127 Summers, 375.

128 Wolfe, 36–8.

129 Wolfe, 36.

130 Wolfe, 35.

131 Wolfe, 574–5.

132 Guiles (1984), 328

133 Spoto, 72.

134 Summers, 357.

135 Wolfe, 32.

136 Wolfe, 32, 149.

137 Summers, 15.

138 Quoted in Summers, 357.

139 Noguchi, 66.

140 McCann, 188.

141 Baty, 174–5.

142 Bronfen, *Over Her Dead Body,* 72.

143 Oates, 878.

144 Spoto, 620, fn.

145 Wolfe, 567.

146 Oates, 934.

147 Southwell and Twist, 15.

148 Fenster, xiv.

149 Ramsay, 20.

150 Leaming, 431.

151 Summers, 463.

152 Baty, 157.

153 Baty, 158.

154 Bronfen, *Over Her Dead Body,* 140–1.

155 Bronfen, *Over Her Dead Body,* 142.

156 Smith (2003), 181–2.

157 Smith (2003), 205.

AFTERWORD

1 Capote, 13.

2 Weatherby, 60.

3 Freeman, 161.

4 Victor, 279.

5 Cunningham, 38.

6 Victor, 52.

7 Victor, 52.

8 Victor, 293.

9 Goodman, 240.

10 Summers, 139.

11 Weatherby, 126.

12 Weatherby, 183.

13 Cunningham, 300.

14 Clark, 111–2.

15 Weatherby, 143.

16 Summers, 51.

17 Spoto, 169.

18 Weatherby, 70.

19 Miller, *After the Fall,* 105–8.

20 Guiles (1984), 111.

21 Meryman, 30.

22 Shaw, 92.

23 Summers, 199.

24 Summers, 199–200.

25 Spoto, 536.

26 Weatherby, 147.

27 Weatherby, 93.

28 Cunningham, 39.

29 Cunningham, 291.

30 Smith (2003), 246.

31 Summers, 219.

32 Summers, 102.

33 Morley and Leon, 104–5.

34 Riese and Hitchens, 73.

BIBLIOGRAPHY

Arnold, Eve. *Marilyn Monroe: An Appreciation* (NY: Alfred A. Knopf, 1987).

Banner, Lois. *American Beauty* (NY: Alfred A. Knopf, 1983).

Barris, George. *Marilyn: Her Life in Her Own Words: Marilyn Monroe's Revealing Last Words and Photographs* (London: Headline, 1995).

Barton, Sabrina. "Face Value," in *All the Available Light: A Marilyn Monroe Reader*, ed. Yona Zeldis McDonough (NY: Touchstone, 2002): 120–41.

Baty, S. Paige. *American Monroe: The Making of a Body Politic* (Berkeley and London: University of California Press, 1995).

Benzel, Kathryn N. "The Body as Art: Still Photographs of Marilyn Monroe." *Journal of Popular Culture* (Fall 1991, vol. 25, no. 2): 1–30.

Bronfen, Elisabeth R. *Over Her Dead Body: Death, Femininity, and the Aesthetic* (NY: Routledge, 1992).

———. "Death: The Navel of the Image," in *The Point of Theory: Practices of Cultural Analysis*, ed. Mieke Bal and Inge E. Boer (Amsterdam: Amsterdam UP, 1994): 79–90.

Brown, Peter, and Patte B. Barham. *Marilyn: The Last Take* (NY: Dutton/Signet, 1992).

Buskin, Richard. *Blonde Heat: The Sizzling Screen Career of Marilyn Monroe* (New York: Watson-Guptil, 2001).

Byer, Stephen. *Hefner's Gonna Kill Me When He Reads This: My Incredible Life at Playboy* (Chicago: Allen-Bennett, 1972).

Capell, Frank A. *The Strange Death of Marilyn Monroe* (NJ: Herald of Freedom of Press, 1964).

Capote, Truman. "A Beautiful Child," in *Music for Chameleons* (London: Hamish Hamilton, 1981): 206–22.

Carpozi, George, Jr. *Marilyn Monroe: "Her Own Story"* (NY: Belmont Books, 1961).

Clark, Colin. *The Prince, the Showgirl, and Me* (NY: St. Martin's Press, 1996).

Conway, Michael and Mark Ricci. *The Films of Marilyn Monroe* (NY: Citadel, 1964).

Corliss, Richard. "Marilyn Lost and Found." Time, 25 May 2001: <http://www .time.com/time/columnist/corliss/article/0,9565,127991,00.html>

Crown, Lawrence. *Marilyn at Twentieth Century-Fox* (London: Comet, 1987).

Cunningham, Ernest W. *The Ultimate Marilyn* (LA: Renaissance Books, 1998).

De Beauvoir, Simone. *The Second Sex*, trans. and ed. H. M. Parshley (London: Vintage, 1997, copyright 1949).

De Dienes, André. *Marilyn Mon Amour* (London: Sidgwick & Jackson, 1986).

Doane, Mary Ann. *Femmes Fatales: Feminism, Film Theory, and Psychoanalysis* (NY and London: Routledge, 1991).

Dougherty, James E. *The Secret Happiness of Marilyn Monroe* (Chicago: Playboy, 1976).

Dyer, Richard. *Stars* (London: BFI, 1982).

———. *Heavenly Bodies: Film Stars and Society* (NY: St. Martin's Press, 1986).

Epstein, William H. "(Post)Modern Lives: Abducting the Biographical Subject," in *Contesting the Subject: Essays in the Postmodern Theory and Practice of Biography and Biographical Criticism*, ed. William H. Epstein (West Lafayette, IN: Purdue UP, 1991): 217–36.

Fenster, Mark. *Conspiracy Theories: Secrecy and Power in American Culture* (Minneapolis: University of Minnesota Press, 1999).

Fiske, John. "The Cultural Economy of Fandom," in *The Adoring Audience: Fan Culture and Popular Media*, ed. Lisa A. Lewis (London and NY: Routledge, 1992): 30–49.

Freeman, Lucy. *Why Norma Jean Killed Marilyn Monroe: A Psychological Portrait* (Mamaroneck, NY: Hastings House, 1992).

Gates, David. "Becoming Marilyn." Rev. of *Becoming Marilyn*, by André de Dienes. *Newsweek*, 12 August 2002: 54–58.

Gilbert, Sandra M. and Susan Gubar. *The Madwoman in the Attic: The Woman Writer and the Nineteenth-Century Literary Imagination* (New Haven and London: Yale UP, 1979).

Goldstein, Bill. Interview with Joyce Carol Oates. *New York Times*, 28 March 2000: <http://www.nytimes.com/books/00/04/02/specials/oates.html>

Goodman, Ezra. *The Fifty-Year Decline and Fall of Hollywood* (NY: Simon & Schuster, 1961).

Gosling, Ray. "You're in Pictures, Honey." Rev. of *Norma Jean,* by Fred Lawrence Guiles. *The Times*, 2 August 1969: 21.

Greene, Milton. *Milton's Marilyn* (Munich: Schirmer, 1994).

Guiles, Fred Lawrence. *Norma Jean: The Life of Marilyn Monroe* (NY: McGraw-Hill, 1969).

————. *Norma Jeane: The Life and Death of Marilyn Monroe* (London: Granada, 1984). (Printed in United States as *Legend: The Life and Death of Marilyn Monroe.*)

Gussow, Mel. *Don't Say Yes Until I Finish Talking: A Biography of Darryl F. Zanuck* (Garden City, NY: Doubleday, 1971).

Hamblett, Charles. *Who Killed Marilyn Monroe?* (London: Leslie Frewin, 1966).

Haskell, Molly. *From Reverence to Rape* (New York: Holt, Rinehart, and Winston, 1974).

————. "Engineering an Icon." Rev. of *Marilyn Monroe*, by Barbara Leaming. *New York Times*, 22 November 1998: 8.

Hoyt, Edwin P. *Marilyn: The Tragic Venus* (NY: Chilton, 1965).

Hudson, James A. *The Mysterious Death of Marilyn Monroe* (NY: Volitant, 1968).

Hyatt, Kathryn. *Marilyn: The Story of a Woman* (NY: Seven Stories, 1996).

James, Clive. "Mailer's *Marilyn*." Rev. of *Marilyn* by Norman Mailer. *Commentary* 56:4 (October 1973): 44–9.

Johnson, Greg. Interview with Joyce Carol Oates. *Atlanta Journal-Constitution*, 12 March 2000: <http://www.usfca.edu/fac-staff/southerr/blonde.html>

Kael, Pauline. Rev. of *Marilyn*, by Norman Mailer. *New York Times*, 22 July 1973.

Kakutani, Michiko. "The Commodified Blonde, or, Marilyn as Text." Rev. of *American Monroe* by S. Paige Baty. *New York Times*, 1 August 1995: C17.

————. "Darkening the Nightmare of America's Dream Girl." Rev. of *Blonde*, by Joyce Carol Oates. *New York Times*, 31 March 2000: E45.

Kaplan, Louise J. "Fits and Misfits: The Body of a Woman." *American Imago* (1993, vol. 50, no. 4): 457–80.

Kennicott, Philip. "Opera Redux: The Old Face of New American Opera," January 1994: <http://www.worldandi.com/specialreport/1994/january/sall801.html>

Kidder, Clark. *Marilyn Monroe: Cover to Cover* (N.P.: Krause Publications, 1999).

Kobal, John, ed. *Marilyn Monroe: A Life on Film* (London: Hamlyn, 1974).

Leaming, Barbara. *Marilyn Monroe* (NY: Crown, 1998).

Lesser, Wendy. "The Disembodied Body of Marilyn Monroe," in *His Other Half: Men Looking at Women Through Art* (London and Cambridge: Harvard UP, 1991): 193–224.

Luce, Clare Boothe. "What Really Killed Marilyn." *Life*, 7 August 1964: 68–78.

Mailer, Norman. *Marilyn: A Biography* (NY: Grosset & Dunlap, 1973).

————. *Of Women and Their Elegance*. With photos by Milton Greene (NY: Simon & Schuster, 1980).

————. "Strawhead." *Vanity Fair*, April 1986: 58–67.

"Marilyn Monroe." *Time*, 11 August 1952: 74–82.

"Marilyn Monroe: A Skinny-Dip You'll Never See on the Screen." *Life*, 22 June 1962: 90–92.

"Marilyn Monroe: The Talk of Hollywood." *Life,* 7 April 1952: 101–4.

"Marilyn Takes Over as Lorelei." *Life,* 25 May 1953: 79–81.

"Marilyn, Part of a Jumping Picture Gallery." *Life,* 9 November 1959: 107.

Martin, Pete. *Will Acting Spoil Marilyn Monroe?* (NY: Bantam, Doubleday, 1956).

McCann, Graham. *Marilyn Monroe* (Cambridge: Polity, 1988).

Mellen, Joan. *Marilyn Monroe* (NY: Pyramid, 1973).

"Memories of Marilyn." *Life,* 17 August 1962: 63–70.

Merkin, Daphne. "Platinum Pain." Rev. of Leaming, *Marilyn Monroe,* and Wolfe, *The Last Days of Marilyn Monroe. New Yorker,* 8 February 1999: 72–79.

Meryman, Richard. "Fame Can Go By." Interview with Marilyn Monroe. *Life,* 3 August 1962: 32–38.

Miller, Arthur. *After the Fall* (NY: Viking, 1964).

———. *Timebends* (London: Minerva, 1987).

Miller, Laura. "Norma Jeane." Rev. of *Blonde,* by Joyce Carol Oates. *New York Times,* 2 April 2000: 6.

Millett, Kate. "Marilyn, We Hardly Knew You," in *All the Available Light: A Marilyn Monroe Reader*, ed. Yona Zeldis McDonough (NY: Touchstone, 2002): 78–82.

"Monroe, Marilyn." *My Story* (NY: Stein & Day, 1974).

"Monroe's Secret Lesbian Fling." Rev. of *Victim: The Secret Tapes of Marilyn Monroe* by Matthew Smith. 10 August 2003 <http://www.suntimes.co.za/2003/08/10/backpage/back01.asp>

Morin, Carole. "If the Most Famous Woman in the World Can Die . . . " *New Statesman,* 5 September 1997: 53.

Morley, Sheridan, and Ruth Leon. *Marilyn Monroe* (Stroud: Sutton, 1997).

Murray, Eunice, with Rose Shade. *Marilyn: The Last Months* (NY: Pyramid, 1975).

Noguchi, Thomas T., with Joseph DiMona. *Coroner to the Stars* (London: Corgi, 1983).

Oates, Joyce Carol. *Blonde* (London: Fourth Estate, 2000).

Ochs, Michael. *Marilyn Monroe: From Beginning to End* (London: Blandford, 1997).

O'Hagan, Andrew. "St. Marilyn." Rev. of *The Personal Property of Marilyn Monroe,* Christie's, *The Complete Marilyn Monroe,* by Adam Victor, and *Marilyn Monroe,* by Barbara Leaming. *London Review of Books,* 6 January 2000: 3–8.

Olivier, Laurence. *Confessions of an Actor* (London: Weidenfeld and Nicolson, 1982).

Pepitone, Lena, with William Stadiem. *Marilyn Monroe Confidential* (NY: Simon & Schuster, 1979).

Piercy, Marge. "Looking Good," in *All the Available Light: A Marilyn Monroe Reader,* ed. Yona Zeldis McDonough (NY: Touchstone, 2002): 103–8.

"Powerful Stars Meet to Play-Act Romance." *Life,* 15 August 1960: 64–7.

Ramsay, Robin. *Conspiracy Theories* (Harpenden: Pocket Essentials, 2000).

Rand, Ayn. "Through Your Most Grievous Fault," in *The Voice of Reason: Essays in Objectivist Thought* by Ayn Rand, ed. Leonard Peikoff and Peter Schwartz (NY: New American Library, 1989: 158–61).

Ratcliffe, Michael. "A Bat Out of Night." Rev. of *Marilyn,* by Norman Mailer. *The Times,* 8 November 1973: 16.

"Remember Marilyn." *Life,* 8 September 1972: 71–4.

Rev. of *Marilyn Monroe,* by Maurice Zolotow. *Times Literary Supplement,* 17 March 1961: 174.

Riese, Randall, and Neal Hitchens, *The Unabridged Marilyn: Her Life from A to Z* (London: Corgi Books, 1987).

Rollyson, Carl E., Jr. *Marilyn Monroe: A Life of the Actress* (London: New English Library, 1986, 1990).

Rooks-Denes, Kathy. *Marilyn* (NY: Bantam Doubleday Dell, 1993).

Rosten, Norman, and Sam Shaw. *Marilyn Among Friends* (London: Bloomsbury, 1987).

Selsdon, Esther. *Marilyn Monroe* (Bristol, UK: Paragon, 1995).

Shaw, Sam. *Marilyn Monroe in the Camera Eye* (NY: Hamlyn, 1979).

Shevey, Sandra. *The Marilyn Scandal* (NY: William Morrow & Co., 1987).

Showalter, Elaine. *The Female Malady: Women, Madness and English Culture, 1830–1980* (London: Virago, 1987).

Siegel, Lee. "Survival of the Misfittest." Rev. of *Blonde,* by Joyce Carol Oates. New Republic, 10 July 2000: <http://www.thenewrepublic.com/071000/siegel@71000.html>

Silver, Brenda R. "The Monstrous Union of Virginia Woolf and Marilyn Monroe," in *Virginia Woolf: Icon* (Chicago: University of Chicago Press, 1999): 236–72.

Slatzer, Robert. *The Life and Curious Death of Marilyn Monroe* (London: W. H. Allen, 1975).

———. *The Marilyn Files* (NY: Shapolsky, 1992).

Smith, Matthew. *The Men Who Murdered Marilyn* (London: Bloomsbury, 1996).

———. *Victim: The Secret Tapes of Marilyn Monroe* (London: Century, 2003).

Snyder, Allan. Foreword to Robert F. Slatzer, *The Life and Curious Death of Marilyn Monroe* (London: W. H. Allen, 1975): xvii–xix.

Solomon, Aubrey. *Twentieth Century-Fox: A Corporate and Financial History* (Metuchen, NJ, and London: Scarecrow Press, 1988).

Southwell, David, and Sean Twist. *Conspiracy Theories* (London: Carlton, 1999).

Speriglio, Milo. *Marilyn Monroe: Murder Cover-Up* (Van Nuys, CA: Seville, 1982).

———. *The Marilyn Conspiracy* (London: Corgi, 1986).

Spoto, Donald. *Marilyn Monroe: The Biography* (NY: HarperCollins, 1993).

Steinem, Gloria. *Marilyn: Norma Jeane.* Photos by George Barris (London: Victor Gollancz, 1987, reissued Orion, 2001).

Stern, Bert. *Marilyn Monroe: The Complete Last Sitting* (Munich: Schirmer, 1992).

Summers, Anthony. *Goddess: The Secret Lives of Marilyn Monroe* (NY: Macmillan, 1986).

Taylor, Roger G. *Marilyn on Marilyn* (London: Omnibus, 1983).

"To Aristophanes and Back." *Time,* 14 May 1956: 74–82.

Trilling, Diana. "The Death of Marilyn Monroe," in *Claremont Essays* (London: Secker & Warburg, 1965): 229–43.

Turim, Maureen. "Gentlemen Consume Blondes," in *Issues in Feminist Film Criticism,* ed. Patricia Erens (Bloomington and Indianapolis: Indiana UP, 1990): 101–11.

Victor, Adam. *The Complete Marilyn Monroe* (London: Thames & Hudson, 2000).

Wagenknecht, Edward C., ed. *Marilyn: A Composite View* (Philadelphia: Chilton Book Co., 1969).

"Walk Like This, Marilyn." *Life,* 20 April 1959: 101–4.

Warner, Marina. *From the Beast to the Blonde: On Fairy Tales and Their Tellers* (London: Chatto & Windus, 1994).

Weatherby, W. J. *Conversations with Marilyn* (NY: Paragon, 1976).

"What Makes Marilyn?" *Playboy,* no. 1, 1953: 17–19.

Wolfe, Donald H. *The Assassination of Marilyn Monroe* (London: Little, Brown, 1998).

Woodward, Richard B. "Iconomania: Sex, Death, Photography, and the Myth of Marilyn Monroe," in *All the Available Light: A Marilyn Monroe Reader,* ed. Yona Zeldis McDonough (NY: Touchstone, 2002): 10–34.

Zolotow, Maurice. *Marilyn Monroe* (London: W. H. Allen, 1961).

———. *Marilyn Monroe.* Rev. ed., with new introduction and new epilogue (NY: HarperCollins, 1990).

ACKNOWLEDGMENTS

This book, like Marilyn herself, has had many lives, and is something of a collaborative effort. Many people have given generously of their thoughts and their time, and this book is certainly the richer for it. For ideas, discussions, reading drafts and support in various guises, I would like to thank: my family (the whole lot of 'em), Nancy Allen, Jon Cook, Anne Margaret Daniel, Walter Davis, Lindsay and John Duguid, Patricia Duncker, Grant Farred, Bill Gleason, Kathy Gleason, Virginia Hickley, Richard Holmes, Eric Homberger, Marion Howard, Will Howarth, Claudia Johnson, Russell Celyn Jones, Louisa Joyner, David Kasunic, Maureen Khadder, Liz Kunkle, Doug Mao, Kristen Mary, Lynn Maxwell, Julian Murphet, Laura Nash, Diane Negra, Arnold Rampersad, Martin Ruehl, John Smelcer, Laura Thompson, Tamsin Todd and Sarah Wood. The argument has also benefited from some extremely engaged and intelligent audiences at seminars, talks and conferences at Princeton, Harvard, Cambridge, Sussex and the University of East Anglia. My thanks to everyone who helped the ideas emerge, and to UEA for a leave of absence that gave me the time to express them.

Special thanks are due to the following people, for materially shaping my ideas about how to tell—and think—this version of Marilyn: to Diana Fuss, Michael Wood and Paul Kelleher for their profound (in every sense) influence on my first attempt; to Dana Guthrie and Julie Burkley for being the only ones steadfast and loyal enough to brave my second attempt, and for their immensely helpful suggestions in how to go about making the third time the charm. But it was Stephen Heath who first made me admit that I was cheating, and rethink the whole. Thanks to Peter Khadder, for being so wrong in an argument that helped me see the shape chapter five should take, and to Kathleen Khadder, for being right and agreeing with me. To Sean Matthews goes more credit than he thinks, especially for helping me see my Marilyn, for getting the joke, for thinking I was an ideal intellectual and for knowing my signature pieces. My gratitude to John Arnold, for several brilliant and sympathetic reads, and for introducing me to George, is boundless. And thanks most of all to Dana for staying so interested in the damn thing, and for seeing me through it.

I have had quite a run of beginner's luck in publishing this book. Thanks as always are due to George Miller and to everyone at Granta who first believed in the book and saw it through to completion and beyond so gracefully and with such care; this book wouldn't be here if it weren't for them. Immense gratitude goes to my agent, David Godwin, for working so much above and beyond the call of duty and for believing in this book so firmly. And now, at Metropolitan Books, Marilyn and I've once again found ourselves in the very safe hands of a team with great taste, elegance and New York style. Thanks to everyone there for the compliment of thinking that Marilyn's many lives were made-to-order for Metropolitan, and for not responding, "But it's not really a biography, is it?" Special gratitude to Shara Kay, for being the book's advocate and for her help with permissions; to Raquel Jaramillo, for a jacket that is even more beautiful than the first; and to Fritz Metsch, for designing a lovely read. Finally thanks to Sara Bershtel, for wisdom, counsel, and for caring about every word. Rumor has it there are only two editors left in the world who do, and I've been fortunate enough to work with them both.

My family are always my biggest fans, and this book is dedicated to them all, especially to my mother, and to my father, for being so proud and for never even hinting that it was taking me an awfully long time, to my grandmother for sanity, and to my sister for keeping a scrapbook.

INDEX

ABOUT THE AUTHOR

Sarah Churchwell was educated at Vassar and Princeton and is now a professor of American literature and culture at the University of East Anglia. A frequent contributor to the *Times Literary Supplement,* she lives in London. *The Many Lives of Marilyn Monroe* is her first book.

BOCA RATON PUBLIC LIBRARY, FLORIDA

3 3656 0336142 7

92 Monroe
Churchwell, Sarah Bartlett,
 1970-
The many lives of Marilyn
 Monroe

APR   2005